STYLE AND SYMBOLISM IN

Piers Plowman

STYLE AND SYMBOLISM IN

Piers Plowman

A MODERN CRITICAL ANTHOLOGY

EDITED BY ROBERT J. BLANCH

THE UNIVERSITY OF TENNESSEE PRESS : KNOXVILLE

Frontispiece: Pieter Brueghel, *The Harvesters.* Reproduced by permission
of the Metropolitan Museum of Art.

To Mrs. Helen Yokell

FROM A GRATEFUL SON-IN-LAW

Preface

IN THE PAST TWENTY-FIVE YEARS, critics of *Piers Plowman* have gradually shifted their focus of attention from authorship, textual, and linguistic problems to the essential literary questions raised by the poem—its theme, purpose, symbolism, and imagery. *Piers Plowman* is universally considered a major work and much worthwhile scholarship has been devoted to it. In fact, the bibliography of recent interpretive studies of *Piers Plowman* affords ample material for more than one anthology like this one.[1]

Since undergraduate and graduate students usually view *Piers Plowman* as the *bête noire* of medieval literature courses, the purpose of this anthology is to elucidate the literary value of *Piers Plowman* as poetry, and it is hoped, to provide the basis for some glimmer of appreciation as a substitute for the usual bewilderment experienced by the student. With the exception of Donaldson's essay, a selection from a *Festschrift* in honor of Margaret Schlauch, the thirteen essays in this volume have been drawn from the scholarly journals in the modern language field.

The first essay on *Piers Plowman,* that by Bloomfield, provides a judicious evaluation of critical treatments of *Piers Plowman* up to 1938 and a point of departure for future studies of the poem. A large part of this essay is devoted to tracing the development of the single or multiple authorship controversy which entangled *Piers* scholarship in the first three decades of this century. In the course of this discussion, Bloomfield notes that many of the disputants in the controversy realized the need for an authoritative text of all three versions of *Piers*—the A-text, the B-text, and the C-text—before further investigation of the authorship problem could be made.[2] Other topics treated by Bloomfield in his essay are the multiplicity of theories on the name and life of the author of *Piers Plowman* and the nature of potential literary influences on Langland. Bloomfield concludes his essay by suggesting that many of the dark mysteries of *Piers Plowman* will be illuminated if the poem is viewed through the

---

1 See, for example, Edward Vasta, *Interpretations of Piers Plowman* (Notre Dame, 1968) .

2 Since the appearance of Bloomfield's essay, the definitive edition of the A-text has been published: *Piers Plowman: The A Version*, ed. George Kane (London, 1960) . Kane's editions of the B- and C-texts are forthcoming.

prism of the theology, philosophy, art, economics, and social history of the fourteenth century.

Smith's essay appears here as the second selection because it marks a *desideratum* for *Piers Plowman* scholarship—the importance of turning away from authorship and textual problems to the literary merits of the poem. In his exposition of the structural development of *Piers Plowman,* Smith construes the theme of the poem as "the Search for Truth and Salvation," the search being symbolized by a pilgrimage. In the course of this pilgrimage, Smith asserts, the poet gradually learns that "the desire for material treasure is the source of worldly evil." After outlining the structure and theme of *Piers,* Smith discusses the use of this poem as propaganda in the fourteenth and fifteenth centuries, the authorship controversy surrounding the poem, and the halting progress of the new "definitive" texts; he concludes that "all these matters affecting the study of *Piers Plowman* . . . have diverted later students from consideration of its literary merit." What places *Piers Plowman* in the mainstream of great literature, Smith maintains, is "the poet's perception of moral values and social principles and his preoccupation with human material, which give the poem its unity and bring a number of seemingly disjoint-ed elements within the compass of a single theme."

Five essays in this collection—those by Coghill, Dunning, Lawlor, Zeeman, and Kean—focus on the meaning and value of the poem as a whole and shed light on the poem's structure and unity. The purpose of Coghill's essay is to delineate the differences between the A- and B-texts, "to show the nature of the transformation of A into B, and how it was dictated in the poet's mind by a long musing over that enigmatic but crucial pardon granted to Piers in the eighth passus of the A-text. . . ." After pondering over the problems inherent in the pardon of the A-text, Langland shifted the scope of his poem from the problems of contemporary England to the problem of salvation, a salvation reached by three ways (Do-wel, Do-bet, and Do-best) . In order to represent effectively in poetry this new line of thinking, Coghill argues, Langland attempted "to re-shape his poem by a known technical expedient of adding a fourth plane of meaning, the anagogical as it was called, the meaning in *aeterna gloria.*"

For Father Dunning, however, the aim of Langland was to reform society. Employing traditional Church teachings on the inner spiritual life of the Christian, Langland modifies this corpus of doctrines to mirror his concern with Christian society and with the problems of fourteenth-century England. Devoting a large part of his essay to the religious traditions of the spiritual life, as seen through the eyes of St. Gregory, St. Bernard, and others, Dunning sees two traditional concepts blending into the structure of the *Vita* of *Piers Plowman*: "the three stages of the soul's progress in the love of God, and the three objective states of life—the Active Life [Do-wel], the Religious Life [Do-bet], and the Life of Prelates [Do-best]." Concurring with Dunning's argument for the unity of theme in *Piers,* Lawlor sees the perception of the connection between the *Visio* and *Vita* as the central problem in *Piers Plowman* interpretation. Noting that the dreamer in *Piers* gradually comes to understand himself and all the truths which form the bulwark of his faith, Lawlor interprets Langland's central theme as the promise of regeneration for mankind.

For Zeeman, the pilgrimage to Truth in *Piers Plowman,* distinctly similar to an allegorical pilgrimage in Walter Hilton's *Scale of Perfection,* represents the main imaginative thread woven into the fabric of *Piers,* for "the activity of travel, whether material or spiritual, preoccupies major as well as minor characters of the allegory." Zeeman, moreover, sees the most important theme of *Piers* as the "exploration of the journey to God through Christ—the reaching of the 'treasure of Truth' along the high-road of Love." Drawing upon medieval political theory and upon the ideal of kingship, Kean's essay, the last in this section, focuses on the theme of law in *Piers,* its affinity with love and mercy, and the relationship of these motifs to Langland's concept of the parallel between divine and earthly kingship.

Six essays in this collection concentrate on a single character, vision, or, in two instances, on a single passage. Examining the character of Piers Plowman, Troyer traces the development, throughout the poem, of Piers as a "multifold symbol"—as an individual man, as a symbol of all mankind, and as Christ. Mitchell, after a brief review of scholarship on Lady Meed, claims that previous critics of Meed have ignored the complexity of her character. The only way to discern the meaning and significance of Meed is "through the action of the poem and the revelation of character and motive." Throughout the episode, Mitchell concludes, Meed is amoral and fails to perceive that she is guilty of wrongdoing. "She has no secure attachments and no antipathies that are dictated by moral principles." Another essay on character, that by Maguire, attempts to show that the significance and function of one figure, Haukyn, have frequently been overlooked by the critics of *Piers Plowman.* While noting the similarities between Haukyn and Piers of the *Visio,* Maguire contends that the two characters are explicitly differentiated by Langland, for Haukyn mirrors imperfectly the true Active Life as represented by Piers. Haukyn "represents its most limited form, what one might call 'Practical Life,' " a life which suggests an inadequate means of attaining salvation. In Maguire's opinion, the Haukyn episode is significant for two reasons: first, it is an integral part of the structure of *Piers Plowman;* and second, since the episode knits together "the various themes and episodes of the *Visio* by referring them in turn to the unifying central figure of Haukyn," it points to and underscores the essential unity of the *Visio*.

Focusing on the second vision in the B-text of *Piers Plowman,* Burrow claims that "so far as its action is concerned, this vision *is* a whole, and that its more difficult episodes make better sense if we see them as parts of it." Furthermore, the well-knit plot of the second vision includes four basic parts—sermon, confession, pilgrimage, and pardon. Burrow concludes his essay by arguing convincingly for a non-literal interpretation of Truth's pardon. Langland's treatment of the pardon, Burrow notes, stems from the fear that "the external form or institution—even though it is acceptable in itself—may come to usurp the place of the inner spiritual reality." The pardon itself, therefore, is merely a "form," a symbol of the spiritual truth of eternal reward for those people who renounce their wickedness and do well.

Kaske draws upon patristic exegesis to interpret a very enigmatic passage (xiii, 151–56) in the B-text of *Piers Plowman.* These lines represent, in part, the reply of Patience to Conscience's invitation to explain the nature and meaning of Do-wel, Do-bet, and Do-best. Donaldson's essay, expressly a rebuttal to R. E. Kaske ("The Speech of 'Book' in *Piers Plowman,*" *Anglia,* LXXVII [1959], 117–44) and R. L. Hoffman ("The Burning of 'Boke' in *Piers Plowman,*" *MLQ,* XXV [1964], 57–65), is concerned not with "the broader issues of theology in which these scholars are interested," but with the syntactical problems raised by Book's speech, especially lines 252–57 of B. xviii.

As was noted earlier in this preface, twelve of the thirteen essays in this collection have been drawn from the scholarly journals, many of which are not available in small libraries. The important critical works of R. W. Chambers *(Man's Unconquerable Mind),* T. P. Dunning *(Piers Plowman: An Interpretation of the A-Text),* Greta Hort *(Piers Plowman and Contemporary Religious Thought),* E. Talbot Donaldson *(Piers Plowman: The C-Text and Its Poet),* Elizabeth Salter *(Piers Plowman: An Introduction),* D. W. Robertson and B. F. Huppé *(Piers Plowman and Scriptural Tradition),* Morton W. Bloomfield *(Piers Plowman as a Fourteenth-Century Apocalypse),* and R. W. Frank *(Piers Plowman and the Scheme of Salvation)* are not included in this anthology because their studies have appeared in book form and are easily accessible.

With the exception of three essays, those by Smith, Mitchell, and Coghill, all essays are reproduced uncut in their text and notes. Sections one and six of Smith's essay, those parts dealing with the beginnings of English studies at University College, are deleted, and the appendix to Mitchell's essay, an extract from the C-text (C. iii, 335–409), is eliminated.

In the case of Coghill's long essay, excisions are indicated by dots or asterisks, and line references enclosed in parentheses are frequently substituted for lengthy quotations from the text of *Piers Plowman*.

In the interests of clarity and consistency, capitalization, caesura markings, and references to the three texts of *Piers Plowman* have been normalized. Obvious typographical errors have been silently corrected, and the American style of punctuation has been followed throughout the text. All unnumbered footnotes have been supplied by the editor.

To aid the student, bibliographical references for further study are provided, when necessary, at the bottom of the first page of the essays. Translations of difficult words or passages in Middle English, and of Latin, German, Italian, Middle French, and Modern French are also supplied by the editor; such translations are enclosed in brackets in the body of the text directly following the passage translated.

As a further aid to the student, references in footnotes to any of the other articles included in this anthology are also made to the page numbers of this book; these cross-references are enclosed in brackets. In addition, cross-references by any of the authors to other passages in their own articles have been changed so that the pages of this volume, and not those of the original journal, are the pages that are cited. This should allow the student to make comparisons and to study with ease the various claims and counterclaims of these writers.

I am grateful to R. E. Kaske for his helpful comments and encouragement. Additional assistance was provided by Susan Wright and Professor Lawrence Ruark of Bentley College; by John Scott Campbell, a graduate student at Boston College; and by Professor Israel Aluf of Northeastern University. I am especially indebted to the contributors and to their publishers for the permissions which they granted for this anthology.

R. J. B.

Boston, Massachusetts
December, 1968

Contents

Illustrations

STYLE AND SYMBOLISM IN

Piers Plowman

1. Present State of *Piers Plowman* Studies

MORTON W. BLOOMFIELD

THE PURPOSE of this paper is to sum up the voluminous research which has been done on *Piers Plowman* in the past thirty-five years in order to make easily accessible the important results of that research and to point the way towards future developments. My own contribution, beyond that of sifting and arranging, is very slight.

I

From Elizabethan times up to recent date, it was assumed that one man, Robert or William Langland, or even Piers Plowman himself,[1] had written the poem which is known as *Piers Plowman*. Although Moore[2] has contended that until 1802 only the B-text was known, variations in the poem were early recognized.[3] Whitaker, in 1787, and Ritson, in 1802, mention two distinct versions, but they did not doubt that they were both by the same author. It is true that, as Moore has pointed out, the former believed the C-text was the original version, yet that is not a serious objection to the validity of his opinion. Richard Price, who was the first to recognize the existence of the A-text in 1824,[4] believed that the three versions were the work of one man.

Thomas Wright, however, unaware of Price's discovery, contended in his edition of the poem that the two versions were the work of two men. George Marsh, the American scholar, in his *Lectures on the English Language* (1860) also maintained a theory of dual authorship. His views

Reprinted, with some revisions by the author, by permission of the author and The Mediaeval Academy of America from *Speculum,* XIV (1939) , 215–32.

See also the classified bibliography in Thomas A. Knott and David C. Fowler's *Piers the Plowman: A Critical Edition of the A-Version* (Baltimore, 1952) . The most authoritative survey of the authorship question is George Kane's *Piers Plowman: The Evidence for Authorship* (London, 1965) .

1 William Webb, *A Discourse of English Poetrie* (1586) . Cf. Skeat, *Piers Plowman,* EETS, o.s. 81, p. xix.

2 "Studies in Piers the Plowman," I, *MP,* XI (1913) , 177 ff. & II, *MP,* XII, 19 ff.

3 See e.g., Thomas Hearne, *Remarks and Collections,* VIII (1722–25) , (Oxford Historical Society L, [1907]) , p. 395.

4 Thomas Warton, *History of English Poetry* (1840) , II, 44, note a, and 60 ff., Note A (from ed. of 1824, written by Price) .

are probably based upon Wright's. In any case, it can be definitely stated that tradition, with one or two exceptions, has favored the assumption of a single author. Too much weight cannot be put upon eighteenth- and nineteenth-century evidence, however, as it is far too late to represent anything but the individual opinion of the critics.

Skeat, in his great edition, has confirmed this view. In his preface to the edition of the A-text (1866–67), he briefly sketched his reasons for believing in single authorship, and his opinion is entitled to the highest respect. In the years that followed, the weight of Skeat's authority fixed this opinion so firmly in the world of scholarship that Hopkins in 1898 could write, "his [Langland's] style and method are so distinct, that there is scarcely an opportunity to question the authorship of any part of it as the work of others is so often questioned." [5]

In January, 1906, Manly, of Chicago, published a short article in *Modern Philology* entitled "The Lost Leaf of Piers the Plowman" which stirred up the muddy waters of scholarship and provoked a dispute over the question of the authorship of *Piers Plowman* which has lasted down to this day. If his contention has not been proved, Manly has, at least, focused attention on a great poem which had been neglected unjustly, and stimulated an interest that has produced notable results, so that we are able to appreciate much that was lost to our predecessors. A few years later, Manly presented his argument more fully, but still inadequately, in Chapter I of Volume II of the *Cambridge History of English Literature*—a rather inappropriate place for a dispute.[6] During the next few years, Manly was engaged in a literary dispute with Jusserand, in the course of which he amplified his arguments.

Manly maintains that five authors wrote the three versions of the poem known as *Piers Plowman*. John But, the only one whose name we know, wrote part of Passus xii of the A-text and left his name. The other authors are unknown, although William Langland might be the name of one of them. Manly writes that "of the A-text only the first eight passus are the work of the first author, the principal part of the vision of Dowel, Dobet and Dobest having been added by another author, and that not only lines 101–12 of Passus xii are the work of Johan But, but that he is responsible for at least one-half of it." [7] Another man, Manly believes, wrote the B recension and yet another the C version. For convenience, I

---

5 E. M. Hopkins, "Notes on Piers Plowman," *The Kansas University Quarterly*, Series B (Philology and History), VIII (1899), no. 1, p. 3. Cf. B. Fehr, review of Görnemann's *Zur Verfasserschaft und Entstehungsgeschichte von Piers the Plowman (Literaturblatt für Germanische und Romanische Philologie* [1916], p. 174).

6 See *ibid.*, p. 174.

7 *MP*, III, 359.

shall call the two sections and two hypothetical authors of the A-text, A-1 and A-2.

Manly bases his conclusion upon the fact that there are considerable differences in style, outlook, dialect, alliteration, and vocabulary between the five sections, and even more conclusively, there are cases where the revisers have distinctly misunderstood their predecessor. In connection with this last statement, Manly has pointed out the fact that in A. v, there is a distinct gap in thought between lines 235 and 236 which can best be explained by the hypothesis of a missing leaf. This missing leaf would account for the abruptness of the transition at this point and would also explain the fact that the confession of Wrath is omitted from the list of the confessions of the seven deadly sins in this passus.[8] Normally, Wrath follows Envy in the list of sins[9] and between the end of the confession of Envy (l. 106) and line 235 there are 129 lines which would adequately fill four pages (of 31 lines each). Thus the missing leaf of a quire would explain the difficulties of Passus v. Knott suggested to Manly that the concluding lines of the confession of Envy, which ends rather abruptly, may have been included in the missing leaf. This explanation is ingenious, and, along with the rest of Manly's theory, received a great deal of attention. His theory, he stated, will make clear that "the fourteenth century was a period of great and widespread intellectual activity, and that poetical ability was not rare." [10]

As regards the differences in the various texts, Manly has never given us his complete data, as it was soon realized that a sound text must be first established before any further work could be done on the authorship dispute.[11] He has listed, however, the different characteristics of each author as he views them.[12] His work has made us more conscious of the merits of A-1 which had been rather neglected since Skeat chose the *Visio* of the

---

[8] This argument is weakened by the fact that Wrath is omitted in the list of sins earlier in the A-text, Passus ii, 60 ff. In any case, there are many precedents for omitting sins from the list of the seven deadly sins. See my unpublished Wisconsin dissertation, *The Seven Deadly Sins in Medieval English Literature*. Dunning, *Piers Plowman: an Interpretation of the A-text* (1937), pp. 78 ff., has an ingenious explanation of this omission of Wrath in both parts of the A *Visio*. I cannot accept his explanation. Although I cannot go into a discussion of his argument here, I must point out that sloth as well as wrath is considered a sin of the irascible faculty by some theologians: see e.g., Belfour, *Twelfth Century Homilies,* EETS, o.s. 137 (1909), pp. 88–89.

[9] This is not necessarily so.

[10] *CHEL,* ii (1908), 38.

[11] A new text is still a need today. The A-text will soon appear, but Professor R. W. Chambers has informed me that it will be still many years before the textual work on the three recensions is finished. [As noted in the Preface of this book, the definitive edition of the A-text has been published: *Piers Plowman: The A Version,* ed. George Kane (London, 1960). Kane's editions of the B- and C-texts are forthcoming.]

[12] *CHEL,* ii, 11 ff., 17 ff., 23 ff., 30 ff.

B-text for his abridged edition. A-1 is brief, direct, and vivid in portraiture and rarely digresses. A-2 is interested in the different theological and philosophical questions of the time and uses figurative language in an entirely different way. B, on the other hand, lacks control and loves to digress. The unsatisfactory ending of that text is proof of his lack of organizing ability, but he is very sincere, which is shown by "the inevitableness with which, at every opportunity, he drifts back to the subjects that lie nearest his heart." [13]

C is more cautious. He has different opinions on some questions than those of the other authors, and throughout, is more prudent. His revision tends to tone down his predecessors' views: "On the whole, it may be said that the author of the C-text seems to have been a man of much learning, of true piety, and of genuine interest in the welfare of the nation, but unimaginative, cautious and a very pronounced pedant." [14]

With these characterizations, though heightened somewhat, no one would be much inclined to disagree, although it is doubtful whether they are incompatible with the conception of a single author writing after lapses of years.[15] Manly, of course, does not base his argument solely upon these differences in literary method and general outlook.

With the publication of Manly's chapter in a publication so widely read as the *Cambridge History of English Literature,* the interest in his hypothesis became so great that the Early English Text Society issued a reprint of the chapter as a supplementary publication with a preface by Furnivall.[16] The dispute which followed was a lengthy one and is not over yet, although a certain quietness has settled upon the field.[17]

Jusserand, who at that time was French Ambassador at Washington, was the first to take up the cudgels. He was one of the foremost students of English life and letters and, particularly, of mediaeval England. In 1894 he had brought out a book entitled *L'Epopée Mystique de William Langland,* which was soon translated into English under a different title.[18] He was, therefore, particularly well qualified to dispute with Manly.

Jusserand[19] accepted the lost-leaf hypothesis, but argued that B had not misunderstood A-1, either in Passus v or ii where Manly had given

13 *CHEL,* II, 29.

14 *CHEL,* II, 31.

15 Cf. Chadwick, *Social Life in the Days of Piers Plowman* (1922) , p. 3.

16 *EETS.,* Extra Issue, 135 b (1908) & o.s. 139 b, c, d, e (1910) .

17 Dunning, *op. cit.,* has recently disturbed the complacency of the supporters of the theory of single authorship who had begun to feel that the alternate theory was dead. See below p. 11.

18 *Piers Plowman, A Contribution to the History of English Mysticism,* Revised and Enlarged by the Author, London (1894) .

19 *"Piers Plowman,* the Work of One or Five," *MP,* VI (1908) , 271–329.

other examples of misunderstanding. The so-called errors in B are due either to Manly's misinterpretation of the passages in question or to the method of publication and the carelessness of the scribes. The differences in outlook and manner of revision are due to the change in the age of the author and these differences have been exaggerated. Jusserand called in the aid of the titles and colophons, the autobiographical references, the improbability of five authors living at the same time and unnoticed,[20] and tradition to support his views.

Bradley, Chambers, Grattan, Knott, and Mensendieck soon entered the lists. Bradley suggested that there was no missing leaf, but a misplaced one, and that lines 236–59 should come after line 145 (the end of the confession of Covetousness) where it would fit into the text.[21] Hall, in 1908,[22] and Carleton Brown, in 1909,[23] independently came to the conclusion that lines 236–41 should be placed after line 253. Chambers, however, believed that "there would seem then to be no ground for disturbing the order of the manuscript in so far as Robert the Robber is concerned." [24] (This refers to A. v, 236–59.) Changes in the order of a text supported by many manuscripts should only be made when the proof is overwhelming and such is certainly not the case here.[25] It must also be realized that the poem is not, by any means, coherently written.

Hall, in 1908, concluded, independently, that the C-text was by a different hand.[26] Teichmann, as far back as 1893, realized how inadequate Skeat's texts were. After pointing out numerous unsatisfactory readings as a result of relying too much upon one manuscript, Teichmann adds, ". . . nicht mehr darf die beste unter den handschriften innerhalb einer redaktion allein die grundlage des textes ausmachen, vielmehr müssen alle guten handschriften geprüft, verglichen, und verwertet werden" [No longer may the best among the manuscripts within one editing alone be the basis of the text, but rather all good manuscripts must be tested, compared, and evaluated].[27]

Knott later realized the necessity of a satisfactory text before the prob-

20 Cf. Chambers' comments on the continuation of the *Roman de la Rose* in Bright, *New Light on "Piers Plowman"* (1928) , Preface, p. 19.

21 Henry Bradley, "The Authorship of *Piers the Plowman*," *MLR*, v (1909) , 202 ff.; Henry Bradley, "The Lost Leaf of *Piers the Plowman*," *Nation*, lxxxviii (1909) , April 29; Henry Bradley, "The Misplaced Leaf of *Piers the Plowman*," *Athenaeum* (1906) , April 21.

22 "Was *Langland* the author of the C-text of *The Vision of Piers Plowman?*" *MLR*, iv (1908) , 1 ff.

23 "The *Lost Leaf* of *Piers the Plowman*," *Nation*, lxxxviii (1909) , March 25.

24 "The Authorship of *Piers Plowman*," *MLR*, v (1909) , 15.

25 *Ibid.*, p. 15.

26 Hall, *op. cit.*

27 "Zum Texte von William Langland's Vision," *Anglia*, xv (1893) , 245. Cf. Kron, *William Langleys Buch von Peter dem Pflüger* (1885) , pp. 20 *et passim*.

lem of authorship could be settled and set to work upon the classification of manuscripts. Chambers and Grattan also saw the need of a new text in the solution of the authorship problem and presented their argument as follows:

> Do these so-called "variants" presume the real reading of the original A-text as it left the author's hands, whilst the alternative readings, which have been adopted in the received A-text, represent the variants of an individual MS. or class of MSS? It has not been represented[28] that the received A-text is not an attempt to reconstruct the original text, as written by the poet.[29] It is a reprint with some corrections of a single MS.—the Vernon (V) —which Professor Skeat selected, believing that its readings were "on the whole, better than those of any other." [30]

Chambers has also maintained that there is a strong possibility that the so-called misunderstandings are the result of a faulty text. In any case, he argues rather successfully that the misunderstandings are not misunderstandings at all, and states that Jusserand has effectively answered Manly's allegations. He also argues for a single authorship from the dialect.[31] Deakin has also come to the same conclusion from her study of the alliteration of *Piers Plowman*.[32] Dobson studied the vocabulary of the poem and reached the following conclusion: "There are certainly no differences of vocabulary which need a theory of dual authorship to explain them." [33]

Bradley and Furnivall were among the early supporters of Manly's theory, but also realized the necessity of a new text. Coulton was not convinced by Manly and his supporters, for he did not believe their evidence was strong enough to overthrow Skeat's view.[34] Mensendieck, arguing from the continuity of the autobiographical element in the Dowel passus of the B-text, favored single authorship. This last is an argument which Chambers, although disagreeing somewhat in the actual interpretation of the several passus in question, has strongly pressed in recent years.[35]

---

[28] See previous note.

[29] See Skeat, *Piers Plowman*, EETS, o.s. 28 (1867), Preface I, p. xvi, where he gives his reasons for choosing the Vernon MS.

[30] Chambers and Grattan, "The Text of *Piers Plowman*," *MLR*, IV (1908), 358.

[31] Chambers and Grattan, "The Authorship of *Piers Plowman*," *MLR*, V (1909), 21–25.

[32] "The Alliteration of *Piers Plowman*," *MLR*, IV (1908), 478 ff.

[33] "An Examination of the Vocabulary of the A-text of Piers the Plowman," *Anglia*, XXXIII (1910), 396.

[34] "Piers Plowman, One or Five," *MLR*, VII (1911), 102 ff. and 372–373.

[35] Chambers, "Long Will, Dante and the Righteous Heathen," *Essays and Studies by Members of the English Association*, IX (1924), 50 ff.; Preface to Bright's *New Light*

He has continued his textual work with the aid of several associates among whom are Blackman, Carnegy, and Allen, and, in 1931, published an important article on the authorship question based upon this work. I shall return to this shortly.

Moore, in two articles in *Modern Philology,* discussed the question of the burden of proof.[36] After a very illuminating investigation, he concluded that the "presumption (in tradition) that has been claimed in favor of the theory of single authorship does not exist." [37] In the absence of any contemporary, fifteenth-, or sixteenth-century reference to the multiple authorship of our poem, as well as a possible different interpretation of tradition,[38] it seems to me that such a presumption in common sense, if not in tradition,[39] does exist.

After a silence of some years, Day wrote several jolting articles. From a study of the alliteration, she comes to the opposite conclusion from that of Deakin; she believes that there is evidence from her study to conclude that the poem is by five authors, but most surprising of all, she finds the greatest difference between two parts of the B-text, which she calls B-1 and B-2 (the rewritten A-text and the B continuation).[40] Day also studied the texts, noting the differences as collated by Skeat, and came to the same conclusion. The difference in the methods of revision,[41] the cases where C misunderstands B, the fact that C and B seemed to have used different A manuscripts, and the changes in the character of Piers,[42] led her to the conclusion that the theory of multiple authorship was correct.

Day's work was a serious effort and certainly seemed to clinch the case for the supporters of Manly's theory, until Chambers and Grattan, breaking a silence of some years, published the article referred to[43] which effectively answered Day, and provided new positive arguments for the theory of single authorship (excluding But). Chambers stated that no "final

---

on *"Piers Plowman"* (1928) ; Chambers and Grattan, "The Text of *Piers Plowman,"* *MLR,* xxvi (1931) , 357 ff. For Mensendieck, see his *Charakterentwickelung und ethisch-theologische Anschauungen des Verfassers von Piers the Plowman* (1900) and "The Authorship of *Piers Plowman," JEGP,* ix (1910) , 404 ff.

36 "Studies in Piers the Plowman," i. The Burden of Proof: Antecedent Probability and Tradition, *MP,* xi, 177 ff.; ii. The Burden of Proof: The Testimony of the Manuscript; the Name of the Author, *MP,* xii, 19 ff.

37 Moore, *op. cit.,* ii, *MP,* xii, 50.

38 See above, pp. 3–5.

39 Seventeenth-century and later evidence seems to me to be of little value one way or the other.

40 Day, "The Alliteration of the Versions of *Piers Plowman* in Its Bearing on Their Authorship," *MLR,* xvii (1922) , 403 ff.

41 Day, "The Revisions of *Piers Plowman," MLR,* xxiii (1928) , 1 ff.

42 Owst, *Preaching in Medieval England* (1926) , pp. 288 ff., and 296, points out that extensions, expansions, and alterations are the common fate of every religious treatise.

43 See pp. 8–9, n. 35.

textual results can be reached without further investigation of the Manu
scripts." [44] He believes, however, that "the question of authorship will
'mainly' have to be settled upon other grounds." [45] The four cases where
Day showed that B has misunderstood A are discussed, and Chambers
disproves one and shows that the other three cases are very unlikely.

By a masterly display of logic, Chambers reduces her arguments, based
upon an investigation of the alliteration, to a *reductio ad absurdum*, by
showing that her tests would make it possible to prove that the B-text was
the work of eight authors. In earlier articles, published since the war,
Chambers has pointed out other arguments for the traditional view. Arguing from the learning, Biblical quotations,[46] dialect, diction, metre,
allegorical method,[47] and intelligibility of the continuation,[48] he comes
to the conclusion that the assumption that B, anyway, is by a different author, is "opposed to much conclusive evidence and supported by none."[49]

Chambers believes, however, that the problem of authorship will not
be solved by the establishment of a sound text.[50] Before the disputants
can rest satisfied, however, a satisfactory text must be provided. Krog, a
recent student of *Piers Plowman,* supports the traditional view.[51]

The fact that organization has been seen[52] in what was once considered
a completely unorganized poem has tended to incline us towards the
theory of a single author, although organization need not imply a single
composer. It is reasonable to assume today that one author (probably

---

[44] Chambers and Grattan, "The Text of *Piers Plowman,*" *MLR,* xxvi (1931) , 23.

[45] *Ibid.,* p. 24.

[46] See Adams, "The Use of the Vulgate in *Piers Plowman,*" *SP,* xxiv (1927) , 556 ff.,
and Sullivan, *The Latin Insertions and the Macaronic verse in Piers Plowman* (1932) ,
pp. 50 ff. *et passim.*

[47] Cf. Owen, *Piers Plowman,* Chap. i and Willis, *Piers Plowman as an Interpretation of Fourteenth Century Life* (1914) , an unpublished M.A. dissertation, McGill
University, Montreal, Canada. This last deserves to be better known.

[48] See Moore, "Studies in Piers the Plowman," ii, *MP,* xii, 26 and above, p. 9, n. 36.

[49] Chambers, "Long Will, Dante and the Righteous Heathen," *Essays and Studies,*
ix, 68.

[50] Chambers and Grattan, "The Text of *Piers Plowman,*" *MLR,* xxvi, 24. Cf. Patch's
remark in his "Review" of Bright's *New Light on "Piers Plowman,"* *ES,* lxvii (1932) ,
112.

[51] *Studien zu Chaucer und Langland (Anglistische Forschungen,* 65 [1928]) and
"Autobiographische oder typische Zahlen in *Piers Plowman,*" *Anglia,* lviii (1934) ,
318 ff.

[52] See H. W. Wells, "The Construction of *Piers Plowman,*" *PMLA,* xliv (1929) , 123
ff.; "The Philosophy of Piers Plowman," *PMLA,* liii (1938) , 399 ff.; Troyer, "Who is
Piers Plowman?" *PMLA,* xlvii (1932) , 368 [see below, pp. 156–73]; R. Hittmair, "Der
Begriff der Arbeit bei Langland," *Neusprachliche Studien,* Festgabe, Karl Luick (*Die
neueren Sprachen,* 6 Beiheft [1925]) ; Carnegy, "The Relations between the Social and
Divine Order in William Langland's 'Vision of William concerning Piers the Plowman' " (*Sprache und Kultur der germanischen und romanischen Völker,* A, Anglistische Reihe, xii [1934]) ; N. K. Coghill, "The Character of Piers Plowman considered
from the B-Text," *Med.AE.,* ii (1933) , 108–135. Dunning, *op. cit.,* etc.

William Langland) wrote *Piers Plowman*. The possibility, however, must be still left open that the three versions were by more than one author, particularly the C-text.[53] There seems little room for further investigation on the authorship question until a new text of the three versions appears. Then with a complete list of variants and a revised text, we can again tackle the question, using the old tests but with careful methodological safeguards which have not always been used in the past. Dunning, who has recently suggested that B is probably by another author A,[54] seems to me not to have proved his point in this regard, although he has written a very illuminating book. A new text will not necessarily solve the problem, but that is the *conditio sine qua non* of further authorship investigation.

A word or two on still another authorship theory. Görnemann, in 1916, brought out a study in *Anglistische Forschungen* entitled "Zur Verfasserschaft und Entstehungsgeschichte von *Piers the Plowman*." She suggests therein that, seeing both Manly's and Jusserand's views present difficulties in the way of acceptance,[55] the three texts and intermediate forms all go back to an original manuscript which the author Robert Langland wrote between 1370 and 1376, although the latter date best fits the social conditions described in the poem.[56] He then died,[57] and various scribes copied his manuscript, changing it as they wished, producing numerous distinct variations, of which three main forms can be distinguished. She emphasizes that the corruption of the texts supports her views,[58] and points out that the differences between the manuscripts of one version are as great as those between the various recensions.[59]

As Chambers has commented,[60] Görnemann's conclusions are serious-

---

[53] Further investigation of the C-text is urgently needed. In the past forty years, it has been neglected in comparison with the work done on A and B. The full implication of John But's comments on Langland, and his own death in 1387 have not been realized in connection with the authorship and date of the C-text. The traditional dates of the C-text, 1393 or 1398, are both open to objection as they are based on very little evidence. Coghill, on no good evidence, holds for 1393–94; see his "Two Notes on *Piers Plowman*," I, *Med.AE.*, IV (1935) , 83 ff. He seems unaware of But's testimony, and, yet, holds to Skeat's authorship theory. Devlin's suggestion, in her thesis, "The Date of the C version of *Piers the Plowman*," *Abstracts of Theses*, Humanistic Series, University of Chicago, IV (1928) , 317 ff., that the C-text was written before 1388, and possibly in 1381, has not been seriously enough studied. Unfortunately, her arguments are not easily available. But speaks of Langland as dead. The force of his testimony, however, only weighs upon those who favor a single author.

[54] See above, p. 5, n. 8 and p. 6, n. 17.

[55] See Görnemann, *op. cit.*, pp. 47–48.

[56] *Ibid.*, pp. 44 ff. and esp. p. 63.

[57] *Ibid.*, p. 119.

[58] *Ibid.*, p. 84.

[59] *Ibid.*, p. 119.

[60] Chambers and Grattan, "The Text of *Piers Plowman*," *MLR*, xxvi, 22.

ly vitiated by the fact that, through no fault of her own, she was unable to examine the manuscripts themselves. Krog, in his recent monograph, in the same series,[61] has refuted a great many of Görnemann's conclusions about the relations of the texts (e.g., that A and C stand closer together in many respects than A and B or B and C). Her theory is improbable, and she forgets to take account of three distinct versions which certainly exist, in spite of some mixed texts.[62] Fehr[63] and Björkman,[64] however, agreed with her argument.

All concur that John But, whom Bradley[65] and Rickert[66] seem to have correctly identified with the King's Messenger of that name, who died in 1387, must have had something to do with Passus xii of Piers Plowman.[67] There is disagreement, however, on the extent of his contribution: Rickert,[68] Chambers,[69] Manly,[70] and Skeat[71] all suggest various answers. In any case, his contribution is a slight one.

The differences in opinion among the various exponents of a theory of multiple authorship do not, of themselves, prove any one such theory false, but they do add to a feeling of doubt. If one does not accept a single author, at least three different courses are open, and none of them seem to rest on sound foundations.

II

Turning to the problems connected with the author's name and life, we must admit that we are still in considerable darkness.[72] Bright has added something to our external evidence in the last fifteen years, but his conjectures are too fanciful for the information and facts he presents. We possess, on the whole, very little external evidence, and much of it is of a conflicting nature. There is no contemporary evidence about Langland, and his name cannot be found in any of the numerous archives of

---

[61] Krog, *Studien zu Chaucer und Langland.*

[62] Cf. Chambers, *Bright's New Light on "Piers Plowman,"* Preface, p. 15.

[63] Review of Görnemann, *Literaturblatt für Germanische und Romanische Philologie* (1916) , p. 174.

[64] *Anglia* Beiblatt, xxvii (1916) , 275–277.

[65] "Who was John But," *MLR*, viii (1913) , 88–89.

[66] "John Butt, Messenger and Maker," *MP*, xi (1913) , 107 ff.

[67] See above, pp. 4 and 11, n. 53.

[68] Ll. 78 ff.

[69] 84 ff. or ll. 89 ff. At one time, Chambers was inclined to attribute the whole of Passus xii to But.

[70] Ll. 57 ff.

[71] Ll. 94 ff.

[72] Cf. Isaac Disraeli, *Amenities of Literature* (1841) , I, 164.

the century.[73] Of course, as has been frequently pointed out, Langland had good reason to be silent about the authorship of an inflammable work like his own,[74] yet it is somewhat surprising that no trace of him whatsoever is found in the records or in the literature of the age. Our external evidence consists of certain comments and titles in the manuscripts, But's testimony,[75] and certain remarks made about the author in the sixteenth century. This sketchy and often conflicting evidence is usually supplemented by internal evidence from the work itself and, more recently, by the few facts and traditions Bright has unearthed. The internal evidence is the chief source of Langland's traditional biography.[76]

What is the value of this internal evidence? There have been, in the main, two natural attitudes towards this question. The first regards the poem as "a great autobiography," [77] while the other denies the value of most of the autobiographical facts culled from the three texts. Wright was the first to deny their value,[78] and, in an extended article, much later, Jack questioned the same element.[79] In the period between, Courthope,[80] Morley,[81] and Saintsbury[82] had expressed doubts of varying intensity, particularly strong in the case of the latter. Manly has agreed with Jack[83] and, as to be expected, his supporters have followed his lead. The autobiographical theory hampers the multiple authorship theory.

On the other hand, Mensendieck[84] and Bright[85] have gone to the other extreme and have interpreted everything autobiographically.

The proper attitude lies somewhere between these two views, for it is

---

[73] See Görnemann, *op. cit.*, p. 121 and G. L. Craik, *A Compendious History of English Literature* (1864) , I, 246. A fresh search of the material available to me has revealed nothing.

[74] See Richard Price in *Warton's History of English Poetry*, II, 62, and Bright, *op. cit.*, pp. 75 ff.

[75] See *ibid.*, pp. 16, 23 *et passim* and above, p. 11, n. 53.

[76] Ten Brink, *Early English Literature* (1883) , p. 352.

[77] Bright, "Langland and the Seven Deadly Sins," *MLR*, xxv (1930) , 133.

[78] T. Wright, *The Vision and the Creed of Piers Ploughman* (1842) , I, x, n. 3.

[79] A. S. Jack, "The Autobiographical Elements in *Piers the Plowman*," *JGP*, III (1901) , 393 ff.

[80] W. J. Courthope, *A History of English Poetry* (1895) , I, 207 ff.

[81] H. Morley, *English Writers*, IV (1889) , 285 ff.

[82] G. Saintsbury, *A Short History of English Literature* (1898) , pp. 131 ff.

[83] "The Authorship of *Piers Plowman*," *MP*, VII, 135 ff.

[84] See above p. 9, n. 35. Cf. Görnemann, *op. cit.*, p. 123.

[85] Bright, "William Langland's Birthplace," *Times Literary Supplement*, Mar. 12, 1925, p. 172; "William Langland's Early Life," *Times Literary Supplement*, Nov. 5, 1925, p. 739; "William Langland's Early Life," *Times Literary Supplement*, Sept. 9, 1926, p. 396; "Source of Piers Plowman," *Times Literary Supplement*, Apr. 24, 1930; "Langland and the Seven Deadly Sins," *MLR*, xxv (1930) , 133 ff., *New Light on "Piers Plowman"* (1928) .

reasonable to assume "Einzelne Reminiszenzen aus des Verfassers Leben sind selbstverständlich darin, wie wohl in jeder wahren Dichtung" [Individual reminiscences out of the writer's life are naturally in it, as in every good poem].[86] Care must be taken, and an endeavor must be made to weigh all assumptions. Bright and Owst, it seems to me, have gone too far on insufficient objective evidence. It is also true, as Jusserand,[87] and, more recently, Chambers,[88] have pointed out, that all the users of the mediaeval dream allegory are the heroes of their own poems. Some of the pitfalls into which we are apt to fall were recently enunciated by Krog[89] in regard to the interpretation of the numbers in the allegory, for, doubtless, many of them are merely conventional.

As regards the name of the author, there have been various opinions expressed. Unless more evidence is adduced, this is a question that will probably never be solved;[90] yet, I think we have a stronger argument for Will, although tradition is divided. The fact that the dreamer, in all the three versions, is called Will, and that it was a convention to use the author's own name in the dream allegory, supports our view.

George Puttenham, in listing the writers of "the first age," mentions "that nameles, who wrote the *Satyre* called Piers Plowman," [91] and I should think that many would like to agree with him. The remarks on the manuscripts give his name as William W., Robert or William Langland, Robert Langland, and William Langland. The "W" after William's name has given rise to much controversy. Probably the most satisfactory explanation is Bright's that it stands for "Wiclefitae," put in by a later hand who misunderstood the purpose of the poem.[92]

The most important and complete of these manuscript notes is one which Sir Frederick Madden discovered in *MS. Dublin D. 4, 1,* in Latin, stating that the author of the poem was William Langland, son of Stacey

---

[86] Görnemann, *op. cit.,* p. 123.

[87] *Piers Plowman,* pp. 196–197, 61 and 74–75.

[88] "The Authorship of *Piers Plowman,*" *MLR,* v (1910), pp. 29 ff.; "The Three Texts of *Piers Plowman* and Their Grammatical Form," *MLR,* xiv (1919), pp. 129 ff.; and *New Light on Piers Plowman,* Preface, pp. 16 ff.

[89] "Autobiographische oder Typische Zahlen in *Piers Plowman,*" *Anglia,* lviii, 318 ff.

[90] See Hopkins, "Notes on Piers Plowman," *Kansas University Quarterly,* Series B, Philology and History, vii, no. 1, p. 1, and Courthope, *A History of English Poetry,* i, 208, n. 2. A note signed Silverstone, in *Notes and Queries,* second series, vi (1858), 229–230, hitherto unnoticed, reproduces annotations written in the margin of a 1561 edition of *Piers Plowman,* in 1577. The comments are not of great importance and seem to come from Bale. The writer speaks of Langland as a Wyclifite. He also suggests that the *Creed* was by someone other than Langland.

[91] *The Arte of English Poetry,* ed. Willcock and Walker (1936), p. 60.

[92] "William Langland's Early Life," *Times Literary Supplement,* Nov. 5, 1925, p. 739, and *New Light,* p. 76.

de Rokayle of Oxfordshire, along with other information.[93] This note will be discussed shortly.[94]

In the preface to his edition of the poem (in 1550), Crowley writes that the author's name was Robert Langland who was born in Cleobury, Shropshire, eight miles from Malvern. It seems likely that John Bale was the source of this information,[95] and in his *Index Brittaniae Scriptorum,* and, later, in his *Scriptorum Illustrium Majoris Brittaniae,* we find the same statement. In Bale's *Index,* Nicholas Brigham, whose writings have not come down to us, is credited, along with William Sparks and John Wysdom, as the source of this information.[96] It is possible that Brigham obtained his information from a manuscript. His testimony, however, in other matters, is reliable[97] and his statement is of worth. Cleobury Mortimer, however, is nearer eighteen (to be exact twenty-three) than eight miles from Malvern.

J. Stow suggested that the author's name was John Malvern, a fellow of Oriel College, Oxford.[98] Webbe suggested that Piers Plowman, himself, was the author, an explicable error.[99] Such is also David Buchanan's patriotic statement that Robert Langland was a Scotsman.[100] Thomas Hearne, in the 1720's, also believed our poet's Christian name was Robert.[101] Tyrwhitt favored William,[102] while Thomas Warton used the name Robert.[103] Joseph Ritson suggested William, unless it be "a personification of the mental faculty," [104] although he uses Robert in the title of his article. Richard Price is doubtful and suggests William, with reservation, quoting Ritson's words with favor.[105] Wright supported Robert.[106] It was Skeat, however, who definitely chose William and set

---

[93] Cargill believes that the information obtained from this note was due to the investigations of Walter de Brugge, Parson of St. Patrick's Trym in Ireland, and right hand man to the Earl of March, "The Langland Myth," *PMLA,* L (1935), pp. 36 ff. His evidence is very slight.

[94] See below p. 17.

[95] See Skeat, *Piers the Plowman,* EETS, o.s. 38 (1869), Preface III, p. xxxii.

[96] For the identification of Sparks and Wysdom, see Cargill, *op. cit.,* pp. 44 ff. See Moore, *op. cit.,* II, 35 ff.

[97] See Cargill, *op. cit.,* pp. 44–45. He attacks Bright's views, *ibid.,* p. 46.

[98] See Skeat, *op cit.,* EETS, o.s. 81, p. 867.

[99] See above p. 3. Cf. Walter Skeat's letter in *The Academy,* no. 1089, Mar. 18, 1893, p. 242. John of Malvern pops up again.

[100] See Skeat, *op. cit.,* EETS, o.s. 81, p. 869.

[101] See *ibid.,* p. 871.

[102] See *ibid.,* p. 871.

[103] *History of English Poetry,* II, 44.

[104] *Bibliographia Poetica* (1802), p. 27. Cargill, "The Date of the A-text of Piers the Ploughman," *PMLA,* XLVII (1932), 354 ff., recently made a similar suggestion.

[105] Warton, *History of English Poetry* (1840, based on the ed. of 1824), II, 60 ff.

[106] *The Vision and the Creed of Piers Ploughman,* I, x, n. 3. Craik, *op. cit.,* I, 246–247, used Robert, but suggested that William is a better choice.

the tradition in that direction.[107] Hence, although tradition had, on the whole, favored Robert, William has been the choice for the last seventy-five years, but not without protest. As has been pointed out,[108] it would be easy enough to explain the use of William by the name of the chief character (although this ignores mediaeval convention), whereas the name Robert could not be so explained. Chambers, however, has called attention to an actual manuscript reading in A. ix, 1, where the misapprehension could have arisen.[109] Skeat had previously suggested that such a misreading could have given rise to the name Robert, as this name had been written in the margin of a B-text manuscript opposite this line *(MS. Corpus Christi College, 201)*.[110]

In recent years, Moore,[111] Macauley,[112] and Görnemann[113] have favored Robert. Moore has made the suggestion that there were two men, Robert Langland and a son of Stacey de Rokayle, who were confused. There is no evidence for this suggestion, and it can only become plausible if we accept a theory of multiple authorship.[114] The arguments for William are stronger, although the possibility of Robert must be left open.

As regards the surname, it was always agreed that the poet's surname was Langland until 1870, when Pearson suggested that it was Langley, arguing from the information in the Dublin manuscript[115] and on the basis of a place, Langley, in Shropshire. Skeat, after a period of doubt, finally rejected the suggestion. Pearson's theory is based on the assumption, then unfounded, that Stacey de Rokayle's family had connections with Shropshire. The de Rokayles were a Buckinghamshire family,[116] but we have since discovered that the Despensers, with whom they were associated, held the Chase of Malvern, with headquarters at Hanley Castle, eight miles from Ledbury, where Bright believes Langland was born.[117] Since Bright's discovery of a farm (or hamlet), Longlands, in

---

[107] *Op. cit.*, EETS, o.s. 28, Preface I, p. xxxiv.

[108] Moore, *op. cit.*, II, p. 43.

[109] "The Three Texts of *Piers Plowman* and Their Grammatical Forms," *MLR*, XIV, 131–132. Cf. Bright, *New Light*, pp. 24–25. This reading also occurs in Bright's own MS.

[110] *Op. cit.*, EETS, 38, Preface II, p. xxviii.

[111] "Studies in *Piers the Plowman*," II, *MP*, XII, 19 ff.

[112] "The Name of the Author of *Piers Plowman*," *MLR*, V (1910), 195 ff.

[113] *Zur Verfasserschaft* (Anglistische Forschungen, 48).

[114] Moore seems unaware that the son need not necessarily take the father's name. His suggestion, too, was made before Bright's discovery of the farm, Longlands, in the Malvern district. Cf. Cargill, "The Langland Myth," *PMLA*, L, 36 ff.

[115] See Skeat, *op. cit.*, EETS, o.s. 81, General Preface, pp. xxiv–xxvi, and above, pp. 14–15.

[116] Moore, *op. cit.*, II, pp. 44 ff.

[117] Bright, "William Langland's Early Life," *Times Literary Supplement*, Nov. 5, 1925, p. 739.

the district, there is no shadow of support for Langley's hypothesis. Even before this discovery, the theory was extremely unlikely, as Skeat[118] and Moore[119] have pointed out that Pearson's hypothesis offers no explanation for the use of the name Langland. William may have been the son of Eustace de Royakle as "the son's surname was not necessarily the same as his father's at this period." [120] There is also a possibility that Langland was illegitimate. Recently, it has been suggested that the author's name was William de Rokayle.[121]

Finally, there is a slight justification for the name William Langland, in the line, "I have lyved in lond, quod I. My name is Longe Wille" (B. xv, 148). The acrostic interpretation of this line has been disputed by several, including Manly,[122] but there is something to be said for Skeat's interpretation that the author here wished to make himself known indirectly. There are other cases of this kind, such as the use of single letters to present Cynewulf and Olivier de Mauny.[123]

Of our poet's biography, little can be said with certainty. It is customary to place Langland's birth in 1332, arguing from the lines in B. xi, 45–46 and B. xiii, 3, in which the poet mentions forty-five years. Since the B-text is assumed to have been written in 1377, it has been a simple arithmetical problem to deduce the date of his birth. Krog has recently shown how tenuous, on the basis of mathematical probability, this assumption really is.[124] We can hardly say that we know with any degree of certainty the date of Langland's birth.

It seems likely that the poet, if not born, was brought up near Malvern.[125] Cleobury Mortimer has been given as his birthplace, and, although there are objections to the correctness of this statement, it is, at least, based upon some evidence.[126] Bright's suggestion[127] that Ledbury, not Cleobury, was meant, has no foundation, although the former town is eight miles from Malvern, as the source of our information announces. If the poet was born in this district, it was probable that he was educated

[118] *Op. cit.*, EETS, o.s. 81, General Preface, p. xxvi.

[119] *Op. cit.*, II, p. 47.

[120] Skeat, *op. cit.*, EETS, o.s. 81, General Preface, p. xxiii, n. 1.

[121] Cargill, "The Langland Myth," *PMLA*, L, 36 ff. Cargill is too dogmatic to be convincing.

[122] "The Authorship of *Piers Plowman*," *MP*, VII (1909), 96–97.

[123] See *The Canterbury Tales*, B, ll. 3576 ff.

[124] "Autobiographische oder typische Zahlen in *Piers Plowman*," *Anglia*, LVIII, 318 ff.

[125] Arthur T. Bannister, "William Langland's Birthplace," *Times Literary Supplement*, Sept. 7, 1922, p. 569.

[126] Bale's *Index* and the quoted sources therein.

[127] "William Langland's Birthplace," *Times Literary Supplement*, Mar. 12, 1925, p. 172, and "William Langland's Early Life," *Times Literary Supplement*, Nov. 1925, p. 739.

at the monastery at Great Malvern. Skeat[128] and Jusserand[129] differ as to the status of the poet. The former, supported by Courthope,[130] believed him to be the son of a freeman, while the latter conceived him to be the son of a bondman.[131] The dispute centered around the interpretation of B. i, 75–76. With the further evidence Bright has since offered, it seems likely Skeat's interpretation is correct.

The remainder of this rather conjectural life is gathered chiefly from C. vi, 1–108.[132] There seems to be little doubt that Langland was in minor orders, as "each of the parts of the work manifests authorship by a cleric." [133] Chadwick writes, ". . . the writer of Piers Plowman, probably himself a clerk in lower orders, showed great interest in these less fortunate ecclesiastics and was inclined to excuse their shortcomings by a sympathetic account of the hardships they endure." [134] Wright suggested that he was a monk,[135] but this is unlikely, although he rarely attacks monks. He also seems to have an intimate knowledge of law which increased as he grew older.[136] Some of his most violent attacks are against lawyers,[137] which fact implies that he was familiar with their profession. He mentions his wife and daughter (C. vi, 2 and B. xviii, 425), but this seems to be a convention.

His close knowledge of London shows that he was a resident of the capital for part of his life.[138] Langland seems to have been poor for a great part of his life[139] and he continually reproaches the weaknesses in his own character.[140] He was intensely self-conscious. Chambers has written, ". . . there is no doubt how far Long Will 'was conscious of the distinction between his creed and that of the people.' " [141] His poem dis-

---

[128] Skeat, *op. cit.*, EETS, o.s. 67 (1877) , p. 32, note on l. 73.

[129] *Piers Plowman*, pp. 63 ff.

[130] *A History of English Poetry*, i, 208, n. 1.

[131] Hanscom, "The Argument of the Vision of Piers Plowman," *PMLA*, ix (1894) , 439.

[132] See Benham, *English Literature from Widsith to the Death of Chaucer* (1916) , p. 595.

[133] J. E. Wells, *Manual* (1916) , p. 265.

[134] *Op. cit.*, p. 21.

[135] *The Vision and the Creed of Piers Ploughman*, i, x.

[136] R. Kirk, "References to the Law in Piers the Plowman," *PMLA*, xlviii (1933) , 322 ff.

[137] See Trevelyan, *England in the Age of Wycliffe* (New Edition, reprinted [1925]) , p. 113.

[138] See C. L. Kingsford, "Review" of Chadwick's *Social Life*, *EHR*, xxxviii (1923) , 106.

[139] See Chadwick, *op. cit.*, p. 82.

[140] See Jusserand, *op. cit.*, p. 102, and R. W. Chambers, "The Three Texts of *Piers Plowman* and Their Grammatical Forms," *MLR*, xiv, 133.

[141] Chambers, "Long Will, Dante, and the Righteous Heathen," *Essays and Studies,* ix, 67.

plays a knowledge of higher social life, which may be attributed to any number of causes.[142]

His personality is best summed up in Krog's words, "Langland ist eine so starke religiöse Natur und hat ein so starkes metaphysisches Bewusstsein, dass es ihn über Fälle subjektiver Problematik . . . schnell zu einer positiv ethischen und aktiven Lösung führt" [Langland is (has) such a strongly religious nature and has such a strong metaphysical consciousness, that it leads him quickly, across instances of the subjectively problematical, to a positively ethical and active solution].[143] His restless and enquiring mind is seen throughout his great work.[144]

We do not know the date of Langland's death, although, if John But is correctly identified, it took place in, or before, 1387.[145] There is no justification for believing, as Skeat did, that Langland wrote *Richard the Redeless*,[146] which would have put his death sometime after 1399. Skeat made the attribution solely on poetic similarities, and, today, that has been shown to be more apparent than real. *Richard the Redeless* was probably written by an anonymous follower.

A great deal more might be written about Langland as Bright and Mensendieck have attempted to do, but further details would be only conjectures. The first passus of the *Vita* of the B-text tell the story of our author's inner life and intellectual struggles, but beyond this nothing else need be said.

III

It is very difficult to trace definite influences upon William Langland. As Cornelius has phrased it, "It is doubtful whether the source of any passage of considerable length in *Piers Plowman* has ever been convincingly identified." [147] There is a vast field of study to which scholars are now turning, in the intellectual climate of the fourteenth century and its relation to the poem. It is here that the most productive work in the coming years can be done. A study of theology, European literatures, art, philosophy, and a fuller consideration of the social and economic facts will throw much light.

---

[142] See Snell, *The Fourteenth Century* (*Periods of European Literature* [1899]) , pp. 384–385 and Hanscom, *op. cit.*, pp. 438–439.

[143] *Studien zu Chaucer und Langland*, p. 7.

[144] See Ker, *English Mediaeval Literature* (Home University Library [1912?]) , p. 199.

[145] See above, p. 11, n. 53.

[146] See Krog, *op. cit.*, p. 174, and J. P. Oakden, *Alliterative Poetry in Middle English*, I (1930) , p. 251.

[147] "*Piers Plowman* and the *Roman de Fauvel*," *PMLA*, XLVII (1932) , 363.

There is no doubt that the Bible, whether directly or indirectly,[148] is the greatest single influence upon our author. His whole thought is pervaded by the Vulgate, and he quotes liberally, if sometimes inexactly, from that source.[149] Adams[150] and Sullivan[151] have made extended studies of Langland's use of Biblical quotations, and the former concludes that the author was a cleric and that his Biblical preferences are those of a humble priest in lower orders. Adams also believes that the majority of his quotations have come from the Breviary and Missal. On the other hand, Sullivan concludes that he shows a first-hand acquaintance with the Bible.[152] We do not know exactly what the Breviary with which Langland was acquainted contained, but it seems natural to assume that he made use of it,[153] although this assumption does not exclude the possibility that he might have known the Bible itself. The choicest and most quotable parts of the Bible are included in the Breviary, so that it is doubtful whether any definite fact can be proved.[154] Langland makes most frequent use of the Psalter and Gospels. Owst has pointed to the fact that quoting from the Psalter was the "general practice of English homilists, writing and preaching under the prevailing influence of Hampole." [155] Langland also quotes from the Latin fathers and from certain hymns, but this need not imply any direct knowledge.

There is little likelihood that he had direct acquaintance with the classical writers of antiquity, although Aristotle, Plato, Porphyry, Cicero, and Ovid are mentioned.[156] These references are mediaeval commonplaces.

Langland has always been conceived of as a very original author,[157] and I think that this is undeniable, although several scholars have disputed it. It depends upon what is meant by original, but by mediaeval (or any) standards, compared to, say, Chaucer or Gower, Langland is extremely original. Marsh has written that "the poem, if not altogether

---

148 There was, and is, a traditional Catholic interpretation of the Bible that was considered fundamental to its proper understanding.

149 See Chadwick, *op. cit.*, p. 98 and Davis, *Piers Plowman* (The University Tutorial Series [1905?]) , p. xv.

150 "The Use of the Vulgate in *Piers Plowman*," *SP*, xxiv (1927) , 556 ff.

151 *The Latin Insertions and the Macaronic Verse in Piers Plowman* (1932) .

152 *Op. cit.*, pp. 50–52.

153 See Chadwick, *op. cit.*, p. 99.

154 Adams, *op. cit.*, pp. 564 ff.

155 *Literature and Pulpit in Medieval England*, p. 572.

156 C. xv, 190, 194; xii, 304; xiii, 173–75; and B. xi, 36. See Jusserand, *Piers Plowman*, p. 172.

157 See Wells' recent statement, "The Philosophy of Piers Plowman," *PMLA*, liii, 341. This recent article is rather confused. His agnosticism on the authorship question (see *ibid.*, p. 340) is unjustified. Dunning has not answered Chambers' arguments at all.

A plowman driving four oxen illuminates a margin
in the Luttrell Psalter, an English manuscript
dating from about 1340.

Courtesy of the British Museum

"Langland's fear," John Burrow observes of the passage concerning Truth's pardon in *Piers Powman,* "is that the external form or institution—even though it is acceptable in itself—may come to usurp the place of the inner spiritual reality." This marginal sketch of a pardoner appears in MS. Douce 104, a fifteenth-century *Piers Plowman* manuscript.

Courtesy of the Bodleian Library, Oxford

original in conception, is abundantly so in treatment." [158] Thomas Warton was the first to point out a possible influence upon our author in gators have suggested links with Grossetete's *Chasteau d'Amour,* Miracle the Latin poems attributed to Mapes and the political poems of the age, particularly the *Poem on the Evil Times of Edward II.*[159] Later investigators have suggested links with Grossetete's *Chasteau d' Amour,* Miracle Plays, French allegories, and certain mediaeval German works. In all these cases, the resemblances are doubtful, and there was certainly a common mediaeval tradition of which the mediaeval artist made use.[160] Owst has denied a great deal of the poet's originality and claims he owes a great deal to the pulpit.[161]

Certain of these similarities, however, are interesting. It was common belief some years ago, and is not dead yet, that Langland was essentially Germanic in tone, thought, and language.[162] The use of such a term as Germanic is unscientific, although one may say that those qualities that are usually considered Germanic are present in his work. As far as language and vocabulary are concerned, however, Langland makes almost as much use of Romance words as his contemporary Chaucer does.[163] He shows the common tendencies of Romance allegory writers, and neither allegory nor the vision framework is particularly Teutonic. Ker has pointed out certain similarities in *Piers Plowman* with the OHG poem *Muspilli,*[164] but, as always, no direct connection is discernible. There are also certain resemblances to Walter von der Vogelweide[165] and the German mystics of the "Free Spirit." [166] These similarities, however, are only the result of the common mediaeval background to which both Langland and the German writers are indebted.

Jusserand also suggests the possibility of acquaintance with the earlier Latin mystics and Joachim de Flora.[167] There is no evidence to this ef-

[158] Quoted by Skeat in Warton, *The History of English Poetry* (ed. W. C. Hazlitt [1871]) , II, 250 (written by Skeat) .

[159] *The Vision and Creed of Piers Ploughman,* I, XV.

[160] See C. S. Baldwin, *Three Medieval Centuries of Literature in England, 1100–1400* (1932) , p. 176.

[161] "The *Angel* and the *Goliardeys* of Langland's Prologue," *MLR,* XX (1925) , 270 ff., *Preaching in Medieval England* (1926) ; *Literature and Pulpit in Medieval England* (1933) .

[162] F. Rosenthal, "Die alliterierende englische Langzeile im vierzehnten Jahrhundert," *Anglia,* I (1878) , 423. This belief is not dead yet, see Dawson, *Mediaeval Religion* (1934) , pp. 161–162.

[163] See Skeat, *op. cit.,* EETS, o.s. 81, p. viii (referring to Marsh) and Jusserand, *Piers Plowman,* pp. 166 ff.

[164] *The Dark Ages* (1911) , p. 241.

[165] See Konrad Burdach, "Über den Ursprung des Humanismus," *Deutsche Rundschau,* CLIX (1914) , 73, and F. J. Snell, *The Fourteenth Century,* p. 383.

[166] Jusserand, *Piers Plowman,* pp. 202 ff.

[167] *Ibid.,* p. 195, and see Wells, "The Philosophy," *PMLA,* LIII, 349.

fect, and the vague parallels are the result of a similar world and a similar goal. This is also the case with certain Spanish and Italian allegories, vague resemblances which Snell pointed out.[168]

A stronger case is presented for direct links between Langland's poem and the earlier French allegories, such as the three *Pèlerinages* of De Guileville, *Le Roman de la Rose,* Rutebeuf's *Le Voie de Paradis,* the *Roman de Fauvel,* and others. Warton,[169] Jusserand,[170] Courthope,[171] Skeat,[172] and Snell[173] have recognized the possibility of this influence. Owen[174] and Cornelius,[175] to a lesser extent, have examined the French allegories closely and have pointed out resemblances. The argument is considerably weakened, however, by the fact that there is no external evidence to show that any of these allegories, with the exception of the *Roman de la Rose,* were known in England at the time when *Piers Plowman* was composed,[176] and also by the fact that there is no evidence that Langland knew any French, for the French expressions he employs are those that anyone living in England, at the time, would know.[177] This last point has been disputed.[178] In any case, "its conscious borrowing from the properly French strain seems to be very slight." [179] The closer resemblances are the result of the closer traditions of mediaeval England and mediaeval France. Some of the results of this investigation have been interesting.[180]

The English poetic allegories, *The Parlement of the Thre Ages* and *Wynnere and Wastour (ca.* 1350), are also possible influences,[181] particularly the last.[182] Langland's references to the Romance of Randolf, the Earl of Chester,[183] and Robin Hood[184] show some knowledge of English literature and tradition.

[168] Snell, *op. cit.,* pp. 379, 383 ff.

[169] Warton, *op. cit.,* (1840) , II, 60.

[170] *Op. cit.,* pp. 190 ff.

[171] *Op. cit.,* I, 238–239.

[172] Warton, *History of English Poetry* (ed. E. Carew Hazlitt [1871]) , II, 263 *et al.*

[173] *Op. cit.,* pp. 379 ff. and *The Age of Chaucer (Handbooks of English Literature* [1912]) , pp. 41–43.

[174] *Piers Plowman, A Comparison with Some Earlier and Contemporary French Allegories* (1912) .

[175] "*Piers Plowman* and the *Roman de Fauvel,*" *PMLA,* XLVII, 363 ff. and (to a lesser extent) , *The Figurative Castle* (1930) .

[176] See Owen, *op. cit.,* Chap. I.

[177] See Wells, *Manual,* p. 265.

[178] See Davis, *Piers Plowman,* p. xv, and Jusserand, *Piers Plowman,* p. 83.

[179] Louis Cazamian, *The Development of English Humor,* I (1930) , p. 85. This statement was made with particular reference to Langland's humor.

[180] For a complete treatment, see Owen, *op. cit.*

[181] See *CHEL,* II, 37.

[182] See Oakden, *Alliterative Poetry,* II, 55.

[183] B. v, 402.

[184] B. v, 402.

Jusserand has called our attention to the resemblance between many of Langland's opinions and those of the Commons.[185] In many respects, he shared their point of view. This, of course, is only natural, as Langland was a man of his age, and the vices and shortcomings of that age would be vividly before his mind as well as before the Commons.

In the use of proverbs, Langland seems to have known those which were in vogue during the fourteenth century, as may be seen from the printing of part of the John Rylands *Latin MS. 394*.[186] Bright pointed out certain parallels in this manuscript to the poem in a letter to the *Times Literary Supplement*.[187] He believes that Langland knew and used this manuscript. B. Hall has shown further resemblances to the B-text.[188] The date of this collection is some time after 1362, so that as far as the date is concerned, indebtedness would be possible. As proverbs are so universal, however, it is hardly safe to draw this conclusion. This collection bears closest resemblance to another proverb collection in the Bodleian Library, *MS. Douce 5*, Fols. 13–31.[189] Langland may have been familiar with another collection resembling these two. Nothing conclusive, however, can be said.[190]

Dante and Langland have often been compared,[191] but it is recognized that Langland could not have known the Florentine.[192] In the use of the dream form, in the condemnation of current vices, in the support of the monarchy and Catholicism, in the mystic view of life, there are general resemblances. There are also more specific ones which I cannot deal with here. The difference in poetic ability and genius between the two poets is obvious. Jusserand has written, "place him at whatever distance you will, he is the only poet of the century whose mystic visions deserve to be mentioned after the epic of the illustrious Florentine." [193]

---

185 *Piers Plowman*, pp. 106 ff.

186 W. A. Pantin, "A Medieval Collection of Latin and English Proverbs and Riddles, from the Rylands *Latin MS. 394*," *Bulletin of the John Ryland's Library*, xiv (1930) , 81 ff.

187 "Sources of Piers Plowman," April 24, 1930, p. 352.

188 "Sources of Piers Plowman," *Times Literary Supplement*, May 1, 1930, p. 370.

189 Pantin, *op. cit.*, p. 85.

190 See *The Year's Work in English Studies*, xi (1930) , 100 ff.

191 See P. Bellezza, "Langland and Dante," *Notes and Queries*, eighth series, vi (1894) , 81 ff.; I. Disraeli, *Amenities of Literature*, i, 168; Ten Brink, *Early English Literature*, pp. 353 ff.; Jusserand, *Piers Plowman*, pp. 13 and 193 ff.; Jusserand, *A Literary History of the English People* (1895) , i, 393–394; Courthope, *op. cit.*, i, 226 ff.; Wells, "The Construction of *Piers Plowman*," *PMLA*, xliv (1929) , 129; Burdach, *op. cit.*, p. 73; Snell, *The Fourteenth Century*, pp. 383 and 385; C. W. Stubbs, *The Christ of English Poetry* (1906) , pp. 89 ff. and note, pp. 117–119; Dawson, *op. cit.*, pp. 169, 175, 178 *et passim;* Chambers, "Long Will, Dante and the Righteous Heathen," *Essays and Studies*, ix, 50 ff. etc.

192 See P. Toynbee, *Dante and English Literature* (1909) , i, xvii, n. 1, and ii, 137.

193 *Piers Plowman*, p. 13.

As regards the Miracle Plays, Grossetete's *Le Chasteau d' Amour,* and the satirical poems, beyond a few doubtful specific resemblances, only the most general parallels can be found. Langland appears, however, to have been familiar with Duns Scotus and St. Thomas Aquinas.[194] Even in these cases, proof is doubtful.

In recent years, Owst has done important work in calling attention to the much neglected pulpit literature of the Middle Ages.[195] It has long been recognized, though frequently forgotten, that the popular sermons of the age influenced our author.[196] Owst, since the early 'twenties, has continually emphasized that our poem "is the fine product of English mediaeval preaching," [197] and "in reality, it represents nothing more or less than the quintessence of English mediaeval preaching gathered up into a single metrical piece of unusual charm and vivacity." [198] Owst traces the use of Scriptural quotations,[199] Langland's realism,[200] his personifications,[201] his social gospel,[202] and the idealization of labor (to a certain extent) to the homilies and homily books of the period. Particularly does he emphasize Langland's debt to John Bromyard[203] and Thomas Brunton, Bishop of Rochester.[204] Although Owst's evidence is impressive, there is, with one or two exceptions, no close parallelism. There is a general agreement as to attitude, but a reformer and a man of deep moral sincerity[205] would naturally resemble the preachers of the age. There is no proof that Langland took anything from the homilists of the age, although he has much in common with them, and may owe something to them. As Brett pointed out in regard to a specific passage,[206] Owst's special reading, and, it must be admitted, the neglect of

194 M. Day, "Duns Scotus and *Piers Plowman,*" *RES,* III (1927) , 333 ff.; Wells, "The Construction," *PMLA,* XLIV, 135 *et passim;* Troyer, "Who Is Piers Plowman?" *PMLA,* XLVII, 372 *et passim* [see below, pp. 156-73]; *The Year's Work in English Studies,* X (1929) , 144; and Dunning, *Piers Plowman, passim.*

195 See above, p. 21, n. 161.

196 See Ten Brink, *op. cit.,* p. 355, and Chadwick, *Social Life,* p. 95.

197 Owst, "The *Angel* and the *Goliardeys* of Langland's Prologue," *MLR,* XX, 271.

198 *Preaching in Medieval England,* p. 295 and repeated in *Literature and Pulpit,* p. 351.

199 *Literature and Pulpit,* pp. 572 ff.

200 *Ibid.,* pp. 445 ff.

201 *Ibid.,* pp. 56 ff.

202 *Ibid.,* pp. 548 and 558 ff.

203 *Ibid.,* pp. 224 and 572 ff.

204 See E. H. Kellogg, "Bishop Brunton and the Fable of the Rats," *PMLA,* L (1935) , 57 ff.

205 See Brink, *op. cit.,* p. 353.

206 "Notes on Old and Middle English," *MLR,* XXII (1927) , 261-262. There are many references of a similar nature to those in the homilies, in literature, secular and religious, before the date of *Piers Plowman.* This fact destroys the value of most of Owst's evidence as far as sources are concerned. For instance, the religious tractates de-

scholars, have made him put undue emphasis upon his contribution to the understanding of *Piers Plowman*.

As regards Langland's learning, it is difficult to be precise. He certainly knew Latin and may have known French,[207] although we have very little definite evidence that he did. His erudition was vast, but not deep,[208] and he was acquainted with that vast medley of mediaeval knowledge which all educated men of the age knew.[209] Recently, Dunning has made out a good case for a close acquaintance with mediaeval theology and philosophy of the writer of the A-text, at least. I do think, however, that Dunning, at times, reads too much into the poem.

The immediate future in *Piers Plowman* scholarship seems to me to be in two directions, omitting for the moment the textual work which is basic and apt to extend over many years: (1) the study of the meaning of Langland's words and lines, and (2) a general study of the backgrounds in folklore, art, theology, homilies, religious tractates, and various literatures, as well as in social and economic history.[210] The basic purpose is not to find sources, necessarily, but to make possible a new understanding of the intellectual and social atmosphere of fourteenth-century England. Much remains to be done in that field.

---

nounce the tavern as frequently as the homilists do; leaving out the question of an independent attack, who can say that Langland is indebted to the homilists and not to the moralists?

[207] See Owst, *Preaching in Medieval England*, p. 295, n. 3.

[208] See Jusserand, *Piers Plowman*, pp. 173 ff. and esp. 80 ff. and Görnemann, *Zur Verfasserschaft*, pp. 138 ff.

[209] Davis, *Piers Plowman*, p. xv.

[210] Literary critics should be cognizant of the scholarship in the field, else their work suffers. D. A. Traversi, "Revaluations (x): The Vision of Piers Plowman," *Scrutiny*, v (1936), pp. 276–291, affords an example of literary criticism which neglects Piers Plowman scholarship and is dogmatic to such an extent as to ignore facts.

G. Hort in *Piers Plowman and Contemporary Religious Thought* (London: Church Historical Society, 1937?) has written a book of some value, but she too has ignored much of the scholarship on *Piers Plowman* and, as a result, falls into error or duplication. See e.g., the comments on Langland's use of the Bible and the Breviary, pp. 43 ff., and appendices. Her study of the theology of the poem is enlightening, although she and Dunning arrive at different conclusions, especially on Synderesis (pp. 71 ff.) .

2. *Piers Plowman* and the Pursuit of Poetry

A. H. SMITH

* * *

II

... I have chosen to address my students on a literary topic which might allow me in passing to point to some of the more permanent elements in our purpose in the study of literature and to illustrate the pitfalls which constantly beset us in our scholarship. My theme is that the academic study of medieval literature, engaged as it often is in the examination of linguistic and technical detail and preoccupied with the rules of Literary Criticism, has diverted students from literature itself, that the pursuit of poetry too often ends in the pursuit of forms and rimes and all manner of technical pedantry, needful as these may be. More particularly, I shall refer to the long fourteenth-century symbolic poem *The Vision of Piers Plowman*,[1] and I have chosen *Piers Plowman* for several reasons. In the first place, it is in itself a poem of singular merit, standing amongst the foremost literary products of our language, and, as an expression of contemporary thought on the eternal problems of mankind, it had a powerful, even if somewhat misleading, influence upon later thinkers, who did not, any more than we do to-day, fully comprehend its meaning; it belongs to a medieval world which is approaching the modern. Secondly, it has been the subject of a very prolonged and, I am inclined to think, unnecessary controversy in the matter of its authorship, where academic ingenuity and the highly subjective interpretation of evidence carefully sifted for its relevance to a particular view have ranged themselves in support of a theory, which is, to say the least of it, improbable. And lastly, as we all know, its study has had very close associations with Univer-

Reprinted by permission of Mrs. Helen Smith, wife of the late Professor Hugh Smith, and University College London. This paper was originally delivered as an inaugural lecture at University College London on Feb. 23, 1950, and was first published in 1951 by H. K. Lewis and Co., Ltd., London.

Some recent essays on *Piers Plowman* as poetry include Elizabeth Suddaby, "The Poem, *Piers Plowman*," *JEGP*, LIV (1955), 91–103; and Nevill Coghill, "God's Wenches and the Light That Spoke (Some Notes on Langland's Kind of Poetry) ," *English and Medieval Studies Presented to J. R. R. Tolkien* (London, 1962) , pp. 200–17.

[1] *The Vision of William concerning Piers Plowman,* ed. W. W. Skeat (Early English Text Society, Original Series, Nos. 28, 38, 54, 67, 81 [1867–84]) .

sity College for some forty years, a study pursued fitfully for long spells, but at times with urgent enthusiasm. It still stands as one of our major research problems, for the College is the inheritor of [R.W.] Chambers's unfinished material[2] and my colleagues and I were enjoined by Chambers many years ago to complete it. To these matters, too, I shall return.

III

The Vision of Piers Plowman, as it is now called, or more correctly, *The Vision of William Langland concerning Piers the Plowman,* is a long fourteenth-century poem in the alliterative measure, and it embodies some eleven visions. By name it is well known; some of us are familiar with the first few passus or sections which are usually prescribed for examinations; a few have even read the whole. But its contents are now more widely known, thanks to Mr. Nevill Coghill's excellent translation[3] and broadcasts. No summary, however, can in fact set forth its complicated theme and its development and treatment, for its plan does not readily emerge from the great mass of detail, the relevance of which is not always easily perceived, from its rich display of contemporary social and historical material, from its religious and moral background, and from its symbolism and its allegory. "The Sence," said Robert Crowley[4] in 1550, "is somewhat darcke, but not so harde, but that it may be understande of suche as will not sticke to breake the shell of the nutte for the kernelles sake."

The theme is the Search for Truth and Salvation and the search is symbolized as a pilgrimage.

In the development of this theme, the poet first sets out his problem in a picture of a world largely dishonest and corrupt. He begins:

In a somer seson . whan soft was the sonne, . . .
Went wyde in þis world . wondres to here.
Ac on a May mornynge . on Maluerne hulles
Me byfel a ferly . of fairy me thouȝte;
I was wery forwandred . and went me to reste
Vnder a brode banke . bi a bornes side,
And as I lay and lened . and loked in þe waters,

2 Chambers's private papers and correspondence relating to this, together with the collations of *Piers Plowman* manuscripts prepared chiefly by Professor J. H. G. Grattan, their photostats and other materials are now in University College Library; they are not yet generally accessible.

3 Nevill Coghill, *Visions from Piers Plowman* (London, 1949) .

4 *The Vision of Pierce Plowman, now fyrste imprynted by Roberte Crowley* (London, 1550) ; the title page bears the date 1505 in error. Crowley was in fact speaking of the language of the poem.

> I slombred in a slepyng . it sweyued so merye.
> Thanne gan I to meten . a merueilouse sweuene.[5]

In his dream the poet saw a great concourse of people, representing Mankind, all busy in their several occupations and thronging a field between the Tower of Truth and the Dungeon of Wrong. Some ploughed and toiled, some prayed. Merchants and minstrels and jesters there were who

> With her bely and her bagges . of bred ful ycrammed,
> Fayteden for here fode . fouȝten atte ale.[6]

There were hermits going off on pilgrimage with their wenches, and parsons complaining that their parishes were too poor since the Pestilence, going to live in London.

> And syngen þere for symonye . for siluer is swete.[7]

Lawyers there were of whom it is said

> þow myȝtest better mete þe myste . on maluerne hulles
> þan gete a momme of here mouthe . but money were shewed.[8]

Such was the world as William Langland saw it, evil from the desire for material treasure most readily achieved by bribery. A lovely lady, Holy Church, to whom he appeals, not for treasure, but about how he might save his soul, replies that

> Whan alle tresores aren tried ... trewthe is þe best.[9]

"Yet," says the Dreamer, "I have no natural knowledge of it." "Thou doltish dafty," she says, "dull are thy wits. It is thy natural understanding that teaches thee to love thy Lord better than thyself, to do no deadly sin. The Father looked on us with love and was merciful; so the rich should have mercy on the poor, for though you be true in speech and deed, unless you love the poor, you have no more merit in your prayers than Malkin in her maidenhood, whom no man desires. Truth is the best of all treasures." [10]

---

[5] I quote from Skeat's edition (the B-text) . This passage is Prologue, ll. 1 ff.: "In a summer season, when the sun was warm, (I) went out into the world, wonders to learn. But on this May morning, on the Malvern Hills, a marvel befell me, of fairyland it seemed. Weary from wandering, I went to rest under a broad bank beside a stream. And as I lay and reclined and looked in the waters, I slumbered asleep, it sauntered so merrily. Then did I dream a marvellous dream."

[6] "With their bellies and their bags crammed full of bread, deceived for their food, fought at their ale" (B. Prologue, 41–42) .

[7] "To sing for simony there, for silver is sweet" (B. Prologue, 86) .

[8] "Thou mightest better measure the mist on the Malvern Hills than get a word from their mouths before thy money were shewed" (B. Prologue, 214–15) .

[9] "When all treasure is tried, Truth is the best" (B. i, 85) .

[10] B. i, 136–82.

To emphasize still more that the desire for material treasure is the source of worldly evil, the poet is shown how to recognize Falsehood, whose bridal with Lady Meed (that is, Bribery) is being prepared. Legal complications over the charter of endowment of the contracting parties with the Lordship of the Deadly Sins carry the whole concourse of corrupt ecclesiastics and lawyers to Westminster. There the king threatens punishment, but Lady Meed is promised forgiveness if she will wed Conscience instead. Conscience lists her faults:

> For she is frele of hir feith, . fykel of here speche,
> And maketh men mysdo . many score tymes . . .
> Wyues and widewes . wantounes she techeth,
> And lereth hem leccherye . that loueth hir ʒiftes.[11]

But, says Lady Meed, "it becomes a king to reward those who serve him; servants are paid their wages, minstrels get their gifts, priests their mass-pennies." Conscience rebukes her, for there is a difference between wages and bribes. But Reason shall reign and shall replace Bribery, and Reason shows there can be no mercy till lords and ladies all love Truth, till harlots choose holiness, and priests prove their teaching in themselves.

In the next stage, the poet develops his theme and proves that this corrupt world he has delineated can be bettered only through repentance, and in a sermon to "the field full of folk" Conscience shows that the way to repentance lies through obedience to the Commandments; it is for their sins that they suffered the Pestilence as well as the violence of the great gale which did so much damage one Saturday night.[12] He bade wasters work, Pernal to leave off her finery and chapmen to chastise their children. Priests and prelates should practise what they preach. So effective was the appeal that the Deadly Sins were all moved to confession and repentance. Even Sir Glutton had but one lapse, when on his way to confession he was accosted outside the tavern by the ale-wife. "I have good ale, gossip. Wouldst thou try it?" Then Glutton went in and found the tavern full of his companions.

> þere was laughyng and louryng . and "let go þe cuppe,"
> And seten so til euensonge . and songen vmwhile,
> Tyl glotoun had y-globbed . a galoun an a Iille.
> His guttis gunne to gothely . as two gredy sowes; . . .
> He myʒte neither steppe ne stonde . er he his staffe hadde;
> And þanne gan he go . liche a glewmannes bicche,

---

[11] "For she is frail in her faith, fickle in her speech, and makes men err many a score times; wives and widows she teaches to be wantons, and to those who love her gifts she teaches lechery" (B. iii, 121–25) .

[12] B. v, 14. This was the gale of 15 January 1362.

> Somme tyme aside . and somme tyme arrere,
> As who-so leyth lynes . forto lacche foules.
> And whan he drowgh to þe dore . þanne dymmed his eighen,
> He stumbled on þe thresshewolde . an threwe to þe erthe . . .
> With al þe wo of þis worlde . his wyf and his wenche
> Baren hym home to his bedde . and brouȝte hym þerinne.
> And after al þis excesse . he had an accidie,
> þat he slepe saterday and sonday . til sonne ȝede to reste.[13]

Being rebuked by his wife, he made confession of his many sins and was moved to repentance and abstinence. And so all the folk after these confessions thronged together, calling for grace to find Holy Truth.

The poet's next problem now unfolds—what should Mankind, having repented, do to be saved, to find Holy Truth and Salvation? There are two stages, and the first is the attainment of the simple life of toil and virtue. But of these folk no one knew the way to Truth except Piers Plowman who directs the pilgrims to the Tower of Truth. The pilgrims ask him to be their guide; he will go when he has ploughed his half-acre. "That's a long time to wait," said one fine lady, "what shall we do?" All must toil, says Piers, for fear of Hunger, who must be fed to be kept away. The poor feed him on peas and beans, but at harvest they feed him well: beggars will eat only wheaten bread and drink best brown ale, labourers only fresh meat and fried fish and they grumble at their wages. "I warn all you labourers," says Piers, "to earn what you can, for Hunger will return and there will be famine." [14] Truth promises a pardon to all who work. The Pardon is the text "These shall go away into everlasting punishment, but the righteous into life eternal." [15] A priest disputes the validity of the pardon. "Piers," quoth the priest, "I can find no pardon except 'do well and have well and God shall have thy soul, and do evil and have evil . . . and the devil shall have thy soul.' "

> And Pieres for pure tene . pulled it atweyne,
> And seyde, *"si ambulauero in medio vmbre mortis, non timeo mala;*
> *quoniam tu mecum es.*

---

[13] "There was laughing and scowling and (cries of) 'let the cup pass,' and they sat thus till evensong and sang bewhiles, till Glutton had gobbled a gallon and a gill. His guts began to rumble like two greedy sows. . . . He could neither step nor stand till he had his staff, and then he walked like gleeman's bitch, sometimes sideways, sometimes backwards, like a man setting lines to snare birds. And when he reached the door, his eyes grew dim, he stumbled on the threshold and fell to the ground. . . . With all the woe of this world his wife and his wench carried him off home to his bed and put him therein. And after all this excess he had a fit of sloth, so that he slept on Saturday and Sunday till the sun went to rest" (B. v, 343–67) .

[14] B. vi, 322–23.

[15] Matt. xxv, 46.

I shal cessen of my sowyng," quod Pieres, . "and swynk nouȝt so harde,
Ne about my bely ioye . so bisi namore.
Of preyers and of penaunce . my plow shal ben herafter." [16]

He decides that the life of Do-well or simple virtue surpasses indulgences. The withdrawal of Piers from the life of industrious virtue marks
the poet's decision to inquire into the higher kind of life, and so ends the
vision of Piers as a poor toiling charitable ploughman.[17]

The second stage in the search for Truth follows upon the attainment
of the life of toil and simple virtue. The poet now enters upon a long
consideration of the three kinds of life which are embodied in the Visions of Do-well (which re-emphasizes the life of simple virtue), Do-
better, and Do-best. Here the movement and device of the pilgrimage
recede before an analysis of the three kinds of life, illuminated and exemplified by the poet's experience and knowledge of the underlying
truths which are greater than simple virtue. The three kinds of life
are considered together in various aspects. After a digression on the doctrine of free will, the Dreamer again falls asleep and dreams. Meeting
Thought, he inquires about Do-well, Do-better, and Do-best and is directed to the castle where they are the masters. After discussions on the
duties to the helpless and the duties of marriage, the conclusion is that
Do-well is to act lawfully and fear God, Do-better to love all and to suffer,
and Do-best to help all and be humble. Another, Dame Study, warns
him of the vexations of Theology and the dangers of Astronomy, Geom-
etry, and Geomancy—three evil things—as well as of Alchemy, all in-
vented to deceive men, and she directs him to Clergy (that is, Learning),
with whom he disputes on predestination and avers that

> Aren none rather yrauysshed . fro þe riȝte byleue
> þan ar þis cunnynge clerkes . þat conne many bokes.
> Ne none sonner saued . ne sadder of bileue,
> þan plowmen and pastoures . & pore comune laboreres.[18]

In the Life of Do-better the Dreamer inquires of Reason about Charity. Now Piers Plowman becomes identified with Christ on Earth through

[16] "And Piers in pure vexation tore it in two, and said 'Though I walk through the
valley of the shadow of death, I will fear no evil, for thou art with me.' I shall cease
from my sowing and toil not so hard, nor busy myself about my belly's pleasure. Hereafter shall my plough be in prayers and penance" (B. vii, 116–19).

[17] *Explicit hic visio willelmi de Petro de Plouȝman. Eciam Incipit Vita de do-wel,
do-bet & do-best secundum wyt & resoun.* [Here ends the vision of William concerning
Piers the Plowman. And also begins the Life of do-well, do-bet, and do-best in accordance with wit and reason.]

[18] "None are more quickly ravished from the right belief than these learned scholars
who know many books. And none are sooner saved nor steadier in faith than plough-
men and herdsmen and other poor common labourers" (B. x, 456–59).

the story of Christ, of the Good Samaritan (who is Charity or Christ) , and through the heroic story of the Crucifixion and the Harrowing of Hell.

In the Life of Do-best, Piers personifies Grace. The whole Christian Church, attacked by the Antichrist, is beset by pride and covetousness and is destroyed, but Conscience, fortified by Hope, determines to wander over the world as a pilgrim until he finds Grace in Piers Plowman. And so Piers Plowman has in turn represented the stages of Mankind's religious life—Do-well or the life of simple virtue, Do-better, the spiritual life in which Charity and Christ on Earth are identified, and Do-best, the state where Piers is Grace and represents spiritual fulfilment. These are the stages by which Mankind can achieve Salvation.

I V

We may ask what the world has made of *Piers Plowman* and gained from it. Although there has been a continuity of interest from the time of its composition, that interest has changed according to the different purposes of its readers.

Some sixty or more manuscripts of the poem, mostly from the fourteenth and fifteenth centuries, testify to its contemporary popularity, as does the fact that it was issued in printed editions by Robert Crowley in 1550 and by Owen Rogers in 1561. It is in the detail of its expostulation against the abuses in Church and State that it most readily lent itself to the service of propaganda, and those features, as every student is aware, are more easily appreciated than the grand conception of Man's religious life or than the genuine orthodoxy of the poet himself. And thus it is those who sought amelioration of the condition of the poor and later on those who sought reform in the Church with whom it was popular. This specialized kind of popularity is attested by several facts. In many manuscripts marginal notes and devices direct attention to passages of particular interest to social and religious reformers. The manuscripts themselves are generally inferior in the quality of their production to those which we might expect to have been prepared at great cost for wealthy patrons, as some of Chaucer's were. Later literature often alludes to the person of Piers Plowman as the embodiment of the down-trodden poor.[19] And Crowley's own preface to the edition of 1550 [20] lays stress upon the significance of the poem in his own days:

it pleased God to open the eyes of many to se hys truth, geving them

19 Cf. Skeat, *op. cit.*, No. 67, 863–8.
20 R. Crowley, *op. cit.*

boldenes of herte, to open their mouthes and crye oute agaynste the worckes of darckenes, as did John Wicklefe . . . and this writer . . . doeth moste christianlye enstruct the weake, and sharply rebuke the obstinate blynde. There is no manner of vice, that reigneth in anye estate of men, whiche this wryter hath not godly, learnedlye, and wittilye, rebuked.

But he singles out for special emphasis the Dreamer's forecast of the Reformation and the Dissolution of the Monasteries:

Ac þere shal come a kyng . and confesse ȝow religiouses,
And bete ȝow as þe bible telleth . for brekynge of ȝowre reule,
And amende monyales, . monkes and chanouns,
And putten hem to her penaunce.[21]

And again,

And þanne shal þe abbot of Abyndoun . and alle his issu for euere
Haue a knokke of a kynge . and incurable þe wounde.[22]

This, says Robert Crowley, is a prophecy of "the suppression of Abbaies."

Thus we are compelled to think of the manifolding of copies of *Piers Plowman* as an expression of early reforming zeal rather than as the enthusiasm to perpetuate an example of great literature.

By contrast with this, the twentieth century has invested the poem with problems of its own creation.[23] The original version of *Piers Plowman,* which we refer to as the A-text, was probably completed about the year 1362 and was followed by two revisions, the B-text from about 1367–69 and the C-text from about 1378. The A-text is in a sense incomplete, for the author was unable at that time to offer more than the life of simple virtue as the way to salvation. But in the B-text, besides some revision, he provides a different and more complicated conclusion, whilst in his last revision he explains in a more intellectual way many of the difficulties left unsolved in the earlier versions. These versions were all considered to be the work of a single author until in 1906 Professor J. M. Manly decided on quite subjective grounds that they were the work of five.[24] It

21 "But there shall come a king and confess you monks, and beat you as the Bible tells for breaking your Rule, and he shall reform nuns, monks and canons, and put them to their penance" (B. x, 317–19).
22 "And then shall the Abbot of Abingdon and all his issue for ever take a knock from a king, and incurable will be the wound" (B. x, 326–27).
23 A very full survey of contributions to the scholarship of *Piers Plowman* is provided by Morton Bloomfield's "The Present State of *Piers Plowman* Studies" in *Speculum* xiv (1939), 215–32 [see above, pp. 3–25] and in E. T. Donaldson's *Piers Plowman—the C-Text and its Poet* (Yale, 1949).
24 J. M. Manly, "The Lost Leaf of Piers Plowman" in *Modern Philology,* iii (1906),

is not necessary to repeat the details of the theory—the ingenious suggestion of a missing leaf in an original manuscript to explain a supposed
abruptness in the Confession of Sloth and the omission of Wrath from
the Seven Deadly Sins, or the supposed changes in literary ability and
treatment, or the supposed misunderstandings of the earlier versions by
the putative revisers—for Manly's theory received undue prominence and
currency by its elaboration in the *Cambridge History of English Literature*. Many scholars like F. J. Furnivall, Henry Bradley, Dr. Knott, Professor Moore, and Dr. Mabel Day, to mention but a few, have sought in
various ways to maintain the theory of multiple authorship, whilst others
like M. Jusserand, and not least Professor Chambers and Professor Grattan, have firmly maintained the unity of composition and revision, as
Skeat had done, and this is now the generally accepted view.[25]

The ingenuity of Manly's suggestion of course flushed some scholars
like Furnivall into a too ready acceptance of the multiple authorship of
Piers Plowman; the latter, though not yielding in the position he had
adopted, freely admitted that Chambers and Grattan "would stop many
folk accepting the Manly-Bradley view as easily as I did" [26] and Bradley
himself, with characteristic intellectual honesty, acknowledged that some
of the arguments were not so overwhelmingly strong,[27] though he maintained his adherence to Manly's conclusion for a long time. "While I
make some concession to your arguments," he wrote to Chambers, "I find
in the main I stand where I did. . . . I honestly think I should not have
been a bit sorry if I had found myself convinced. For, like yourself, I do
not quite relish giving up the portrait of 'Long Will' which is so full of
interest and so humanly credible." [28] In the end Bradley came near to
Chambers's view.[29]

359–66; "Piers Plowman" in *The Cambridge History of English Literature* (Cambridge, 1908) II, 1–42; etc.

25 Allowance, of course, is always made for John But's lines at the end of the A-text.
Both Bradley, who favoured multiple authorship, and Jusserand, who did not, felt also
that there might be some episodic insertion. Bradley had "a suspicion that the Rat-
Parliament episode may have been written and published as part of an occasional
pamphlet, something like *Wynner and Wastour* or *Mum, Soothsegger,* and afterwards
inserted, not altogether appropriately, in the Prologue to Piers Plowman" (University
College Library, Chambers Papers, No. 27, 2 February 1910) . It is proper to mention
here that the Chambers Papers contain a good many private letters from various
scholars which are strikingly illuminating for this learned controversy.

26 Chambers Papers, No. 15 (1 July 1909) .

27 "What you and I desire," he wrote to Furnivall, "is truth, not the confirmation of
our own theories" (Chambers Papers, No. 14, 30 June 1909) .

28 Chambers Papers, No. 27 (2 February 1910) .

29 Bradley wrote to W. P. Ker in 1917: "However, there is at least one important
point on which I believe Chambers has permanently convinced me. He has satisfied me
that the plan followed in A x and A xi is continued through the following books of

Manly never published his full material and arguments, as he had promised to do, but, according to statements made by Chambers to Professor A. G. Mitchell and myself in 1938, Manly too had finally abandoned the theory of multiple authorship. The discrepancies which led to this theory are in fact only apparent ones; there is little or nothing in the poem which is incompatible either with the coherent unity of the main theme of the poem or with those changes in circumstances, in interest, in outlook, and in knowledge that befall a man or his audience over the years of his life.

Chambers and Grattan saw at the beginning of this long controversy the need for a reliable text of the three versions, as this was and still is a singular omission from the armoury of all the scholars.[30] "It all comes to this," wrote Skeat to Chambers in 1909,[31] "we cannot profitably discuss a question till we know precisely what we are talking about. And we cannot discuss Text A till we know precisely what Text A is." With the encouragement of Skeat, whose own edition would thus be supplanted, Chambers and Grattan began to prepare an edition of the A-text in 1909, and some of this was in type as long ago as 1910.[32] Although Grattan had prepared the major part of the collations of all the relevant manuscripts, for various causes no great progress was made towards the completion of the final edition. Thus, it was only after the work was started that a better manuscript could be chosen as the basis. It also became clear after a time that to edit the A-text the B-text would also be needed, and so Mrs. Blackman began work on the B-text. These difficulties of course became more evident when the principles of editing had been evolved out of the experience and conclusions of Westcott and Hort, and much effort was directed to that end; yet it was not until 1930 that Chambers became convinced that Grattan's theory of the Substitution of Similars was right.

---

the B text, in a way that almost proves identity of authorship" (Chambers Papers, No. 40, 7 October 1917).

30 Skeat's A-text is from the unsatisfactory Vernon manuscript with selected collations from other manuscripts; yet this has never been replaced. [Since the appearance of Smith's essay, the definitive edition of the A-text has been published: *Piers Plowman: The A Version,* ed. George Kane (London, 1960). The basis of the text is Trinity College, Cambridge, MS R.3.14, corrected from other manuscripts, with variant readings.]

31 Chambers Papers, No. 3 (26 April 1909). Bradley, too, expressed the same view: "Until we get a sound critical edition of each of the three texts, any detailed argumentation on the question of authorship is sure to contain much that is fallacious. . . . Strong as my conviction is that I am right, I flatter myself that I am open-minded enough to yield at once if real proof can be produced against me" (*ibid.,* No. 8, to Furnivall, 1 June 1909).

32 Furnivall expressed his willingness to accept the edition for the Early English Text Society in May 1909 (Chambers Papers, No. 4, to Grattan, 10 May 1909; No. 7, to J. H. Robertson, 25 May 1909).

Meanwhile, a growing distaste for work of an analytical character turned Chambers to other fields and the work lagged, especially after Grattan's departure to Liverpool, except for fitful pricks of conscience. "It is a reproach," wrote Chambers in one letter to Grattan in 1928, "that scholars had to base their results on Skeat's old collations and build on sand," and again in 1930, "we must do our duty to old William Langland (and to Skeat) before the night comes when no man can work." Although Chambers's visit to California to examine the Huntington Library manuscripts of *Piers Plowman* revived a temporary activity, he was, as he wrote, "feeling amazingly lazy" after a serious illness, but he was hopefully enthusiastic about the edition's being completed when we were joined by A. G. Mitchell and G. J. Kane in 1937–38. Between us we have carried the programme a good deal further forward; the A-text, completed by Professor Grattan and Dr. Kane, will soon be ready for the printer, and the remaining texts by Dr. Kane and Professor Mitchell have advanced considerably; these will be followed by a linguistic study by Mr. C. R. Quirk and myself, as well as by a commentary and studies of the poem, in which we hope to have the help of other scholars.

All these matters affecting the study of *Piers Plowman*—its early propagandist use, "the bog of scholarship" over the authorship problem, the effort to provide an adequate text—have diverted later students from consideration of its literary merit.

V

The study of poetry has two aims, one the understanding, and the other the appraisal, of a poet's endeavour. The historical approach, which is characteristic of what may be termed the "academic" study of poetry, shows how we may distinguish tradition from genius. An artist's work cannot be appraised without regard to its context, for the simple reason that few artists indeed can be said to have remained uninfluenced by their environment or cultural background. The academic student, therefore, follows on the one hand the evolution of human thought, and more especially of its artistic expression, and on the other hand the peculiar contribution made by a particular author.

To this, William Langland's work is no exception. The details of his work cannot possibly be comprehended without a knowledge of his fourteenth-century world, literary, political, and ecclesiastical; the greatness of his theme, without knowing his Church and his religion; his meaning, without being familiar with the essentials of his education and with the books that he knew. Yet only through these can we isolate and estimate his own peculiar merit. It is by this appreciation that *Piers Plow-*

man becomes itself a pathway to knowledge and enjoyment, to stimulation of the mind through the assimilation of his experience. The revelation springs from the peculiar merits of the aptness of its form and style and treatment and especially from the understanding of its content.

These are matters that properly pertain to Literary Criticism, which I do not propose to discuss, but about which it may not be inappropriate to make one or two remarks, because they may be relevant to the student's approach to *Piers Plowman*. Literary Criticism embraces what the learned of many ages, by skilful analysis of creative literature, have evolved as the criteria by which those literary productions might be judged and valued. That these criteria are fundamentally sound and reasonably permanent comes not only from the display of great analytical powers but also from knowledge and historical perception. It is perhaps the growth of the body of literature itself that endows the study of Literary Criticism with its dangerous hold, and the immeasurable wealth of literature of all degrees of excellence or poverty may well drive the student, as we know he is driven, to works of literary analysis as to books of rules. The danger reveals itself in its specialized jargon, for Literary Criticism has, like every other branch of knowledge, very rightly created its own terminology. In science and technology, where we can deal with concrete matter and concrete processes, the use of words can be and is exact, but when it is a process or idea that can be neither demonstrated physically nor perceived by the senses, or else involves almost inhuman conceptions of time, space, and the like, the adaptation of old words and the invention of new ones, unless defined in terms generally known in human experience, become very nearly a meaningless device. Although we know that man's mind usually seeks to understand what is unknown in terms of what is known, the not uncommon trick of explaining by loose or imperfect analogy is no adequate substitute for properly disciplined definition. In literature, we may be dealing with even more intangible concepts and the risk of using ill-defined or half-understood terms is the greater, especially when the mind of the user is not illumined by that same knowledge of literature or by that same measure of experience as that possessed by the creator of the term. When Gladstone said of Homer that "there is a singular transparency of the mind, as there is also in the limpid language" his meaning is clear and certain, but to extend the term *limpid* to other writings where it is patently inappropriate to the style, as students have done, is a confession of failure to understand the term or, as is not unlikely, to have read the writings.

The more direct methods of Literary Criticism as applied to *Piers Plowman* would lead me to speak of its diction, which in its fitting directness and colloquialism lacks the ornamental effects of the language

of other contemporary alliterative poetry, of its prosody, which in its
close agreement with the rhythmical patterns of speech does not distract
by elaborate trickery and stunts, of the use of allegory and symbolism
which are not so formal as to destroy the sense of reality, or of the special
devices in satirical treatment. But these are better dealt with when we
know more about the precise text of the poem.[33] I would, however, refer
particularly to one feature that has seemed to me as to others to be the
mark of great literature—that is the poet's perception of moral values and
social principles and his preoccupation with human material, which give
the poem its unity and bring a number of seemingly disjointed elements
within the compass of a single theme. It shows itself in his accurate, truthful, and realistic presentation of human actions or the motives of such
behaviour, as in his appreciation of what we call moral standards. What
we mean by moral standards is the sum of the duties enjoined by the Ten
Commandments and the New Testament teachings on Love and Charity;
it has its origins in the traditional instruction we receive in behaviour,
and in our western civilization its essence is Christian teaching. This has
given our moral outlook a degree of permanence which is of the greatest
importance in English literary history, for the revelation of moral values
in the delineation of character and action is one of the things that places
our great writers in their high rank.

The poet of *Piers Plowman* is one of these. Everywhere, of course, he
upholds a strict adherence to the doctrines of the Catholic Church and
nowhere does he condone heresy. Yet he could be adduced in support of
the Reformation, because he reveals and reproves the abuses that spring,
not from doctrinal error, but from lapses in the common standard of
good social conduct which originates in charity and love. His sympathy
lies with the poor and oppressed; yet he can castigate them for their idleness and bad husbandry. His fierce condemnation of corruption in the
Church is not an attack on the Established Faith; it is rather on the
Church's failure to inspirit the practise of its religion with love, grace,
and forgiveness. With the rich it is their lack of charity; and with all who
seek material advancement, it is bribery and excess that call forth his
reproof. The standard by which he measures mankind is a moral one,
and his finest and most moving verses are those aroused by love and charity, which are the fulfilment of the moral outlook.

> For þouȝ ȝe be trewe of ȝowre tonge . and trewliche wynne,
> And as chaste as a childe . þat in cherche wepeth,
> But if ȝe louen lelliche . and lene þe poure,

---

[33] Some of these points are dealt with by Dr. G. J. Kane in his *Middle English
Literature* (London, 1951) .

Such goed as god ʒow sent . godelich parteth,
ʒe ne haue na more meryte . in masse ne in houres,
þan Malkyn of hire maydenhode . þat no man desireth. [34]

Though there is a layer of allegorical nomenclature in his characters, the realism of description furnishes them all with human quality. Though many are enshrouded in human weakness, even as in the case of Sir Glutton to the point of grossness, his satirical reprobation invests his work with a propriety inspired by his moral attitude, which we can accept as one of the marks of his greatness.

These are the qualities that merit the student's and the scholar's attention, and we should not be deflected from them or fail to seek them through being too narrowly engrossed in the technicalities of our work.

*   *   *

[34] "For though you be true in your speech and live honestly, and be as pure as a child that weeps in church, unless you truly love the poor and give to them, and liberally share such goods as God has sent you, you shall have no more merit in your mass nor in your hours than Malkin in her maidenhood, whom no man desires" (B. i, 177–82) .

3. The Pardon of Piers Plowman

NEVILL K. COGHILL

I

IT MAY SEEM SIMPLE to ask again what the visions of *Piers Plowman* are about, yet it is a question that has been a little over-borne by its younger sister "who wrote them?" By putting the elder question twice, first to the A-text and then to the B, the natural assumption that they are both about the same thing begins to dwindle and vanishes as our reading proceeds; for not only does it become gradually clear that the main theme of the B-text is very different from that of the A, but, which is more important, one perceives that the two poems belong to separate species of poetry, to different orders of the imagination (in consequence of their different themes), and therefore call for different kinds of response from their readers, as they called for different kinds of treatment by their poet.

These differences in purpose and quality are the subject of this paper and I shall try to show the nature of the transformation of A into B, and how it was dictated in the poet's mind by a long musing over that enigmatic but crucial Pardon granted to Piers in the eighth passus of the A-text, the Pardon that is Piers' reward for setting the world to work....

This paper is not offered as a contribution to the long-drawn controversy over the authorship of *Piers Plowman*. It is offered as an investigation of poetry. The metamorphosis from A to B is striking, beautiful, and unique and will here be studied for its own sake. It may be that some readers, interested in controversy, will find or draw an argument for one theory or the other from this investigation, but no such corollary is intended here. It is, however, my opinion that the present state of this

Reprinted in abridged form by permission of the author and The British Academy from *Proceedings of the British Academy*, XXX (1944), 303–57, published by Oxford University Press. This paper was originally delivered on Feb. 28, 1945, as a Sir Israel Gollancz Memorial Lecture.

For other discussions of the Pardon, see Robert W. Frank, "The Pardon Scene in *Piers Plowman*," *Speculum*, XXVI (1951), 317–31; John Lawlor, "Piers Plowman: The Pardon Reconsidered," *MLR*, XLV (1950), 449–58; and Donald R. Howard, "The Body Politic and the Lust of the Eyes: *Piers Plowman*," in *The Three Temptations* (Princeton, 1966), pp. 175–78.

battle authorizes me still to believe that both texts were written by the same man, William Langland, and I shall use his name freely throughout on this assumption; this will not invalidate the inquiry into the nature of these poems as poetry, and those who adhere to the theory of multiple authorship can mentally substitute A 1, A 2, Johan But, B 1, B 2, and C for the name Langland whenever they wish to do so, without losing anything of the argument.

I was led to think about these poems in the way proposed by a passage in the preface to Sir Israel Gollancz's edition of *Wynnere and Wastoure* and I cannot do better than begin by quoting it, for it is not only a true critical starting-point for my subject, but also a fair foundation for a paper given, as this is, in honour and memory of his scholarship.

> When *Wynnere and Wastoure* was a new poem, it seems to have stirred the heart of a young Western man, and perhaps to have kindled in him the latent fire of a prophet-poet, destined to deliver a weightier message to his fellow-countrymen. Ten years later than *Wynnere and Wastoure* the first version of *The Vision of Piers Plowman* set before all classes of the realm the evil conditions of the time, pointed to the corruptions in Church and State, and denounced even greater evils than those dealt with dramatically and dispassionately by our poet. The old man of *Wynnere and Wastoure* inspired Langland, the prophet-poet of England.[1]

WYNNERE AND WASTOURE AND THE A-TEXT OF PIERS PLOWMAN

No reader of *Wynnere and Wastoure* and of the A-text of *Piers Plowman* can fail to be struck by their general resemblances to each other, and any who follows Gollancz's suggestion far enough to make a close comparison will be led to support his view that these resemblances are too many and too exact to be attributable to an ambient literary tradition that the poets happened to share. Langland must have known the old man's poem itself; in his early twenties it must somehow have fallen upon his ears, or even into his hands, as the poem travelled those hilly Western regions, that were the last home of our more ancient style of poetry; in that style it set him dreaming. A great tradition is common property and there was no theft in his appropriation of images and phrases from the older poem; the summery brilliance of the sun, the drowsy gaze of a man lying beside a stream on a May morning among the Malvern Hills, lay to his hand:

Als I went in the weste, wandrynge myn one,

1 *Winner and Waster*, ed. Sir I. Gollancz, Oxford, 1931.

Bi a bonke of a bourne, bryghte was the sone,
Vndir a worthiliche wodde, by a wale medewe;
Fele floures gan folde ther my fote steppede. . . .
Bot as I laye at the laste, then lowked myn eghne,
And I was swythe in a sweuen sweped be-lyue.
Me thoghte I was in the werlde, I ne wiste in what ende,
One a loueliche lande that was ylike grene,
That laye loken by a lawe the lengthe of a myle. . . .[2]

Or again there was another flavour to be borrowed, a foretaste of Glutton in the Ale-house:

And thou wolle to the tauerne, by-fore the toune-hede,
Iche beryne redy withe a bolle to blerren thyn eghne,
Hete the whatte thou have schalte, and whatt thyn hert lykes,
Wyfe, wedowe, or wenche, that wonnes ther aboute.
Then es there bott "fille in" & "fecche forthe," Florence to schewe,
"Wee-hee," and "worthe vp," wordes ynewe.[3]

. . . each fashions his narrative allegory in what seems, at first sight, a similar manner, namely by advancing two meanings to be apprehended simultaneously (the literal and the transferred) , of which the first is to be accepted as a fantasy and the second as the actual state of affairs in contemporary England; their world is this world and their time the present. A chief theme, common to both (indeed the only theme of *Wynnere and Wastoure,* is the proper use of wealth, argued in the manner of a poetical debate (also a part of long tradition) , accented with invective and satire. The A-text of *Piers Plowman* ends with a longish moral *significacio,* and such an ending Gollancz believes also to have concluded *Wynnere and Wastoure,* more briefly, however.

2 *Wynnere and Wastoure,* Fitt I, 32–35, 45–49.
  As I went in the west, wand'ring alone,
  Along the bank of a brook,—bright was the sun,—
  'Neath a wondrous wood, by a winsome mead;
  Many flowers enfolded where my foot stepped. . . .
  But at last, as I lay, lock'd were mine eyes;
  And swiftly in a dream swept was I thence.
  Methought I was in the world, wist I not where,
  On a lovely lawn, all alike green,
  Immurèd with mountains a mile round about.
3 *Ibid.,* Fitt II, 277–82.
  But thou betakest thee to the tavern before the town-head,
  Each one ready with a bowl to blear both thine eyes,
  To proffer what thou shalt have, and what thy heart pleases,
  Wife, widow, or wench, that is wont there to dwell.
  Then is it but "Fill in!" and "Fetch forth!" and Florrie appears;
  "We-he!" and "whoa-up!," words that suffice.
              (Tr. Gollancz.)

Probably very little of the poem is lost. The dreamer no doubt was roused from his vision by the sound of trumpets, and found himself resting by the bank of the burn, the tale ending with some pious reflection, by way of conclusion.[4]

These are indeed great resemblances; what are the differences? There is a formal difference and a difference in the degree of genius shown. With regard to the formal difference, the A-text outsoars *Wynnere and Wastoure* by the addition of a further level of meaning of which every reader must become presently aware; it adds a continuous moral counter-point to the other two levels already mentioned, the literal and the transferred. This is not simply to be explained as a chance difference in visionary power between the two authors; it is a technical difference in poetical construction, a difference in allegorical convention. . . . there existed a richer kind of allegory, much used in preaching and biblical exegesis, by which a moral is continuously implied and drawn from the story; in Langland, indeed, it is forever bursting forth, as when Lady Meed promises a Church window in which her name is to be engraved in return for absolution from a Friar, and the indignant author intrudes upon the incident with:

> But god to all folk . such graving defendeth
> And saith, *Nesciat sinistra quid faciat dextera*.[5]
>
> (A. iii, 54–55.)

There may, as Gollancz suggests, have been "some pious reflection" at the end of *Wynnere and Wastoure,* but it is not a poem morally imbued all through. . . .

* * *

Apart from the greater merit of his poem in its formal construction in three voices, the degree of Langland's personal genius was incomparably greater than that shown by the poet of *Wynnere and Wastoure,* though the latter shows himself a glittering performer in the coining of alliterative phrase; Langland's superiority is, however, always to be seen in his grasp of affairs, even on the most secular level. The other poet has nothing real to tell us about wealth and its uses. . . . The disputants seem perfectly satisfied that the whole problem of wealth turns on the question of spending or saving it, and Waster's interest in the poor is momentary, a debating-point. In Langland the problem is more deeply seen in the antitheses of wealth and want, means and ends. Nothing is concluded

---

4 *Wynnere and Wastoure,* Preface.

5 Quotations from *Piers Plowman* have, for convenience, been modernized throughout, except where the established text of Skeat is necessary to the argument.

in the argument of the older poem, though the debate is wound up by the King with summary but frivolous advice....

In contrast to the colourful incoherence of *Wynnere and Wastoure,* the A-text is a masterpiece of intellectual organization. When those vivid things in Langland that give him rank as an artist with Pieter Brueghel the Elder have been listed, such as are rough laughter, a gift in proverbs, peasant sympathy, Christian faith, irony, skill in visualizing (crowds especially and tumultuous landscapes), a rich colour-sense, a deep pity, and so forth—it still remains to praise his best power (and Brueghel had it too), namely a strong architectural instinct for planning and carrying out a great composition, a design enormous in itself and wild with detail. It is not he who loses himself in a tangle of digressions, or if he does it is seldom; the unaccustomed modern reader, missing some association of idea, may cry out that he is lost, that the poet has no control; but however many and however long his digressions, he seems like a man giving himself more room, rather than like one who has lost his way. There are, however, some exceptions to this impression in both texts, which will be touched upon later.

*   *   *

II

THE STRUCTURE OF THE A-TEXT

Langland's narrative has a strategy; it is presented not in disorderly "Fitts," but by passus, each a real step that carries the reader logically onwards to the next. The main problems he propounds are four, each with its subdivisions. They are the purpose of wealth, the abuses of government, the sins of society, and the fear of famine; the narrative leads logically through these themes to that Pardon which, it is here contended, was the root-cause of the rewriting of the poem. It moves in a single on-rush or trajectory, the changes of scenes within it notwithstanding. Although this part of the poem is familiar to many readers, a brief analysis may have place to show the essential shapes within it, and how they are organized into the allegory.

(i) *The purpose of wealth.* (A. Prologue and Passus i)

The whole world of English life is gathered into a field which almost all are using as a Tom Tiddler's Ground with varying degrees of honesty and success. The main body is of beggars, business-men, several sorts of ecclesiastical swindler, lawyers, trades-people, barons, and bondmen; their whole activity is the amassing of wealth. Noble exceptions are a poor plowman or two and a few hermits who live "for loue of vr lord."

On either side of the field are set the Tower of Truth and the Deep Dale, to one or other of which all must eventually come; but the folk he pictures in the field seem unaware of them just as Bunyan's man with the muck-rake is unable to look any way but downwards.

When the question "What is the purpose of wealth?" is set in this context of Heaven and Hell, it leads beyond itself to further questions which only the Church can answer and it is logical that she, clothed in awe and beauty, should be the first visitant and instructress of the questioning Dreamer. Her replies go to the roots of human need and purpose. God has given man five senses *to worship Him with*.[6] As He has given these senses, so He has given their simple worldly satisfactions, namely food, drink, and clothing; these may be worked for, they are the constituents of wealth; but this kind of wealth is a means and not an end.

> All is not good to the ghost . that the body liketh.
>
> (A. i, 34)

The just debts of the body, like Caesar's penny, may be paid, but the soul has an over-riding debt to God; real wealth is wealth of the spirit.

> When all treasure is tried . truth is the best;
> I do it on *Deus Caritas* [God is love] . to deem the sooth.
>
> (A. i, 83)

That God is love and truth our treasure is too difficult a saying for the Dreamer, so he asks another question, Pilate's question, about truth and how it can be known.

> "Yet have I no kind knowing," [7] quoth I . "thou must teach me better,
> By what craft in my corpse . it commenceth and where."
>
> (A. i, 127)

To which the Church answers roundly that truth and love are known by simple intuition, by a natural recognition in the human heart (A. i, 129). An answer that Blake would have understood. Thus ends the catechism of the first passus which has dealt with the general ends of life and how we know them. Now, by a verbal ingenuity in which he is seldom deficient, the poet turns to his next problem, and the narrative steps forward into another field of inquiry (still, however, related to the abuses of wealth), namely the corruptions of government as seen in Lady Meed and Wrong.

(ii) *The abuses of government*. (A-text. Passus ii, iii, iv)

These brilliant passus are so well known as to need little analysis. With

[6] A. i, 16.
[7] "Yet I have no natural knowledge."

a rollicking irony the poet indicts English officialdom of simony and bribery from bishops and civil lawyers down to Randolph the Reve of Rut-
land; all are guests at the wicked wedding of Lady Meed and False, an
alliance of reward and dishonesty egged on by flattery and guile. Her
wedding present, by a fine stroke of allegorical vision, is a charter, estab-
lishing the bridal couple as lords of the Seven Deadly Sins. Langland re-
serves comment on their effect upon society at large for a later passus.
Meanwhile he has to speak of graft and outrage. The former has a passus
to itself, pictured in the trial of Lady Meed before the King; first she is
taken to Westminster, where she makes easy friends with judges, lord-
ings, and friars and gets herself shriven at the cost of putting up a Church
window. Brought before the King she is charged by Conscience with the
perversion of justice and the corruption of religion and we see a picture
of England given over to the fraudulent official, the rascal Summoner,
the simoniac parson, the gaoler and the hangman, and every other func-
tionary that money can buy.

The solution propounded for this state of affairs is that Meed should
marry Conscience, and Conscience is to bring Reason to his aid; but
while the debate is still in progress, a new character appears; it is Peace
with her complaint against Wrong, that is, against a particular form of
outrage or aristocratic oppression exercised through "Purveyors," who
made arrangements for the commissariat of feudal retinues in their peri-
odical cross-country journeys from one estate to another; they are accused
of billeting themselves without mercy or honesty on innocent and helpless villages, raping the women, robbing the stable and the fowlyard,
breaking into barns and commandeering wheat. Goneril utters a like
complaint against the hundred knights of Lear. The petition of Peace
was no dream of Langland's, nor even a piece of conventional invective
(as the charges of corruption, for their generality, might be considered);
it was a matter of recent history and the rolls of Parliament for 1362 bear
the poet out, at least in respect of non-payment for exactions.[8]

Langland's King listens to Peace with a just attention and Reason
prompts his judgment and verdict (A. iv, 148). As always with Langland the answer to a practical problem is a practising change of heart.

(iii) *The sins of society.* (A. Passus v)

Langland now takes us back to have a look at Lady Meed's wedding

---

[8] *Rotuli Parliamentorum*, vol. ii, p. 267, items 10–17. Attempts to curb the abuse
of Purveyance go back to *Magna Carta* at least; see McKechnie, *Magna Carta*, p. 386.
Item 10 of the *Rotuli Parliamentorum* for 1362 contains the petition "q le heignous
noun de Purveiour soit change & nome Achatour" [that the hateful name of Purveyor
be changed and called Buyer]. The petition of Peace against Wrong seems to be a
reminiscence of these transactions in Parliament, and may be held to support the traditional dating of the A-text to shortly after 1362.

present. The scene is once again the Field of Folk, where Conscience with a cross preaches to the throng; Repentance runs to rehearse his theme and William the poet weeps water at his eyes. The Deadly Sins make their confession; the link between them and Lady Meed is not restated but implied; such linkages are common in this poet; for instance the last words in the sermon of Conscience are,

> Seek Saint Truth . for he may save you all,

a penance manifestly linked to the advice previously given by Holy Church, as the writer expects you to understand. We shall see many examples of this, for all his poetry is shot through with such foretastes and echoes which are there for the reader to discern as he may; they resemble the tentative statement of a theme by one group of instruments in an orchestra, taken up and developed later in the symphony by another. This is, however, not a perfect analogy, for the musical composer effects it by a conscious technique of musical artifice, by utter skill; there is no reason for thinking that these echoes and foretastes in Langland are placed where they are to suit an exact theory of composition; but it is an element so frequent in his writing as to call for notice; to explain it one is driven to say "that is how his mind worked"; it is as though, on the way to one idea, he would pause or even turn aside a little to see how he could use another, recognize it as a true part of his thought, and pass on with an intention to revisit it when the right moment came. There is something whole and strong in his thought; he does not waste any part of it, for every part of it was also a part of him and of what he believed, and therefore in some way connected with every other of his thoughts, consistent with them. At moments it may seem that "his speech was like a tangled chain; nothing impaired, but all disordered"; if we remember that he was playing with a plait of three threads it may sometimes help us to see that the disorder is often less his than ours. Allegorical thinking needs practise.

The confession of the Deadly Sins which occupies the bulk of this passus needs little analysis for the present purpose of showing the architecture of the poem; it must be understood that these seven Hogarthian phantoms that make confession are intended as the transgressions of the field full of folk embodied or taken as it were in bulk, and divided into the normal medieval categories of self-examination. Thus the seven sins are not new characters in the poem; they are the sins of the crowd he had pictured in the Prologue, and have been with them all the time (thanks to Lady Meed) . They make their crude and blundering acts of contrition as best they may, each a little masterpiece of presentation and a source-book for the social historian; to Langland, however, what mattered was that the hearts of his sinful folk were changed, for a moment at least; they must press on to their penance (A. v, 260).

(iv) *The fear of famine.* (A. Passus vi, vii)

The next passus at last introduces the hero of the poem, the man whose name is given to these visions taken as a whole, Piers Plowman. Langland has kept him back until now for a clear reason. Of the problems he has so far raised, only the Church could satisfy the first, only Conscience and Reason the second, and only Repentance the third. But his fourth question was a question in economics, which meant, for Langland, in things agrarian; so he chose a simple Christian plowman to solve it; the same perhaps of whom there is a "foretaste" in the opening lines of the poem:

> Some put them to the plough . and played full seldom
> In harrowing and in sowing . swonken full hard.

Now, in Passus vi, he is at last ready to develop this touch, and the almost forgotten plowman, the strength of Langland's economy, steps forward into the poem to take control. Silent hitherto and unperceived, he knows what the farmers of Devonshire call "the Three Ups of Life," when to stand up, when to speak up, and when to shut up. He also knows St. Truth and works for him (A. vi, 33–41). For Piers and his Master, Truth and Love are practical things, concerned with digging and delving and garnering corn, but there are also moral guides to practise that he knows by heart, namely the two Great Commandments and the laws of Moses; to him who works by them Piers promises (A. vi, 75–84). But the crabbed pilgrim's progress to the Tower of Truth described by Piers is not suited to all tastes:

> "By Christ," quoth a Cut-purse . "I have no kin there!"
> (A. vi, 118)

and others more reasonably say:

> "This were a wicked way . but whoso had a guide."
> (A. vii, 1)

So Piers promises to lead them, but first they must help to plow his half-acre; this is of course another symbol for the working world. In the early sixties of the fourteenth century there had been a new outbreak of plague, killing men rather than women and thus aggravating a shortage of labour already acute; corn was fetching famine-prices.[9] Langland's so-

---

[9] Walsingham, *Historia Anglicana,* vol. i, Rolls Series.

lution was that all must work, each in his degree, to avert starvation. It is in exact pursuance of what Holy Church had told the Dreamer in Passus i. Work is honesty and that is practical Truth. Harvest will bring food for all and that is practical Love.

There is no reason to suppose that Piers stands here (in the A-text) for anything more than an ideal type of English country Christian whose work pleases God and succours man. . . . He knows how to handle men and get his field plowed; he has a wife and children; he is a good son of the Church.

Work will avert famine, but what of those who cannot or will not work? Shortage of labour does not solve all the problems of unemployment; there are always the cripples and the wasters. They have their say; the former

> . . . complained them to Piers . with such piteous words
> "We have no limbs to labour with . we thank our lord for it.
> But we pray for you, Piers . and for our plough too
> That God for his grace . our grain multiply
> And yield you a return . for the alms you give us here!"
>> (A. vii, 116–20)

The latter, more brazenly,

> "I was not wont to work," quoth a Waster . "Yet will I not begin!"
>> (A. vii, 153)

Piers has an answer for both. The blind or broken-shanked or bed-ridden,

> They shall have as good as I . So me God help.
>> (A. vii, 132)

but for the wasters his first impulse is to hand them over to hunger.

> Hunger in haste . hent Waster by the maw
> And wrung him so by the womb . that both his eyes watered.
>> (A. vii, 161)

This is a kind of solution to the problem, but not a Christian kind and Piers repents it:

> . . . "They be my blood-brethren . for God bought us all,
> Truth taught me once . to love them each one,
> And help them in all things . according to their need."
>> (A. vii, 196)

And so a better solution is propounded; for the love of God even wasters are to be supported, if not with plenty, at least with a dole sufficient for life (A. vii, 202–6) .

With these solutions and with this seventh passus ends Langland's survey or vision of his England in triple allegory; he had mapped her evils and shown their remedy in true life; it would be hard to imagine a more clear-sighted survey in so short a space, in language better suited, or in imagery more memorable. . . .

THE PARDON. (A. Passus viii)

We are now led to the crucial passus of the Pardon sent to Piers. It is represented in the poem as a puzzle as well to him as to the Dreamer. It has been a puzzle to all his commentators and, I suppose, a surprise, at the least, to every reader. I do not think it can be fully understood except in the light shed upon it by the B-text, and for this I offer the good reason that it was the Pardon and his ponderings upon it that in the end forced the revising poet to recast the whole work, not merely by augmentation and the rewriting of individual lines, but by adding a mode of meaning that was to transmute it into a new species of poetry, the greatest imaginable to a medieval mind, of which Holy Scripture itself was the exemplar.

All our understanding, then, depends upon a study of this Pardon and how the reader is to take it. Unfortunately there are variant readings in the manuscripts of the very lines upon which the weight of interpretation must fall, and therefore the larger architectural survey of the poem which is attempted in this paper must here give way for a moment to a closer scrutiny.

The new critical edition, eagerly awaited, of the A-text, upon which the late Professor Chambers and Professor Grattan were so long at work, has not yet appeared and the present conjectures must therefore of necessity be based on the information given in Skeat's edition, which may be deemed standard until the new one is available.*

By any text, the gist of the eighth passus is as follows: Truth hears tell of the work done by Piers and his fellow helpers from the Field of Folk, and as a reward a Pardon is granted to him and to them and to their heirs forever. Piers takes the Pardon trustfully but when it is unrolled at the request of a priest among his followers, it is contained in two lines of Latin:

> *Et qui bona egerunt, Ibunt in vitam eternam;*
> *Qui vero mala, in ignem eternum.*

---

* Since the appearance of Coghill's essay, the definitive edition of the A-text has been published: *Piers Plowman: The A Version,* ed. George Kane (London, 1960) , Part I of *Piers Plowman: The Three Versions,* General Editor, George Kane.

[And those who have done good will go into eternal life;
Those who have done evil, into eternal fire.]

A dispute arises as to its meaning; the priest denies that it is a pardon
at all and Piers tears it up in mortification. The noise of the disputes
wakes the Dreamer, who is left meditating the meaning of his vision. All
readers of the poem are left to do the same.

The question is, *Was it a valid pardon?* and the variants in the text
force us to inquire into this more deeply than the Dreamer himself,
whose chief concern was *What did the Pardon mean?* Our first question,
however, must be *Where did it come from?* Did Langland mean us to
think it came from Truth Himself? For if so it must be considered as in
some way valid, whatever logical trap the priest set for Piers about it.
This question leads us to the variant readings.

Passus viii of the A-text in Skeat's edition opens thus:

> Treuthe herde telle her-of . And to Pers sende,
> To taken his teeme . and tilyen the eorthe;
> And purchasede him a pardoun . *A pena et a culpa*
> [from punishment and from guilt]
> For him, and for his heires . euer more aftur.
> And bad holden hem at hom . and heren heore leyȝes,
> And al that euere hulpen him . to heren or to sowen,
> Or eny maner mester . that mihte Pers helpen,
> Part in that pardoun . the Pope hath I-graunted.
>
> (A. viii, 1–8)

There seems to be some confusion here, even in the author's mind. First
we are told that it is Truth who purchases and sends the Pardon; then
that it is the Pope who has granted it. Which of these is meant? The
whole question of its validity depends upon our being sure. That it was
purchased by Piers from the Pope, and not by Truth, is supported by the
readings in three manuscripts where the third line (above) reads:

> And purchace him a pardoun.
> (Trin. Coll. Cambridge, R. 3. 14, and Harl. 875)
> And purchasen him a pardoun.
>
> (Univ. Coll. Oxford)

If we accept either of these alternatives the meaning becomes: "Truth
heard tell hereof and sent (a message) to Piers to take his team and till
the earth and purchase himself a pardon (from the Pope)." A reading
of this kind seems to be preferred by Chambers, for he writes of this passage:

The poet goes on to tell how Truth heard of Piers setting folk to work, and bade him purchase a pardon from the Pope; all Piers' helpers are to have a share in it.[10]

If this is indeed the true intention of the passage, then we can but note that this all-important Pardon, whether papal or not, is at least backed by the authority of Truth who told Piers to buy it; to that extent it is warranted genuine, whatever it means.

If on the other hand the true reading is as Skeat printed it in his text ("And purchasede him a pardoun"), then it was Truth who bought it and there can be no dispute as to its efficacy as an instrument of grace, even if its application is enigmatic. But a different question arises, name-ly, *Where and when did Truth purchase this pardon?* I believe we must look to the preceding passus for the explanation, to a line already quoted in another context:

> And heo beoth my blodi bretheren . for god bouȝte vs alle.
>   (A. vii, 196)

"God bought us all" at the Redemption and our pardon was "pur-chased" not in Rome but on Calvary, a pardon held to be valid for all generations of Christians,

> For him, and for his heires . euer more aftur

an hereditary force that no merely papal pardon can have.

This is the meaning that I think the poet intended us to take and it remains for us to consider how the Pope came into the business at all. I can only suggest that it was the momentary aberration of a poet who, seeking to alliterate his line, overlooked the fact that he was blurring his thought. It is noticeable that the line is revised in the B-text; the Pope is removed, but the alliteration wrecked:

> Pardoun with pieres plowman . treuthe hath ygraunted.
>   (B. vii, 8)

In the C-text all difficulties are evaded:

> Pardon with peers plouhman . perpetual he graunteth.
>   (C. x, 8)

If it be thought that these arguments establish that it was indeed Truth who bought and sent the Pardon for Piers and his fellows, then its efficacy cannot be questioned; truth lies in it somewhere and the priest who impugned it, causing Piers to destroy it "for puire teone" is the vil-

---

10 R. W. Chambers, *Man's Unconquerable Mind*, p. 117.

lain of the piece,[11] a sophist who understands the letter but not the spirit; more than that, he is an ignoramus (though he should be a man of learning) , for he gives no sign of recognition that the Pardon is nothing but a quotation from the Athanasian Creed.[12] For all that, it may seem a grim joke to offer as a piece of Heaven's forgiveness the most threatening sentence from the *Quicunque vult*. Sheep are to enter bliss and goats to burn. Where is the pardon for a goat?

Piers, perhaps because he could not read, had not unrolled the Pardon; he had taken it on faith. But now that he had had it explained to him (in its bleakest sense) by the meddling priest whose office and learning he should be able to trust, he tears it up, exclaiming:

"*Si Ambulauero in medio umbre mortis, non timebo mala, quoniam tu mecum es.*
I shall cease of my sowing," quoth Piers . "and swink not so hard
Nor about my livelihood . so busy be no more!
Of prayer and of penance . my plough shall be hereafter. . . ."
                                                    (A. viii, 102–4)

Of this passage Chambers writes:

Piers' pardon had been a reward promised in exchange for righteous deeds done. But the priest has denied that the document is a pardon at all, and the voice of authority seems to be on the side of the priest. So Piers abandons his charter. It is disputed; so be it; he will trust no longer to parchment, to bulls with seals, but to the Psalmist's assurance that death can have no terrors for the just man.[13]

Just so; but who is just? A point instantly taken by Langland.

---

[11] But see T. P. Dunning, *Piers Plowman, an Interpretation of the A Text*, pp. 145–52, where an interesting defence for the priest is advanced; as Father Dunning says, "the priest is obviously the proper person to interpret the pardon"; but in fact he does not interpret it, he "impugns it, all by pure reason" (A. viii, 155) , that is, he points out that it is written, not in the form of a pardon, but in the form of a statement of cause and effect, viz. "if you do well, you will be saved." Whether the document was a pardon or not, therefore, depends on what is meant by doing well, a matter which the priest omitted to explain and which Langland himself was only able to resolve by writing the B-text, as will be seen.

[12] Piers' Pardon is taken verbatim from the thirty-ninth verse of the Athanasian Creed (*vide* D. Waterland: *A Critical History of the Athanasian Creed*, ed. J. R. King, 1870) , which Skeat, who refers instead to Matthew xxv. 46, and Father Dunning, who refers to John v. 29, seem to have overlooked. The sentence appears to have had some vogue as a catch-phrase about salvation towards the end of the fourteenth century and a little later, as it is used at the climax of the last scene of the *Castle of Perseverance*, scene viii, lines 3637–8 (E.E.T.S. Extra Series XCI, *The Macro Plays*) .

[13] *Man's Unconquerable Mind*, p. 119.

"*Contra*" [I dispute that!], quoth I as a Clerk . and commenced to dispute,
   "*Sepcies in die cadit iustus* [The just man falls seven times a day]:
Seven times a day, saith the Book . sinneth the righteous man."
                                                (A. ix, 16–17)

If none can do well, if all are goats, what is the force of a Pardon for sheep? Thus the story of Piers, at its first telling, came to an abrupt end in paradox, leaving the poet to supply what explanation he could.

>   All this maketh me . to muse on dreams
>   Many a time at midnight . when men should sleep,
>   And on Piers the Plowman . and what a pardon he had.
>   (A. viii, 152–4)

And he roamed about, looking for an explanation,

>   All a Summer season . For to seek Do-well.
>   (A. ix, 2)

THE SIGNIFICACIO. (A. Passus ix, x, xi)

*   *   *

When we ask ourselves what these passus of *Significacio* are about, we are forced to say that they touch on many topics not very obviously related to each other or to the story of Piers. At first the going is easy; the Dreamer meets a couple of Friars and puts his question, much as the Field of Folk had questioned the ignorant Palmer about St. Truth. The two Friars give a sort of answer; in the parable of the Man in the Wagging Boat, they seem to say that although a just man may sin seven times a day, he does no *deadly* sin,

>   for Do-well him helpeth
>   That is charity the Champion.   (A. ix, 40–1)

If a man's will is not turned against Charity (Do-well), his soul is safe though he stumble; they seem satisfied with this, but not so the Dreamer; the equation of Do-well with charity is too simple; he takes leave of them, turned in upon his own thought. Thought instantly shows him that he is entering upon three fields of inquiry, not one.

>   "Art thou Thought?" quoth I then . "canst thou me tell
>   Where that Do-well dwelleth . do me to know?"
>   "Do-well," quoth he, "and Do-better . and Do-best the third
>   Be three fair virtues . and be not far to find. . . ."
>   (A. ix, 67–70)

Not far to find! It was to take him perhaps fifteen years to find them in their fullness.[14] Meanwhile his task of commentary had tripled itself in a sentence. By that grammarian's trick, Thought had added to the *qui bona* of the Athanasian Creed a *qui meliora,* a *qui optima,* of which nothing had been said in the Pardon to Piers. Yet this new trinity, that seems in the poem to take its origin in a verbal whim, corresponded to a reality defined in the *Meditationes Vitae Christi* and in St. Thomas Aquinas, whose work was certainly known, at least by hearsay, to Langland. St. Thomas had already distinguished three types of human life, that of Martha who did well and that of Mary who did better; and that third life which combined the virtues of both, a Mary-Martha life that did best of all, the Active, the Contemplative, and the Contemplative-returned-to-Action.[15]

How long Langland had foreseen this branching of his thought it is impossible to say; I do not think it can have been a part of his original design, even though the Dreamer seems to accept it without surprise. It was a development, however, that once perceived could neither be disregarded nor suppressed; yet how difficult to include it in the compass of a *significacio!* Setting out to show what pardon the Active life of the Laity in England might hope for, he found himself involved with the Clergy and the Episcopate, for these, as Thought also told him, were Do-better and Do-best. But there was more than that. In the wake of the Three Lives there followed other necessary but intractable topics, as old and as vast . . . Faith and Works . . . Learning and Simplicity . . . Wealth and Poverty . . . Free Will and Predestination . . . the Righteous Heathen . . . the nature of Charity . . . somehow they were all involved, they branched out intertwiningly from the three great limbs of his thought.

*   *   *

How was all this new material to be organized? He knew at least how his own mind worked: by rumination. Rumination could be given a poetical cast by making an allegory of the growth of his mind, of the stages in his thinking; so he imagined a series of ghostly advisers each figuring one such stage . . . Thought—Wit—Study—Learning—Scripture. It was a way of organizing his inquiry. Perhaps, for us, these shadowy figures are

[14] This guess is based on the opinion of Skeat who dates the A-text to shortly after 1362 and the B-text to 1376–7. Mr. J. A. W. Bennett, following Dr. Huppé, advances some reasons for supposing that the A-text "must have been in process of composition by 1370, even if it was not finished by then" (*P.M.L.A.* lviii, no. 3) and that the B-text was being written between the years 1377 and 1379" (*Med. Æv.,* vol. xii) .

[15] Attention was first called to these by H. W. Wells in *P.M.L.A.* xliv, no. 1, "The Construction of Piers Plowman," where relevant quotations from St. Thomas (*Summa,* Part III, Quaest. XL. A. I) and from the *Meditationes* are given.

not easy to identify with precision;[16] but however tenuous they seem to us, for him they were a help in forming and unifying his work; they gave it a sort of shape.

He struggled to find other images for what he had to say; after rejecting the parable of The Man in the Wagging Boat offered by the two Friars, he tried again in the parable of the Castle of *Caro* [Flesh]. It starts brilliantly. In the Castle lives *Anima* [Soul] the beloved of God, and Sir Do-well is Lord of the Marches to protect her against Sir *Princeps huius mundi* [Prince of this world]; Do-bet is her lady-in-waiting, daughter to Do-well; these with Do-best are Masters of the Manor. There is also a Constable of the Castle to keep them all, Sir Inwit, and he has five sons called See-well, Say-well, Hear-well, Work-well, and Go-well. These are promising *dramatis personae* and lure the reader into a hope for some adventure in the manner of *The Bludy Serk*. That poem, however, was still unwritten. The *Pilgrim's Progress,* too, was still in the future.

No adventure befalls the Lady *Anima;* her story falters and dissolves before an untimely interruption into what is perhaps the least well managed passus in the poem. Untimely it may be to the reader hoping for a romantic parable, but to Langland it seemed more important to tell of Kuynde who made this Castle,

> That is the great God . that beginning had never
> (A. x, 29)

the creating Father who made man in His own image—gave him ghost of his Godhead—and gave him Conscience, Constable in Chief:

> After the grace of God . the greatest is Inwit
> (A. x, 48)

and this moves him to think of those who lack this leadership within, the sots who have drowned it in drink; children and half-wits, over whom the fiend has no power, for they are not, or not yet, responsible. From this he is led to think of education and the wisdom that is begun in the fear of God; learning and teaching recall Do-better to his mind, the clerkly life, and some of the dangers of knowing too much; yet it is by knowledge that Do-better springs from Do-well, and Do-best from both (A. x, 119–23) . Do-better is the child of Do-well not only in this sense, however, but also in the literal sense; priests are the children of layfolk.

It is by this roundabout of meditation that Langland has returned to the theme proposed, namely, "What is Do-well?" and has marked out its first essential character, namely, that it is a family life of Christian mar-

---

16 For a study in identification see *Journal of English and Germanic Philology,* ix, no. 3, "The Authorship of Piers Plowman," by A. Mensendieck.

riage; a sermon upon this ends the passus with that kind of practical advice we always find in this poem, where common sense flows from spiritual vision.

In this eleventh passus a second essential character of Do-well is also marked out with equal positiveness; Do-well is defined in terms of active manual labour:

> "It is a well fair life" quoth she . "among these simple folk"
> *Active* it is called . husbandmen use it.
>
> (A. xi, 179 et seq.)

Now, in the twelfth passus, he passes to a third, namely, the unlearnedness of Do-well. As the purpose of his *significacio* was to explain and justify the Pardon granted to those *qui bona egerunt,* he did not, at that first writing of his poem, see why he should not fulfil this purpose at the expense of those grammatical intruders, Do-better and Do-best; so in defence of Do-well for his unlettered simplicity, Langland adopted a strategy of denying the efficacy of Learning as a means of salvation. He argued this partly from his own observation of the clergy of England who (he thought) used their learning to such ill purposes that they endangered their own souls and those of other people, and partly from what happened to Solomon and Aristotle, who, for all their learning, were said to be in Hell. Happier are the ignorant, the "lewd jots" whose simple *Paternosters* pierce Heaven; it is the argument used also by Andrew Marvell:

> None thither mounts by the degree
> Of Knowledge, but Humility.[17]

Thus was victory for Do-well gained at the cost of slighting the attainments of clergy. It was a truth halved by prejudice.

A lesser man than Langland might have rested in his anticlericalism all his life; he believed himself to have grounds enough for it, and it had been the burden of his song from the Prologue, where the Parish Priest is described as asking leave to live in London,

> To sing there for Simony . for silver is sweet

to the Pardon, which an officious priest had impugned. Yet there was something in Learning that the poet felt bound to honour, as he shows in the very drift of his allegory. Thought, Wit, Study, Clergy, and Scripture, however abstractly personified, are an abstract of instruction; wisdom, says Dame Study, is one of the precious pearls that wax in Paradise.[18]

[17] *A Dialogue between the Resolved Soul and Created Pleasure.*
[18] A. xi, 12.

But this question of the place of Learning in the scheme of salvation brought other questions into Langland's mind; it would be truer perhaps to put it thus, that at the time of writing the A-text he had in mind a number of notions, as yet not very distinct to him, but all in some way fundamental to his Christianity; and as he pondered on Learning, these other notions began to move in his mind by a sort of sympathy as if every thought that came to him in the matter of Learning disturbed, touched, and mingled with all his other thoughts, much as one aching tooth will set others on to ache. The resulting complex of his thoughts may be shown in brief tabular analysis:

I. Learning is nowadays pursued for the sake of its rewards in wealth:

> Wisdom and wit now . is not worth a rush
> But it be carded with Covetousness.
>
> (A. xi, 17)

(The same complaint as that of the Prologue:

> I saw there Bishops bold . and Bachelors of Divinity
> Become Clerks of Account . the King for to serve.)

Therefore Learning in alliance with worldly gain is somehow mixed up with and introduces the contrary notion of true Christian poverty, a subject treated at length in the revised poem.

II. Learning leads to an intellectualism which allows men to chatter about God, though they have Him not in heart:

> Clerks and acute men . carp often about God
> And have Him much in their mouth . but mean men in heart.
>
> (A. xi, 56)

Learning is thus linked with the question of practising what you preach, of which the reviser has also much to say.

III. But the test of entry into Heaven is neither one of Wealth nor of Poverty, but of Belief and Baptism:

> Paul proveth it is impossible . rich men in Heaven
> But poor men in patience . and penance together
> Have heritage in Heaven . and rich men none.
> "Contra!" quoth I, "by Christ! that I can tell you,
> And prove it by the Epistle . that is named Peter;
> *Qui crediderit et baptizatus fuerit, salvus erit."*
> [He who believes and is baptized will be saved.]

"That is *in extremis*," quoth Scripture . as Sarasens and Jews
May be saved so . and so is our Belief.

(A. xi, 225)

Thus Faith becomes important in the argument, and the Righteous Heathen. This also is much developed in B.

IV. But Do-well is defined as the Active Life of Work,

True tillers on earth . tailors and cobblers
(A. xi, 181)

and thus is introduced the antithesis of Faith and Works.

V. But however well a man works,

For how so I work in this world . wrongly or otherwise
I was marked without mercy . and my name entered
In the legend of life . long ere I was
(A. xi, 252)

which glances at the topic of Predestination (one on which, for a wonder, Langland had less to say than Chaucer).

VI. Solomon was a man of learning; he did well "in work and word":

Aristotle and he . who wrought better?
And all Holy Church . holds them to be in Hell!
(A. xi, 262)

whereas St. Mary Magdalen, Dismas the Penitent Thief, and

Paul the Apostle . that no pity had
Christian kind . to kill to death?
And none (to say sooth) . are sovereigns in Heaven
As are these, who wrought wickedly . in the world, when they were.

(A. xi, 281)

All these were saved by their Faith. (David has also somehow got into this category, though more properly he belongs with Solomon his son.) Thus Learning, previously opposed to Unlearned Works, is now opposed to Unlearned Faith, and linked with the problem of Heathen Salvation too. All these topics, paradoxes, and contradictions were in solution in Langland's mind and began to crystallize as he pondered the place of brains in the scheme of Salvation; for the moment he was only able to mention his difficulties and pass them by on his way to the climax he was seeking, namely, corroboration for the Pardon and justification for Do-well. He passed them by. Perhaps he was impatient to finish his poem, and indeed, to some extent, "the latter end of his commonwealth forgets the beginning"; beautiful as it is, it suggests haste, for whereas the Pardon had been sent as a reward (apparently) for the work done on Piers' half-acre by the Field of Folk, yet if we consider the last lines of the twelfth passus, it would seem that they were finally saved, not by their works but by their simple faith.

> Are none rather ravished . from the right belief
> Than are these great clerks . that con many books;
> Nor none sooner saved . nor sadder of conscience
> Than poor people as plowmen . and pastors of beasts.
> Cobblers and tailors . and such lewd jots
> Pierce with a *paternoster* . the palace of Heaven
> Without penance at their parting . into high bliss!
> *Brevis oracio penetrat celum.*

Whatever doubts had been raised as to the meaning of Do-well, and whether the followers of Piers were saved by their Faith or by their Works, a high visionary assurance over-rules argument in an outburst of poetry and sees poor people saved by sincerity in prayer.

Visionary assurance is not intellectual proof. Langland had not so much finished as finished off his poem. If we feel that his *significacio* is not of equal force with that which it was to explain, we shall be feeling no more than he felt himself; not because he had explained too little, but because Thought had driven him to see how much more there was that needed explanation; he had tripled his problem and this would force him to triple his poem. He had matter for a meditation that was to change his cherished opinions and alter the poetical centre of gravity of his work, not merely by addition in length but by addition in depth also; it would need a new kind of poetry.

The twelfth, last, and hastiest passus of the A-text is of slight impor-tance, at least to our present study. Preserved in only one manuscript it is remarkable also for its concluding lines in which one Johan But puts forth his head.

> And so bad Iohan but . busily wel ofte,
> When he saw thes sawes . busyly a-legged
> By Iames and by Icrom . by Iop and by othere,
> And for he medleth of makyng . he made this ende.
>
> (A. xii, 101–4)

How many lines were added by this interloper is still in dispute; that
they were added at some time later than 1377 seems certain from the line

> Furst to rekne Richard . kyng of this rewme.
>
> (A. xii, 108)

The passus, as a whole, has two purposes: first, another mild rebuke to
the Dreamer for his presumption in seeking to know Do-better, coupled
with the advice to hold fast to that which is good; *quod bonum est tenete,*
almost as if *quod melius* were no business of his, and secondly to bring
the poem to an end by the simple literary device of killing off the author,
who, meeting with hunger and fever, perishes abruptly:

> Deth delt him a dent . and drof him to the erthe
> And is closed vnder clom . Crist haue his soule!
>
> (A. xii, 99–100)

The passus adds nothing to any of the problems raised previously and is
no more than a trick-ending of immeasurable inferiority to the close of
Passus xi, whoever wrote it or had part in writing it.

III

ADDITIONS AND ALTERATIONS WHERE THE TEXTS RUN PARALLEL

Now the B-text runs parallel to the A-text (apart from additions
and alterations made by B) to the point where this vision appears,
telling how the search for Do-wel was abandoned. This "Vision of
how the abandoned search was resumed" is the beginning of the B-
continuation. (R. W. Chambers and J. H. G. Grattan, *Modern Language Review,* vol. xxvi, no. 1, p. 9.)

When a poet alters his own work, we cannot always see, or even feel,
the reason for the change. Why, for instance, did Chaucer find it necessary to rewrite the Prologue to the *Legend of Cupid's Saints?* A question
as easy to trip on as a text in the Galatians (to take a phrase from Brown-
ing). In the case of *Piers Plowman* we can at least be sure that the B version was written after the A, which is more than we know of the versions
of the Prologue to the *Legend.* If we assemble and consider the changes
made by Langland in the earlier part of his poem, we should therefore be
able to assess in some degree the new directions in which his mind was
working; but since the manuscripts are so full of variations from each

other, only the larger changes (that cannot be due to scribal interference) will help us in attempting such an assessment.

*   *   *

The major additions seem to be of the following kinds.[19] First, those which fill out the picture of English society; secondly, those which enforce or elaborate some point in Christian morality; thirdly, what I can only call *Foretastes;* insertions, that is, into the early part of the poem, of ideas which are only developed in their fullness at the very end of the B-continuation; and lastly those additions that show something of "The supernal things of eternal glory," to use a technical term from medieval criticism of allegorical poetry.[20] These classes of addition are worth a detailed consideration.

The picture of English society

In comparing the A-text with *Wynnere and Wastoure* it became clear that both were topical narrative allegories, the former enriched by a moral meaning, about the state of England. The B-text additions of our first category most emphatically bear this out; this part of the poem is more in England than ever, and it may be here useful to point out the Time-Place scheme of the B-text as a whole which is exactly parallel to the scheme by which the character of Piers seems to change; for just as he seems at first to be a simple Christian farmer, then Christ, and finally St. Peter and the Popes who succeeded him, so the time and place in the first part of the poem (in both versions, but more emphatically in B) is fourteenth-century England; in the second part (not in A) it is Jerusalem in the First Passion Week; and in the third part it is unspecified Christendom at any time between the Coming of the Holy Ghost and the Coming of Anti-Christ. This increasing shadowiness in person, time, and place gives the poem an extraordinary sense of growing dimension; and this is made possible by the fact that we start so firmly in England; for as we see the reign and Kingdom of Richard II caught gradually up into the

---

19 For lists of alterations and additions made in the B-text, see E.E.T.S. original series 28, *Piers Plowman A Text,* ed. by Skeat, reprinted 1932, pp. 156–8, and also T. P. Dunning, *Piers Plowman, an Interpretation of the A Text,* 1937, pp. 195–6 where some deviations from A are noted in B to support the view that they are by different authors, a view which Father Dunning has recently withdrawn in his extremely interesting article "Langland and the Salvation of the Heathen," *Med. Æv.,* vol. xii, 1943.

20 Dante, *Convivio,* Second Treatise, ch. i. The "supernal things of eternal glory," so manifestly a part of the B revision, are no doubt the "mystical developments" to which Dr. Mabel Day refers (*Mod. Lang. Rev.* xxiii) , in seeking to establish that the B reviser could not have been the author of A. It does not seem impossible that "the growth of a poet's mind" might include mystical development in the course of the long meditation between the writing of the two texts.

"universal world" so we also see common humanity caught up into the life of God and of His Church.

The first major interpolation is in the Prologue (B. Prol. 87–209) and its function is obvious; it completes the original picture of contemporary England by the inclusion of the King, the Knighthood that "led" him and the might of the Commons "that made him to reign." Rebuke veiled in advice is offered by "a lunatic" (clearly the poet himself), and an Angel, the voice of Heaven, who reminds the King that he is no more than the Deputy of Christ,

> *O qui iura regis . Christi specialia regis*
> [O you who administers the special laws of Christ the King]

(a touch which binds England to those supernal things, which it was also a part of the revising poet's intention to enforce). There follows immediately the highly topical (and terrestrial) fable of the Cat and the Ratons, which puts the political situation of 1376–7 in a brief sardonic fancy.[21]

Another series of large additions that adds rich English colour to the allegory is found in the additions to the confessions of the Seven Deadly Sins which are much enlarged; the missing penitence of Wrath is added for completeness; it is mainly devoted to a description of the jangles in Convents and Monasteries (of which the former are the more spiteful) ; there is a touch of London life added to Envy, and of the common practices of business morality to Avarice; in like manner, Sloth is greatly expanded by many dark details of contemporary abuse. The reviser has thrust in fifteen years' worth of social observation.

The second class of large additions, that reinforce the moral teaching of the poem, is obvious and frequent and need scarcely be illustrated by examples.

The third, which I have ventured to call "foretastes," is less easily perceived, but when once it is so, is strange and striking.

Foretastes

We have seen already that it is a character of Langland's writing to throw out hints and images to be developed later in the poem, and some of the larger insertions in the B-text strongly suggest that this was, or became, a conscious device. It should here be said that we cannot be sure whether he started his revision from the Prologue, having in mind some plan for how the visions were to continue after the point at which the A-text comes to an end, or whether he started on the continuation itself,

---

[21] In spite of the argument advanced by Mr. J. A. W. Bennett in *Med. Æv.* xii, I cling to this view.

and, having written or roughed it out, returned to the early part of the poem and revised it in the light of what he had added. Some inserted passages seem to point faintly towards the latter procedure; but if that was how he worked, it is strange that he has missed some important opportunities for clarifying his meaning at an early stage; examples of this will presently be offered, but first some of these strange "foretastes" may be shown.

There are two interpolated passages in the B Prologue which run thus:

> I perceived of the power . that Peter had to keep,
> To bind and to unbind . as the book telleth,
> How he left it with love . as our Lord commanded,
> Among four virtues . the best of all virtues,
> That cardinal are called. . . .
>
> (B. Prol., 100–4)

Then, after a brief fling in pun-fashion at those other Cardinals of the court (whose Pope-making he declines to impugn), he goes on to describe the spiritual basis of society thus:

> And then came Kind-Wit . and clerks he made
> For to counsel the King . and the Commons save. . . .
> The commons contrived . by kind-wit crafts
> And for profit of all the people . plowmen ordained
> To till and labour . as true life asketh.
> The King and the commons . and kind-wit the third
> Shaped law and loyalty . each man to know his own.
>
> (B. Prol., 114–22)

Thus within twenty-two lines we have the following association of somewhat unusual ideas into one connected argument: the binding-and-loosing power of the Church, the cardinal virtues, the natural gifts of the spirit, which give counsel to the King, Clergy, and Commons, shape the law, till the earth, and bind society.

Exactly the same association of ideas, expanded, not to say expounded, at much greater length, comes at the very end of the poem, where its treatment clears some of the mystery from the meaning of Piers' Pardon, to solve which was the grand motive of the B-text.

> And when this deed was done . Do-Best he taught
> And gave Piers power . and pardon he granted
> To all manner of men . mercy and forgiveness, . . .
> . . . In covenant that they come . and acknowledge to pay
> To the Pardon of Piers Plowman . *redde quod debes* [Pay
>   back what you owe].

Thus hath Piers power, . be his pardon paid,
To bind and to unbind....

(B. xix, 177–84)

Almost immediately there follows the Coming of the Holy Ghost and the gifts of the spirit and how they are to be used (exactly as the Prologue insertion suggests) (B. xix, 208–41). And then, after again insisting on *redde quod debes,* and equipping Piers and his Farm of Holy Church with four oxen (the Evangelists), four stotts (the Fathers) and the two harrows of the Old and New Testaments, the author brings the similarity of these two passages full circle with:

And Grace gave grains . the cardinal virtues
And sow them in man's soul....

(B. xix, 269)

Were these later passages written to expand the interpolation in the Prologue, or was that interpolation thrust in as a foretaste of his grand conclusion? Which is the voice and which the echo? There are other examples. There is, for instance, a large interpolation in Passus v, continuing thirty lines. They are among the words of Repentance at the end of the confession of the Seven Sins. Within them occur so many "foretastes" or "echoes" of what is to come later, that it is impossible to conceive of either passage having been written without the other in mind, and both are central to the whole argument of pardon and redemption. The earlier passage is as follows: (See B. v, 485–515). Can anybody doubt that this was written in direct relation to Passus xviii and xix, to Langland's account of the Harrowing of Hell and its consequences? Phrase recalls phrase and image recalls image; for instance "our suit" (human flesh), the armour in which Christ is to do "doughty deeds," rings forward to

This Jesus of his gentle birth . will joust in Piers' arms
In his helm and his habergeon . *humana natura*

(B. xviii, 22–23)

or again the blinding of Lucifer by the Light shining in darkness recalls the earlier passage thus:

Dukes of this dim place, . anon undo the gates
That Christ may come in . the King's son of Heaven
And with that breath, Hell brake . with Belial's bars
In spite of guard and guardian . wide open the gates,
Patriarchs and prophets . *populus in tenebris* [the people in darkness]
Sang St. John's song . *ecce agnus dei* [behold the Lamb of God]

Lucifer might not look . for light so blinded him.
(B. xviii, 317)

One or two such similarities might be dismissed as accidental, since the Harrowing of Hell was a well-known story, but such a clenching together of images that were to be used again at greater length at the peak of the poem can hardly be other than a deliberate anticipation, a piece of purposeful revision; and the purpose is clear enough. It is to link the Confession of the Field of Folk, that is, of Do-well, with the pardon purchased on Calvary, and with that binding and unbinding power which Langland says was won by Christ's conquest over falseness and death and Hell.

This technique of anticipation, the casting of a seed into the poem that it may flower again later, may be seen in many places; for instance, the first hint we are given in anticipation of the jousting of Jesus at Jerusalem (fully described in B. xviii, 10–30) , comes far earlier, in these lines:

And then spake Spiritus Sanctus . in Gabriel's mouth
To a maid that was called Mary . a meek thing withal,
That one Jesus, the son of a judge . should rest in her chamber
Till *plenitudo temporis* [the fullness of time] . were fully come,
That Piers' fruit flowered . and fell to be ripe.
And then should Jesus joust therefore . by judgment of arms
Whether of them should take the fruit . the fiend or himself.
(B. xvi, 90)

Another example may be seen in the lines:

Such arguments they move, . these masters in their glory
And make men misbelievers . that muse much on their words
Imaginative here-afterward . shall answer to your purpose.
(B. x, 113)

which not only foreshadows the coming of Imaginative some seven hundred and fifty lines later, but also the Doctor on the Dais, God's Glutton of Passus xiii.

Against this notion of revisionary foresight it may be urged and must be admitted that if the poet knew what was coming he missed some important opportunities very strangely. For instance, in the third passus of the B-text there is a large addition celebrating the rule of love that is to come on earth, when there shall be "peace among the people and perfect truth"; it is difficult to know when this Golden Age is to be. I am unable to believe with Skeat that it has something to do with the jubilee of Edward III, and incline to think it eschatological; for before this happy time is to come about, "men shall find the worst" (B. iii, 323) and if this refers to the Coming of Anti-Christ, as perhaps it may, it is so feeble a foretaste of that event as pictured in B. xx, 51, that one would suppose the poet ignorant at the time of revision how the poem was to end. So, too, when he came to revise the line

> Actyf lyf or contemplatyf . Crist wolde hit alse
> (A. vii, 236)

he was content to rewrite it thus

> Contemplatyf lyf or actyf lyf . Cryst wolde men wrouʒte
> (B. vi, 251)

which does nothing to prepare the reader for the fact that these Lives are the basis of Do-well, Do-better, and Do-best, of which he presently has so much to say, for they are the backbone of the whole B revision from the eighth passus onwards.

The Supernal Things of Eternal Glory

Into the morning daylight of his English scene the reviser has flung a shaft here and there from that further world to which Do-well, Do-better, and Do-best are the roads. Even in the A-text, as has been said, that world had been adduced as the type, end, and sanction of Christian life, and particularly in its moral aspect, that is, the solving of contemporary problems by Christian principles; but now this moral note is softened and exalted by touches, rare as they are, which add a quality lyrical and contemplative to what before was mainly admonitory. One such passage, the foretaste of the Harrowing of Hell, has already been considered, of which the key-note is redemptive love; another interpolation on the same subject is put into the mouth of Holy Church:

> For truth telleth that love . is treacle of Heaven
> May no sin be on him seen . that useth that spice. . . .
> For Heaven might not hold it . it was so heavy of itself
> Till it had of the earth . eaten its fill.
>   And when it had of this fold . flesh and blood taken
> Was never leaf upon linden-tree . lighter thereafter
> Light to bear and piercing . as the point of a needle
> That no armour can keep out . nor no high wall;
> Therefore is love leader . of the lord's folk in Heaven. . . .
> And, to know it in its nature, . it begins in a power
> And in the heart is its head . and the high well.
> (B. i, 146)

This is, perhaps, the finest passage in the revised Prologue; another such glimpse may be caught in a passage where the Church, traditionally the Bride of Christ, is seen in Heaven as the Bride of Man also:

> My Father the Great God is . and ground of all graces,
> One God without beginning . and I his good daughter,
> And hath given me mercy . to marry as I will
> And whatsoever man is merciful . and loyally loves me
> Shall be my lord and I his love . in the high Heaven.
>
> (B. ii, 29)

Gathering together what has been said of all these classes of addition we may discern the following trends and qualities in the revising poet so far: an insistence on the Englishness of his scene, as it is and as it ought to be; a great emphasis upon the need, fullness, and efficacy of confession, a hinting consciousness of the great vision of Redemption to come later, and a more touching sense of the enfolding and creative love of God the Father. These things are made into a poetry that has moments of lyrical contemplation, suggestive of a mystical rather than a moral vision, in so far as these can be distinguished.

IV

THE POINT AT WHICH THE TEXTS BEGIN TO DIVERGE

The A-Text is not a brief first draft of the B-Text. It is a fragment of a poem which, had it been continued, would presumably have been continued in much the same way as the completed B-Text. For the accounts of Do-wel and Do-bet and Do-best in the A-Text forecast a continuation on the same lines as we ultimately get.

The A-Text breaks off so suddenly in the middle of Do-wel, because the poet feels unable to solve the problems he has raised. (R. W. Chambers and J. H. G. Grattan, *M.L.R.,* vol. xxvi, no. 1, p. 10.)

It is my present purpose to suggest that the A-text is indeed "not a brief first draft of the B-Text," but was undertaken by the author, under the stimulus of *Wynnere and Wastoure,* as a topical narrative allegory about the moral condition of England; his narrative went vigorously forward to its climax, which was a Pardon for that moral condition, granted to the Field of Folk. This Pardon, however, was enigmatic, even to Langland, so he set himself to ponder and explain it; but as he did so, other immense and unexpected problems arose before him; he grappled with them as well as he then knew how, without swerving more than he could help from what seemed to be his poetical task, namely the justification of the followers of Piers and the assertion of the truth of their pardon. As we have seen, this high assurance was reached at the end of his eleventh passus, but only by denigrating clergy and by evading the issue whether the simple were pardoned for their works or their faith.

Langland's honesty did not allow him to rest for ever in such a conclusion; as the years went by he continued to ponder and, as he did so, his thought insensibly changed its objective; he found himself committed to a poem not about England but about Salvation and the Three Ways that led to it, of which up till then he had explored but one. To make this new theme effectual in poetry, he found himself driven to reshape his poem by a known technical expedient of adding a fourth plane of meaning, the anagogical as it was called, the meaning in *aeterna gloria*. More will be said of this later; for the moment let us consider his effort to achieve the difficult grafting of the new vision on to the old at their point of divergence. We have seen that some at least of his alterations forecast the distant shape of his final solution, but between that and his retouchings of the story of the Field of Folk lay a perplexing middle that was to be the intellectual core of the poem, in that its chief business was to expound the moral nature of the Three Lives (with fairness to each), and to give hearing to some of those other problems (Faith, Works, Learning, Wealth, Poverty, and the rest) that had already forced their way into the A-text. This would involve much theological speculation; neither nature, nor perhaps education had fitted Langland to be an exact theologian, yet theology had to be faced; the poet had already confessed his difficulties through the mouth of Dame Study, who had frankly admitted:

> Theology hath troubled me . ten score times
> For the more I muse thereon . the mistier it seemeth
>   (A. xi, 136)

and this must be accepted as an apology for that bewilderment which makes him "break off so suddenly in the middle of Do-wel, because the poet feels unable to solve the problems he has raised."

The divergence between the two poems begins to be very marked where A. x is being converted into B. ix, that is, exactly where the theologizing starts; and it is not until B. xi, where the author leaves the older poem behind and launches into new work that his firmness of grasp seems increasingly to return to him; it is as if he were encumbered rather than helped by what lay before him in A. x and xi. To deal with A. xii was simple enough; it could be scrapped altogether; and except for a few touches—the scornful character of Scripture (A. xii, 12, to B. xi, 1), the hint of on-coming age in the Dreamer (A. xii, 60, to B. xi, 59), a tag from 2 Corinthians and another from Thessalonians, both used in other contexts in B (A. xii, 22, to B. xviii, 393, and A. xii, 56, to B. iii, 335) —it was scrapped.

But how to deal with A. x and xi was another matter; they both contained much that he still wanted to say, and yet they had somehow led him to a conclusion that was in a sense false, or incomplete; to detect exactly at what point a ramified argument is going astray is always one of the most difficult problems in revision, and I am bound to think the revising poet's second thoughts, particularly in B. xi, have strayed even farther from his distant objective than did the A-text before him. Indeed the impression is sometimes given that he had no text before him, that he was revising this part from memory; as he seems to have been unhappy in the new conduct of his argument, so also his power as a poet seems temporarily occluded. Interpolations such as those at B. ix, 35–44, 61–72, 96–129, and 143–59 are like the movements of a pedestrian who in leaving a track that seemed to be leading him astray, strays even farther, with uncertain foot. In B. x, however, he returns to his path, his interpolations are better managed and his poetical vision returns in some degree. I would instance two such interpolations, one for its change in emphasis and the other for its imaginative sympathy, deeply related to the new turn of his argument.

The former is a re-definition of the Three Lives that begins at B. x, 230. If this is compared with the far briefer sketch of them given in the corresponding passage in A. xi, 179–200, it will be seen that Do-wel is now seen as a life based on elementary faith (particularly what the Church teaches of the Trinity and other articles of the faith as warranted by the Gospels and St. Augustine) as opposed to the mere activities of "trewe tilieries on erthe . taillours and souteris, and alle kyne crafty men" recommended as Do-wel in the A-text (A. xi, 181–82). The purpose of this seems to be an insistence that simple plowmanship is not enough and that some instruction to the lewd is absolutely necessary to salvation; and this prepares the reader for the wisdom of Imaginative later on who points out that Do-wel is lost without Do-better to instruct him in the articles of the Church "that falleth to be knowe."

> Take two stronge men . and in Themese caste hem,
> And bothe naked as a nedle . her none sykerer than other,
> That one hath connynge . and can swymmen and dyuen,
> That other is lewed of that laboure . lerned neuere swymme;
> Which trowestow of the two . in Themese is in most drede?
>
> (B. xii, 161–65)

Without Do-better, Do-well would drown, for ignorance. So too Do-bet is redefined in terms of suffering and practising what you preach, pointing thus more surely to the life of Christ as Do-bet, which is to come, rather than simply saying (as A does) that it consists in feeding the hungry, healing the sick, and obeying the rules of conventual life. The alterations in Do-best insist on the moral qualities that underlie his episcopal authority rather than on the fact stressed in A that he controls benefices. All these changes are well wrought to make a better coherence with the later developments of the revised poem.

The second interpolation, that is so poetically striking and shows the returning vision that seemed to be failing in B. xi, takes up the story of Noah from A. x, 159 again and gives it a marvellous new twist in the direction of the great argument he is now conducting, whether their learning, which had helped to build the wisdom of mankind, had saved Solomon and Aristotle (B. x, 399–406 and B. x, 411–33) . This anticipates the *et vidit deus cogitationes eorum* [and God saw their thoughts] of B. xv, 194–95. An imagination that touches home so closely as to think with compassion on the labourers of Noah who were lost for all their labour, and to see in them an analogy for such as Solomon and Aristotle, whose wisdom supports a faith that can save others but not them, unless indeed their love, known only to God, has lifted them into his hand, such an imagination shows the returning powers of the poet.

AFTER THE DIVERGENCE OF THE TEXTS

So far in following the process of revision we have only considered some interpolations made in the B version before it finally parts company with the A. When it does so, although some arguments are new and some opinions reversed, the life of the poem is nevertheless not interrupted, for the revising poet has continued the allegory of his own maturing mind (so far pictured in Thought, Wit, Study, Clergy, Scripture) by the introduction of a further figure, Imaginative, which claims to have followed the poet for five and forty winters; it is to be associated with the concept of Memory, the memory of an adult man reviewing his opinions in the light of his experiences.[22] It is through this figure that the author retracts and redresses the injustices done in A. xi by the denigration of Clergy, retaining the course of his allegory while changing the course of his argument, an ingenious and poetical way of saving his work from self-contradiction.

The study of the author's revisionary method that has been offered has been suggestive rather than exhaustive, and its purpose to show such

22 "Throughout we find the Imagination—mediating as the character in Piers Plowman between the senses and the reason." H. S. V. Jones, "Imaginatif in Piers Plowman," *J.E.G.Ph.* xiii, no. 4. See also R. W. Chambers, *Man's Unconquerable Mind*, p. 139.

changes as seem to bear on the transformation of the poem from one
about England into one about the search for eternal life; in the course of
this transformation, Langland found himself faced with many new problems, as we have seen; two of the most important of which are an understanding of Do-wel, Do-bet, and Do-best, and an understanding of the
part in them played by Faith, Works, and Learning. The great additions
of the B-text are too many and too complex to be treated fully here, but
something may be said of his handling of each of these two problems, to
show how he has lifted them into the fourth plane of allegory already
mentioned, that is, into the supernal things of eternal glory.

DO-WEL, DO-BET, AND DO-BEST

There is a particularly strange passage in the A-text that so far as I
know has received little attention; it runs:

> And as Do-wel and Do-bet . duden hem to vnderstonde,
> Thei han I-Corouned A kyng . to kepen hem Alle,
> That ӡif Do-wel or Do-bet . dude aӡeyn Do-best,
> And were vnbuxum at his biddinge . and bold to don ille,
> Then schulde the kyng comen . and casten hem in prison,
> And puiten hem ther In penaunce . with-outen pite or grace,
> Bote ӡif Do-best beede for hem . a-byde ther for euere!
> Thus Do-wel and Do-bet . and Do-best the thridde
> Crounede on to beo kyng . and bi heor counseil worche,
> And Rule the Reame . bi Red of hem Alle,
> And otherwyse elles not . bute as thei threo assenten.
>
> (A. ix, 90–100)

This seems a very dark saying; but that it was clear in meaning to the reviser seems certain, for he repeated it almost verbatim in the corresponding passage of the B-text. The sense seems to be:

> And as Do-wel and Do-bet gave them (the wicked) to understand,
> they have crowned a King to control them all, so that if Do-wel or
> Do-bet rebelled against Do-best, and were disobedient to his bidding
> and bold to do evil, then the King should come and cast them into
> prison, and put them to their penance without pity or grace, where
> they should stay for ever, unless Do-best prayed on their behalf.
> Thus Do-wel, Do-bet, and Do-best, all three, crowned one to be King
> and to work by their counsel, and rule the Kingdom by the advice of
> them all, and otherwise not, except by their assent.

On the face of it, it seems an obscure statement of some form of social contract, and we are incited to ask who is this King? When was he

crowned by these three lives? What is this pitiless prison that only the prayers of Do-best can save the disobedient from? And if he is King why should he be controlled by those who have crowned him?

There is another passage, if anything darker still, that seems to give a partly similar message; it is one of the interpolations at the point of divergence of the two texts:

Ac there shal come a kyng . and confesse ʒow religiouses,
And bete ʒow as the bible telleth . for brekynge of ʒowre reule,
And amende monyales . monkes and chanouns,
And putten hem to her penaunce . *ad pristinum statum ire* [to return to
    their original state],
And Barounes with Erles beten hem . thorugh *beatus-virres*[23] techynge,
That here barnes claymen . and blame ʒow foule.

(B. x, 317–22)

and then, after a brief and excessively difficult passage about the donation of Constantine and the Abbot of Abingdon, irrelevant to our present purpose, the passage ends:

    Ac ar that kynge come . cayme shal awake.
    Ac dowel shal dyngen hym adoune . and destryen his myʒte.

(B. x, 329–30)

I confess that the lines here quoted seem to me very hard to translate and it may be that some textual corruption has made them untranslatable. I offer, nevertheless, what may be accepted as a rendering:

But there shall come a King and bring you Religious people (i.e. Do-bet) to confession, and make you better (possibly "beat," but I think the sense is against it) for breaking the Rule of your Order, and amend nuns, monks, and canons, and put them to their penance (namely to) return to their former state (? obedience to their Rule), and make barons and earls better themselves (?) through the teaching of the First Psalm (in respect of) what their children claim, blaming you (Religious people) foully (? for having defrauded them of their inheritance) . . . . But ere that King shall come, Cain will awake; but Do-well shall ding him down and destroy his power.

The similarity of thought in these two prophecies, vague though they be, suggests that the second is some sort of recollection or development of the first; a King is to come and bring to penance those who are disobedient, especially the Religious Orders, though a part of the Laity also will

---

23 ["Blessed is the man": the first few words from the First Psalm.]

come under reproof. The second passage adds that before this is to happen, Cain shall awake; but Do-well will deal with him.

Conjecture as to what these things meant to Langland must be insecure,[24] but by reference to the end of the poem an interpretation can be found which gives a good sense. In Passus xx there is a vision of the coming of Anti-Christ:

> And the Religious reverenced him . and rung their bells
> And all the convent came forth . to welcome that tyrant
> And all his followers as well as himself . save only fools.
>
>   (B. xx, 58)

It is true that in the event, the fools, though called upon by Conscience to come into Unity, make no attempt to "ding him adown," and he passes like a tornado through the poem leaving all in havoc save Conscience. There is, however, some whiff of similarity to the passage quoted about Cain, and if that hint be accepted, we may conjecture that all these three passages are linked in meaning, and that their meaning is eschatological. From this we may infer that the King who is to come and "confess the Religiouses" is Christ at His Second Coming. This would answer our questions, who is this King and what his prison? The question whether Do-best can pray them out of prison is more difficult; it is raised again in the case of Trajan, who

> . . . had been a true knight . (and) took witness at a Pope
> How he was dead and damned . to dwell in torment. . . .
> Gregory knew this well . and willed to my soul
> Salvation for the Truth . that he saw in my works.
>
>   (B. xi, 136)

However in Trajan's case, Langland seems to think the prayers of Do-best were not enough, for he adds:

> Not through prayer of a Pope . but for his pure Truth
> Was that Saracen saved . as St. Gregory beareth witness.
>
>   (B. xi, 150)

Perhaps we are safe in suggesting that the "prison" in A. ix, 94, is Purgatory and not Hell, in which case the prayers of the Church are held to have efficacy. This leaves only one question to be answered, namely, when

---

[24] I have attempted a more detailed elucidation along similar lines in *Med. Æv.* iv. 2, p. 84, suggesting the identification of Cain with Anti-Christ, and am indebted to Mr. J. A. W. Bennett for reminding me of a passage in *Beowulf* (line 1261 et seq.) , associating Cain with those ancient giants of evil, of whom Grendel was one, and thought of as the enemy of God and man.

was Christ "crowned" and controlled by Do-wel, Do-bet, and Do-best, and in what sense? Again the answer seems to be given at the end of the poem. After the vision of the Harrowing of Hell, the poet goes to hear Mass, and there has a dream of Jesus as Christ Conqueror which is expounded to him by Conscience. "In His youth," says Conscience

> this Jesus . at a Jew's feast
> Water into wine turned . as Holy Writ telleth,
> And there began God . of His grace to do well.
> (B. xix, 104)

Later, says Conscience.

> He made lame to leap . and gave light to the blind,
> And fed with two fishes . and with five loaves
> More than five thousand . sorely hungred folk.
> Thus he comforted the care-stricken . and caught a greater name
> Which was Do-bet. . . .   (B. xix, 121)

At last, having been crowned on Calvary [25] and having won His triumphs over Hell, He returned in resurrection to Galilee and to the Disciples,

> And when this deed was done . Do-best He taught
> And gave Piers power . and pardon he granted
> To all manner men . mercy and forgiveness
> (And gave) [26] him might, men to assoil . of all manner sins
> In covenant that they come . and acknowledge to pay
> To the Pardon of Piers Plowman . *redde quod debes.*
> (B. xix, 177)

Thus, by taking all these scattered passages together, the full meaning of the first becomes clear. Christ, by living Do-well, Do-bet, and Do-best in His own person, is crowned by them on Calvary, having been obedient to those ways of life and having appointed them as the advisers by which His Kingdom is to be ruled.

FAITH, WORKS, AND LEARNING

These are matters powerfully entangled in both A- and B-texts. As has already been noticed, the Field of Folk seem to receive their Pardon for their Work under Piers; Piers had begun their instruction by telling them that the way to Truth is by obedience to the Commandments (and this, as we shall see, counts as "Works") ;[27] on the other hand he adds

25 B. xix, 41.
26 For this bracketed emendation, see "The Text of Piers Plowman" by R. W. Chambers and J. H. G. Grattan, *Mod. Lang. Rev.*, vol. xxvi, no. i, p. 4.
27 See below, p. 79.

that when they come at last to "the Court, clear as the sun, where Truth is in" they will find it

Buttressed with the Belief . wherethrough we may be saved

(A. vi, 79)

which clearly gives importance to Faith. So too, when Piers turns from his work of labour in the fields, quoting the psalm of trust *"si ambula-vero in medio umbre mortis, non timebo mala,"* he glances also at a text from St. Matthew:

Ne soliciti sitis [Be not solicitous] . he saith in his gospel

(A. viii, 112)

which is a pointer to the verse that ends "Shall he not much more clothe you, O ye of little faith?"

Faith and Works are thus alternately stressed, and it is far from clear, as we have seen already, whether it is the "true tilling" of Do-well or his simple *paternoster* that has the greater power of his justification in the eleventh passus of the A version. But these two conceptions, from the very start, are complicated by a third, namely that of Learning. For when Piers quotes the psalm about the valley of the shadow, the derisive priest retorts upon him for his show of Latin and suggests in mockery that Piers should turn priest himself and preach on the theme *Quoniam litera-turam non cognovi* [Seeing that I have not learned the alphabet].

When Langland comes to consider the effects of Learning on the learned, he finds that their skill in the subtleties of the Faith does not issue in those Works to which it commits them (A. xi, 42 and 53). But their lack of inward charity is not the only count against the learned nor even their failure to practise what they preach. Their Learning itself is a danger to Christendom. It is the old business of the *Song of Nego,*

> Now o clerk seiith *nego* [I deny];
> And that other *dubito;*
> Seiith another *concedo;*
> And another *obligo,*
> *Verum falsum* sette therto;
> Than is al the lore i-do.
> Thus the fals clerkes of har hevid,
> Makith men trewth of ham be revid.[28]

Subtleties in discussion, as whether Two Members of the Trinity could be held to have conspired to slay the Third,[29] or why God allowed the

[28] *Political Songs of England,* Camden Society, 1839, p. 211.
[29] A. xi, 40.

Serpent to seduce Eve[30] (says Langland), must shake the Faith of simple folk.

> Such motions they move . these masters in their glory
> And make men misbelieve . that muse on their words.
>
> (A. xi, 70)

Better not to know such things; *Non plus sapere quam oportet sapere* [Not to be more wise than is proper to be wise]. Christ Himself had spoken against learning when He said "Take no thought beforehand what ye shall speak" [31] and St. Augustine had confessed *Ecce, ipsi ydiote rapiunt celum, ubi nos sapientes in infernum mergemur* [Behold, the fools themselves seize heaven, while wise ones are plunged into hell].[32]

And thus, through a tangle of thoughts on the effect of Learning on Faith and Works, the Author had passed to his first conclusion, the justification of Do-wel by his simplicity, and the damning of the Doctors.

In this conclusion, however, he was unable to rest; he came in middle age to see that without Learning there could be no Faith, not even the simple Faith that reposes on a Paternoster; for who is to teach a tinker how to say his prayers except a learned priest?

> And as a blind man in battle . beareth weapon to fight
> And hath no hap with his axe . his enemy to hit,
> No more can a man of natural wit . unless clerics teach him
> Come for all his wit . to Christendom and be saved
> Which is the coffer of Christ's treasure . and clerics keep the keys.
>
> (B. xii, 107)

This is the advice of Imaginative, the power of a man in middle age, to see the images of memory in their true perspective. The Dreamer stands self-rebuked for his earlier contempt of Learning.

We have seen in outline the complex of ideas centering round Faith, Works, and Learning in the A-text; we have seen that in the A-text, aiming at the justification of the Pardon of Piers, Langland made what might be called a false landing and finished off his poem as best he might, justifying Do-wel at the expense of Do-bet; and we have seen that the reviser has not suppressed any of these things, although he was obviously of a different opinion; true to the existing organization of the poem on the lines of a spiritual autobiography, he leaves on record the prejudices of his youth in all their insolence and passes on to his maturity and the

---

30 *Ibid.*, 66.
31 A. xi, 287.
32 *Ibid.*, 295.

change of his views. That is why the next passus in the B-text (B. xi) deals with his wayward worldly life, giving the passage of time,

> Till I forgot Youth . and hastened into Eld
>
> (B. xi, 59)

and met with Imaginative.

But even Imaginative cannot finally resolve the whole problem, for all his arguments about the Penitent Thief, Trajan, and Aristotle, classic examples of Faith, Works, and Learning respectively. The trouble was that poetically speaking these three historical figures, though they made an argument, did not make a picture; without a picture, without a story, the argument hung fire, for Langland's thinking was always clearer to him when it came under an allegory, a narrative; we have seen this not only in his organization of the English scene, but also in his effort to dress his later arguments in a sort of autobiography. He was never really at home with *nego, dubito,* and *concedo.* He was, however, given to thinking in terms of trinities: Do-wel, Do-bet, and Do-best; Faith, Works, Learning. It was in puzzling over these and how to match them with each other that he suddenly hit upon a new trinity and a new story that could embrace his whole thought; the trinity was that of the three virtues, Faith, Hope, and Charity, and the story was the story of the Good Samaritan.

> (I do it on *Deus Caritas* . to deem the sooth.)

Most delicately, most gradually, the allegory is introduced; the unsuspecting reader can hardly see it happening until it has happened. First, as if in continuation of the series of his ghostly companions (Wit, Study, Imaginative, Conscience, Patience, and the rest), Piers Plowman returns into the poem

> and all for pure joy
> That I heard name his name . anon I swooned after
> And lay long in a lone dream . and at last methought
> That Piers the Plowman . all that place showed me.
>
> (B. xvi, 18)

He teaches the ravished Dreamer how to understand the tree of Charity and its Triune support and the first notes of the theme of the Incarnation are sounded:

> Then spake *Spiritus Sanctus* . in Gabriel's mouth
> To a maid called Mary....
>
> (B. xvi, 90)

The life of Christ is then swiftly told up to the crucifixion; very naturally this is followed by the coming of Faith, in the form of Abraham its great exemplar, and he too teaches the dreamer the nature of the Trinity and speaks of the Incarnation and the Sacrament of the Altar; in his bosom lie many, Lazarus, the Patriarchs, and Prophets, in safe keeping against the day when Christ descending into Hell shall release them from the power of the Fiend. And, as that is matter for hope, it is Hope who immediately appears, in the form of Moses.

Why should Moses stand for Hope? He bears the tables of the Law, *Dilige Deum et proximum* [Love God and your neighbor], which link exactly with those words spoken by Piers when he first set the world to *work*.

> You must go through meekness . both man and wife,
> Till you come into conscience . that Christ knows the Truth
> That you love Him more dearly . than the life in your hearts,
> And then our neighbours next. . . .
>
> (A. vi, 51)

Abraham is to Faith as Moses is to Works; each justifies his claim to have saved many souls; and so it is argued:

> And as we went thus in the way . wording together
> Then saw we a Samaritan . sitting on a mule
>
> (B. xvii, 47)

who brings a parable within a parable to tell the story of Faith, Hope, and Charity. Of all the subtle foretastes in which this poem abounds, the phrase *sitting on a mule* is the most pregnant; it is the first hinting that the Samaritan, Charity, is Christ Himself. But the story is not yet far enough told for a full identification; so great a vision must open with extreme gradualness, and except for this hint, the true identity of the Good Samaritan is held in reserve. Meanwhile we see him tend the man who fell among thieves while Faith and Hope play the parts of the Priest and the Levite:

> Faith flew away . and Spes his fellow too
> Forsight of the sorrowful man . that had been robbed by thieves.
>
> (B. xvii, 88)

Who is this sorrowful man but the human race, fallen among thieves in their first garden?

> For in my palace, Paradise, . in person of an adder. . . .
> Thievishly thou didst rob me. . . .
>
> (B. xviii, 333)

And neither Faith nor Hope is sufficient for the wound:

"Have them excused," said the Samaritan . their help may little avail
No medicine upon earth . can bring the man to health,
Neither *Faith* nor fine *Hope*, . so festered are his wounds,
Without the blood of a boy . born of a maid.

(B. xvii, 90)

So the Samaritan begins his teaching, and in image upon image tells of
the death of Death (*O mors, ero mors tua* [O Death, I will be your
death]) , and of the mystery of the Trinity (like a Hand: fist, finger, and
palm; like a Torch: wax, wick, and flame) , and of repentance and pardon. In this story and in this teaching that crowns it, Faith, Works, and
Learning are made one with Faith, Hope, and Charity; Allegory has resolved argument.

But there is a climax still to come, the hinted identifications have still
to be made manifest; it is kept back for the next passus, the next dream,
for the Good Samaritan has spurred his mule

And went away as wind . and there-with I awaked.
(B. xvii, 350)

Weary and wet-shod, Langland "went forth after, all my lifetime" until
again he slept:

And of Christs passion and penance . reaching to the people
(Resting myself and deep asleep . till *ramis palmarum* [Palm Sunday]),
Of children chanting *gloria laus* . I greatly dreamed. . . .
One semblable to the Samaritan . and something to Piers the Plowman
Barefoot upon an ass's back . unbooted came riding. . . .
Then was *Faith* in a window . and cried *"A! fili David!"*
As doth an herald of arms . when the adventurous come to joust
Old Jews of Jerusalem . for joy they sang
    Benedictus qui venit in nomine domini
Then I asked of *Faith* . what all this affair meant. . . .
"Is Piers in this place?" said I . and he peered upon me,
"This Jesus of His gentle birth . will joust in Piers' arms,
In his helm and in his habergeon . *humana natura.*"

(B. xviii, 1–23)

At last Charity and Learning, the Good Samaritan and Piers, are made
one with Christ, and He one with humanity. This is (I suppose) the top
of all English allegorical writing, the greatest gathering of the greatest
meanings in the simplest symbols.

Thus in the B-text, the seeds set so unregardingly in the A have grown to their flower and fruit. It would indeed be true in a certain sense to say that there is no material in the revised poem which is not present or implicit in the earlier one. Yet it might not have been given to the revising poet to see it all so clearly, to let it grow to its natural organic shape. The *Canterbury Tales* are unfinished; a hundred more stories are implicit in its plan; but of all those untold tales we could not name one that is implied by the structure of the poem in the sense that the story of the life and passion of Christ is implicit in the A-text of Piers Plowman, as are also the stories of the Harrowing of Hell, the building of Piers' Barn of Holy Church, and the Coming of Anti-Christ, given the allegorical genius to see them there. From the moment when Thought first told the Dreamer of Do-well, Do-better, and Do-best, the stories of the Incarnation and the founding of Christendom were inevitable *exempla* for who could perceive and tell them. In the course of the years they were perceived and told.

It need hardly be said that they are the most striking additions made in the revision; if one were to imagine the A-text published with the B Prologue, the resulting poem would still be near in kind to *Wynnere and Wastoure*. But these other additions have outsoared what is topical and temporal, albeit the Prologue is more securely anchored to fourteenth-century England than ever; the author has found the ways to Paradise "by way of Kensal Green."

Allegory is a way of thinking, parallel thinking, thought directed to a subject on several levels of reality at once. It seems to have arisen out of Christianity and spread to science and poetry; but in Holy Scripture was its home. Origen distinguished three meanings, the historic, the moral, and the spiritual,[33] that is the verbal, the moral, and the mystical.

In the dedication to Leander of Seville of his lectures on the Book of Job, Gregory the Great put forward a similar view.[34]

> You must know that there are some parts which we explain historically, others we search out by allegory, investigating symbolical meaning, in others we open out only moral lessons, allegorically conveyed, while there are some few which we discuss in all these ways together, exploring them by a three-fold method.

A fourth way of interpretation was also discovered, especially for biblical exegesis, popularly expressed in the tag:

[33] "He was familiar with the Pauline distinction of 'body, soul, and spirit.' He finds such a distinction in the senses of scripture. There too we have a bodily or historic sense, a moral sense, which—perhaps without any very special propriety—he classes with the soul; a higher element, the spiritual meaning." R. B. Tollington, *Selections from the Commentaries of Origen,* 1929.

[34] *Gregory the Great,* by F. Homes Dudden, vol. i, p. 193.

> Littera gesta docet, quid credas allegoria
>
> Moralis quid agas, quo tendas analogia[35]
>
> [The literal explains actions; the allegorical explains
> what you should believe;/The moral explains what you should
> do; the anagogical explains where you should aim]

and this is elaborated in the *Summa* of St. Thomas, Question 1, Article 10, and quoted in Mr. H. W. Troyer's extremely suggestive article "Who is Piers Plowman?" [36] An even clearer account of the fourfold method of interpretation appears in the *Convivio* of Dante.

> . . . Writings may be taken and should be expounded chiefly in four senses. The first is called the literal, and it is the one that extends no further than the letter as it stands; the second is called the allegorical, and is the one that hides itself under the mantle of these tales, and is a truth hidden under a beauteous fiction. . . . It is true that the theologians take this sense otherwise than the poets do, but since it is my purpose here to follow the method of the poets I shall take the allegorical sense after the use of the poets.
>
> The third sense is called the moral, and this is the one that lecturers should go intently noting throughout the scriptures for their own behoof and that of their disciples. Thus we may note in the Gospel, when Christ ascended the mountain for the transfiguration, that of the twelve apostles he took with him but three; wherein the moral may be understood that in the most secret things we should have but few companions.
>
> The fourth sense is called the anagogical, that is to say "above the sense"; and this is when a scripture is spiritually expounded which even in the literal sense, by the very things it signifies, signifies again some portion of the supernal things of eternal glory. . . .[37]

I have assembled these few accounts of the nature of allegory not because I imagine, or think I can prove, that Langland had access to any of them, but to show that it was so current a commonplace of medieval exegesis that it would be no wonder if our author knew of it; he may indeed have known it more intimately than we can, who, by reading, can apprehend it intellectually but cannot easily let it live in us as a way or habit of thinking and feeling. Langland was, perhaps, no great reader, but he gives the effect of a great listener. "His knowledge must have been

35 Encyclopaedia of Religion and Ethics, vol. i, p. 331.

36 *P.M.L.A.*, xlvii, no. 2 [see below, pp. 156–73].

37 Dante, *Convivio*, Second Treatise, ch. i. tr. P. H. Wicksteed.

largely derived from what he heard in sermons or got from conversations with other men." [38]

The allegorical method was then a regular method of presentation and analysis for the makers of sermons and the renderers of the Bible; but to reverse the process, to use it as a method not of criticism but of creation in this its most complex, fourfold manner, seems to belong to Langland alone in the field of English poetry. To know that Holy Writ may have four meanings and to discern them is one thing, but to create a great work on this biblical scale is a feat of poetry almost above ambition.

*   *   *

It remains to link the analysis here attempted with ideas already advanced elsewhere as to the structure of the poem. The existence of a fourth voice within it (so much more important than a fourth author) was first discerned by Mr. Wells, albeit he did not fasten upon it the official name, the *sensus anagogicus* [anagogical sense] of medieval theory; that was the work of Mr. Troyer.[39] Both of these scholars see the same truth, but in different ways; for whereas Mr. Troyer sees Christ as God in the image of Man, for whom he believes Piers to be "a multifold symbol," Mr. Wells stresses that man is made in the image of God; either of these approaches is valuable, but that of Mr. Wells the more fundamental, for if we follow its implications under the guidance of Mr. Wells, the poem as a whole takes anagogical shape, into which the character and meaning of the symbol Piers easily fits; whereas if we follow the line suggested by Mr. Troyer, we reach an answer only in respect of the symbol Piers, which it must be said in fairness to Mr. Troyer is the special point of his inquiry. The doctrine that man is made in the image of God is fully stated in both the A and B versions of the poem (A. x, 27–37). Wells expounds the importance of this idea to the reviser of the poem thus:

> He evidently considered that, since God is a Trinity, man must in some sense also be a trinity. Each of the three parts of the *Vita* begins with allusions to the interrelation of the three parts of the Trinity and each is clearly dedicated to a special Person of the Trinity. At the conclusion of the *Vita de Do-well* we are told that even the Saracens believe in God the Father. It is this Person of the Trinity who clearly presides over the Life of Do-wel. Christ as Piers the Plowman is the central theme of the *Vita de Do-bet*. In this part of the poem

[38] R. W. Chambers, *Man's Unconquerable Mind,* p. 104.
[39] *Op. cit.*

the life of Christ, his crucifixion and the harrowing of hell supply the chief narrative elements. The *Vita de Do-best* is no less clearly dedicated to the Holy Spirit. . . . Such is the spiritual trinity of man according to *Piers Plowman,* a thought of no inconsiderable importance in the organization of the work.[40]

It would seem that although the writer of the A-text knew well enough that God is a Trinity and that Man is made in His Image, the notion that Do-well, Do-better, and Do-best were in some sense parallel to the functions of the Three Persons of the Trinity did not dawn upon him, or at least become a part of his poem, until the process of revision began. But once he had apprehended it, it became the thought upon which the whole revision was moulded; once more there was an equation of Trinities. We may even make a simple table of the organization of the new poem:

Sensus literalis:	Piers the Farmer	Piers the Teacher	Piers the Builder of the Barn
Sensus allegoricus:	Laity	Clergy	Episcopate
Sensus moralis:	Do-wel	Do-bet	Do-best
Sensus anagogicus:	God the Father	God the Son	God the Holy Ghost

If to this tabular presentation we add that it is indeed only a table, that all the meanings harmonize and interplay their counterpoint, mingle, vanish, reappear, and combine in every variety, and that every combination is graced with images of intense poetical force and told in language equal to the design, it becomes possible to view the whole poem in one complex imaginative act, to see it as a great and single vision made of many visions, held and harmonized in the mind of the revising poet, and written down so that we can hold it in the same way.

The uniting symbol is Piers;[41] choosing him for hero was the masterstroke of the revising hand. The simple farmer about whom the A-text poem on England had centred, became the changeable but constant centre of the three ways of Christian salvation.

It has been seen in this inquiry that the revision of the poem was dictated by the enigmatic character of the Pardon sent by Truth to the Field of Folk; in what light do we now see this Pardon, after studying the revision? Are we any nearer to knowing whether it was a pardon or not? If our analysis has been correct, in the Vision of Pentecost and the Build-

---

[40] *P.M.L.A.,* xliv, no. 1, "The Construction of Piers Plowman," by H. W. Wells.
[41] For a detailed demonstration of this see *Med. Æv.* vol. ii, no. 2, "The Character of Piers Plowman," by Nevill Coghill.

ing of the Barn of Unity ("Holy Church in English") , Piers was the *exemplum* for Do-best, as in the Vision of the Incarnation and especially of the Passion, Piers was the *exemplum* for Do-bet. But Piers had also been the symbol of the first vision, the vision of England, and in this, as we can now see, he stands for Do-wel, or in Latin *qui bona egerunt;* it is his very name, and the Pardon is truly his. But there is more in it than this: his followers have to be considered.

If we turn to the first advice given to them by Piers we find him use this allegory of entry into Heaven:

> Grace is the guard on the gate . a good man in truth;
> His man is called Amend-you . for many men know him;
> Tell him this token . for Truth knows the sooth:
> "I performed the penance . that the priest enjoined;
> I am sorry for my sins . and so shall I ever
> When I think thereon. . . ."
>
> (A. vi, 85)

Penance includes one more of those trinities in which Langland so often thought; it has three parts, *contritio cordis* [contrition of the heart], *confessio oris* [confession of mouth], and *satisfactio operis* [satisfaction of work]; at one time in his revision he began to play with this thought, seeking in it an analogy for Do-wel, Do-bet, and Do-best.

> "And I shall ken thee," quoth Conscience . "of contrition to make,
> That shall clean thy cloak . of all kinds of filth,
> *Cordis contricio etc.*
> Do-wel shall wash it and wring it . through a wise confessor,
> *Oris confessio*
> Do-bet shall beat it and cleanse it . as bright as any scarlet,
> And dye the grain with a good will . and God's grace to amend thee
> And afterward send thee to satisfaction . to sew it up,
> *Satisfaccio* Dobest"
>
> (B. xiv, 16)

But he leaves this fancy, and comes back to a simpler statement:

> *Ergo,* Contrition, Faith and Conscience . is the nature of Do-wel,
> And are surgeons for deadly sin . when shrift of mouth faileth.
> But shrift of mouth more worthy is . if man be inly contrite;
> For shrift of mouth slayeth sin . be it never so deadly. . . .
> But Satisfaction seeketh out the root . and both slayeth and voideth it
> And, as if it had never been . bringeth deadly sin to nought.
>
> (B. xiv, 87)

Now when the Pardon was sent to Piers, his followers had already shown
Contrition and made Confession through the figures of the Seven Deadly
Sins, and were even then engaged on the search for St. Truth, which
seems their act of Satisfaction. The revising poet therefore has made clear
that such men are also written in the Pardon by the name of Do-wel, *qui
bona egerunt,* even though they had sinned; for they were "inly contrite," they had made their shrift of mouth, and they were "seeking out
the root" in satisfaction. They were "kyndelich Do-wel." The Pardon
Truth had sent them was their Pardon; He had bought it and they had
earned it.

In this new light upon their repentance, let us look at their Pardon
once again. All in two lines it lay:

> *Et qui bona egerunt, Ibunt in vitam eternam*
> *Qui vero mala, in ignem eternum.*
> [And those who have done good will go into eternal life;
> Those who have done evil, into eternal fire.]

Understood on the human planes of the A-text, here is justice, but no
mercy, for on any human plane justice and mercy are at variance; one
must yield to the other. But on that further plane of *aeterna gloria,* in
the life of God, where justice and mercy are one, Langland saw them
manifested with equal power in the Incarnation, the Atonement, and in
Pentecost; by these the simple followers of Piers, "blustering forth as
beasts" on their pathless penance, are to find mercy as well as justice in
the Pardon of Truth. To show the richness of its meaning and the
strength of its foundation, Langland had to write not only a new poem,
but a new kind of poem, one that can awaken in the reader a new kind
of attention to some portion of those supernal things of which Dante
wrote.

4. The Structure of the B-Text of
Piers Plowman
T. P. DUNNING, C.M.

IT IS NOW very generally agreed that the organizing factors in the B-text of *Piers Plowman* are the concepts of the Active, Contemplative, and Mixed Lives as distinguished by the medieval theologians and spiritual writers. There is, however, no general agreement as to how these factors operate in determining the structure of the poem.[1] Certain questions still present themselves, of which the most insistent is concerned with the relationship between the two main parts into which the poem is divided, the *Visio de Petro Plowman* and the *Vita de Dowel, Dobet, et Dobest.* If Dowel, Dobet, and Dobest represent the Active, Contemplative, and Mixed Lives, with what aspect—if any—of the spiritual life of man is the *Visio* concerned? And in what sense and to what extent do the three divisions of the *Vita* represent the traditional divisions of the spiritual life?

I hope to show that a closer examination of the terms "Active," "Contemplative," and "Mixed" Lives in their fourteenth-century connotation will throw some further light on these questions.

I

It is first useful to recall that Langland had a vast body of uniform spiritual teaching on which to draw. One of the many services which Mr. Pantin's recent work on the English Church in the fourteenth century has accomplished for students of medieval English literature is to make clear how the teaching of the Fathers and doctors had, by that time, be-

Reprinted by permission of the author and The Clarendon Press, Oxford, from *Review of English Studies*, N.S., VII (1956) , 225–37.

1 For an excellent summary of the different interpretations of these concepts proposed by critics of the poem, see E. Talbot Donaldson, *Piers Plowman: The C-Text and its Poet* (New Haven, 1949) , pp. 156–61; and for an admirable discussion of the various views, see S. S. Hussey, "Langland, Hilton, and the Three Lives," *R.E.S.*, N.S. vii (1956) , 132–50. Mr. Hussey reaches the conclusion that "neither the triad active, contemplative, and mixed lives, nor the triad purgative, illuminative, and unitive states, nor a combination of the two is completely satisfactory as a definition of Dowel, Dobet, and Dobest . . ." (p. 146) . The present article will suggest that the definitions of the active, contemplative, and mixed lives so far put forward by critics of *Piers Plowman* have not fully taken into account the connotation of those terms in Langland's time.

come available to a very wide public in a great number of semi-popular and popular manuals and compendia.[2]

Properly to understand the poet's use of this body of teaching on the Christian life, which is essentially the inner life of the individual, one must take into account the scope and purpose of the poem. The one is indicated in the Prologue; the other in Passus i. From the beginning, Langland shows that his subject is Christian society, or the Church; and that his concern is with the reform of society. It would seem that he largely takes for granted the traditional teaching on the spiritual life of the Christian; and while using this as the framework of his poem in such a way as never to distort its systematic character, he constantly modifies it to reflect his preoccupation with (a) Christian society, and (b) the society of his own time and its peculiar problems. Two examples may serve to illustrate the point.

The first is from Passus xix. Langland has here come to the final stage of the spiritual life: we have moved from Contrition, Confession, and Satisfaction through Patience and Poverty to Faith, Hope, and Charity; and now to the Cardinal Virtues. According to the traditional *schema*, the final element of the spiritual equipment is the seven Gifts of the Holy Ghost. But instead of describing these gifts—Wisdom, Understanding, and the rest, which guide the soul to the higher flights of mysticism— Langland describes the gifts of the Holy Ghost as the talents each man receives for a particular work in the world; and he makes the giving of these gifts the starting-point for building up again at the end of his poem that composite picture of Christian society we saw in the Prologue. This time, in Passus xix, first the ideal; then, as in the Prologue, the contemporary. And so his end, like Mr. Eliot's, is in his beginning.

The other example is from the *Vita de Dowel*. This represents the beginning of the spiritual life proper; and a principal feature of such a beginning, according to all the spiritual writers, is coming to know oneself. In the *Benjamin Major,* for instance, Richard of St. Victor points out in some detail how the knowledge of oneself is first necessary if one wishes to lead a spiritual life worthy of the name. The diversity of our human

---

2 W. A. Pantin, *The English Church in the Fourteenth Century* (Cambridge, 1955) , pp. 189–262. I should like to mention three works in particular which became vade mecums of the clergy during the fourteenth century and which I have consulted for this paper: Hugh of Strasbourg's *Compendium Theologicae Veritatis*, a summary of St. Thomas's *Summa*, mentioned by Richard Rolle, and popular for over 300 years; John of Freiburg's revision of Raymond of Peñafort's *Summa Confessorum*, a useful and most popular compendium of Canon Law, recommended by the pope to every priest engaged in pastoral work; and William of Pagula's *Oculus Sacerdotis*, written *c.* 1320, of which some 50 manuscripts survive in England (Pantin, op. cit., pp. 195– 205; L. E. Boyle, "The *Oculus Sacerdotis* and some other works of William of Pagula," *Trans. Royal Hist. Soc.*, 5th Series [1955], 81-110) .

faculties, the multiplicity of affections, the perpetual mobility of the mind are elements which must be understood if one wishes to control them. Besides, concupiscence having veiled the eye of the intelligence, how are we to distinguish the good from the bad, how can we judge the movements of the heart, how discern their provenance? A reconnaissance of the terrain where one is to exercise the inner life is indispensable. Richard judges that *discretio* and *deliberatio* take charge of that necessary work.[3] It seems that Passus viii–xii really constitute that phase of the Christian's development where the dreamer comes to know himself. Scripture says at the beginning of Passus xii, "Multi multa sciunt sed seipsos nesciunt" [Many people know much, but they do not know themselves]; and the same point is underlined by Ymagynatyf throughout Passus xii. One might also refer to the effects of concupiscence on the intelligence, vividly described in Passus xi. This is, however, the framework. Within this framework, Langland has embodied two of the main intellectual preoccupations of his day: the place of learning in the good life and the problem of Predestination.[4] These are represented as the chief clouds which obscure the dreamer's vision of the ground he has to cover.

Such manipulation of the body of traditional teaching presupposes among the poem's first readers a familiarity with the main lines of that teaching. The same assumption underlies the poem's outward structure. Its significance may be better understood by examining the terms "Contemplation" and "Action."

II

"The traditional doctrine of the two ways of life, the one of Action, the other of Contemplation, is so clearly suggested in the incident of Martha and Mary that it must be considered to have its origin in the Gospel itself."[5] Nevertheless, during the early centuries, especially at Alexandria,

---

[3] *Benj. Maj.*, iii, c. 23, 132 B–C–D. Summarized and discussed in G. Dumeige, *Richard de Saint-Victor et l'idée chrétienne de l'amour* (Paris, 1952), pp. 54–56. "Le 14e siècle est tributaire de la notion de contemplation élaborée durant les siècles précédents: à travers les définitions et les classifications de saint Thomas et de saint Bonaventure, on a conservé notamment la trace de Hugues et de Richard de Saint-Victor" [The fourteenth century is the tributary of the notion of contemplation elaborated during the preceding centuries: alongside of the definitions and the classifications of St. Thomas and of St. Bonaventure, one has preserved, particularly, the mark of Hugo and Richard of St. Victor] (François Vandenbroucke, *Dict. de Spiritualité* [Paris, 1952], ii. 1988).

[4] Discussed in Pantin, op. cit., pp. 123–35. See also T. P. Dunning, "Langland and the Salvation of the Heathen," *M.Æ.*, xii (1943), 45–54.

[5] H. Bérard, "Action et Contemplation," *La Vie Spirituelle*, xx (1929), 135. The most comprehensive discussion of this complex subject is in the *Dict. de Spiritualité*,

Christian thought on the subject was profoundly influenced by Neoplatonic philosophy. In the pagan tradition, the Contemplative Life meant a life of study, consecrated to philosophical speculation; the Active Life, one devoted to external works and especially to political affairs. The influence of this tradition on the Christian theologians at Alexandria may be seen in the high speculative quality they attributed to the Contemplative Life, by reason of the *gnosis,* which for them distinguished the perfect Christian. Cassian, on the other hand, in resuming the teaching of the Egyptian monks on Christian perfection, puts forward a somewhat different view. The life of the Egyptian coenobites was, in fact, not contemplative in the Alexandrian sense, being very little speculative and very much given up to manual labour. In his fourteenth *Conference,* Cassian divides the Contemplative Life into two parts, actual and theoretic. By the theoretic *(theoria),* he means the act of contemplation itself. He is quite clear that this act is not continuous: one cannot, as it were, *live* this kind of life. One achieves the act of contemplation from time to time. The actual life is the cultivation of virtues. This is, as it were, the setting of the contemplative life. Cassian does not seem greatly concerned with the precise character of this setting: it may be a hermitage; but it may also be the reception and care of strangers—what we should now call active good works.[6]

It would seem that the teaching of St. Gregory on the spiritual life, from which the Western tradition chiefly derives, is a development of these ideas of Cassian. For "Gregory, the great clerk," as Langland calls him, the Active and Contemplative Lives are not lived separately by two distinct categories of people, but should be united in the lives of everyone; for the life of pure contemplation is quite beyond the power of human nature.[7] In his view, contemplation is an act wherein the mind, having disengaged itself from the things of this world and fixed its attention on spiritual things, is by a great effort raised above itself to a direct and simple intuition of God, not by a process of reasoning but by a close union of love. This perception of the "unencompassed Light" "as through a chink" is momentary; and then the mind, exhausted by the effort and blinded by the vision of the Light, falls back wearied to its

---

ii. 1643–2193. See also: P. Pourrat, *Christian Spirituality* (3 vols., tr. London, 1922–6) ; Dom Cuthbert Butler, *Western Mysticism* (London, 2nd edn., 1927) .

6 Cassian, *Conferences,* tr. Robert (London, 1847) , ii. Conf. xiv.

7 St. Gregory's teaching on the spiritual life is to be found chiefly in his *Homilies on Ezechiel* and in his *Morals on Job.* The latter book was written for monks, and Langland refers to it in regard to monks, in Clergye's speech in x, 292–99. The *Homilies,* however, were not addressed to monks, but to the ordinary people of Rome; and they embody the same teaching. In the present article I am indebted to Dom Butler's study of St. Gregory's teaching in *Western Mysticism,* pp. 91–133.

normal state, to recuperate its spiritual strength by exercising the works of the active life, till in due time it can again brace itself for the effort of another act of contemplation.[8]

The Contemplative Life, then, in St. Gregory's mind, is not that solely which excludes the external works of the Active Life to devote the greater part of the time to actual contemplation: it is that which has Contemplation for its proper end, abstracting altogether from the amount of time given respectively to external works and to prayer. Contemplation is possible in a life crowded with external activity—as were, no doubt, the lives of many of those whom St. Gregory addressed; as were, for instance, the lives of St. Catherine of Siena and St. Bridget of Sweden and other contemporaries of Langland who achieved the highest Christian perfection. St. Gregory's distinction is based on the principle that in the moral order it is the end which specifies the acts. So was begun the great Western tradition of spirituality. St. Bernard, the Victorines, St. Bonaventure, and St. Thomas Aquinas are fully in accord with St. Gregory.[9]

The importance of this teaching is that Contemplation is open to all: the Contemplative Life is conceived as the perfection of the ordinary Christian life, charity in a high degree.[10] Some Christians, such as monks and hermits, lead a kind of life which is deliberately ordered towards Contemplation as its end: their state will be often referred to as "the Contemplative Life." Nevertheless, their lives, too, must necessarily be a blend of Action and Contemplation. And Contemplation is not confined to those in the monastic state.

[8] *Homilies on Ezechiel*, II. ii, tr. Butler, op. cit., pp. 93–95. Cf. II. v: Butler, pp. 98–101.

[9] St. Thomas's teaching on the subject is very substantial, comprising not only forty-eight articles in the *Secunda Secundae* of the *Summa*, but also a number of *opuscula* on the Religious Life and the Religious State, ed. R. M. Spiazzi, *Opuscula Theologica S. Thomae Aquinatis, II: de re spirituali* (Rome, 1954). For an analysis of two treatises contemporary with Langland, see W. A. Pantin, "Two Treatises of Uthred of Boldon on the Monastic Life" in *Studies in Medieval History Presented to F. M. Powicke* (Oxford, 1948), pp. 363–85.

[10] Hence St. Gregory says: "The contemplative life means the keeping of charity towards God and our neighbour, and the fixing of all our desires on our Creator," *Mor. in Job*, vi. 18 (tr. mine). This is the main theme of Langland's poem. "Loue is leche of lyf," says Holy Church at the end of Passus i, "and also the graith gate that goth into heuene" (B. 202–3). Not merely is this theme constantly reiterated throughout the poem and especially stressed when the poet is defining Dowel, Dobet, and Dobest, but there will be found a progressive strengthening and deepening of the teaching on Charity, culminating in the speech of the Samaritan in Passus xvii (note particularly ll. 250–92), and having as its climax the Passion and Death of Christ and its redemptive effects, as described in Passus xviii. Cf. Vandenbroucke in *Dict. de Spiritualité*, ii. 1988: "A la suite de saint Bonaventure, sans doute, l'amour prendra au 14ᵉ siècle une place prépondérante dans la notion de contemplation" [After Saint Bonaventure, undoubtedly, love will assume in the fourteenth century a preponderant position in the notion of contemplation].

The perfection for which man can hope on earth is, however, only relative, because "as long as we are on earth, there is always room in us for an increase of charity." Hence, "if the perfecting of our spiritual life be nothing else than growth in justice and charity, then its essential law will be progress." [11] This concept of progress brings forward the notion of stages on the journey. These stages were discussed and analysed by the doctors from early Christian times; and by Langland's time the notion of three main stages in the progress of the soul towards God had become a traditional view. These stages constitute one aspect of the triple division Dowel, Dobet, and Dobest.

Since, in St. Gregory's view, the good Christian life at even its highest stage on earth is a blend of Action and Contemplation, in what sense can Dowel be considered to represent the Active Life? Or in what sense, if any, does the *Visio* represent the Active Life, as Mr. Coghill would have it? [12]

It must be noted that the terms "Action," "Active Life," as used by St. Gregory, St. Bernard, St. Thomas, and other spiritual writers, refer to the *spiritual life:* the "action" denoted is not any kind of action, such as manual labour, but the active practice of virtue. The distinction is not between *otiosa* [leisure] and *negotiosa* [work]: the good works of the Active Life are works of religion and devotion.[13] In other words, the Active Life is the ascetical life.

The Active Life may be considered under two aspects. First, these good works—vocal prayer, mortification, the service of the neighbour, the practice of the virtues—constitute the normal conditions under which the spiritual life is lived on no matter how high a plane. Whether the spiritual life of any individual have the character of Active or Contemplative does not depend on the absence of activity but on the presence of contemplation.[14] Secondly, the term Active Life is used in a more restricted sense. The spiritual writers are agreed that to achieve union with God in prayer we must remove in ourselves the obstacles to the working of God's grace in us. This we do by severe self-discipline in the spiritual formation of our character—that is, by the good works of the Active Life. In this sense, the Active Life is a state in which contemplation is not yet present. And in this restricted sense, the Active Life is conceived as a stage of the spiritual life, the beginning of the spiritual life proper: Dowel. The transition from Dowel to Dobet is the transition from Action to Con-

11 Pourrat, op. cit., i. 186–7.

12 "The Character of Piers Plowman," *M.Æ.*, ii (1933) , 108–35.

13 Dr. Wells already noted this important point in "The Construction of *Piers Plowman,*" *P.M.L.A.*, xliv (1929) , 123–40; but it seems to have been largely overlooked by some later writers on the same subject.

14 Butler, op. cit., p. 323.

templation; this is indicated in Passus xv, the Prologue to Dobet, though Langland is careful also to indicate that the good works of the Active Life do not cease to be performed.

Now, there are other works which man must perform which are not works of the spiritual life at all. A consideration of this aspect of man's situation gives us the key to the *Visio*. As St. Paul says, "prius quod animale, deinde quod spirituale" [before, that which is physical; afterward, that which is spiritual] (1 Cor. xv. 46). Man is not a pure spirit, but a being composed of soul and body. He therefore finds himself compelled to take thought for the needs of the body. This primary necessity gives rise to the arts and crafts—the provision of food and clothing and all those major occupations which absorb most of the energies of men in civil society. We have only to live to become aware of the imperious demands of this necessity: and *necessitas* is the term St. Bernard, for example, uses for this care or love of the body: a necessity *quae urget nos* [which drives us]. It is to these facts of life Holy Church refers in Passus i, 17–57. This necessity must be distinguished—as Lady Holy Church points out—from another form of carnal love which arises from concupiscence and for which the technical term is *Cupiditas*—a cupidity *quae trahit nos* [which draws us]. "As the normal state of the body is health, so the normal state of the heart is purity," or *simplicitas* [guilelessness]. "It is unhappily a fact that human desire only very rarely observes the limits of either. Instead of remaining canalized in the bed of natural necessity"—within the limits, that is, set out by Holy Church in Passus i, 20–60—"the will goes off in pursuit of useless pleasures; that is, of pleasures not desired because required for the due exercise *(in mesurable manere)* of the functions that preserve life, but pleasures desired for their own sake as pleasures." That the will has overstepped the limits of natural necessity may be recognized when it has no longer any right reason for its desires: "For riȝtful reson schulde rewle ȝow alle." [15]

The first stage, then, in the spiritual journey of man is the limiting of his natural appetites, by reason, within the limits of the *necessitas quae urget nos* [necessity which drives us]—"Measure is medicine," as Lady Holy Church says: and the rejection of Lady Meed, *quae trahit nos* [which draws us] by her meretricious beauty. Most of the folk in the field have been drawn to Lady Meed; but guided by Reason, they repent and go to Confession, and then set out in a body to seek St. Truth. Their guide is, appropriately at this stage, a poor ploughman, himself concerned with the provision of the basic necessities of life and whose condition is not one in which he is greatly tempted by cupidity. The way he

[15] B. i. 54. See E. Gilson, *The Mystical Theology of St. Bernard* (tr. London, 1955), pp. 40–42, to which I am much indebted in this paragraph.

outlines to Truth is the way of the Commandments, the first stage of the
Active Life, the lowest plane of the spiritual life. But having been only
just converted from servants of Meed to seekers after Truth, the folk in
the field, before they can advance at all, must first be grounded in that
carnal love which is of necessity and is therefore legitimate. They must
be taught the lesson of Lady Holy Church's opening lines. And so, before the pilgrimage can start, we have in the ploughing of the half-acre
an exposition of how the different ranks of society are to be provided
with food and clothing in a measurable manner *so that* they may serve
God. But the service of God in a positive fashion has not yet begun.

Two points may be noted at the end of B. Passus vi:

(a) It is true that Piers began by outlining a way to Truth; it is, however, merely the beginning of the way, the way of the Commandments,
the way of those who, as Guillaume de St. Thierry says, "being either
moved by authority or stirred by example . . . approve the good as set before them without understanding it." [16] The next stage is where the spiritual life proper begins, when a man starts to progress along this way by
beginning to understand the import of some of the truths in which he believes (an understanding that comes to Piers only as a result of Truth's
"Pardon," at the very end of the *Visio*) . Thus he moves from the *animale*
to the *spirituale,* and becomes a "rational" man in the spiritual life, as
Guillaume puts it. And he moves forward, not merely by the practice of
virtues, but "by the progressive understanding of himself and of those
things which in the teaching of the faith have been laid before him." [17]
This development takes place during the long debates of the *Vita de Dowel.*

(b) The second point to be noted is that the pilgrimage outlined by
Piers does *not,* in fact, take place in the *Visio*. The reason is, I think,
because the reform of society is not possible on a corporate basis: it is
achieved when each individual reforms himself. For Langland, Christian
society is the Church; and the reform of the Christian is the beginning
and growth of a truly fervent spiritual life. Now the spiritual life by definition is the *inner* life of the individual. This pilgrimage to Truth must
be made by each of the folk on his own. It is the *Vita de Dowel, Dobet,
et Dobest.*

The Pardon episode in Passus vii seems to be clearly a call by God to
Piers to lead a truly spiritual life—to move on from the way of the Commandments: to do well, in the sense in which St. Gregory and St. Ber-

---

[16] *The Golden Epistle of Abbot William of St. Thierry*, tr. Shewring, ed. Dom
Justin McCann (London, 1930) , p. 27. Cf. Ruysbroeck, *The Seven Steps of the Ladder
of Spiritual Love,* tr. F. Sherwood Taylor (London, 1943) , pp. 40–43.

[17] *The Golden Epistle,* p. 28.

nard, St. Thomas and St. Bonaventure would interpret *bona agere:* to spend more time in prayer and penance; that is, to progress in Charity by the mortification of desires and the practice of virtue. And the message seems to bring to Piers in a flash a new understanding of old truths: *Fuerunt michi lacrime mee panes die ac nocte* [My tears have been for me my bread day and night]. . . . *Ne solliciti sitis* [Be not solicitous]. . . . The Pardon initiates a new kind of pilgrimage: the progress of the soul in the spiritual life.

The *Visio,* then, is concerned with the *animalis homo* and with the first stage in his regeneration. The *Vita de Dowel, Dobet, et Dobest* is concerned with the spiritual life proper. And at the end of Dowel, the people in the plain of Passus v are recalled in the person of Haukyn;[18] and we are reminded that the pilgrimage to Truth has been, in fact, for some time under way, but in a different mode—the only possible one. In this manner, the two parts of the poem are intimately bound together as one whole.

III

We now come to consider the significance in the poem of the threefold distinction of Dowel, Dobet, and Dobest. The poet has guided us here by a number of definitions, for the *Vita* begins with the Dreamer's search for Dowel and his questioning of various characters as to its nature. The definitions which are given may be divided into two main classes. Outside this division fall two definitions which may be termed accidental, and one rather mysterious definition given by Piers Plowman, who reappears in the *Vita de Dobet* as a symbolic figure, representing the human nature of Christ.[19]

First, to consider the two definitions which I have termed "accidental," since they define Dowel in a particular case. The first of these is the tentative definition of the Dreamer towards the end of Passus xi. Dowel, he says, "is to see much and suffer more." Ymagynatyf, who has just appeared, tells him that if he *had* suffered, Reason would have further explained to him what had already been told him by Clergye. There is clearly no finality about this definition.[20] The second comes in Passus xiv where Conscience identifies Dowel, Dobet, and Dobest with the three parts of the sacrament of Penance—Contrition, Confession, and Satisfac-

---

[18] On the relationship between Passus xiii, xiv, and the *Visio,* see the very stimulating article by Stella Maguire, "The Significance of Haukyn, *Activa Vita,* in *Piers Plowman,*" *R.E.S.,* xxv (1949) , 97–109 [see below, pp. 194–208].

[19] Piers's definition is reported by Clergye, B. xiii, 118–29.

[20] B. xi, 398–429.

tion.[21] The meaning appears to be that at this stage the sacrament of Penance is what is most essential for Haukyn. For the sinful man, regeneration begins with this sacrament, which restores the infused virtues of Faith, Hope, and Charity, to the soul.[22] And we note that immediately afterwards Conscience does in fact begin to exhort Haukyn to a higher life, to Patience, Poverty, and Charity—to the life to which Piers Plowman was called in the *Visio,* by the "Pardon."

To turn now to the two main classes of definitions. The first class consists of:

1. Definition of Friars, viii, 18 ff.
2. Definitions of Wit, ix, 94–97; 199–206.
3. Definitions of Study, x, 129–34; 187–88.
4. Definitions of Ymagynatyf, xii, 30–40.
5. Definitions of Patience, xiii, 136–71.

All develop the first definition of the Friars, for all define Dowel, Dobet, and Dobest as growth in Charity. Patience's definitions not merely end this series, but end the whole series (apart from a reference to Dowel, Dobet, and Dobest in the life of Christ in Passus xix, 104–93). These definitions, then, furnish one aspect—and the chief aspect—of the threefold division of the second poem in the *Liber de Petro Plowman.* The *Vita* is essentially concerned with spiritual reform; this must be the spiritual progress of the individual. We have reference here, then, to the distinction of three main stages in the Christian's progress in the love of God, whether considered, as St. Bonaventure considers them in his book *De Triplici Vita,* as the Purgative Way, the Illuminative Way, and the Unitive Way; or, in the terms of an earlier distinction, the condition of *incipientes* [beginning], of *proficientes* [progress], and of *perfecti* [perfection]. The Purgative Way of St. Bonaventure is concerned with the expulsion of error and sin, and leads to peace; the Illuminative Way is concerned with the deeper knowledge and more exact imitation of Our Lord; the Unitive Way is the achievement of union with God through the operation of the Holy Ghost.

The second class of definitions comprises:

1. those given by Thought in viii, 78–102;
2. Wit's first definition—leading on from Thought—in ix, 11–16;

---

21 Xiv, 16–24.

22 See, for example, Uthred of Boldon, *De perfectione vivendi:* "Man's *via* is two-fold: (1) of first innocence, (2) of *reparacio graciosa* [restoration of grace] through Christ. By sin, man was wounded in his natural and intellectual powers, and despoiled of gratuitous and moral virtues (cf. *Sent.* dist. ii, c. xxv); by penitence the theological virtues are regained. Perfection consists in the practice of the three theological virtues." (Summary by Pantin, *Studies . . . Presented to F. M. Powicke,* p. 375.)

3. the definitions given by Clergye in x, 230–65;

4. the definitions of the Doctor, xiii, 115–17.

To these may be added the distinction of Dowel, Dobet, and Dobest in the life of Christ, xix, 104–93.

In considering Langland's point of view in these definitions, we shall be helped by recalling that the phrase "Contemplative Life" may also denote a manner of corporate living ordered to the primary end of facilitating and promoting the exercise of contemplation; such a state of life is created by the stable observance of the evangelical counsels, by means of vows publicly taken. This objective state is referred to juridically as "religion" and the members of such a society as "religious." [23] The contemplative life is not the exclusive prerogative of such persons; but in virtue of their vows they are constituted in an objective state of perfection: *in statu perfectionis acquirendae* [in the state of acquiring perfection].[24] Hence they are in the *Vita de Dobet,* but they are not the only persons there: Langland never identifies the *Vita de Dobet* with the religious state. (See Passus xv, Prologue to *Dobet.*)

A higher state than the religious life is the office of a bishop or abbot or other ecclesiastical prelate. This is the most perfect state of all. And here we come to the *only* sense in which the majority of the doctors will use the notion of a "Mixed" life of action and contemplation. As we have seen, the contemplative life as actually lived—even in religion—*is* a mixed life; but the relation between Action and Contemplation in the life of a prelate is a very special one. The function of a prelate is to exercise *spiritual* authority: it is, therefore, as John of Freiburg expresses it, a *magisterium perfectionis* [office of perfection] and presupposes perfection.[25] That is to say, it ought to be the overflowing of contemplation. *Contemplata tradere* [to deliver up to contemplation] is the phrase St. Thomas uses of true ecclesiastical government,[26] and the phrase is often repeated in the *Specula* and *Compendia* used in the fourteenth century. Hence a prelate is said to be constituted in *statu perfectionis acquisitae* [the state of having acquired perfection]: in the *Vita de Dobest.*

Priests with the care of souls share in the authority of the bishop; but

[23] These canonical terms had already become colloquial by the fourteenth century. Langland frequently uses them: see, for example, B. x, 312–13.

[24] St. Thomas Aquinas, *S.T.,* ii–iii. clxxxiv. 5.

[25] "Status religionis ad professionem pertinet quasi quedam via tendendi in perfectionem. Status autem episcopalis ad perfectionem pertinet tanquam quoddam perfectionis magisterium" [The state of religion pertains to a profession as if it were a way of aiming for perfection. The state of a prelate, however, pertains to perfection as if it were an office of perfection]. Joannes de Friburgo, *Summa Confessorum,* lib. iii, titl. xxviii, questio iiii. Cf. *S.T.* loc. cit., art. 7.

[26] *S.T.* ii–ii. clxxxiv and clxxxv.

since they may resign their care at any time (and he may not, unless in very exceptional circumstances), they are not constituted in an objective state of perfection. Juridically, they are in the Active Life. However, by reason of their functions they are bound to be in a subjective state of perfection.[27] Hence we meet them often in the *Vita de Dowel;* but their functions are discussed with those of religious in the Prologue to *Dobet.*

Walter Hilton inevitably comes in here; but I suggest that in regard to the meaning of Dowel, Dobet, and Dobest he will bring only confusion. In the *Scale of Perfection,* written for a religious sister, Hilton distinguishes merely two kinds of life, the Active and the Contemplative. In his treatise *Mixed Life,* written for a wealthy man living in the world and apparently exercising a good deal of temporal sovereignty, Hilton seems to liken his reader's state to that of a bishop; and in thus confounding the two, seems to deny to prelates the most perfect state of all.[28] This may be a compliment to his reader; or it may be simply an example of somewhat loose thinking in a popular treatise.[29] Whatever the explanation, Hilton's concept of the Mixed Life seems not to be found in Langland: a surer guide to Langland's view is given in the extract from the *Meditationes Vitae Christi,* quoted by Dr. Wells.[30]

If we now consider the second class of definitions of Dowel, Dobet, and Dobest, we may see, foreshadowed in them, the blending in the structure of the *Vita* of the two traditional concepts: the three stages of the soul's progress in the love of God, and the three objective states of life—the Active Life, the Religious Life, and the Life of Prelates.

Thought distinguishes the three objective states clearly. In Wit's first definition, Dowel and Dobet are defined in subjective terms, but Dobest is "a bisschopes pere" (ix, 14). We are moving towards the more important concept, that of progress in love; and Wit's further definitions in Passus ix belong to this class. Clergye again defines Dowel and Dobet in

---

[27] *S.T.* ii–ii. clxxxiv. 8.

[28] Walter Hilton, *Mixed Life,* ed. D. Jones in *Minor Works of Walter Hilton* (London, 1929), ch. v, 16–17; ch. vi, 22–23. S. S. Hussey clearly illustrates the discrepancy between Hilton and Langland (loc. cit., esp. pp. 135–7, 139–42). Mr. Hussey, however, is surely mistaken in treating Hilton's definition as authoritative: as he notes himself, St. Gregory "recognized all three lives although he never called the mixed life by that name" (p. 135). So did many other doctors, whose views St. Thomas synthesizes in *S.T.* ii–ii. clxxix–clxxxii. For a writer contemporary with Langland in the same tradition, see Uthred of Boldon in Pantin, op. cit., pp. 374–80.

[29] It is unlikely that Hilton is here recalling an earlier definition of the Mixed Life given by St. Augustine, discussed and dismissed—as an unnecessary distinction—by St. Thomas, *S.T.* ii–ii. clxxix, "Of the division of life into the Active and the Contemplative." See also Butler, op. cit., pp. 291–304.

[30] H. W. Wells in *P.M.L.A.,* xliv. (1929), 134–5. The passage is from cap. xlv. See Pseudo-Bonaventure, *Meditations on the Life of Christ,* tr. Sister M. Emmanuel, O.S.B. (London, 1934), pp. 219–20.

general fashion—the Contemplative Life is not the special prerogative of religious nor of priests—but Dobest includes "alle manere prelates" (x, 267) . The Doctor's definition in Passus xiii is a general statement of the three juridical states, as we might have expected.

From this examination, it seems that Langland begins in the *Vita* by indicating the pilgrimage of the soul towards God. The first stage in the spiritual life of any individual is an emergence alike from intellectual error and moral disorder. This is the *Vita de Dowel*. I have earlier referred to the dissipation of intellectual error in the first part of *Dowel*, Passus viii–xii. In Passus xiii we meet moral disorder in the person of Haukyn, and the situation described in Passus v is recalled. As in Passus v, but now in a more explicit manner, this disorder is repaired by the sacrament of Penance. The moral virtues which will sustain Haukyn and also help him to make progress are put before him: Poverty, or the spirit of poverty in some degree; and Patience.[31]

With the Prologue to *Dobet* (Passus xv) we have already progressed. Priests and religious come in for a large share of the discussion, for they make proclamation of leading the Contemplative Life. Langland summarizes the discussion conducted through Passus x–xii on the place of Learning in the good life and applies the conclusions to the obligations of the clergy in Christian society. The highest evangelical ideal of poverty, put by Patience before Haukyn, is here presented in practice, in the lives of religious, anchorites, and hermits.

We are thus led on to a more comprehensive view of Charity in the *Vita de Dobet*. Perfection is represented in the redemption wrought by Christ and is rightly conceived as a growth in Faith, Hope, and Charity in the speech of the Samaritan. Piers Plowman appears as the human nature which the Wisdom of God assumed to redeem mankind.

---

[31] Of Patience, St. Gregory says: "Perfection springs out of patience. He that maintains patience possesses his soul, in that henceforth he is endued with strength to encounter all adversities so that by overcoming himself he is made master of himself." (*Morals on Job*, v. 33. Oxford tr. i. 266–7.) Echoed by St. Thomas in *S.T.* II–II. cxxxvi. 2, ad 2. Langland has already brought out that it is the hardships of life which make it difficult for Haukyn to keep from deadly sin. There is another reference in St. Thomas to Patience which seems to indicate the background of Langland's mind here and the link which binds Passus xiii and xiv with v and vi: "The inclination of reason," St. Thomas says, "would prevail in human nature in the state of integrity. But in fallen nature the inclination of concupiscence prevails, because it is dominant in man. Hence man is more prone to bear evils for the sake of goods in which the concupiscence delights here and now, than to endure evils for the sake of goods to come which are desired in accordance with reason; and yet it is this that pertains to true patience." (*S.T.* II–II. cxxxvi. 3 ad 1. Dominican tr.) Here we have the point of Reason's entry into the vision of Meed (Passus iv) ; and of Reason's sermon in Passus v, leading to repentance. Now, Patience is put forward as the virtue which will render his teaching stable and make progress along the road to Truth possible.

Then, instead of leading us on to the third stage of the spiritual life, as do Rolle and Hilton, Tauler and Suso, the mystical stage in which the Holy Ghost works unimpeded in the soul, the poet, in the *Vita de Dobest,* quietly turns—as the definitions of Wit and Clérgye had foreshadowed—to the third objective state, the life of prelates.

There is no sharp break. There is a gradual moving away from the figure of the Dreamer's progress during the latter part of *Dobet* to the meaning for all men of the Passion and Death of Christ. This is reflected in the objective fashion in which these events are narrated. After the Samaritan's speech to the Dreamer, the objective tone becomes apparent and continues right through Passus xviii. There the language takes fire, as Langland describes the Redemption by Christ and the Harrowing of Hell in memorable verse, ending with the debate between Mercy and Truth, Peace and Righteousness—a debate traditional since St. Bernard but which again Langland re-tells in his own way. Then, in the *Vita de Dobest,* while dedicating Passus xix to the activity of the Holy Ghost and thereby indicating one aspect of Dobest, Langland describes how the Holy Ghost through the agency of Piers builds up the structure of the Church. For unlike Tauler and Suso and Hilton, Langland's concern is not with religious sisters, but with Christian society. Piers in xix and xx represents the ideal pope, in whom Christ continues to be represented on earth; and our attention is drawn to the government of the Church. The blending of the two traditional triple distinctions in the concepts of Dowel, Dobet, and Dobest has been extremely well done; and it has been made to serve the poet's purpose in the poem.

The beginning of Dowel is love; by love, love is increased, until we come to the perfection of love, which is Dobet; while Dobest is superabundant love, overflowing into the works of the apostolate, cultivating the Christian life in the souls of men and raising the edifice of the Church. Such is the ideal. And it is a traditional one. Almost at once, in Passus xx, Langland recalls the real: the siege-scarred Christendom of his own time, first pictured in the Prologue. And the poem ends with the poet going out into the world to seek, apparently, a true pope who will effect a reform: the Piers Plowman described in *Dobest.*

5. The Imaginative Unity of
Piers Plowman
JOHN LAWLOR

I

IT IS TO BE HOPED that the considerations advanced by Fr. T. P. Dunning in a recent article will win general assent.[1] Fr. Dunning has given in brief space an account of the unity of theme in *Piers Plowman* which should safeguard us from exploring false paths and repeating old errors. In particular, his identification of "active life" with "the spiritual life" will prevent that confusion of 'active life' with mere activity, action as opposed to contemplation, in which a good deal of comment upon *Piers Plowman* has been entangled. Much of the difficulty over the "definitions" of the three lives might have been spared if those who followed Wells's decisive lead had observed, as he did, that, in Fr. Dunning's words, "the good works of the Active Life are works of religion and devotion."[2] There is thus room for the blending of two traditional triads—active, contemplative, and "mixed" lives, and purgative, illuminative, and unitive ways. Indeed, so far from rejecting the one to provide for the other,[3] we must see their very interdependence if we are to advance at all with the Dreamer. But confusion came from another source, Walter Hilton's special conception of "mixed life": and here, too, Fr. Dunning does a notable service by showing that "in regard to the meaning of Dowel, Dobet, and Dobest [Hilton] will bring only confusion."[4] The recent contribution of Mr. S. S. Hussey, in which Hilton's views are taken as authoritative, illustrates the difficulties which beset *Piers Plowman* criticism.[5]

Reprinted by permission of the author and The Clarendon Press, Oxford, from *Review of English Studies*, N.S., VIII (1957), 113–26.

For other discussions of the structure of the poem, see A. C. Spearing, "Verbal Repetition in *Piers Plowman* B and C," *JEGP*, LXII (1963), 722–37; and Jay Martin, "Wil as Fool and Wanderer in *Piers Plowman*," *TSLL*, III (1962), 535–48.

1 "The Structure of the B-Text of *Piers Plowman*," *R.E.S.*, N.S. vii (1956), 225–37 [see above, pp. 87–100].

2 *Ibid.*, p. 230 [p.92].

3 Professor Howard Meroney, insisting upon the spiritual life as the poet's dominant concern, finds it necessary to reject the triad of "lives" as "a false and mischievous analogy which has stultified *Piers Plowman* criticism for twenty years." ("The Life and Death of Longe Wille," *ELH*, xvii [1950] 1–35.)

4 Loc. cit., p. 235 [p. 98].

5 "Langland, Hilton, and the Three Lives," *R.E.S.*, N.S. vii (1956), 132–50.

Mr. Hussey perceives well enough that "active life" must include "much of what Langland's critics usually assign to Dobet." But for him this serves only to throw doubt on any claim for the three lives as truly satisfactory equivalents of Dowel, Dobet, and Dobest, a doubt which is reinforced when "the idea of mixed life" (that is, Hilton's idea of it) is correctly seen to be "too limited" to apply to Dobest.[6] The root cause is plain: it is the definitions of the active, contemplative, and mixed lives so far put forward by Langland's critics that are at fault.[7] Mr. Hussey's contribution is more valuable for his criticism of those definitions than for any firm conclusions he himself can offer: for, correctly understanding the nature of "active life," he cannot see its applicability to Langland's Dowel, a term which, he holds, "must refer to the majority of Christians who have no special religious calling." [8] We are back, though by a less familiar route than usual, at that central stumbling-block of *Piers Plowman* interpretation, the connexion between the *Visio* and the *Vita*. There is no possibility of advance until we see that the "doing well" which refers to *all* Christians consists in that conformity to the rule of "riȝtful reson" which the Plowman of the *Visio* at once exemplifies and helps to bring about. This is the necessary condition of and the preparation for that further "doing well" which, while it is open to all Christians, is essentially the progress of the individual soul in the spiritual life (and thus admits of degrees of "perfection"). Mr. Hussey is, I am sure, wholly right to stress the penetrating simplicity which invests Langland's term Dowel (and hence the progression, Dobet, Dobest). It is evident, above all, in that concern for the *practice* of the Christian life which I comment on below. But we shall be making an impossible demand if we insist that the Christian life, as the Dreamer begins to inquire into it in the *Vita,* must involve no complexities. The truth is that Langland's Dowel is no invariable term. His concern is with right conduct, a "doing well" which, first apprehended as the obedience to God's law required of all men, is deepened into awareness of the spiritual life—that life which may be expressed as obedience to the Counsels rather than the Commandments, conformity to God's will in the spirit of a son rather than a servant. As such, Langland's "doing well" joins with and becomes indistinguishable from the "doing well" of the spiritual life; and the progression to a "better" in this sphere is easily and naturally achieved. But it is the lasting appeal of Langland's work that in the conclusion he turns aside from the ideal, the "best" of the spiritual life, to the real, the leadership which is required by the suffering and sinful humanity we first en-

---

6 *Ibid.,* pp. 139–40.
7 Cf. Dunning, loc. cit., 225, n. 1 [p. 87, n. 1].
8 Loc. cit., p. 139.

countered in the Prologue. Langland's poem has thus a design all its own: and we rightly reject those "definitions" that would "provide a ready-made guide" to his thought.[9] But we shall make no headway with Langland's thought until we grasp the connexion between the "doing well" that is enjoined upon the folk of the *Visio* and the prospect of "doing well" that is revealed to their leader, the Plowman. Fr. Dunning has, I believe, given us the firmest ground we have yet been offered for resolving the purely "doctrinal" questions, What is the "theme" or "content" of the *Liber de Petro Plowman?*, and, What is the relationship in those terms between the *Visio de Petro Plowman* and the *Vita de Dowel, Dobet, et Dobest?* Langland's theme is "doing well," an insistent probing of man's capacity for the good life; and this is prepared for by presenting in the *Visio* the *animalis homo* and "the first stage in his regeneration."[10]

If this is the relation between *Visio* and *Vita* in terms of Langland's thought we may be better enabled to ask, How is this relation effected in the poem?—and thus, of *Piers Plowman* as a whole, By what distinctive appeal to imagination does the poet initiate and conduct the "argument" of his poem? Fr. Dunning has very well demonstrated how Langland, employing "as the framework of his poem" "the traditional teaching on the spiritual life of the Christian," modifies it to his purpose, "his artistic preoccupation with *(a)* Christian society, and *(b)* the society of his own time and its peculiar problems."[11] What that "artistic preoccupation" may be it is no part of Fr. Dunning's immediate purpose to inquire. But it should be a question worth raising; for *Piers Plowman* is not a treatise, remarkable only for clothing deep truth and penetrating observation in memorable verse. To be sure, some who have perceived poetry in *Piers Plowman* have yet withheld the designation "poem." Professor C. S. Lewis has praised Langland for "sublimity," and for a "largeness" of vision which pertains to "the 'intellectual imagination.' " But Langland, he concludes, "is confused and monotonous, and hardly makes his poetry into a poem."[12] Similarly, Professor G. Kane speaks of a "paradox of total greatness and local failures."[13] A unity of theme, or "doctrine," and hence a mutual relationship of the major parts of the work, will not, assuredly, of themselves serve to counter these objections. We must try to clarify the imaginative appeal of Langland's work—to find, if we can, the focus of imaginative attention, the vantage-point from which we, with the writer, look out upon his world.

9 Hussey, loc. cit., p. 147.
10 Dunning, loc. cit., p. 232 [p. 95].
11 *Ibid.*, p. 226 [p. 88].
12 *The Allegory of Love* (Oxford, 1936), pp. 160–61.
13 *Middle English Literature* (London, 1951), p. 185.

It should be the more useful to make this inquiry in as far as the poem, if there is one, may need to be rescued from overmuch elucidation. A work as long as *Piers Plowman* (in its B- and C-texts) and as comprehensive in its main issues may well reward approaches from widely differing standpoints. But critical evaluation is likely to fare ill in this pressure of interests.[14] There is a further consideration. Readers—not always untutored—who have been conscious of the explorations as well as the affirmations that the work contains have thought of *Piers Plowman* as a kind of spiritual autobiography, in which the author hammers out his best understanding of what often appears to puzzle and even, sometimes, to elude him. Against these, there have not been lacking interpreters who, rightly insisting upon a body of traditional teaching informing Langland's thought, seem at times to come very close to suggesting that Langland is a writer of clear purpose, involving his readers in perplexities that were for him only apparent, in order to win their better understanding. It is, unless I am greatly mistaken, to the second group that Fr. Dunning belongs, in his maintaining that Langland "largely takes for granted the traditional teaching on the spiritual life of the Christian." [15] The question here is not one of degree (the mere extent, covered by Fr. Dunning's "largely," to which Langland might be thought *not* to "take for granted" traditional teaching) but rather of kind, the kind of activity we are to envisage in the writer. It would require a considerable hardihood on our part to discredit Langland when he tells us of his setbacks and vexations, the problems he cannot solve, as well as the truths he can confidently affirm. Yet it is true that his "teaching" at all points appears conformable to what had long been maintained and was more generally accessible in his own day than has always been realized.[16] The question is, finally considered, insoluble: but in its present terms it is certainly ill put. The mere dichotomy, "Poem or Autobiography? " will never take us very far; but with some kinds of poem we can hardly apply it all. If, then, we can see what imaginative unity *Piers Plowman* may have, we must go on to determine the kind of poem we have been dealing with.

14 As Professor Kane observes, "To consider *Piers Plowman* as a poem is not only the safest but also the most fruitful means of studying it, and should precede the detailed consideration of its single features and qualities." It may, however, be felt that Professor Kane's attempt "to isolate the main features" of the poet's "personality" is itself allowed, unhappily, to precede consideration of the poem (op. cit., pp. 185, 192).
15 Loc. cit., p. 226 [p. 88].
16 Fr. Dunning (p. 225 [p. 87]) draws attention to W. A. Pantin's account of manuals of instruction for parish priests and vernacular religious and moral treatises (*The English Church in the Fourteenth Century* [Cambridge, 1955], pp. 189–243). Mr. Pantin's general observation (p. 189) is especially worth pondering: "It is impossible to exaggerate the importance of the educated layman in late medieval ecclesiastical history." For a treatment of the "intellectual history" thus involved, see G. de Lagarde, *La Naissance de l'esprit laïque au déclin du Moyen Age* (Paris, 1934–).

II

It will be best to begin with the *Vita de Dowel:* not only because it is, by common consent, one of the most difficult parts of the whole work, but because in it we are given some account of the Dreamer himself, pondering the significance of what has been seen in the *Visio,* and in that pondering some of the problems which the Dreamer presents as vexing him are well to the fore. What deserves our notice at once is the series of rebuffs the Dreamer receives from the authoritative persons he interrogates after his first colloquy, that with the Friars. From the Friars he has received practical counsel in the parable of the man in the storm-tossed boat—counsel which is designed to turn the inquirer away from the high theoretical question, How shall a man avoid sin? to the humbler recognition of common experience implied in the distinction between sins of frailty and deliberate sins. The Dreamer is not content, and seeks to know more: but we should note, in view of the scoldings he is to receive, that all he seeks to know is where he can find Dowel, so that, as he humbly says, he may learn of these high matters by direct observation: "if I may lyue and loke . I shal go lerne bettere." It is a sentiment which is repeated after Thought's "explanation":

> I coueite to lerne
> How Dowel, Dobet, and Dobest . don amonges the peple.
> (viii, 108–9) [17]

Wit's account of the matter is no more helpful to this Dreamer who seeks examples from practice. In the wooden allegory of Sir Dowel inhabiting the Castle of Kind, we may detect a similarity to the Plowman's allegory of the Ten Commandments, delivered to the Pilgrims of the *Visio.* In either case, the predicament of the listener is the same. Like the Pilgrims, the Dreamer seeks a living embodiment of the good, not mere discourse, however apt. It is therefore a striking irony that Dame Study, waiting with unconcealed impatience for the end of Wit's discourse, should soundly berate the Dreamer as a seeker after mere knowledge. But the irony is deepened when we perceive that the Dreamer is eventually drawn into debate, so that Study's warning against high speculation, unfairly levelled at the Dreamer on first encounter, is later amply justified. Her very words, "Non plus sapere quam oportet" [not to be more wise than is proper] (x, 116), are repeated at the end of the *Vita de Dowel* by Anima, rebuking a Dreamer who has sought to know all (xv, 63–67). Similarly, Ymagynatyf is able to point, unopposed, the moral of the Dreamer's experience:

---

[17] Except as otherwise indicated, all references are to the B-text.

for thine entermetyng . here artow forsake,
Philosophus esses, si tacuisses.
(xi, 406)
[you are now left here alone because of your interruptions.
You might be a philosopher if you could keep silent.]

We see very readily that, in his being drawn into debate, the Dreamer has
fulfilled Clergye's prediction:

The were lef to lerne . but loth for to stodie.
Thou woldest konne that I can . and carpen hit after,
Presumptuowsly, parauenture . a-pose so manye,
That hit myȝthe turne me to tene . and Theologie bothe.
(A. xii, 6–8)
[You would be glad to learn, but reluctant to study;
you would like to know all that I know, in order to retail
it to others, and perhaps to question so many people in a
presumptuous manner that it might turn to harm
both Theology and me.]

As Miss Maguire has remarked, in an article which firmly grasps the tension between the speculative and the practical in the *Vita de Dowel,* the
Dreamer we meet at the beginning of Passus xiii "still seems to hold to
his faith in the possibility of an intellectual resolution of his problems."
So, as she observes, the turning-point must come with the entry of a moral
virtue, Patience, upon the scene of the Banquet.[18] But we should not fail
to notice that experience itself has already given the Dreamer a foretaste
of patience. At his meeting with Ymagynatyf he could ruefully contribute his own finding concerning Dowel: " 'To se moche and suffre more .
certes,' quod I, 'is Dowel!' " (xi, 402) . If we look back, we see that the
Dreamer is one who has been drawn aside from his original purpose,
from the question Where is Dowel? to discourse upon What is Dowel?
But the situation in which he was placed, *vis-à-vis* Wit, Study, &c., is not
simple; rather, it is one of cross-purpose. Just as his interlocutors mistrusted him, a seeker, as it appeared, after mere knowledge, so the Dreamer mistrusted them, the learned and authoritative. Christ was a carpenter's son; what, then, is the place of learning in the good life? In this,
of course, Langland is echoing controversies of his own day,[19] but it is
his achievement to communicate the universal sense of unchangeable
cross-purpose between authority and the ardent inquirer. So we follow a

18 "The Significance of Haukyn, *Activa Vita,* in *Piers Plowman," R.E.S.,* xxv (1949) ,
99–100 [see below, pp. 196–97].
19 See Pantin, op. cit., pp. 123–35.

Dreamer who, meeting no direct answer to the over-simple question he proposes, finds himself involved in debate, to reach that point of ultimate weariness, foretold by Study, where all exercise of reason threatens to appear as profitless subtilizing:

> The more I muse there-inne . the mistier it semeth
> And the depper I deuyne . the derker me it thinketh;
> It is no science for sothe . forto sotyle inne.
>
> (x, 181–83)

He must learn to be constant to his own initial purpose, the search for a truth revealed in practice: but it is no easy matter. It is his final lesson, at the hands of Anima, that the search for knowledge may be not merely immoderate but even positively harmful; for

> the more that a man . of good mater hereth
> *But he do ther-after . It doth hym double scathe.*
>
> (xv, 57–58)

In all this the Dreamer has been less fortunate than the repentant sinners of the *Visio.* They found a guide, in the Plowman who is "of flessh oure brother." The Dreamer's questioning will avail him little until, all subtilizing exhausted, he is brought to contemplate Incarnate Deity, the Saviour who

> wole Iuste in Piers armes,
> In his helme and in his haberioun . *humana natura.*
>
> (xviii, 22–23)
>
> [will joust in Piers' armor,
> in his helmet and mail, human nature.]

It is the last irony that those he had interrogated at the very outset of his journey had given a sufficient answer to his desire to find examples from practice:

> "I have no kynde knowyng," quod I . "to conceyue alle ȝowre wordes,
> Ac if I may lyue and loke . I shall go lerne bettere."
> "I bikenne the Cryst," quod he . "that on the crosse deyde."
>
> (viii, 57–59)

The imaginative appeal of the *Vita* in its whole extent resides not in any answer to the Dreamer's inquirings, though there is, as we have seen, a decisive turn in the *Vita de Dowel* when the shift is made from speculative to practical considerations. The truly imaginative appeal is in the very failure of inquiry so long as the initiative is with the Dreamer. It is he, who at the outset insisted on the practice of the good life, who is in

the end brought to understand what his earlier interlocutors had dogged-
ly maintained as the ground of their reserve towards him—that practice is
all. Then, and only then, is he ready to apprehend as vision what eluded
him as discourse. And this, in its turn, will mean that his search, so far
from ending, must have a new beginning.

III

If this is the imaginative appeal, what is its focus? What particular
aspect of human nature serves as an entry upon and sustains the *Vita?* To
answer that question, we may with advantage turn back to the beginning
of Langland's work as a whole, not only to see afresh the relation of *Visio*
and *Vita,* but to place the rebukes of the *Vita de Dowel* in their full setting. In the Prologue, the Dreamer has acutely observed a world whose
law is self-interest: now, in the first Passus of the *Visio,* Holy Church is to
"explain." In doing so she will encounter questions from the Dreamer
which are inappropriate to his understanding; for the Dreamer desires
all-embracing answers, but his gaze is directed outwards, while the real
situation requiring redress is within the heart of man. The colloquy deserves to be taken in some detail, for it contains indications which are
central to our inquiry.

Holy Church, as yet unknown to the Dreamer, begins with the simple
and sufficient statement that to do right is to live according to Truth's
teaching, and this is at once given its particular application to the world
the Dreamer has seen—men are to observe "mesure" in the use of creature
comforts. The Dreamer at once asks a large question—and this is to be
characteristic of him: To whom does the wealth of the world belong?
The answer is, as was Holy Church's first statement, that the individual
is to look to himself: he is to render unto Caesar the things that are
Caesar's. As she concludes her "explanation" of the "field," the Dreamer
asks her who she is: and the reply he receives carries its own mild reproof:

> "Holicherche I am," quod she . "thow ou3test me to knowe,
> I vnderfonge the firste . and the feyth tau3te."
>
> (i, 75–76)
>
> ["I am Holy Church," she said. "You ought to recognize me,
> I received you first and taught you the faith."]

The Dreamer at once cries to be taught how to save his soul. Holy
Church's answer is in keeping with baptismal simplicity. Those who do
good and purpose no evil to their fellow men shall have their reward.
What she adds is very important for the implications that are later to
come to the Dreamer of the *Vita de Dowel;* the truth she has uttered is

common knowledge to all men, Christian and Pagan alike: "cristene and vncristne, clameth it vchone" (i, 93) . We should not miss the gentle rebuke that this implies. But it is not dwelt upon: Holy Church continues by emphasizing the obedience to Truth which all men must give, and concludes that those whose actions show their true faith will go to heaven, where Truth is enthroned. Nothing simpler or more directly connected with the practice of the individual soul could be conceived. But the Dreamer responds with another of his large questions, How does Truth come to man?, and disclaims any natural knowledge upon the point: he does not know "By what craft in my corps . it comseth and where" (i, 137) .[20] Now Holy Church is less gentle: how stupid, she declares, to say he does not know something revealed by common experience! This is the first scolding the Dreamer receives, and the first of many that are to come in the *Vita de Dowel.* An apparently radical question has been asked: and the answer is, in effect, "look in your heart." Something known to all men has been overlooked by this searcher after knowledge:

> "It is a kynde knowyng," quod he . "that kenneth in thine herte
> For to louye thi lorde . leuer than thi-selue;
> No dedly synne to do . dey thouȝ thow sholdest."

The Dreamer's question is foolishness indeed. But he is not left without one concession to his desire for knowledge. Holy Church concludes,

> "This I trowe be treuthe . who can teche the better,
> Loke thow suffre hym to sey . and sithen lere it after.
> For thus witnesseth his worde . worche thow there-after."
>   (i, 140–45)
> [This, I trust, is the truth. If anyone can teach better,
>   Be sure you allow him to speak, and learn accordingly;
>   For God's word is the witness by which you must live.]

The lesson should be clear to the reader, if it is long in coming to the Dreamer. There is something "better" than this "treuthe"—not better than truth, absolutely considered, but better than the truth that is all that can be revealed to the Dreamer in his present condition. And in the moment that Holy Church withholds the "better" she gives her reasons for doing so: it is a teaching which must be carefully attended to, and it must be *practiced.* At the outset of the work, the Dreamer is established for the purposes of the poem in one line by both the neat glance at his impetuosity—"suffer hym to sey"—and the sterner counsel to pass from

20 The C-text has the sadder recognition, "By what wey hit wexith . and wheder out of my menyng."

theoretical inquiry to earnest application. We are prepared for the last lesson the Dreamer of the *Vita de Dowel* is to grasp. In him the desire to intervene, to search out the imagined heart of the problem, consistently overbears the simple and prior necessity of an individual attempt to practice the life about which he would know all. Again, the vexation of Holy Church with this inquirer who overlooks the knowledge written ineffaceably in his own heart may remind us of the "pure tene" of the Plowman when realization[21] breaks upon him. The focus of imaginative attention in *Piers Plowman* is upon our habitual incapacity to grasp that what we know as doctrine bears directly upon us, and hence our search for a truth which shall be comprehensive while in fact, and all unwittingly, we would exclude ourselves from the reckoning.

What I have called the "focus" of imaginative attention is therefore perfectly adapted to the doctrines the poet communicates. As Fr. Dunning observes, a "principal feature" of beginning "the spiritual life proper" "according to all the spiritual writers, is coming to know oneself." Some men, at the outset, will "approve the good as set before them without understanding it"; and progress is made when a man begins "to understand the import of some of the truths in which he believes." When the transition is made from the *animale* to the *spirituale,* man moves forward, "by the progressive understanding of himself and of those things which in the teaching of the faith have been laid before him." [22]

We begin to see that Langland's work offers a remarkable combination. His theme is of the greatest solemnity: man is a creature destined for regeneration. Hence we have the distinctive appeal to imagination—vision must show forth what remains hidden to discursive thinking. But it is Langland's genius to initiate and conduct his poetic argument by showing us man as determinedly ratiocinative, seeking the causes of all things, and overlooking what lies nearest home. The kind of poem we are dealing with is thus not easily determined. If we approach it by asking what is the poet's dominant faculty, we must answer, in however unfashionable terms, the satiric intelligence.

IV

The satire abounding in the *Visio* is not always squarely faced by crit-

[21] I keep this term "realization" throughout in order to stress the imaginative appeal the poet achieves. In terms strictly applicable to the spiritual life, the word "conversion" may be used, always provided that it is not misunderstood as a "turning from" unbelief to the Christian faith.

[22] Dunning, loc. cit., pp. 226, 231, 232 [pp. 88, 94, 94].

ics elaborating a claim for the unity of *Piers Plowman*. True, there is general recognition that the perception of widespread wickedness prompts, by a natural reaction, the question "How may I save my soul?" But the connexion between *Visio* and *Vita* may be thought to go deeper. Certainly, if we are to claim for *Piers Plowman* an imaginative unity, we must ask again how the work of the satirist is related to the thinker's task of construction. Some critics may feel that the satire of the *Visio* is an involuntary concession to the age in which Langland wrote: and it is noticeable that as scholarship has attended closely to *Piers Plowman* it has become increasingly absorbed in the matter of the *Vita* in its three great divisions. We are so much concerned with the issues Langland unfolds that we may be in danger of neglecting the simplicity with which he begins. Professor Lewis states clearly what is implied by others when he invites us to consider Langland in these terms:

> He is writing a moral poem, such as Gower's *Miroir de l'homme* or Gower's Prologue to the *Confessio Amantis,* and throwing in, as any other medieval poet might have done, a good deal of satire on various "estates." [23]

This is a striking reaction from those earliest critics who, dwelling with satisfaction on the poet's more obvious satirical targets, hailed him as a great reformer and thus, in Fuller's phrase, "by *Prolepsis* a Protestant." But each side misses the mark: for Langland's satire is more radical than Professor Lewis allows, and covers a wider range than Fuller perceived. What is central to Langland's whole design is the observed discrepancy between what we believe and what in fact we are. His poem has its focus in this aspect of the human condition. He therefore proceeds at the outset of the poem by way of external observation—the misdeeds of others—until he has amply shown the necessity of repentance. At this stage, he advances a step farther in the whole inquiry, by bringing forward the one good man the world of his poem can produce in its deepest need—only to humble him. In the realization that comes upon Piers we may see that we have not reached a final limit when goodness is found—for the goodness is now seen to be relative: the only absolute is Perfection. The Plowman who began by instructing others in the way of law (the stiff, signpost-like allegory of the Commandments in Passus v) has perceived that the law condemns unless it is perfectly fulfilled. He therefore turns—or rather, he is turned—away from Justice to the Divine Mercy: and his "confession of evil works" is, in St. Augustine's phrase, "the beginning of

[23] Op. cit., p. 158.

good works." For Piers there has opened a road to the Promised Land which leads beyond Sinai.

The satire of the *Visio* is emphatically not "thrown in." Langland, indeed, begins well within the customary usages of satire. But his genius is to carry the argument beyond those limits. If all men profess the truth and few appear to practice it, we must pass from censure to inquiry: for this universal condition must make us ask, What is man's capacity for the good life? It is in that light that we see the shortcomings of the best man the world of the *Visio* could produce, the Plowman whose Pardon brings an equal and undeviating assurance of reward and punishment. And it is thus that we are prepared for the next appearance of "Piers Plowman"; for it is the Redemption, perfectly fulfilling inexorable law, which allows the Plowman to seek a Mercy which is also Justice. But the satiric intelligence has not done: what we have seen in the *Visio* is slow to declare itself to the Dreamer of the *Vita de Dowel*. In Langland imagination and logic are uniquely joined: his characteristic capacity is to imagine absolutely. The Pardon that is a "pardon" only on condition that law can exact no punishment reveals the external world for what it is in the moment that we pass beyond it. There remains the Dreamer, hitherto the observer, on whom realization is yet to fall: and throughout the *Vita de Dowel* there is the continual play of a satiric intelligence, that comes upon us at many turns and with a varying range of effect—from tonic scorn and impassioned rebuke to the practiced facility of the dialectician, in whose mind there is always ready to start up the *contra!* of swift objection. Langland appears to have solved a capital problem, to communicate in imaginative and poetic terms the central riddle of our experience. It is not only that we everywhere approve and seldom practice the good: much more, it is that the realization of our own predicament is the last discovery we make. The Dreamer searches long and confusedly for what the Plowman saw in a moment: but the Plowman was ready for this knowledge, by reason of his long perseverance in simple well-doing. The strength of the *Vita de Dowel, Dobet, et Dobest* is that the Dreamer in his turn is *brought* to know the truth when all his efforts have been apparently fruitless. He must contemplate Incarnate Deity before his ultimate questioning is at rest. But he is then freed to continue his own pilgrimage, long postponed, to find the human creature who comes closest to the ideal. Langland's poem propounds an answer not to the simple, though profound, question, How do we know ourselves?, but to the question which lies closer to real experience, How shall we be brought to know ourselves?

To put the primary difficulty in Fr. Dunning's words,

> . . . how are we to distinguish the good from the bad, how can we judge the movements of the heart, how discern their provenance? A reconnaissance of the terrain where one is to exercise the inner life is indispensable.[24]

Langland's "answer" is in effect twofold. Firstly, that we "distinguish the good from the bad" all too easily—where others are concerned. This is his *Visio,* where the reader, with the Dreamer, is the spectator of vice and folly. But when we think we have found a good man, then the standard that is at once in question will surprise us into examining not the vices of others, but our own. The reader is involved in this development in a way comparable with that employed in *Gulliver's Travels.* In each instance, the standpoint of the observer is decisively shifted. Dislodged from a comfortable vantage-point, our guide, and thus we, find ourselves involved, no longer able to interpose between ourselves and reality that "glass wherein beholders do generally discover everybody's face but their own." But what for Gulliver comes as a progressive understanding in a world of sober discourse comes to the Dreamer all at once as action on the part of the Plowman—an action which continues to perplex the Dreamer until action is perfected in the Crucifixion and made triumphant in the Harrowing of Hell. The logical imagination of Langland can move easily from sardonic observation to exalted wonder. The quality of his poetry is an unswerving fidelity to the facts of particular experience: for its centre is in the hard fact that the human condition is to find self-knowledge the all-but-impossible undertaking. Of this kind of poem we are tempted to say that the poet succeeds by calling Reason to the aid of Imagination.

V

Piers Plowman, then, appears to traverse two major kinds of poetry to which we are accustomed. On the one hand, its greatest things, as Professor Lewis has observed, come from the region of "the 'intellectual imagination.' " So, we may add, does its continuing energy, the play of a logical imagination in a predominantly satiric mode. But this introduces us to the other aspect in which the poem must be viewed. The satire is concerned with the truths we claim to know and yet do not apprehend: so, at the turning-points, vision must play the decisive part. Thus, for some modern readers great Romantic poetry may be the best entry upon

24 Loc. cit., pp. 226–27 [p. 89].

the complexity of experience to which *Piers Plowman* is faithful—the penetrating simplicity of "realization," and its uncovenanted nature, the sharpness of the sense of defeat—which at once redoubles awareness of what we seek while it falsifies all our contriving—and, rarely but centrally, the exaltation of vision. We must not classify Langland's work with the poetry that merely expounds a system of beliefs. It is in its essentials more like that genuinely new "kind" for which the treatise poem of the eighteenth century prepares a way—a poetry which is concerned not with the exposition of doctrine as a contribution to the reader's knowledge, but with the individual reader's apprehension of truth, his growing into awareness, as the poem proceeds, of a path inescapably opening before him. These different kinds may resemble each other at certain points; and we run the risk of confusing them whenever we paraphrase for discussion their "content." It could hardly be otherwise, when the poet himself cannot adequately safeguard from misinterpretation his theme of "Imagination,"

> Power so called
> Through sad incompetence of human speech.

But there is yet a difference between *The Pleasures of Imagination* and *The Prelude* which is not merely the difference between a greater poet and a less. Fr. Dunning does well to recall us from an unreflecting acceptance of *Piers Plowman* as spiritual autobiography. But we must not be diverted from the real centre of imaginative excitement, the difference between "knowledge" and "realization," between the doctrines so long accepted and the significances at last apprehended. We may well, if we choose, identify the poet behind the Dreamer, manœuvring the reader through his guide until vision is inescapable. But we should be very sure that we allow for the activity of the poem itself, bringing to the poet, in the act of telling, new relations and significances. Our criticism will be beside the mark if we do not see that the poem succeeds by communicating the mind, not behind, but *in* the poem—a poem which is always, in a sense, unfinished. As it is a poem piercingly clear in its central issues, so it is multiple in its implications.

It is with those "implications" that we encounter the charge of passages that are "confused and monotonous," the "paradox of total greatness and local failures"; and we shall do well to heed Dr. Tillyard's warning that it is possible to be "too tolerant of Langland's repetitions and irrelevant moralising." [25] Not everything in Langland can be defended: indeed, one would wish to hear less in some modern criticism of Lang-

---

[25] *The English Epic and its Background* (London, 1954), p. 168.

land as a master-craftsman of multiple allegorical meanings, perception of which will somehow enable us to see merit in what might otherwise appear otiose or redundant. But before judgement is given on such particular passages as appear faulty, it would be as well to place them in the setting of Langland's whole endeavor. His undertaking must be not merely to state the apparent perplexities and nearly insoluble difficulties, but to communicate the very sense of weariness and apparent purposelessness that any stage of the journey may afford, if it is looked at neither from the end nor the beginning, but as it was encountered. Perhaps, too, our modern practice of concentrating upon the *Vita de Dowel, Dobet, et Dobest* increases the difficulty of apprehending the whole work serially, experiencing its crises as they occur and not as they may be extracted from their setting for the purposes of cross-reference and detailed comparison. It is the merit of Langland's poem that we share the sense of confusion and apparent repetition of experience: for how otherwise shall we see that man must be brought to simple practice? But this is not to claim that Langland works of set purpose and in thorough detail, like a modern artist who would communicate the sense of reality as complex and ambiguous by fostering a degree of complexity and ambiguity in the very communication itself. There is no question of that capital verdict of criticism, *pauper videri Cinna vult et est pauper* [Cinna wishes to seem poor and is poor]. Langland is faithful to a central purpose, our blindness to what resists all our inquiry until we are brought to practice it: and for this fidelity we may be thankful. When penetrating clarity and largeness of vision are found side by side with the very taste of purposelessness we may feel that what is monotonous and confused is the necessary, but excessively rare, complement of those heights of "intellectual imagination" which thereby gain in authenticity and are saved from any suspicion of the merely austere.

In the same way, our understanding of Langland will be sounder if, as we come to judgement, we can concern ourselves less with the doctrines with which the Dreamer wrestles, and more with the nature of his progress towards his goal. The poem deals in mysteries, but the focus of attention is not upon man's ignorance of what is too dark for him; it is upon his insentience of what has been brought into the light of common day. Langland's poem thus succeeds in communicating not a cumulative effect of discursive thinking, but the very pressure of experience itself. However it may have been with Langland himself, his Dreamer is one who is forced, in the words of a later allegorist, "not to propound, but to live through, a sort of ontological proof." [26] Langland's hand is there,

---

[26] C. S. Lewis, *The Pilgrim's Regress* (London, 1943) , p. 10.

certainly: but it is his greatest single achievement that at the turning-points we see that the preparation is not the creature's but the Creator's. Until the living example is set before us, all our inquiries serve only to mislead. So the Plowman, and after him the Saviour Himself, are sent to meet our need. It is thus fitting that the Dreamer goes forth at the end to seek a true exemplar. Langland's last and most individual stroke is in deepest conformity with his whole design. By it he draws that design conclusively away from a formal into a truly imaginative unity.

6. Piers Plowman and the Pilgrimage to Truth

ELIZABETH ZEEMAN

THE SENCE is somewhat darcke, but not so harde, but that it may be understonde of suche as will not sticke to breake the shell of the nutte for the kernelles sake." In spite of these confident words with which Robert Crowley prefaced his mid-sixteenth-century edition of *Piers Plowman*, the effort to reach the kernel of its meaning continues. While critics agree basically on the fact that the poem must be given a number of interpretations—the deepest of which is of a most subtle spirituality—we are still far from a complete understanding of Langland's intent and procedure.

That the orthodox contemplative writings of the medieval church may resolve some problems is already recognized. Walter Hilton's definitions of the various kinds of Christian life have been used to clarify certain terms used in the poem[1] and a recent study of the C version discusses Langland's basic theme in the specific context of Bernardian mysticism.[2] The general line of inquiry is rewarding if pursued with care. There are

Reprinted by permission of Elizabeth (Zeeman) Salter and The English Association from *Essays and Studies by Members of the English Association*, N.S., XI (1958), 1–16. Volume XI was originally published by Messrs. John Murray, Ltd., for the English Association and has recently been reprinted by Messrs. Wm. Dawson and Sons, Ltd., of Farnham, Surrey.

For further explanation of the views expressed here, as well as discussions of other themes in the poem, see Elizabeth Salter's *Piers Plowman: An Introduction* (Cambridge, Mass., 1962). Some other recent studies are D. W. Robertson, Jr., and Bernard F. Huppé, *Piers Plowman and Scriptural Tradition* (Princeton, 1951); Robert W. Frank, Jr., *Piers Plowman and the Scheme of Salvation*, YSE, Vol. 136 (New Haven, 1957); David C. Fowler, *Piers the Plowman: Literary Relations of the A and B Texts* (Seattle, 1961); Morton W. Bloomfield, *Piers Plowman as a Fourteenth-Century Apocalypse* (New Brunswick, 1961); John Lawlor, *Piers Plowman: An Essay in Criticism* (New York, 1962); A. C. Spearing, "The Art of Preaching and *Piers Plowman*," *Criticism and Medieval Poetry* (New York, 1964), pp. 68–95; Edward Vasta, *The Spiritual Basis of Piers Plowman* (The Hague: Mouton and Company, 1965); Donald R. Howard, "The Body Politic and the Lust of the Eyes: *Piers Plowman*," *The Three Temptations* (Princeton, 1966), pp. 163–214; E. Talbot Donaldson, *Piers Plowman: The C-Text and Its Poet* (New Haven, 1949); and Ben H. Smith, Jr., *Traditional Imagery of Charity in Piers Plowman* (The Hague: Mouton and Company, 1966).

[1] R. W. Chambers, *Man's Unconquerable Mind* (London, 1939), pp. 104–6.

[2] E. T. Donaldson, *Piers Plowman. The C Text and its Poet* (New Haven, 1949), Chapter VI.

strong connexions between the development of the allegory in *Piers Plowman* and mystical processes, but it is a mistake to insist on close equations with any particular doctrine.[3] Working as a poet, with the greatest freedom and imaginative range, Langland is not to be circumscribed in this way; we must be prepared for comparisons to reveal divergence of outlook and method as often as agreement. With these reservations, the treatises of the English mystics, Langland's contemporaries, do throw light on some of his most vital concepts and aims. Especially important, they show us how much emphasis should be placed on certain parts of the allegory if our reading is to be soundly based and comprehensive—confirming, for instance, how necessary it is, if we are to have a proper grasp of the enigmatic character of Piers Plowman himself, to take seriously the directions he gives, early on in the poem, for the momentous Pilgrimage to St. Truth:

> Ac if ʒe wilneth to wende wel . this is the weye thider,
> That I shal say to yow . and sette yow in the sothe.
>
> (B. v, 568–69) [4]

This Pilgrimage to Truth is undertaken by reader and poet-dreamer no less than by Piers and his crowd of penitent, stumbling pilgrims, and the going is sometimes rough. As always with Langland, however, the difficulties lie in the details of the route, not in the statement and achievement of main objectives. For the broad features of his spiritual geography are well-marked. In the "toure on a toft" lives Truth, who is God, as Holy Church points out to the inquiring dreamer:

> "The toure vp the toft," quod she . "treuthe is thereinne,
> . . . . he is fader of feith . fourmed ʒow alle. . . ."
> ["The tower on the hill," she said, "is the home of Truth,
> . . . he is the father of Faith, who created you all . . ."]
>
> (B. i, 12, 14)

The need to seek Truth is the first clear theme which emerges from the poem; when the dreamer asks how he may save his soul, Holy Church replies:

---

[3] Warnings of this are given by T. P. Dunning, "The Structure of the B-Text of *Piers Plowman*," *R.E.S.*, N.S. vii (1956) , p. 225 [p. 87], and by J. Lawlor, "The Imaginative Unity of *Piers Plowman*," *R.E.S.*, N.S. viii (1957) , pp. 113–14 etc. [pp.101–102]. Donaldson, op. cit., who wishes to find in the poem three stages corresponding to St. Bernard's humility, charity and unity, has to admit "this progress seems to have stopped short of its goal" (p. 197) .

[4] The text of the poem used throughout is that of W. W. Skeat, *The Vision of William concerning Piers the Plowman in Three Parallel Texts* (Oxford, 1886) .

> Whan alle tresores are tried . . . trewthe is the best.
>
> (*ibid.,* 85)

She says, further, that the way to Truth is love:

> Loue is leche of lyf . and nexte owre lorde selue,
> And also the graith gate . that goth into heuene. . . .
> [Love is the physician of life, the power nearest to our Lord himself,
> and the wicket gate that goes to heaven.]   (*ibid.,* 202–3)

Nothing in *Piers Plowman* ever contradicts these words; in a very real sense they are final. And they are richly associative; the approach to God through love, recommended here so decisively as the only possible direction of activity, is not only recommended but experienced and analysed by men and women such as Richard Rolle, Dame Julian of Norwich, or the author of *The Cloud of Unknowing.* The words of Holy Church are echoed in

> By loue may he be getyn & holden; bot bi þouȝt neiþer.
> (*The Cloud of Unknowing,* 26/4–5) [5]

and in

> . . . the soul that of his special grace seyth so ferforth of the hey mervelous godenes of God, and that we arn endlesly onyd to hym in love . . . .
> (Julian Of Norwich, *Revelations of Divine Love,* f. 60) [6]

But this is a general correspondence only; it is particularized when, after the examination and confession of the Seven Deadly Sins, the search for Truth takes full allegorical shape as a pilgrimage:

> A thousand of men tho . thrungen togyderes;
> Criede vpward to Cryst . and to his clene moder
> To haue grace to go with hem . Treuthe to seke.
> (B. v, 517–19)

For this large, miscellaneous body of pilgrims the way to Truth must be defined exactly. And Piers, making his dramatic entry into the poem as guide for the journey, gives detailed instructions which, though they may be grounded in ordinary homiletic teaching on the good Christian life, reach out to spiritual matters within the compass of the mystic alone.

---

[5] Ed. P. Hodgson (E.E.T.S., O.S., 218, 1944) .

[6] Since no good edition is yet accessible, the text of the *Revelations* has been taken from British Museum MS., Sloane 2499.

At this stage a similar allegorical pilgrimage in Walter Hilton's manual for the contemplative life, the *Scale of Perfection*,[7] becomes relevant. The pilgrim in Hilton's book is anxious to set out for Jerusalem which "be tokenyth contemplacyoun in parfyte loue of God . . . a syght of ihesu. . . ." And like Langland's pilgrims, he looks for a guide:

> Ther was a man þat wold gon to Ierusalem| And for he knew nout the weye . he cam to an othir man that he hopid knew þe weye thedyr| And he askyd hym if he myth comyn to that cyte|
> (f. 119b)

His guide speaks of the route with assurance and authority, claiming:

> And if þu wylt holdyn this weye and don as I haue seyd. I undirtake thyn lyf . that þu shalt nout be slayn . but wol comyn to þat . that þu coveytyst.
> (f. 120a)

So, too, in *Piers Plowman,* when the ordinary plowman addresses the hopeful crowd of travellers, his words are by no means ordinary. He shows a far deeper knowledge of religious mysteries than we might expect from even the best of the obedient sons of Holy Church; the springs of growth and change are already in Piers when we first meet him. The way to St. Truth, as he describes it, lies first through meekness and conscience and the commandments; man begins to travel to God through belief and obedience. The verse in which Langland sets these directions is hardly beautiful, but it is clear. The allegory is kept simple; it is a map such as a child could understand, and this in itself is a virtue, for the pilgrims who wait, listening to Piers, have become "as a little child" in order that they may be received into the kingdom of Heaven:

> ʒe mote go thourgh Mekenesse . bothe men and wyues,
> Til ʒe come in-to Conscience . that Cryst wite the sothe,
> That ʒe louen owre lorde god . levest of all thinges,
> And thanne ʒowre neighbores nexte . in none wise apeyre,
> Otherwyse than thow woldest . he wrouʒte to thi-selue.
> And so boweth forth bi a broke . Beth-buxom-of-speche,
> Tyle ʒe funden a forth . ʒowre-fadres-honoureth, *Honora*
>   *patrem et matrem,* etc.
> Wadeth in that water . and wascheth ʒow wel there,
> And ʒe shul lepe the liʒtloker . al ʒowre lyf-tyme.
> And so shaltow se Swere-nouʒte- . but-if-it-be-for-nede-
> And-namelich-an-ydel- . the-name-of-god-almyʒti.

---

7 The text of the *Scale of Perfection* used in this article is that contained in Corpus Christi College, Cambridge, MS. 268.

Thanne shaltow come by a crofte . but come thow nouʒte
    there-inne;
That crofte hat Coveyte-nouʒte- . mennes-catel-ne-her-
    wyves
Ne-none-of-her-servauntes- . that-noyen-hem-myʒte;
Like ʒe breke no bowes there . but if it be ʒowre owne.
Two stokkes there stondeth . ac stynte ʒe nouʒte there,
They hatte Stele-nouʒte, Ne-slee-nouʒte . stryke forth by
    bothe;
And leue hem on thi left halfe . and loke nouʒte there-after;
And holde wel thyne haliday . heighe til euen.
Thanne shaltow blenche at a berghe . Bere-no-false-witnesse,
He is frithed in with floreines . and other fees many;
Loke thow plukke no plante there . for peril of thi soule.
Thanne shal ʒe se Sey-soth- . so-it-be-to-done-
In-no-manere-ellis-nouʒte- . for-no mannes-biddynge.

                                      (B. v, 570–93)

If this were all, then there would be reason to agree that Piers' description of the highway to Truth "has been little more than an outline of the virtuous active life." [8] But he continues with more significant material. By now the pilgrims are within sight of "a courte as clere as the sonne"; it is the dwelling of Truth, the "toure on a toft" seen so sharply in the opening panorama of the vision. Piers then completes his account of the approach to God in plain, reduced poetry, which echoes most strongly the spiritual directions given to Hilton's aspiring contemplative. For Piers sends the travellers across the moat of mercy, by means of a bridge of prayer; the walls of the court which faces them are of wit, buttressed by belief and christendom. The entrance has pillars of penance, and the gates hang on hinges of alms-deeds. The whole court is roofed with love:

Thanne shaltow come to a courte . as clere as the sonne,
The mote is of Mercy . the manere aboute,
And alle the wallis ben of Witte . to holden Wille oute;
And kerneled with Crystendome . man-kynde to saue,
Boterased with Bileue-so . or-thow-beest-nouʒte- ysaued.
And alle the houses ben hiled . halles and chambres,
With no lede, but with Loue . and Lowe-speche-as-bretheren
The brugge is of Bidde-wel- . the-bette-may-thow-spede;
Eche piler is of Penaunce . of preyeres to seyntes,
Of Almes-dedes ar the hokes . that the gates hangen on.

---

[8] Donaldson, op. cit., p. 168, Lawlor, op. cit., p. 122 [p. 111], also sees Piers' account of the route as inadequate—"stiff, signpost-like allegory"—and thinks that he later rejects it.

[Then you shall come to a court as bright as the sun. The moat which circles the manor is of mercy. All the walls are wisdom, to keep out passion; it has battlements of Christendom to save mankind, and is buttressed with believe-or-you-cannot-be-saved. All the houses are tiled, both halls and chambers, not with lead, but with love and lowly-speech-of-brothers. The bridge is of ask-and-you-shall-receive; each pillar is made of penance and prayers to the saints, and the gates hang on hinges of alms-deeds.]   (B. v, 594–603)

Hilton's guide has also stressed obedience, meekness, prayer, repentance:

The begynnyng of þe heigh weye in which þu shalt gon . is reform-yng in feyth grounded mekly in the feyth . and in þe lawys of holy cherche.   (f. 120a)

. . . a soule be first smet doun fro the heite of þe self by drede and meknesse and be wel examynid and brent in the fyer of desyer and as it were puryfied from alle gostly fylthe by long tyme in deuout preyerys and othir gostly exercise.   (f. 129a)

And love must work with meekness:

Thanne yf þu wylt spedyn in thyn goyng . and makyn goode iornys . þe behouith to holdyn these to thyngis oftyn in thyn mende mek-nesse and loue.   (f. 120b)

Piers brings his pilgrims up to the gates of the court, and, as the climax draws near, the poetry noticeably warms and relaxes. Grace is the porter—"a gode man for sothe"—and his servant is Amende-ȝow:

> Biddeth Amende-ȝow meke him . til his maistre ones,
> To wayue vp the wiket . that the woman shette,
> [You must ask amendment to beg his master
> to open the wicket that the woman shut]

> Tho Adam and Eue . eten apples vnrosted . . .
> And if Grace graunte the . to go in this wise,
> Thow shalt se in thi-selue . Treuthe sitte in thine herte,
> In a cheyne of charyte . as thow a childe were . . . .
>   (B. v, 610–12, 613–16)

These last lines give bold and elliptical expression to a profound spiritual concept, familiar in mystical writings—man's discovery, by divine grace and through divine love, of the divine within himself. Hilton speaks of it frequently: "the trewe lith is the perfite loue of Jesus felt thurgh grace in a manys soule" (f. 124b). His pilgrim is told of the "in-

dwelling" of Christ in the soul—Christ who is the real source and centre
of energy for the search at the same time as he is the goal, Jerusalem, to
be striven after:

> Coveite þu this ȝifte of loue principaly as I haue seid ffor if he wil
> of his grace ȝevyn it on that maner wyse . it shal opynyn the reson
> of thyn soule for to seen sothefastnesse that is Jesus . and gostly
> thyngys. . . .
> And it shal werkyn in thyn soule only as he wold and þu shalt
> holdyn hym reuerently with sothfastnesse of loue and sen how he
> doth. Thus biddith he be his prophete that we shuld don. seying
> thus. . . .
> Behold ȝe me ffor I do al. I am loue and for I loue . I do al þat I do
> and ȝe don nout. And that this ys soth . I shall wel shewyn ȝow ffor
> ther is no good dede don in ȝow . no good thout felt in ȝow . but
> if it be don thurgh me that is thurgh myth wisdam and loue. I only
> do all ȝoure good dedys . and ȝoure goode thowtis . and goode louis
> in ȝow . and ȝe don ryth nout.   (f. 148a)

Where Hilton is writing directly towards those in the religious life,
Langland has in mind a more varied public; his pilgrimage must attract
all classes of men—the finding of Truth must be possible on many levels
of experience. But the lines

> Thow shalt see in thi-selue . Treuthe sitte in thine herte
> In a cheyne of charite . . .

coming as they do after the painful stress on penance, amendment,
prayer, have greatest power of meaning as the climax of a process akin,
if not identical to that described by Hilton. Piers sees the pilgrimage to
Truth in a far wider context than that of "obedience to the tables of the
law." [9] The poem has multiple allegorical sense, and the discovery of
long-sought Truth, bound by love, in the pilgrim's own heart, asks for
various interpretations. On the plane of ordinary Christian morals, it
may be understood as the achievement of a life controlled and shaped
from the inside by God's truth and love. On a rare spiritual plane, however—that of Hilton's pilgrimage to Jerusalem—it speaks most coherently
of the mystic's apprehension of God in himself, the mapping of the divine into the human, brought about by grace.

   If, however, this passage is to justify itself completely, it must not only
gather up and re-express with greater precision what has been said earlier
in the poem about the "way to Truth." The lines of action it prescribes

9 Donaldson, loc. cit.

must be traceable, somehow, over the rest of the allegory. And here we begin to deal in complexities, for from this point onwards Langland turns his full creative powers to the exploration of the search for Truth. The allegory becomes increasingly complicated; there appear, at times, to be not one but a score of themes and sub-themes. As far as we know, these particular pilgrims, instructed by Piers, never embark upon their journey. Yet the pilgrimage to Truth, once announced, is never abandoned. It is the great imaginative motif of the whole work; the activity of travel, whether material or spiritual, involves the major characters of the allegory—Piers and the Dreamer, no less than minor figures such as Conscience and Patience[10] and Hawkin,[11] the unreformed man of active life. The successive searches for the three lives or states, Dowel, Dobet and Dobest, are only sub-divisions of the large search for Truth. Struggle towards illumination, on every level—moral, theological, mystical—is a constant element in the shifting dream-world to which Langland admits us. And the main pattern of this journeying is forecast by Piers, as he describes in the simplest terms what he knows of the approach to and the dwelling-place of God.

So, in a general sense, the dreamer and many of those connected with him are taught the difficult lessons of obedience, humility, repentance as they make their way towards Truth. At the Feast of Learned Doctors (cooked by Contrition) the dreamer is given the sour bread of penitence to stomach;

> He sette a soure lof to-for-us . and seyde "agite penitenciam"
> [do penance].   (B. xiii, 48)

Hawkin's sinful cloak is cleansed by Conscience, and he takes humbly "fiat voluntas tua" [thy will be done] to sustain him ever after.[12] The dreamer is persuaded, gradually, that "Truth dwells in him, in love," for his inmost comprehension of divine matters is only achieved through love. The passage in which one of his many anxious inquiries about the meaning of Dowel, Dobet and Dobest is met by Clergye with the simple reply "Piers and his doctrine of love" [13] tells us of the transformation of Piers, but also of the growth of understanding in the dreamer himself. His journey to Truth on its own limited but sound level, is being fulfilled in the name of love; and the power to love, as he was first informed by Holy Church, is created in man's heart by God:

10 B. xiii, 215. "Conscience tho with Pacience passed . pilgrymes as it were."
11 Hawkin moves toward good, with the help of Patience; see B. xiii, 220 onwards
12 B. xiv, 36 onwards.
13 See below, p. 126.

And in the herte, there is the heuede . and the heiȝ welle;
[And in the heart is its home and fountainhead]
. . . And that falleth to the fader . that formed vs alle,
Loked on us with loue . and let his sone deye
Mekely for owre mysdedes . to amende vs alle.

(B. i, 162, 164–66)

As confirmation of what he is learning about divine love and truth, he is allowed to witness the Crucifixion and the Harrowing of Hell; the gates are indeed opened to him, by grace, as he *sees* Truth bound by charity, Christ willingly sacrificed in love, so that he may gain entry to man's heart. Piers' words:

And if Grace graunte the . to go in this wise,
Thow shalt see in thi-selue . Treuthe sitte in thine herte,
In a cheyne of charyte . . .

prophesy the dreamer's experience in no uncertain manner.

But there is another way in which the pilgrimage to Truth takes place over the rest of the poem. This way is mystical in concept, although its literary form could only have been devised by an essentially poetic imagination. For Langland has his plowman-guide, Piers, suffer in person and on the most exalted level, all he dictates to others about the search for and the finding of Truth; he enlarges the significance of Piers until he becomes a symbol of the operation of the divine upon the human—God's relationship with man through Christ. At his most powerful, he is neither wholly man nor God; he represents much more the state of grace in which both are united. Piers, in the highest spiritual sense discovers (both to himself and to us)

Treuthe sitte in thine herte,
In a cheyne of charyte. . . .

He not only gains but *is* the apprehension of God within, worked by love. What we watch, in Piers, is

þe eendles merueilous miracle of loue, þe whiche schal neuer
take eende . . .   (*The Cloud*, 19/10–11)

by which

oure soule, bi vertewe of þis reformyng grace, is mad sufficient
at þe fulle to comprehende al him by loue. . . .

(*ibid.*, 18/17–18)

Now especially, in this process of spiritual alchemy, the writings of men such as Hilton or the *Cloud* author confirm and clarify. We see Piers, who has already shown, by his knowledge of the route to St. Truth, some acquaintance with mysteries, beginning his long transformation in Passus vii. And he dedicates himself to a life of prayer and penance. He is no longer using the metaphor of the pilgrimage in such detail as before, but his opening quotation: "si ambulauero in medio umbre mortis, non timebo mala, quoniam tu mecum es" reaffirms the idea of travelling. In fact, although his experiences take place in a finer context, he will, as he advised others, seek his God, St. Truth, across the bridge of prayer and come face to face with the pillars of penance:

> Of preyers and of penaunce . my plow shal ben herafter,
> And wepen whan I shulde slepe . though whete-bred me
>   faille.
> The prophete his payn ete . in penaunce and in sorwe
> . . . *Fuerunt michi lacrime mee panes die ac nocte.*
> [. . . My tears have been for me my bread day and night.]
>   (B. vii, 119–21, 123)

His absence in the next section of the poem (Passus viii–xv) [14] does not remove him from the consciousness of either dreamer or reader. He is kept in mind by skilfully placed references which seem to indicate that he is in some kind of activity, and certainly increasing in power and significance. By Passus xiii he has progressed far enough through and beyond prayer and penance to represent the doctrine of love itself:

> For one Pieres the Ploughman . hath impugned vs alle
> And set alle sciences at a soppe . saue loue one,
> And no tixte ne taketh to meyntene his cause,
> But *dilige deum* [love God]. . . .
>   (B. xiii, 123–26)

Far from deserting the dreamer, he is still acting as guide; those taking part in the narrative of events reach out to him as to the resolution of all problems:

> Thanne passe we ouer til Piers come . and preue this in dede. . . .
>   (B. xiii, 132)

And this intangible leadership is most strongly reminiscent of the part played by Christ in Hilton's Pilgrimage to Jerusalem; with these words

---

14 In the C-text he makes one brief appearance (C. xvi, 138–50) which does not contribute much to the main development of the narrative.

indeed, Hilton might be describing the function of Piers in this part of the poem:

> behold hym wel . he goth beforn the nout in bodily lyknesse . but un-
> seably bi[15] priue presens of his gostly myth. Therfore se hym gostly
> if þu may and ellys trowe hym and folwe hym whydir so he goth ffor
> he shal ledyn the in the ryth weye to jerusalem.
>
> (f. 124b)

It is no surprise when, in the next passus, Reason says of charity:

> With-outen helpe of Piers Plowman . . . his persone seestow
>   neuere.   (B. xv, 190)

And neither dreamer nor reader can be entirely unprepared for the positive words which follow:

> There-fore by coloure ne by clergye . knowe shaltow hym
>   neuere,
> Noyther thorw wordes ne werkes . but thorw wille one.
> And that knoweth no clerke . ne creature in erthe,
> But Piers the Plowman . *Petrus, id est, Christus.*
>   (B. xv, 203-6)

It is not, I think, in mistaken enthusiasm that Langland gradually per-
suades us to think of Piers in terms of love and Christ.[16] He is dealing
with ideas very close to those of Hilton when he says to his pilgrim:

> If þu wost wetyn thanne what this desier is . sothly it is Jesus for he
> makith this desier in the and he it is that is desyryd and desiryth . he
> is al and he makith al. If þu mytist sen hym þu dost nout . but suf-
> feryst hym werkyn in thyn soule . assentyst to hym with gret glad-
> nesse of herte . that he wold vouchesaf for to don so in the . þu art
> nout ellys but a resonable instrument . wherinne that he werkyth.
>
> (f. 124a)

Piers is by now a large symbol of spiritual activity. He is the "Christ
element" in man which aspires, searches, goes on pilgrimage—"he it is
that . . . desiryth." So Piers pledges himself to pilgrimage twice over—

---

[15] The Corpus Christi College MS. reading here is "onsaciably priuy"; the emendation has been made from Trinity College, Cambridge, MS. B. 15. 18.

[16] Donaldson, op. cit., p. 195: "emphatic, and misleading, couplings of Piers with
Christ which culminate in the phrase *Petrus, id est, Christus.*" It is true, as he says,
that this phrase disappears in the C-text but Langland's alterations at that stage were
as often prompted by extreme caution as by a radical change of attitude. The B-text
stands consistent, although audacious, in its main approach.

first when he offers to travel with the confused penitents on their lowly way to St. Truth:

> "And I shal apparaille me," quod Perkyn . "in pilgrimes
> wise,
> And wende with ʒow I wil . til we fynde Treuthe."
> (B. vi, 59–60)

and then at a high point of devotion, setting out on the hard contemplative path to God: *"si ambulavero in medio umbre mortis. . . ."* He is the Christ-guide who leads and moreover *is* the way—"he goth beforn the . . . unseably bi priue presens of his gostly myth"—and he is even Christ the object of the search—"he it is that is desyryd. . . ." So Piers directs to St. Truth, and, almost imperceptibly, *becomes* the "way" which Holy Church first sketched in outline, and he completed; he draws all with him, for he becomes love, "the graith gate . that goth into heuene. . . ." And at the very end of the poem he is to be sought for as urgently as St. Truth was at the beginning.

But now, after the decisive statement, *"Petrus, id est, Christus,"* the re-entry of Piers into the poem is awaited. The dreamer, beginning to grasp something of what Piers symbolizes, reaches a crescendo of excitement as the moment comes near. The question is "What charite is to mene" (B. xvi, 3) , and Piers is mentioned:

> "Piers the Plowman!" quod I tho . and al for pure ioye
> That I herde nempne his name . anone I swoned after.
> [I fainted as soon as I heard his name.]
> (*ibid.,* 18–19)

It can be objected that when the moment does arrive, in Passus xvi, Piers, although in a position of great authority,[17] is not able to take such an ambitious interpretation as that suggested above. Moreover, the figure who

> Barfote on an asse bakke . boteless cam prykye
> [Barefoot on an ass's back came riding along bootless]
> (B. xviii, 11)

is firmly defined by Langland as Christ, and not Piers. Christ simply assumes the human nature of Piers for the "jousting in Jerusalem":

> This Iesus of his gentrice . wole Iuste in Piers armes,
> In his helme and in his haberioun . *humana natura.*

---

[17] He has the Tree of Charity under his care (B. xvi, 15–16) and the fruit of mankind which is to be wrested from the Devil is "Pieres fruit."

[Jesus, out of chivalry, will joust in Piers' armor
and wear his helmet and mail, human nature.]
(B. xviii, 22–23)

The Piers symbol, built up accumulatively over the poem, now seems
to be weakened.

Here the differences between Langland, the poet-allegorist, and Hilton, the prose-writer become clear. Langland's allegory cannot long remain purely didactic; its natural movement is towards drama. He has, therefore, a far more difficult problem of communication to meet and overcome. The vital comment on the nature of Christ, made so succinctly by Hilton (see page 127, above) must, if rendered as a play of personages, appear full of paradox, and, if then judged by either realistic or symbolic standards, full of complexity. In fact, there is a paradox at the root of the matter: the co-existence of human and divine in the being of Christ, and, through grace, in the nature of man. Such a subject needs delicate handling; neither Hilton nor Langland could have wished to say without reservation that the pilgrim travelling to Truth by way of love is identical with Truth and love, that Piers and Christ are exactly the same person, and that man can become divine by his own efforts. The dangers of heresy would have been sufficiently clear to any Christian of the later fourteenth century. Yet they do wish to say that through the sacrifice of Christ and the grace obtained for man thereby, a divine element exists potentially in even the simplest of creatures. The prose writer is able to make the distinction brief and clear:

he is al and he makith al . if þu mytist sen hym þu dost nout . but sufferyst hym werkyn in thyn soule . . . þu art nout ellys but a resonable instrument . wherinne that he werkyth.

Hilton's words are paralleled in other contemplative texts; the author of *The Cloud of Unknowing* expresses himself with economy:

only bi his mercy wiþ-outen þi desert arte maad a God in grace, onyd wiþ him in spirit wiþ-outen departyng, boþe here & in blis of heuen wiþ-outen any eende. So þat, þouȝ þou be al one wiþ hym in grace, ȝit þou arte ful fer bineþe hym in kynde.
(120/16–20)

Dame Julian of Norwich with meticulous care:

And I saw no difference atwix God and our substance but as it were al God, and yet myn understondyng toke that our substance is in God, that is to say that God is God, and our substance is a creature in God. (f. 74)

Langland has a more daring plan; he sets out to show us, in full imaginative and dramatic form, how this "working in the soul" takes place.
We are allowed to understand how the devout human being, Piers,
changes in significance from plowman to the principle of divine love in
man: Christ works so perfectly in his soul that indeed in this sense *"Petrus, id est, Christus,"* Piers is "maad a God in grace." But although we
can be told of this in his absence, we cannot be allowed to see Piers dis-
played before us as the total sum of divine love. The living and speaking
Piers must remain separate from the divine force which operates mysteriously and triumphantly in him. Man's aspiration and God's condescen-
sion meet in the soul—but they are not the same thing: "our substance is
a creature in God."

Consequently, the Crucifixion and the Harrowing of Hell, in Passus
xvi–xviii, are experienced by Christ, not by Piers the Plowman. And in
the last few passus of the poem, Piers is intimately connected with the
Holy Spirit, but is not identical with it. He has discovered God's Truth
within—Truth "sits in his heart"—but he is not to be mistaken for its
divine essence, St. Truth himself.

The deepest theme of *Piers Plowman* might, then, be viewed as an exploration of the journey to God through Christ—the reaching of the
"treasure of Truth" along the highroad of Love: a study of the way in
which Christ, with his doctrine of love, enables the pilgrim to Truth and
his goal, Truth, to become one:

> "I am via et veritas," seith Cryst. "I may auaunce alle."
>
> (B. ix, 159)

The powerful welding of the two concepts of the going out towards
God, and the ultimate finding of God within, is not unique to Langland;
it can be found in both Hilton and Dame Julian:

> ... he shewid him in erth thus as it wer in pilgrimage that is to say
> he is here with us bidand[18] us and shul bin till whan he hath browte
> us all to his bliss in hevyn . he shewid him dyvers tymes regnand as
> it is aforn seyd but principally in mannys soule he hath taken there
> his risting place and his worshipful cyte out of which worshipfull
> see he shall never risen nor removen without end.
>
> (f. 106)

Langland, however, *is* unique in that he not only tries to express but
also to personify it through the Piers-Christ figure—a powerful, composite symbol which he manipulates freely and sensitively, so that it commands moral, mystical and poetic significance.

18 This should probably read "ledand."

In some ways, the fact that Langland always needed to turn to the drama of flesh and blood was a serious limitation; the difficulty of animating subtle spiritual truths is formidable, and there are minor failures and inconsistencies in *Piers Plowman*. But in other ways his instinct for drama was sure and triumphant. However rarified the doctrine he presents to us, we never lose touch for long with the warm humanity of the plowman who first "put forth his head" and offered to lead us to St. Truth. Even if we are not destined to know the fulness of God's love in contemplative rapture, we can all travel with Piers the Plowman, who, "wiþ þe drawʒt of þis loue & voise of þis cleping," [19] leads us irresistibly through an experience as rich as it is sometimes perplexing and challenging.

19 *The Cloud*, 14/19.

7. Love, Law, and *Lewte* in *Piers Plowman*

P. M. KEAN

So comune cleymeth of a kyng thre kynne thynges,
Lawe, loue, and leaute, and hym lord antecedent.

THESE LINES (381–82) from the C-text of *Piers Plowman* contain, it is clear, a purely political idea, expressed in a triple formula which had echoed through the B-text of the *Visio* with almost the persistence of "Dowel, Dobet, and Dobest the thridde" in the *Vita*.[1] Since it is now sometimes claimed that Langland's interests were entirely theological or even clerical, it seems worth tracing out the ideas which develop around this formula in the B *Visio*.[2] This seems all the more desirable since there is no agreement among editors and translators as to the meaning of *Lewte*, although it is an often repeated and an obviously important word in *Piers Plowman*.

The first mention of Law and *Lewte* in the B-text is in the B Prologue, in a passage which introduces the figure of the King, and which brings together a number of the commonplaces of medieval political theory:[3]

Reprinted by permission of the author and The Clarendon Press, Oxford, from *Review of English Studies*, N.S., XV (1964), 241–61.

See also Rudolf Kirk, "References to the Law in *Piers Plowman*," *PMLA*, XLVIII (1933), 322–28.

[1] I do not think that "Law, Loue, and *Lewte*" has previously been noticed as a *leitmotiv* in the *Visio*. As in the case of "Dowel, Dobet, and Dobest" all three elements are not always present. The instances are (numbers in brackets after the reference indicate whether all three or only two occur): Pr. 120–26 (3); Pr. 212–13 (2); i, 157–59 (2); ii, 21–22 (2, or 3 if *lemman* is taken as implying love); ii, 32–33 (2, *lelly* implying *lewte*); iii, 289 (2); iii, 292–98 (3); iv, 35 (2); iv, 147–48 (2); iv, 161 (2); iv, 180–84 (2); vi, 223–30 (2); vii, 39–49 (2); vii, 62–64 (2); vii, 89 (2). I am only concerned here with the *Visio* (B. Prol.–vii) because, although the triad does occur again later, it does so only occasionally, and is used in a different way as the poet's thought and purpose develop.

[2] All quotations are from Skeat's B-text (Oxford, 1886). I have concentrated on B because, though I think they are present, the ideas with which I am concerned are not much developed in A, and the thought of B must, evidently, be established before C's treatment of it is explored—a matter of some interest in this case, but beyond my present scope.

[3] A really detailed study of Langland's political thought is much to be desired. See E. T. Donaldson, *Piers Plowman: the C-Text and its Poet* (New Haven, 1949), pp. 85 ff. and the references given there.

Thanne come there a kyng, knyȝthod hym ladde,
Miȝt of the comunes made hym to regne,
And thanne cam kynde wytte and clerkes he made,
For to conseille the kyng and the comune saue.
The kyng and knyȝthode and clergye bothe
Casten that the comune shulde hem-self fynde.
The comune contreued of kynde witte craftes,
And for profit of alle the poeple plowmen ordeygned,
To tilie and trauaile as trewe lyf asketh.
The kynge and the comune and kynde witte the thridde
Shope lawe and lewte, eche man to knowe his owne.

(112–22)

The King here derives his power from the "comune," and, if we can take this as the commonwealth, the community as a whole, most authorities would agree with Langland.[4] The clergy are to counsel the King and to "save the comune," and in this context they certainly act within the frame of the State.[5] The community itself is not without obligation: it must provide for the needs of the body and ensure that everyone has the basic necessities of life—and this, I believe, is meant in the plainest of literal senses.

This task falls to the lot of the Plowmen, whom we have already met in lines 20–22 of the Prologue, in which the whole Field of Folk is divided into "Winners and Wasters": those who get for the community what should be used according to every man's basic needs, and those who grab more than their share. In both passages the Plowmen are certainly, I think, to be taken literally[6] except in so far as they stand for all those employed in what St. Thomas Aquinas calls the labour "quod pertinet ad commune" [which belongs to the community].[7] Holy Church expresses the same idea when she says that Truth

fourmed ȝow alle,
Bothe with fel and with face, and ȝaf ȝow fyue wittis
Forto worschip him ther-with, the while that ȝe ben here.
And therfore he hiȝte the erthe to help ȝow vchone

---

4 Cf., e.g., A. P. d'Entrèves, *The Medieval Contribution to Political Thought* (Oxford, 1939), pp. 32 ff.; Donaldson, op. cit., pp. 93 ff., and, for the inclusion of the "assent of the commons" in the English coronation ceremony, pp. 106–7.

5 On the medieval idea of the moral function of the State see T. P. Dunning, *Piers Plowman: an Interpretation of the A-Text* (Dublin, 1937), pp. 88 ff.; d'Entrèves, op. cit., p. 9.

6 In spite of D. W. Robertson and B. F. Huppé, *Piers Plowman and Scriptural Tradition* (Princeton, 1951), pp. 17 ff. Cf. E. T. Donaldson in *Critical Approaches to Medieval Literature*, ed. D. Bethurum (New York, 1960), p. 10.

7 *Summa Theologica*, II. II, q. 66 a. 2.

>   Of wollen, of lynnen, of lyflode at nede'
>   In mesurable manere, to make ʒow at ese;
>   And comaunded of his curteisye in comune three thinges.
>
>   (i, 14–20)

Every man has an inalienable right to food, drink, and clothing in so far
as he needs them to maintain the body so that the soul can fulfil the purpose for which it was created. This purpose is implied, as we shall see, by
the phrase "trewe lyf." It is for the State to ensure the proper provision
and distribution of the necessities which God has ordained to be used in
common by all men.[8]

Finally, in the last two lines of the passage, Langland introduces the
idea of Law:

>   The kynge and the comune, and kynde witte the thridde
>   Shope lawe and lewte, eche man to knowe his owne.

Robertson and Huppé interpreted this passage as a criticism of the
existing order. They equated "eche man to knowe his owne" with 1 Cor.
x. 24, "Nemo quod suum est quaerat" [Let no man seek what is his own],
and with the "amor sui" of St. Augustine, which is the opposite of true
charity.[9] This leads them to interpret the speeches of advice and warning
to the King which follow as flattery or satire. But I believe that in this
passage, as in the Prologue as a whole, Langland is making a straightforward statement of ideas which are essential to the plan of his poem.

If we do take lines 121–22 literally we have in the creation of Law with
the help of Kynde Witte a formula which is not unlike St. Thomas's "ius
humanum, quod est ex naturali ratione" [human law, which is derived
from natural reason].[10] St. Thomas distinguishes between human and
divine Law, giving examples of the kind of thing which arises through
each: "Dominium et praelatio introducta sunt ex iure humano; distinc-
tio autem fidelium et infidelium est ex iure divino. Ius autem divinum,
quod est ex gratia, non tollit ius humanum." [Power and authority are
institutions of human law; the distinction between faithful and unfaith-
ful, however, springs from the divine law. Moreover, the divine law,

---

    [8] Cf. Dunning, op. cit., pp. 54–57, for passages illustrating the idea that men only
have a just title to their basic needs.
    [9] Op. cit., pp. 27 ff. This is, I think, an instance of the way in which these two
scholars tend to introduce Augustinian ideas into a context which they do not really fit.
    [10] *Summa*, II. II, q. 10 a. 10. "Kynde Witte" and "Reason" in *Piers Plowman* are,
as T. P. Dunning points out (pp. 39–40) , very close in meaning, and both are nearer
to modern "Conscience" than modern "Reason," since both imply knowledge of right
and wrong.

which is the law of grace, does not abolish the human law.][11] According to Langland, Law in this sense is linked to *Lewte,* and, beyond noting that, in my opinion, *Lewte* is something of which he approves very strongly indeed, it will be best to leave the translation of this term for the moment.

The puzzling phrase "eche man to knowe his owne" supplies the object of the creation of Law. Donaldson thought that it meant "so that each man might know his own place," that is, his position and duties in society. This fits the general context well, since it is the organization of the State that is in question, but I think that the immediate context, with its mention of Law, and the duty of the community to see to the provision of the body's necessities, calls for something a little different. This impression is reinforced when we remember the passage in which Holy Church comments on the needs of the body. It would, I think, be more natural to take *his owne* as "his own property," that is, the material things which, by Law and *Lewte,* can justifiably be considered a man's own. This, as T. P. Dunning has shown, is very much the problem with which Holy Church is concerned in Passus i.[12]

St. Thomas, too, is concerned with the relation of the holding of property to the organization of society. For the management of external things, he says, it is necessary to have "the power of getting and of distributing"—two activities which are certainly of importance in the Prologue, and which become personified in the good Plowman who later undertakes the organization of society's physical needs. And to this end "licitum est quod homo propria possideat" [it is lawful for man to possess property]. It is even necessary because, among other reasons, "per hoc magis pacificus status hominum conservatur, dum unusquisque re sua contentus est." [13] A society made peaceful because each man is content with his own, seems to correspond closely to the kingdom in which, as a result of the establishment of Law and *Lewte,* "each man knows ('acknowledges,' 'accepts') his own."

"*Lewte*" and "Law" are now picked up by the three figures who advise the King: the Lunatic, the Angel, and the Goliardeys, whose advice has been interpreted as ironical, or as flattery. Setting aside for the moment the problem of what the three figures mean, it seems to me worth considering whether what they say could not be taken at its face value, and

11 On the relation of human Law to natural Law, and the "lumen rationis naturalis quo discernimus quid sit bonum et quid malum" [the light of natural reason whereby we perceive what is good and what is evil], see *Summa,* I. II, q. 91 a. 2–3.

12 Op. cit., pp. 31 ff.

13 *Summa,* II. II, q. 66 a. 2.

whether it is not a development of what is clearly the leading idea in this part of the poem, the relation of King and Comune to law.

The words of the Lunatic are, after all, unexceptionable:

> Crist kepe the, sire kyng, and thi kyngriche,
> And leue the lede thi londe so leute the louye,
> And for thi riȝtful rewlyng be rewarded in heuene.
>
> (125–27)

They are in fact a terse summary (whether Langland knew it or not) of St. Thomas's discussion of the proper rewards of kingship. Worldly riches are naturally to be rejected—the desire for them is sinful: even honour and glory, though nearer to virtue, would be a poor reward and an insufficient motive for good rule. He concludes that the bliss of heaven is the only proper reward for a good king.[14] There is no irony in the Lunatic's speech as it stands, and certainly no flattery. Nor need there be irony in the immediate transition to the problem of the restraint of a bad king in the fable that follows; this is, in fact, a standard subject in any treatise on Government. The *de Regimine* devotes some space to the question, and it is impossible to suspect St. Thomas of ironical intentions. His conclusion, too, is precisely that of Langland's fable.[15]

One other point from the Lunatic's speech must be noted here: it introduces, in the word *lede,* an idea which is to become increasingly important in the *Visio.* This idea of the "leader" in relation to Love and Law is developed in a way that is, I think, original to Langland, but he could have found the suggestion for it in the *de Regimine:* St. Thomas is fond of speaking of the King as directing, or steering (he compares him to the steersman of a ship), the realm in the right direction, that is towards the common good.[16]

The Angel who speaks from heaven can certainly not be suspected either of flattering the King or of in any other way giving him bad advice. It is, I think, best to interpret the reference to the common people:

> for lewed men ne coude
> Iangle ne iugge, that iustifie hem shulde . . .
>
> (129–30)

as meaning that the Angel speaks on behalf of those who cannot speak

---

[14] *De Regimine,* i. 7 ff. I quote from A. P. d'Entrèves's edition of Book I (*Aquinas: Selected Political Writings* [Oxford, 1959], pp. 36 ff.) .

[15] *De Reg.,* i. 6 (d'Entrèves, pp. 28 ff.) : the deposition of a tyrant, even if justified, is bad as it may cause strife and discord among the populace (cf. Prol. 195 ff.) and there is a danger that the tyrant will be followed by a worse one (Prol. 185 ff.) .

[16] *De Reg.,* i. 1 and 2 (d'Entrèves, pp. 2 and 10) ; but these are commonplaces.

for themselves.[17] In fact, I think that the Angel's speech follows logically on that of the Lunatic and indicates the way in which the King can so "lead his land" as to gain the proper reward of a good rule. Now, the Angel simply reminds the King of the end towards which his actions should be directed: the justice which he administers should be compatible with the "special laws of Christ the King" (Skeat's translation), and this means that human justice must be administered with mercy.[18] This is, of course, a legal commonplace. St. Thomas, quoting the *Digest,* makes the point clear:

> Sicut supra dictum est, omnis lex ordinatur ad communem hominum salutem, et intanto obtinet vim et rationem legis; secundum vero quod ab hoc deficit, virtutem obligandi non habet. Unde Iurisperitus dicit quod "nulla iuris ratio ut aequitatis benignitas patitur ut quae salubriter pro utilitate hominum introducuntur, ea nos duriori interpretatione, contra ipsorum commodum, perducamus ad severitatem." [19]
>
> [As was stated above, every law is directed toward the common welfare of men, and derives the force and nature of law accordingly; but if it fails in this aim, it has no binding power. Hence the Jurist says that "by no reason of law, or favor of equity, is it allowable for us to interpret harshly, and render burdensome, those useful measures which have been enacted for the welfare of men."]

Thus the King has been promised heaven as a reward if he rules well; he has been given conventional advice about the administration of Law, and it remains for the third speaker to raise a point which often occupied the minds of political theorists: the King is in a sense above Law, since he is the source of Law in the community. How then is he to be restrained and persuaded to submit to Law? This problem is perfectly clearly expressed in the words of the Goliardeys: the King takes his very being from the act of ruling—that is, of providing and administering Law:

> rex a regere dicatur nomen habere

but he would be no true King—he would have the name without the

---

[17] So G. R. Owst, "The 'Angel' and the 'Goliardeys' of Langland's Prologue," *M.L.R.,* II (1925), 270. Owst identifies the King's three advisers with contemporary figures, including the poet, and the undoubted presence of topical allusions in this part of the poem is a complicating factor. I have left it out of consideration here because I do not think that Langland intended more than a passing glance at current events, and the identification of these references does not affect the development of his ideas.

[18] I do not think that there is any doubt that *pietas* here means "mercy." See Donaldson, *Piers Plowman: the C-Text and its Poet,* p. 114 and n. 1.

[19] *Summa,* I. II, q. 96 a. 6. The quotation is from the *Digest,* I. iii. 25 (Modestinus).

thing itself ("nomen habet sine re") —unless he fulfilled his obligation
to keep the Law ("nisi studet iura tenere") . This is not flattery, nor is it
irony. It is simply a statement of the generally accepted principle that,
although no one else can restrain a King legally, he himself should voluntarily accept the restraint of the Law. Again, St. Thomas puts the position clearly:

> princeps dicitur esse solutus a lege, quantum ad vim coactivam legis;
> nullus enim proprie cogitur a seipso; lex autem non habet vim coac-
> tivam nisi ex principis potestate. . . . Unde quantum ad Dei iudi-
> cium, princeps non est solutus a lege, quantum ad vim directivam
> eius; sed debet voluntarius, non coactus, legem implere.[20]
> [The sovereign is said to be exempt from the law, as to the coercive
> power of the law, for, in a proper sense, no man is coerced by him-
> self; and law, moreover, has no coercive power except through the
> authority of the sovereign. . . . Hence, in the judgment of God, the
> sovereign is not exempt from the law, as to its directive force; but he
> should follow the law voluntarily, not under compulsion.]

But we do not even need to go to St. Thomas for formulations of these
ideas. There are other, more popular sources, of a kind which Langland
must certainly have known.

The advice of the Lunatic is, in fact, very like some versions of the
opening formula of the *Secreta Secretorum*. It is hardly likely that a poet
with Langland's interests did not know some version of this extremely
popular work, though most of the surviving English ones are later than
Piers Plowman. One of these begins thus:

> God almyȝty kepe oure kynge to ioye of his ligeys, and make fast his
> kyngdome to defende þe lawe of god, and make hym dwellynge to
> enhye þe worschipe and louynge of gode men.[21]

Another version lays stress on the King's duty to administer the laws
rightly,[22] and all insist on the need for virtue and the rule of reason in
the King: this indeed is the purpose of the whole work.

The advice of the Goliardeys is closely paralleled in the English coronation oath. In the Latin form: Concedis iustas leges et consuetudinis
esse tenendas . . . ?" [Do you grant that just laws and customs will be preserved . . . ?], and in the French: "Sire, graunte vous a tenir et garder le

---

[20] *Summa*, I. II, q. 96 a. 5. Here, too, St. Thomas is reproducing established legal
opinion. This time he quotes from the *Codex*, I. xiv. 4.

[21] *Three Prose Versions of the Secreta Secretorum*, ed. R. Steele, E.E.T.S., E.S., lxxiv
(1898) , p. 47, 1–4.

[22] *Ibid.*, p. 127, 34 ff.

Loys, et les custumes droitureles, les quiels la Communauté de vostre Roiaume aura esleu?" [Sire, do you agree to keep and preserve the Law and the righteous customs, which the Community of your Realm will have elected?][23]

The kind of punning poem attributed to the Goliardeys is, too, as Skeat pointed out, quite common;[24] all turn on the need to persuade the King to rule in accordance with Law.

Donaldson, following C. Brett,[25] considered that the Goliardeys contradicts the Angel, and urges "nudum ius" [naked justice] on the King. This, however, could hardly be the meaning of *iura tenere;* it means "preserve," "guard" the Law, as it does in the coronation oath. The difficulty lies in the introductory lines. The Goliardeys "greued hym," and this could be taken as "angered the angel," to whom he makes answer. I would suggest taking "greued hym" as reflexive, referring to the Goliardeys himself, who, made angry by an obvious omission, hastens to make it good, and in this sense "answers" the Angel. True, on this interpretation the reaction of the Goliardeys seems over-emphatic, but I think that we can find a tendency to over-emphasis of this kind elsewhere in the poem.[26]

The words of the Commons "Precepta Regis sunt nobis vincula legis" [The king's decrees are the chains of law to us] have usually been interpreted as ironically intended—Skeat, for instance, remarked "they know just as much (Latin) as is good for them." Certainly, as the fable shows, the lot of the Commons will depend on the extent to which the King follows Conscience and Reason in the interpretation of the Law of which he is the fountain-head, but their words are, as a matter of fact, another legal commonplace. They paraphrase a sentence of the *Digest,* "Quod principi placuit legis habet vigorem" [What is pleasing to the sovereign has the force of law] (I. iv, I, Ulpianus) . St. Thomas explains this dictum in terms which are curiously near the edge of allegory:

> Ratio habet vim movendi a voluntate, ut supra dictum est: ex hoc enim quod aliquis vult finem, ratio imperat de his quae sunt ad finem. Sed voluntas de his quae imperantur, ad hoc quod legis ra-

23 Quoted and discussed by Donaldson, *Piers Plowman: the C-Text and its Poet,* p. 106. He does not, however, interpret the speech of the Goliardeys in relation to it.

24 Cf. especially "Nomen habes sine re, nisi te recteque regas, rex" [O king, you have the name without the thing itself unless you rule properly] (T. Wright, *Political Poems* [London, 1859–61], i. 278) , and "Non a regnando rex est, sed iure regendo" [Not by exercising royal authority is there a king, but by ruling rightly] (*ibid.,* i. 57) . Cf. Gower, *Confessio Amantis,* vii. 3067 ff., esp. 3073–5, which also looks like a paraphrase of a verse of this kind.

25 "Notes on Old and Middle English," *M.L.R.,* xxii (1927) , 261.

26 Cf. x. 3: Study "was wonderly wroth"; A. xii, 12: Scripture "skornfully . . . set vp here browes" (cf. B. xi, 1–2) .

tionem habeat, oportet quod sit aliqua ratione regulata. Et hoc
modo intelligitur quod voluntas principis habet vigorem legis: alio-
quin voluntas principis magis esset iniquitas quam lex.[27]
[Reason has the power of moving from the will, as was stated above:
for it is due to the fact that someone wills the end, that the reason
issues its commands concerning things ordained to the end. But in
order that the volition of what is commanded may have the nature
of law, it needs to be in accord with some rule of reason. And in this
sense it is understood that the will of the sovereign has the force of
law: otherwise, the will of the sovereign would be more so injustice
than law.]

The Commons, thus, are not sweeping aside what has already been said
about the King and Law, but are merely restating the case by using the
formula best adapted to their particular position within the State.

It is natural enough to follow their words with a fable which shows
what happens when the Prince's will becomes "magis iniquitas quam
lex" [more injustice than law].

In the C-text the King and Conscience go straight to the law-courts
where, apparently, they hear the case of the mice and the cat. This, I
think, is one of C's less happy alterations, though it does serve to emphasize the importance of the relation of the King to Law. In B the reference
to the lawyers and the courts stands after the fable, and is not directly
connected to it; but it is connected through its phrasing with the earlier
passage on Law and the King:

> Seriauntz...
> Pleded for penyes and poundes the lawe
> And nought for loue of owre lorde vnlese here lippes onis.
> (211–13)

[Sergeants ... plead the law for pennies and pounds, and never once
did they unlock their lips out of love for our Lord.]

We have already seen that Law should be such that it earns the *Loue of
Lewte* and that it should be in accordance with the Law of God. But we
still might be tempted to think that lawyers are entitled to a fair profes-
sional fee. Minstrels may "get gold with here gle synneles" (Prol. 34), the
circulation of money by merchants is allowed by Conscience: "It is a per-

---

27 *Summa*, I. II, q. 90 a. I. For a brief discussion of St. Thomas's position on the commonly debated question of the King's relation to Law, see d'Entrèves, *Aquinas: Selected
Political Writings,* pp. xxvii ff. Langland does not use any phrases resembling such formulas as "princeps legibus solutus" [the sovereign exempt from laws] (*Summa,* I. II, q.
90 a. I, &c.) or Bracton's "Lex facit Regem" [Law makes the King].

mutacioun apertly, a penyworth for an othre" [It is simply a mutation, one pennyworth for another] (B. iii, 256) . Why then is there no fair hire for lawyers? The answer is, because Law, since it arises through natural reason out of the very nature of man as a social animal,[28] with the function above all of ensuring the proper working of the community, is something which is the due of every man, and to withhold this due until payment should be produced is, in Langland's view, comparable to withholding man's daily bread. This becomes even clearer if we compare the passage on lawyers in Passus vii where their share in the Pardon of Piers Plowman is debated, especially in the lines:

> Ac to bugge water, ne wynde, ne witte, ne fyre the fierthe,
>   [Do not sell water nor wind nor wit nor fire]
> Thise foure the fader of heuene made to this folde in comune;
> Thise ben treuthes tresores trewe folke to helpe,
> That neuere shal wax ne wanye withoute god hymselue.

>   (52–55)

This is a paraphrase of Holy Church's speech of i, 12 ff., and echoes her often-repeated formula of the "treasure of truth." In Passus i Holy Church says that Truth "hyȝte the erthe to help ȝow vchone" [has commanded the earth to provide for all men] and goes on to speak of the three things, food, drink, and clothing, which arise from the cultivation of the earth, and are "in common" to all mankind. To say that Truth has provided the four elements in common is to say much the same thing, since it is of the four elements that the Creator has compounded the world and all that is in it. But here Langland adds a further twist to his paraphrase by inserting into the familiar list of the four elements something which does not belong there, but which he has already established as bearing a natural relation to that other great provision of the Creator which all men should enjoy in common: viz. Law.[29]

Before we come to consider the allegorical development in the Meed episode of a plot very like that sketched out by St. Thomas, we must examine one more passage on the theme of Law and Love. In this Holy Church links them to the idea of the leader, which was already briefly indicated in the passage on the King.

> For-thi is loue leder of the lordes folke of heuene,
> And a mene as the maire is bitwene the kyng and the comune;

[28] See, e.g., *de Reg.*, i. i (d'Entrèves, pp. 2 ff.) ; *Summa,* i. ii, q. 96 a. 4.

[29] "Wit" here is, I think, the Kynde Wit of Pr. 121, and we are again reminded of "ius humanum quod est ex naturali ratione" [human law, which is derived from natural reason].

> Right so is loue a ledere and the lawe shapeth:
> Vpon man for his mysdedes the merciment he taxeth.[30]
>
>   (i, 157–60)

Love is a leader of God's people to heaven just as Moses was the leader of God's people to the promised land (the comparison is implied in line 149): thus here Love stands for Christ (of whom Moses is a type), as mediator between God and Man. So, in the earthly state, the mayor is mediator between King and Commons, and by these intermediaries human and divine Law is "modified."

The whole passage is particularly rich in word-play and word association. For the moment, however, we must restrict ourselves to its contribution to the ideas connected with Law, and only note in passing the introduction of the mayor as *mene* (cf. ii, 76), and the pun in *merciment,* followed by the repetition of *mercy, mekeli, meke* (i, 166, 168, 171, 173; cf. iv, 142 with its play on *mede, mercy, mekenesse*). *Merciment* is picked up later, at an important point, in Piers's address to the Knight in Passus vi:

> "Loke ȝe tene no tenaunt, but Treuthe wil assent.
> And thowgh ȝe mouwe amercy hem, late Mercy be taxoure,
> And Mekenesse thi mayster, maugre Medes chekes. . . ."
>
>   (38–41)

Knights, Lords, "ȝow Riche," are for Langland the executors of the Law, either for the protection or persecution of the poor. For Langland this is the concrete reality of all abstract theory about the State, and almost all his statements about Love and Law end with the relation of Rich and Poor, Powerful and Weak.[31]

The Prologue and Passus i have thus established the importance of the theme of Law, its association with love and mercy and, through the idea of the Leadership of the King, has instituted a comparison between divine and earthly Kingship and Law. These ideas, and even the words in which Langland expresses them, are neither original nor "advanced." They belong to accepted legal and political theory and some of the formulas Langland uses can be traced to such standard sources as the *Digest* and *Codex.*

---

30 Holy Church's reference to love as "shaping the law" is reminiscent of the *Divina Commedia* (*Paradiso,* vi. 11–12) on Justinian "che, per voler del primo amor ch' i' sento, d'entro le leggi trassi il troppo e 'l vano" [who, by the will of the Primal Love that I feel, drew from the laws the superfluous and the useless]. Langland's *shapeth* seems likely in the context to mean "modify." The same idea is found in Jean de Meun's *Roman de la Rose:* Justice without love would destroy too much (ll. 5549–50).

31 Cf. B. i, 173 ff. (the conclusion of Holy Church's speech on Love and Leadership); xi, 152–53 (the moral of the story of Trajan, cf. 165 ff.); xiv, 145 ff.

II

In the episode of Lady Meed the King is again an important figure, and the theme of Law is further developed. The first lines describing Meed, it is true, show her as active throughout society, but as the episode continues she is only actually seen in contact with: Lawyers and "clerkes" employed in legal affairs (iii, 12 ff.) ; Friars as confessors (iii, 76 ff.) ,[32] "Meires and maceres that menes ben bitwene The kynge and the comune to kepe the lawes" [mayors and officers, who are the means conjoining the king and the people in keeping the laws] (iii, 76 ff.) ; and purveyors of food, whom she attempts to corrupt through the mayors, and who deal in a basic, common property of mankind. Meed is finally defeated through the operation of the law in the case of Peace and Wrong, which is tried before the King.

The False who is pointed out by Holy Church as Truth's opposite and Meed's associate is not evil in general, although the Tower of Falsehood was certainly the Devil's stronghold. He relates, rather, to the False Life, as Truth does to the True Life, that is to a life directed not towards God's reward for man in heaven, but towards the temporary advantages of the world seized without thought of the welfare of one's neighbour. That Langland should marry Meed to a False of this kind is not surprising. He had, like St. Thomas, developed a theory concerning temporal goods in which, as we have seen, the cardinal sin against society becomes the exploitation for personal advantage of what God has ordained, as a means towards a clearly defined end, for the common benefit. Meed herself stands for this reward of the False Life, won by the perversion of God's gifts. She is thus "False Reward" in a very specialized sense. She is not merely "wealth"; not merely "the power of the purse," and not, in fact, "cupidity" though she must always call cupidity into being: she is the reward of a life directed to the wrong end.

The opponents of Meed, therefore, use two arguments to confound her. First, that there is a just use of necessary material goods in society. Langland, like St. Thomas, recognizes that in a developed society this legitimately goes further than the bare provision of food, drink, and clothing. Both justify the activity of the merchant.[33]

Secondly, the true and only worth-while reward available to mankind, the goal of the True Life, is God's reward—"do wel and haue wel." This is the good Meed of Theology's speech (ii, 114 ff.) and of Conscience's rebuke to the King. Theology's speech is a riddling one—for Langland it

---

[32] Langland seems to regard Confession as comparable to Law in that it is also a provision of the Creator to mankind in common. Cf. Prol. 64.

[33] iii, 255 ff. and vii, 18 ff.; cf. *Summa*, II. II. q. 77 a. 4.

is "no science, for sothe for to sotyle inne" (x, 183) —but her ambiguities are firmly resolved by Conscience, a plain man, and the King's faithful guide: "There aren two manere of medes, my lorde, with ӡoure leue" (iii, 230).

The episode of Meed begins with an attempt to introduce disorder among the people of the Field as a whole. It soon becomes centred on the person of the King. If he succumbs to temptation the destruction of society is assured. As Morton W. Bloomfield says, "the king as the key to the political problem is a favorite subject of medieval admonition." [34] For Langland the successful restraint of the King by Conscience and Reason is, essentially, the fulfilment of the coronation oath and the Goliardic advice of the B Prologue. "I wil haue leute in lawe" (iv, 180) is both the triumphant conclusion to the debate and the starting-point of the good kingdom.

The episode of Lady Meed and the King is, then, devoted to a further consideration of the problems raised in the B Prologue and in Holy Church's sermon. The fundamental question is still how the State can be organized so as to fulfil its function of enabling men to live the True Life with its reward from God. Like other political writers Langland sees the King as the key figure, and his main concern is, therefore, with the problems and temptations of the King. These largely concern his relationship to Law, and to the Commons, by whose assent he rules, for good or ill.

The first reference to Law and *Lewte* in the Meed episode is an important and measured statement, with the authority of Holy Church behind it:

> "That is Mede the mayde," quod she, "hath noyed me ful oft,
> And ylakked my lemman that Lewte is hoten,
> And bilowen hire to lordes that lawes han to kepe."
> ["That is Meed the maiden," she said, "who has injured me often,
> slandering my dear friend Honesty and lying to the lords who have
> to keep the laws."]

> (ii, 20–22)

Her meaning is clear: through the temptations of Meed the natural guardians of Law, the "lordes," betray their trust, and *Lewte,* here exalted as the "lemman" of Holy Church, is brought into disrepute. A possible breach between Law and *Lewte* is implied here, with "lords" on one side, and "love" (implied in "lemman") , on the other.

Theology's riddling speech makes no mention of *Lewte* or Law,

---

[34] *Piers Plowman as a Fourteenth Century Apocalypse* (New Brunswick, 1961), p. 110.

though it emphasizes the link between God's reward and Truth (= the True Life, 1. 119) , and stresses the important text *"dignus est operarius* [the laborer is worthy] his hyre to haue." The true-living labourer whose hire is justified is a figure we shall meet again.

In Conscience's great speech in the next passus the ideal rule is described under which Meed is banished, and Love, Lowness, and *Lewte* control human affairs:

> Shal na more Mede be maistre, as she is nouthe,
> Ac loue and lowenesse and lewte togederes,
> Thise shul be maistres on molde treuthe to saue.
> And who-so trespasseth ayein treuthe or taketh aȝein his wille,
> Leute shal don hym lawe, and no lyf elles.
> Shal no seriaunt for here seruyse were a sylke howue,
> Ne no pelure in his cloke for pledying atte barre.
> [No longer shall lawyers wear a silk hood in their service,
> Nor fix fur on their robes for pleading at the bar.]
> Mede of mysdoeres maketh many lordes,
> And ouer lordes lawes reuleth the rewmes.
> Ac kynde loue shal come ȝit, and conscience togideres,
> And make of lawe a laborere, suche loue shal arise,
> And such a pees amonge the peple and a perfit trewthe,
> That Iewes shal wene in here witte and waxen wonder glade.
> That Moises or Messie be come into this erthe,
> And haue wonder in here hertis that men beth so trewe.
>
> (iii, 288–302)

Meekness, "lowenese," is to replace mastery, that is might as right; the human exponents of Law, the actual lawyers and "lords" will act in accordance with Truth (the requirements of the True Life) ; *Lewte* will control the administration of Law, and will render it like the true humble labourer whose hire is justified. All this will lead to such a state of peace and hope that it will seem as if Moses had come to lead the people to the promised land, or rather that greater figure, the Messiah whom Moses typifies. We have already, in Holy Church's speech in Passus i, seen Moses used to stand for the greatest of all mediations, that between the strictness of the Law of God and His people, just as the mayor mediates between the human King and his.

The next important contribution to the theme of Love, Law, and *Lewte* is in Reason's speech to the King, but there are one or two minor references which it will be best to take first. In iv, 33 ff. Conscience, speaking to Reason, emphasizes the opposition of Meed to Love and *Lewte*. Wisdom and Witty, he says,

> with Mede thei dwelleth;
> There as wratthe and wranglyng is there wynne thei siluer,
> Ac there is loue and lewte thei wil nouȝte come there. . . .
>   (33–35)

Wisdom and Witty, in contrast to the good "wisdome and witt" of Theology's speech (ii, 133 ff.), stand for the misuse of the Wit which Langland places in his list of the elements, and considers a part of God's endowment to mankind in common. The figures are linked to the mercenary lawyers of the Prologue by the wording of the lines that follow:

> For, wot god, thei wolde do more for a dozeine chikenes . . .
> Than for loue of owre lorde or alle hise leue seyntes.
>   (37, 39)

Again, Wrong's words at iv, 66 gain irony from the chain of associations which has by now been established. Wrong, faced with a lawsuit, hopes to get the "loue of my lorde thy kynge." In such a context love suggests a kind of law which would hardly suit Wrong, though the law that he does want is by now firmly associated with "lords."

Reason, consulted by the King over the case of Wrong's assault on Peace, sums up epigrammatically what Conscience has already said:

> . . . Lawe shal ben a laborere, and lede a-felde donge,
> And Loue shal lede thi londe, as the lief lyketh.
>   (iv, 147–48)

Law is to become the Labourer whose hire is justified, and whose function is, like that of the good plowmen of the Prologue, to ensure the provision of the basic necessities of the True Life. The King is to delegate even the "leadership," which for Langland expresses his true relationship to his people, to Love, whose function, as we have seen, is one of mediation between Law, whether human or divine, and the people.

Meed makes a final attempt to rally the men of law on her behalf, but the King agrees with the judgement pronounced by Love and *Lewte* in person:

> Loue lete of hir liȝte and Lewte ȝit lasse,
> And seide it so heiȝe that al the halle it herde. . . .
>   (iv, 161–62)

The King has now only to express his assent, which he does in the formula: "I wil haue leute in lawe, and lete be al ȝowre Ianglyng!" (iv, 180). Conscience, however, reminds him that his obligation towards Law includes a respect for that assent of the Commons through which he became King:

> Quod Conscience to the Kynge, "but the comune will assent,
> It is ful hard, bi myn hed here-to to brynge it."
>
> (182–83)

Conscience belongs to the King as an individual. Reason, however, is God's common endowment to mankind; and through it (as Kynde Witte), Law and State arose in the first place. Rule according to Reason must, therefore, ensure the "assent of the commons," and Reason duly asserts: "But if I reule thus ʒowre rewme, rende out my guttes!" (186). The passus ends with the compact between the King, Reason, and Conscience: "Als longe as owre lyf lasteth, lyue we togideres" (195), and we are brought back, with our ideas much enlarged, to the statement of the Prologue,

> The kynge and the comune, and kynde witte the thridde,
> Shope lawe and lewte, eche man to knowe his owne.
>
> (121–22)

But we have left *Lewte* untranslated long enough. Before we look at Langland's idea of it in action, it is time to try to define what he meant by it.

III

The activities of Lady Meed and her upholders have been directed against Law and *Lewte,* and *Lewte* has been paired with Love in effective opposition to her. These two, it seems, are the forces which ensure that the State performs its true function. It is clear, therefore, that Langland's *Lewte* implies a breadth and importance of meaning which enables us to rule out at once a translation like "strict adherence to the letter of the law." [35]

"Loyalty," "fidelity," [36] even in their sometimes limited modern senses, are important virtues whose neglect is certainly fatal to the good order of society, yet they do not really give a modern reader the sense of Langland's *Lewte.* We can speak of a "misplaced loyalty," or of "loyalty to a

[35] Donaldson, *Piers Plowman: the C-text and its Poet,* p. 66, n. 4. Cf. J. J. Lawlor, *Piers Plowman* (London, 1962), p. 31, "*lewte,* scrupulous regard for law" (but, "lewte in lawe, steadfast compliance with justice," p. 40).

[36] So Skeat, though he distinguishes other senses: see the glossary to his edition. H. W. Wells, *The Vision of Piers Plowman* (London, 1938), and N. Coghill, *Visions from Piers Plowman* (London, 1949), both use "loyalty" in their translations.

bad cause." We are accustomed to see "clashes of loyalty," and would feel no surprise to find loyalty to the State on one side, loyalty to the Church on the other. This would not do for Langland.

"Justice," in view of the constant linking of *Lewte* and Law seems more hopeful,[37] but "justice" has more than one meaning and it needs careful definition if it is to serve a useful purpose as a rendering of *Lewte*, as the hesitation of its supporters shows, and before accepting it, it will be best to look closely at Middle English usage outside *Piers Plowman*.

Lewte was never a common nor, probably, an unlearned word in Middle English, but it does occur in contexts which throw an interesting light on Langland's usage.[38]

In *Cursor Mundi* God promises to save Noah "for ȝour treu leute." [39] Now Noah was not saved because he was particularly "loyal," nor because he was a strict legalist, but because, in contrast to an evil and corrupt generation, he was "vir iustus atque perfectus" [a just and perfect man] (Gen. vi. 9). In fact, as St. Thomas would have put it, he "lived well," or in Langland's terminology "did well," or lived the True Life, and so earned God's reward. *Lewte* here, therefore, stands for a virtuous way of life, and has a general rather than a particular sense.

In Barbour's *Bruce, Lewte* occurs again in a famous passage which is headed in Skeat's edition for the Early English Text Society "the praise of fidelity." Yet if we take fidelity in any accepted modern sense, the passage would imply a surprising limited scale of values. Barbour is praising the Douglas, and after a list of his virtues which culminates in the statement "And our all thing luffyt lawte," he breaks off to praise "lawte" itself:

> Leavte to luff is gretumly;
> Throuch leavte liffis men rychtwisly:
> With A wertu [of] leavte
> A man may ȝeit sufficyand be:
> And but leawte may nane haiff price,
> Quhethir he be wycht or he be wys;

[37] See R. W. Frank, *Piers Plowman and the Scheme of Salvation* (New Haven, 1957); Bloomfield, op. cit., p. 109, "integrity and justice, perhaps."

[38] See *O.E.D.*, s.v., "Lewty," "Lawty." Curiously, the examples from *Piers Plowman* were not included. There is interesting material in the English *Secreta* versions, but as these are all later than *Piers Plowman*, and as the thought in them is confused and needs careful analysis, I have left them out of consideration. In romances *Lewte* tends to be emptied of meaning and is used in tag phrases, "by or for my, thy (&c.) lewty" = "by, my (thy) truth." When it is meaningful, as in *Gawain and the Green Knight*, 2366, 2381 (cf. *Testament of Cresseide*, 547), the sense ("faithkeeping," "faithfulness") is nearer to modern "loyalty."

[39] MS. Göttingen 1655. Cotton and Trinity omit "treu." Fairfax reads "for þi riȝ-twisnes and þi lewte."

The episode about Lady Meed in *Piers Plowman,* says A. G. Mitchell, reaches "a satisfying conclusion both on the human plane of the story and the allegorical plane. . . . In a dramatic and colourful story the great questions about Meed have been raised, thrashed out, and settled." The initial description of Lady Meed in the A-text appears in the first seventeen lines reproduced here from the Vernon Manuscript.

Courtesy of the Bodleian Library, Oxford

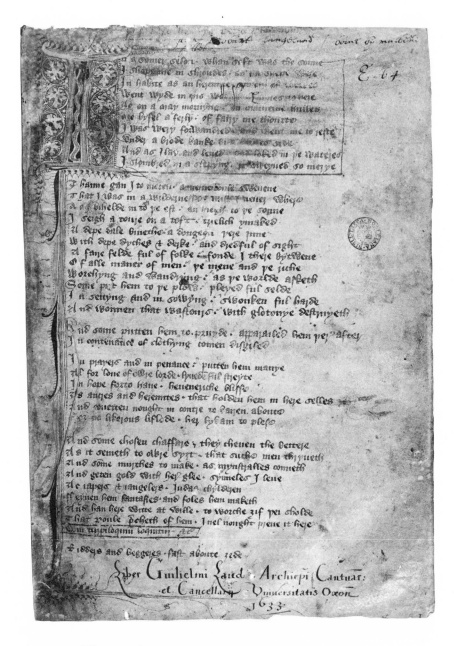

The opening lines of the Prologue to *Piers Plowman*
in the B-text, describing the dreamer and his
vision, are elegantly illuminated in the
first folio of MS. Laud Misc. 581.

Courtesy of the Bodleian Library, Oxford

For quhar It failӡeys, na wertu
May be off price, na off valu,
To mak A man sa gud, that he
May symply gud man callyt be.
(i, 365–74)

In the context, of course, faithkeeping, and the loyal relationship of master and man are important, and Barbour goes on to stress these aspects.[40]
Nevertheless, virtue through which men "live righteously" and whose
presence is needed to "mak A man sa gud, that he/May symply gud man
callyt be" suggests the same kind of well-doing which entitles Noah to be
called *perfectus*.

To sum up, *Lewte* in Middle English can stand for virtue, for living
well, in a wide sense. In the case of Noah in the *Cursor Mundi* the word
has no political implications, but in the *Bruce* (and in the *Secreta* versions), it is associated with man as a social animal. In all these instances
Lewte has a width of meaning which would justify even further exten-
sion in *Piers Plowman*. I think that Langland does, in fact, use it to represent a concept which was probably not in the minds of the other Middle English writers—though Barbour is perhaps an exception—but on
which *Lewte,* as they use it, impinges. This, I believe, is the Aristotelian
virtue of Justice, which would be familiar to a reader of St. Thomas.[41]

Now the Aristotelian Justice, as it is defined in the section of the *Nico-
machean Ethics* on which St. Thomas bases his discussion, is "complete
virtue, but not absolutely, but in relation to our neighbour. And therefore justice is often thought to be the greatest of virtues . . . and proverbially 'in justice is every virtue comprehended.' And it is complete virtue
in its fullest sense, because it is the actual exercise of complete virtue. . . .
Justice in this sense then, is not part of virtue but virtue entire, nor is
the contrary injustice a part of vice, but vice entire." [42]

This conception of justice, as distinct from "the justice which is a part
of virtue" (*Ethics,* v. ii. 1130ᵃ), could certainly be understood from the
Summa with its frequent quotations from *Ethics,* v. i, ii, &c., without direct recourse to the works of Aristotle. St. Thomas also cites another authority in Cicero, whose work was, presumably, more easily available
than Aristotle's. This is a paraphrase, from *de Officiis,* i. vii, of Aristotle's
remark in *Ethics,* v. i, which St. Thomas uses twice: "In iustitia virtutis
splendor est maximus, ex qua boni viri nominantur" [The greatest splen-

---

[40] Cf. i, 376 ff. See also xx, 516 ff. (the story of Fabricius, where *Lewte* is opposed to
actual treason). Even here Barbour is careful also to contrast it with wickedness in
general (551 ff.).

[41] See, e,g., *Summa,* II. II, q. 58.

[42] v. I. 1129ᵇ–1130ᵃ (tr. W. D. Ross, Oxford, 1925).

dor of virtue lies in justice from which quality good men are named].[43]
This looks very like Barbour's source for the final couplet of his praise of
Lewte.

The main points which Aristotle makes concerning this "justice in a
wide sense," and which St. Thomas reproduces, may be summed up as
follows: it is coextensive with virtue *(Ethics,* v. i, ii; *Summa,* ii. ii. q. 58 a.
5–6) ; it is virtue directed towards one's neighbor *(Ethics,* v. i; *Summa,*
ibid., a. 12) ; it is linked to Law because

> practically the majority of the acts commanded by the law are those
> which are prescribed from the point of virtue taken as a whole; for
> the law bids us practise every virtue and forbids us to practise any
> vice.[44]

Justice in this sense fits Langland's use of *Lewte* well. As *tota virtus*
[the whole of virtue] *(Summa,* ii. ii, q. 58 a. 6) , *praeclarissima virtutum*
[the most resplendent of the virtues] *(ibid.,* a. 12) it is a fitting "lemman" for Holy Church. It is also fittingly opposed to "vice entire," as far
as one's relation to one's neighbour is concerned, in the persons of False
and Lady Meed. It links naturally to Law, and, when the King, the Commons, and Kind Wit "Shope lawe and lewte, eche man to knowe his
owne," we can note that, if Law ensures the peaceful enjoyment of what
is rightly a man's own, it is the function of justice "reddere unicuique
quod suum est" [to render to each one what is his own] *(Summa,* ii. ii,
q. 58 a. 11) . The King's oath to have "leute in law" is thus the promise of
the good rule in the fullest possible sense.

In Conscience's speech *Lewte* is linked to peace, in a description which
to our ears sounds apocalyptic in tone,[45] and which suggests the millennium rather than any possible human political achievement. Yet here,
too, we can now see that we are within the normal frame of reference of
medieval political writing. The aim of the good rule, the result of the organization of the State in full accord with *justitia,* was peace. "The attainment of such 'unity of peace'—like the withering away of the state in
the Marxist millennium—would really have meant the abolition of politics altogether, at least in any modern sense of the word." [46] It is clear

43 *Summa,* ii. ii, q. 58 a. 12. Cf. q. 58 a. 3, where the same passage is quoted in a
slightly different form.
44 *Ethics,* v. ii. 1130[b], cf. 1129[b]; *Summa,* ii. ii, q. 58 a. 5.
45 So Bloomfield, op. cit., pp. 110 ff.
46 A. P. d'Entrèves, *Dante as a Political Thinker* (Oxford, 1952) , p. 31. Cf. Jean de
Meun's *Roman,* where the triumph of Love over Law and Justice (used in a more
limited sense than *Lewte* in *Piers Plowman*) results in the elimination of the State:

> paisible e quei
> Trestuit cil dou monde vivraient,
> Jamais rei ne prince n'avraient

that Conscience envisages just such a "withering away" of the State in the golden age presided over by *Lewte*. It is worth noting that Dante, too, was moved to extravagance of language by this conception. He wrote, in Epistle vii, of the Emperor not only as the restorer of justice and peace, but even as the new Messiah: "Then my spirit rejoiced within me, when I said secretly within myself: 'Behold the Lamb of God which taketh away the sins of the world.' " [47] It may well be, as d'Entrèves suggests, that Dante came to repent of this too particular identification of "the mission of a man with that of the divine Saviour," and Conscience certainly does not go so far; but for both Dante and Langland the ideal State and the ideal King are linked to the idea of the Messiah.

IV

Ad bonam autem unius hominis vitam duo requiruntur: unum principale, quod est operatio secundum virtutem (virtus enim est qua bene vivitur) ; aliud vero secundarium et quasi instrumentale, scilicet corporalium bonorum sufficientia, quorum usus est necessarius ad actum virtutis [Two things are required, moreover, for an individual man to lead a good life: the first and most important is to act in accordance with virtue (for virtue is that by which one lives well) ; the other requirement, which is secondary and instrumental, is namely a sufficiency of those bodily goods whose use is necessary for an act of virtue].[48]

This sentence makes a good summary of the final episodes of the *Visio*. Through the preaching of Repentance and the Confessions of the Sins the people of the Field are brought to face in the right direction for a life of virtue, represented by the pilgrimage to Truth which they are so anxious to undertake. The pilgrimage represents the True Life, the doing well of man the social animal. The Good Plowman, the Winner on whom society depends if it is to function at all, naturally knows the way, and his directions, though they serve as a guide to virtue in general, are

---

[. . . peaceful and quiet
All the inhabitants of this fair world would live;
They would never have any king or prince.]
(5556–8)

In the Bodley version of Mandeville, Alexander finds the virtuous inhabitants of the Isle of Bragman in the same situation (though they have a king) : "We han ouer us a kyng, not for no right to don to ne fro, for amongis vs no man doth othir wrong but as he wolde he dede to hym . . . And therfore from vs mayst thow reue nothing but pes" (ed. M. C. Seymour, E.E.T.S. 253 [1963], p. 115, ll. 9–13) .

47 D'Entrèves, *Dante as a Political Thinker*, p. 51.

48 *De Reg.*, i. 15 (*Aquinas: Selected Political Writings*, ed. d'Entrèves, p. 80) .

weighted on the side of good done to one's neighbour.[49] Further evidence
of the social nature of the pilgrimage is provided by the objectors to
Piers's directions: they are a "cutpurs," an "apeward," and a "wafreste"—
Wasters of the most obvious sort.

But Pilgrimage is preceded by ploughing and, in so far as the Ploughing of the Half-Acre represents the establishment of the State in accordance with *justitia,* a practical purpose meets with practical difficulties.
What these difficulties are St. Thomas tells us with precision. First, men
are mortal and may at times be genuinely incapable of playing their part
in the work of the community. Secondly:

> Aliud autem impedimentum boni publici conservandi ab interiori
> proveniens in perversitate voluntatum consistit, dum vel sunt de-
> sides ad ea peragenda quae requirit respublica, vel insuper sunt paci
> multitudinis noxii, dum transgrediendo iustitiam aliorum pacem
> peturbant [Another impediment to the preservation of the public
> good, coming from within, consists in the perversity of the wills of
> men, inasmuch as they are either too lazy to perform what the state
> demands, or, in addition, they are harmful to the peace of the mul-
> titude because, by transgressing justice, they disturb the peace of
> others].[50]

Finally, the State can be threatened by attack from outside. This last
problem does not arise for the Good Plowman, but he is concerned with
the other two. Much space is devoted to his need to distinguish between
those who, through their real infirmity, are in need of the State's support,
and the "perverse wills" who are trying to waste without doing their
share of winning.

When Repentance has done his work, the people are ready to start the
Good life ("virtus est enim qua bene vivitur" [for virtue is that by which
one lives well]) , but, since they are men, and man is a social animal, it
will be useless for them to "bluster forth as beasts." [51] They must first
find a guide who will show them how the social organization can help
them. It is here that the somewhat enigmatic figure of the Good Plowman steps in. It is clear that Piers is in charge of the provision of the
"sufficiency of material goods" which man needs, and thus stands as Reason did for an aspect of the activity of the Ruler of the State. But the
choice of the Plowman-Labourer to hold this position brings with it, of

49 Passus v, 568 ff. The route to Truth runs, of course, through the Ten Commandments, the sacrament of Confession, and the Seven Virtues. But cf. 589–91, where false-
swearing is linked to legal abuse, or 603 on alms-giving.

50 *De Reg.,* i. 15 (ed. cit., by d'Entrèves, p. 80) .

51 The comparison is significant. Cf. *de Reg.,* i. I. Man differs from all other animals
in naturally requiring a social organization.

necessity, a train of associations established by earlier passages. It links back to the Winner-Plowmen of the Prologue; to the labourer who is worthy of his hire, on whom so much of the argument between Meed and Conscience turns; and, finally, if in the ideal State Law is to become a labourer "to lede a-felde donge," the Good Plowman has, surely, something of that labourer too.

The result of this conversion of Law was, above all, to ensure that right relation of Rich and Poor which Langland sees as the heart of the political problem. Piers returns again and again to this relation; in his speech to the Knight, in all his dealings with Hunger, and especially when he speaks even of the Wasters as his "blody bretheren." This phrase places him as the mediator between Love and Law whom we have already seen compared to Moses and to the Messiah—as we recall later in the poem when we read that all mankind became the "blody bretheren" of Christ on Calvary (xi, 193 ff.), and how "blode may nouȝt se blode blede, but hym rewe" (xviii, 393).

Piers's opening speech in Passus v brings together the ideas of the True Life, under the guidance of Natural Reason and of Conscience; of the proper provision of the essential food and clothing of mankind;[52] of the labourer's justified hire and of the superabundance of God's reward to the good man ("and other wilesmore," 1. 557); of love and meekness ("as lowe as a lombe") in the treatment of the poor (ll. 558–60); and it keeps closely twined together the two threads which Langland twists through the *Visio,* of parallelism between earthly and heavenly justice.

> "Peter!" quod a plowman, and put forth his hed,
> "I knowe hym as kyndely as clerke doth his bokes;
> Conscience and Kynde Witte kenned me to his place,
> And deden me suren hym sikerly to serue hym for euere,
> Bothe to sowe and to sette, the while I swynke myghte . . .
> Ich haue myn huire of hym wel, and otherwhiles more;
> He is the prestest payer that pore men knoweth;
> He ne with-halt non hewe his hyre that he ne hath it at euen.
> He is as low as a lombe and loueliche of speche". . . .
>
> (v, 544–48, 557–60)

The contrast of true and false hire is once more pointedly made in the exchange between Piers and the would-be pilgrims. Piers, the worthy labourer who willingly takes the hire of Truth, expresses horror at the idea of payment for guiding the pilgrims to him:

> "ȝe, leue Pieres," quod this pilgrymes, and profered him huire,

---

52 Cf. ll. 552–55 of Piers's speech. A plowman is naturally concerned with the production of food, but not with that of cloth and the making of clothes.

> For to wende with hem to Treuthes dwellyng-place,
> "Nay, bi my soules helth," quod Pieres, and gan forto swere,
> "I nolde fange a ferthynge for seynt Thomas shryne!
> Treuthe wolde loue me the lasse a longe tyme thereafter!"
>
> (v, 563–67)

The idea that labour in the service of Truth is for love not hire is further developed in B. vi, in the Ploughing of the Half-Acre,[53] as is also the close association of this labour with the provision of the divinely ordained basic physical necessities of food and clothing.

Piers also directs the provision of what Langland regards as the other basic necessity to be enjoyed in common by mankind—Law. It is significant that his speech to the Knight is not concerned with the military function of his order (as we have already noted Langland does not deal with the threat to the good order of the State which comes from outside), but with its duty to maintain Law. Lines 38 ff. in Passus vi urge on the Knight the necessity for Truth and Mercy in his dealings with the poor, that is, for *Justitia,* rather than a rigid interpretation of particular Law.[54] When the Knight is called into action to protect Piers's organization he threatens Waster not with the strong arm but with Law:

> Curteisly the knyȝte thanne, as his kynde wolde,
> Warned Wastoure, and wissed hym bettere,
> "Or thow shalt abugge by the lawe, by the ordre that I bere!"
>
> (vi, 166–68)

In fact, Waster is subdued not by the Knight, but by that natural order of things which is the cause of man's need for the State.

With the episode of the Pardon[55] Langland's direct concern with the State is near its end. The first Pardon, a lengthy allegorical document,[56] still relates to man in society. It deals with the separate occupations, first with those, lay and clerical, responsible for rule within the State (vii, 9 ff.) ; secondly with the merchants, whose position in society is justified, and even necessary, but who must perform good works as well (28 ff.).

[53] Cf. vi opening, especially 21, 27, and cf. vii, 62 f.

[54] The phrasing shows that he has Law in mind: for *amercy* . . . *Mercy* see above, p. 249; the presents suggest passages like Prol. 210 ff.; cf. vii, 48 ff.

[55] The many problems of this episode have been ably discussed elsewhere, and are beyond my present scope. See, especially, N. Coghill, "The Pardon of Piers Plowman," (Sir Israel Gollancz Memorial Lecture), *British Academy Proceedings,* xxx (1944), 303 ff. [see above, pp. 40–86], and R. W. Frank, "The Pardon Scene in *Piers Plowman," Speculum,* xxvi (1951) , 317 ff., and *Piers Plowman and the Scheme of Salvation,* ch. 3.

[56] The discrepancy between this and the Pardon "al in two lynes" does not really need rationalization. The objects of allegory are frequently treated with this kind of freedom.

The lawyers, who come next, could be justified in the same way as the merchants. But Langland sees their position as a key one, and he is more emphatic as to the danger in which they stand: they will get no pardon at all if they abuse the common rights of man (39 ff., and especially 52–55). The True Living Labourers have exactly the same absolution as Piers himself (62–65) : that is, they are those who use the frame of society for its true purpose and lead the True Life fully ("virtus est qua bene vivitur"). Lastly, those who do not play their part in the community are considered at some length (66 ff.). The problem is discussed in the same terms as it was in the actual Ploughing scene. Society must support those who cannot support themselves, and, thus enabled to live the True Life, they will share in Piers's own Pardon. But the frauds, the "perverse wills," are to gain nothing from the State, although here, again, Law is tempered with mercy: it is not always possible for man to distinguish truth from falsehood:

For wite ȝe neuere who is worthi, ac god wote who hath nede.

(vii, 78)

After this, the Pardon which the Dreamer reads over Piers's shoulder, and which seems no Pardon to the Priest, is logical enough. The Good Life is not possible without the State, but, even when the State has been properly constituted, it remains for the individual to live well or ill. The promise of the Athanasian Creed to the Christian who seeks "How I may saue my soule" loses none of its force. "Dowel and haue wel" is no literal pardon, but it is nevertheless the end and justification of the political life.

A. P. d'Entrèves reminds us that "it has been said that there are no 'politics' of St. Thomas Aquinas," [57] and the warning is even more necessary in the case of Langland. For him, as for St. Thomas, politics are "a part of morals," and for him this is their only interest. But that, with these provisos, his interest is a keen one, and that he gives it effective expression through the formula "Love, Law, and *Lewte*" round which he builds up so much of the *Visio,* seems to me an inescapable conclusion.

[57] *Aquinas: Selected Political Writings,* p. viii.

8. Who is Piers Plowman?

HOWARD WILLIAM TROYER

I

PERHAPS NO CHARACTER in English Literature commissioned by his author to be the title bearer of his work has fulfilled his commission more effectively than Piers the Plowman. Even to the layman, ungiven to "Lettrure and longe studie," there is pleasant connotation in the name, while to the scholar, moving in the uncertainties of authorship and text, the title of Piers the Plowman and the central importance of his figure in the poem stand as one thing sure. Still one may ask questions. Just why should this poem of political and religious satire have been called the vision or book concerning Piers the Plowman? From the angle of his presence in the action of the poem, he is but a minor character. Conscience, Kynde Witte, and Longe Wille, any of them are more consistently recurrent. Just who is Piers anyway? And what is his significance in the poem?[1]

As with many another query in the field of English Literature, the answer may begin with Skeat. He, in the preface to his first edition of *Piers the Plowman,* summarized the significance of Piers as being in the *Visio* "no more than the type of ideal honest man . . . so dear to God the Father on account of his unswerving integrity and faithfulness that he is actually qualified to guide the pilgrims . . . on a search for Truth" and explained him in the *Vita* as the result of the author's perception "that the true guide to God the Father . . . had already come to men in the person of Jesus who must therefore be his true Piers." And though the central import of this interpretation has been accepted by subsequent writers on the poem, it is obvious to any reader of the work that it is somewhat inadequate. In the first place such an interpretation allows for only two of the multifarious rôles which Piers actually assumes throughout the poem. In the second place it suggests that there is an abrupt and definitive transition from the plowman of the earlier passus to the Christ

Reprinted by permission of the Modern Language Association from *PMLA*, XLVII (1932) , 368–84.

1 The author wishes to express his thanks to Dr. H. W. Wells of Columbia University for his valuable criticisms and suggestions in the preparation of this article.

of the later, a suggestion the text itself hardly warrants.[2] And more than either it makes no suggestion for any organic unity which might underlie the apparent variations and transitions of the rôle. Certainly Piers is something more in the *Visio* than merely an ideal honest laborer, and certainly in the *Vita* he is often something less than Christ. If his predominating rôle in the *Visio* is that of a plowman, he has at times, as we shall see, attributes rather of the overseer and landlord, of the civil and ecclesiastical ruler, of the saviour of man, and of the entire race itself. Nor are such attributes foreign to him in the *Vita*. If the most important designation here is the incarnate Son of God, the plowman Piers and the laborer, the ruler and ecclesiastic, the racial aggregate are not forgotten. And any formula attempting to establish the identity and significance of Piers must, to be adequate, allow not only for select aspects, important though they may be, but for all the diverse variants of this interesting rôle.

The question of who Piers is involves first of all the question of the unity or disparateness of these variants in the Piers symbol. Is he a plowman, a magistrate, the holy see, humanity, in a somewhat haphazard and confusing fashion, owing his varied forms merely to the undisciplined fancy of the author, who uses him when he thinks about it and then forgets about him at intervals, only to call him back in a new dress? Or is there in the conception of the Piers symbol an essential unity in which these varied aspects find logical existence and correlation?

There are two factors in medieval thought and religion that relate directly to this question. The first has to do with the relation between the two most diverse rôles of Piers in the poem, i.e., those of man and Christ. If we may assume for Piers such rôles as plowman, king, overlord, the pope, St. Peter, and Adam, at this point of the argument (allowing the verity of their existence to wait until a later division of the article) we may note that all such rôles have in common their humanity, and that they are but individual members of the larger aspect which Piers sometimes assumes—man as a race. His rôle as Christ, however, distinctly adds another element, i.e., the divine. Now the modern mind, having relegated the mystery of the twofold nature of Christ to the realm of religious fancy, is not apt to feel perturbed by a consanguineous association of Christ with an ideal honest man, such as Piers is, whatever station in life he assumes. But to the author of the poem and to his medieval reader such an association was possible only because the humanness of Christ

---

[2] Skeat's interpretation of this rôle is accepted in principle by Jusserand, Ten Brink, Morley, J. E. Wells, and Manly. Both Morley and Wells imply, however, that the transition is not a hard and fast one, Morley characterizing it as a *rise* from the former to the latter.

was a vital and dynamic fact, grounded in the verity of an historic incarnation. The relation between Christ the saviour and man whom he came to save had been made for the medieval mind a very actual one—Christ was as human as he was divine. Testifying to this is the medieval distinction between the terms *Son of God,* the second part of the Trinity, *Jesus,* the human being in whom God became incarnate, and *Christ,* the proper designation for the resulting union of Godhead and manhood.[3] That the author of *Piers the Plowman* felt the vitality of such distinctions is apparent from the use he makes of them in his own poem. Especially is this true of those passus in which we are told of Christ's life, death, and victory over hell, a passage sometimes referred to as the triumph of Piers the Plowman. Here there is a definite distinction between the Son of God, the second part of the Trinity, and Piers as man, in whose armor, that is in whose flesh and blood, the Son of God fought.

At the opening of the Lenten dream the dreamer sees come riding "one sembable to the Samaritan," who (we have been told in the preceding passus) is the Son of God, and "some-del to Piers Plowman." Faith answers the direct question of the dreamer concerning his identity, by saying:

> This Iesus of his gentrice wole Iuste in Piers armes,
> In his helme and in his haberioun *humana natura;*
> That Cryst be nouȝt biknowe here for *consummatus deus*
> [Almighty God].[4]

And in the resurrection scene after the return of the soul of Christ from the harrowing of hell into the physical body of Jesus, the dreamer sees again one Piers the Plowman, covered with blood and bearing the cross of victory, "lyke in alle lymes to owre lorde Iesus." [5]

---

[3] This distinction as made by Thomas Aquinas is as follows: "Nomina vero concreta supponunt hypostasim naturae; et ideo indifferenter praedicari possunt ea quae ad utramque naturam pertinent, de nominibus concretis; sive illud nomen de quo dicuntur, det intelligere, utramque naturam, sicut hoc nomen *Christus,* in quo intelligitur et Divinitas ungens et humanitas uncta; sive solum divinam naturam, sicut hoc nomen *Deus,* vel *Filius Dei;* sive solum naturam humanam, sicut hoc nomen *homo,* vel *Jesus"* [Concrete words certainly stand for the hypostasis of the nature; and for that reason, we may indifferently predicate of concrete words what belongs to each nature— whether that word of which they are predicated refers to each nature, as the word *Christ,* by which is signified both the Divine Nature anointing and the human nature anointed; or to the Divine Nature alone, as this word *God,* or the *Son of God;* or to human nature alone, as this word *man* or *Jesus*].—*Summa Theologica,* Quaest. xvi. Art. v.

[4] B. xviii, 22–25.

[5] The author here seems to use the term *Jesus* as synonymous with the term *Christ,* though a distinction corresponding with the one in the quotation from Thomas Aquinas above is made in the lines immediately following.

Is this Iesus the Iuster? that Iuwes did to deth?
Or it is Pieres the Plowman! who paynted him so rede?

And Conscience answers:

... "thise aren Pieres armes,
His coloures and his cote-armure ac he that cometh so blody
Is Cryst with his crosse conqueroure of Crystens"![6]

This passage indicates clearly upon what basis the author includes the figure of Christ within the Piers symbol. As the terms Christ and Jesus indicate here the Godhead of the *suppositum* [hypostasis], so Piers indicates the manhood. In so far as the Godhead assumed manhood in the incarnation the symbol of Piers is applicable to Christ.

There is in Thomas Aquinas an expression of this relation of Godhead and manhood in Christ and an interesting equivalent usage of the terms Jesus and Peter to designate the latter, that is suggestive at least of their similar usage in *Piers the Plowman*.

... dictur autem quod Christus est homo, sicut et quod Christus est Deus. Deus autem significat habentem Deitatem, et homo significat habentem humanitatem. Aliter tamen habens humanitatem significatur per hoc nomen *homo,* et aliter per hoc nomen *Jesus* vel *Petrus.* Nam hoc nomen homo, importat habentem humanitatem indistincte, sicut et hoc nomen *Deus* indistincte importat habentem Deitatem; hoc autem nomen *Petrus* vel *Jesus,* importat distincte habentem humanitatem, scilicet sub determinatis individualibus proprietalibus; sicut et hoc nomen *Filius Dei* importat habentem Deitatem sub determinata proprietate personali. [... but it is said that Christ is a man just as Christ is God. God, moreover, signifies one having the Godhead, and man signifies one having manhood. Yet one having manhood is differently signified by the word *man* and by the word *Jesus* or *Peter.* For this word *man* implies one having manhood indistinctly, just as this word *God* implies indistinctly one having the Godhead; but the word *Peter* or *Jesus* implies one having manhood distinctly; namely, with its determinate individual properties, just as the phrase *Son of God* implies one having the Godhead under a determinate personal property.] [7]

The terms *Jesus* and *Peter* belong then to the entity of manhood and designate the unit of manhood in which the *Son of God,* a unit of the Godhead, became incarnate. May not the applicability of Piers as a sym-

[6] B. xix, 10–15.
[7] *Summa Theologica,* Quaest. xvi, Art. v.

bol of Christ be then his humanity? In his human essence he was a blood brother to the laborer, the plowman, the king, and the pope, and alike reducible to the common denominator of man. The unity of the Piers symbol lies then, we may say, in the humanness of all of its variants. Piers is man.

The second factor that will help us to understand the Piers character has to do with the diverse variants within the common symbol. If we assume that Piers is a symbol for man, we have left to deal with the phenomenon of the multifold aspects. If Piers in his generic aspect is man, he is often specifically a man or several men, each in his own way representative of the various spheres and activities which the race had developed for itself. We may ask then whether or not there is a principle underlying this transition from one rôle to another or this merging of several rôles in one. Why should Piers a laborer become a few lines later Piers an overseer, or how is it that he suggests now being the race and then again but one member of it, or that Piers the Christ and Piers the laborer give a common utterance fraught with meaning peculiar to each?[8] The answer here is to be found in the working method of the symbolism penetrating all phases of thought and artistic creation in the middle ages.[9] For the fourteenth-century mind every fact and event in nature or in scripture was but a symbol for a deeper meaning beyond and behind its reality, and duly contemplated opened pathways for the mind of man to penetrate the mysteries of the eternal story. Every such fact contemplated or expressed carried in addition to its palpable meaning, others more veiled and spiritual, and of even deeper verity than the obvious one. So firmly established was this approach to eternal verities through the symbol that the truths derived from such contemplation and the methods of attack became the subjects of extensive categories and grammars. Symbols were arbitrary, descriptive, or insight symbols according to their relation to the truths they revealed. The truths themselves were categorized as natural, moral, or divine, based upon whether they related to man's relation to the natural world, man's moral obligations to other men, or man's divine relation to his creator.[10] Thomas Aquinas, for instance, lists such a catalogue of values.

Secundum ergo quod ea quae veteris legis significant novae legis, est

---

[8] A case in point is B. vi, 133–34. There are many others.

[9] For a brief but comprehensive introduction to the general question of symbolism in the middle ages, see H. O. Taylor, *The Mediaeval Mind.*

[10] Formally they were known as interpreting the symbol on its allegorical, tropological, or anagogical level. For a very able and illuminating discussion of the medieval symbolism and its importance in medieval thought and literature, see H. Flanders Dunbar, *Symbolism and Medieval Thought* (Yale University Press, 1929).

sensus allegoricus; secundum vero quod ea quae in Christus sunt facta, vel in his qui per Christum significant, sunt signa eorum quae nos agere debemus, est sensus moralis; prout vero significant ea quae sunt in aeterna gloria est sensus anagogicus. [Therefore, so far as these things of the Old Law signify these things of the New Law, there is the allegorical sense; so far as these things which have been done in Christ or those things which signify Christ are types of what we ought to do, there is the moral sense; but so far as they signify what relates to eternal glory, there is the anagogical sense].[11]

Now to the author, Piers the Plowman was just such a symbol. He knew the story of man told in holy scripture and in theological tradition; he knew too, the men of his own fourteenth-century England. For man at his best he set the symbol of Piers, and then as he worked he allowed Piers to become plowman and overseer, pilgrim and prophet, secular king and holy see, the race of Adam or its redeemer as he saw in the various rôles the truths he meant to convey. In the plowman was one truth, in the pope was another, and Piers was made to speak them in order for one and yet all.

Indeed the words of Thomas Aquinas quoted above are in principle quite as applicable to the poem *Piers the Plowman* as they are to the holy scripture. Piers is to be interpreted quite in the manner of the medieval interpretation of the Old Testament fathers. Piers is allegorically a symbol for man the race. The Piers who signifies the things we ought to do, i.e., the perfect laborer, the charitable lord, the righteous magistrate, and the conscientious pope, is the symbol on its *moral* interpretation, and the Piers-Christ who guides man to God is the *anagogical* revelation of man's redemption through Christ. As the story of man in the scriptures had its multifold meanings, so the story of Piers is multifold in its teachings.

There is, of course, something illogical to the modern mind in such a conception and in such multiplicity of meanings. The procedure can not be reduced to any exact scientific principles. Where there are many interpretations the modern mind insists on asking which one. To the medieval mind, looking not for one but for many, the question was irrelevant. In the merging and superimposing of meanings the modern mind asks by what logic are these things done. To the medieval mind the only logic involved was one of suggestion, or intuition. It is well for the student repeatedly to fortify himself with the words of Professor Taylor: "The Medieval man thought and felt in symbols, and the sequence of his thought moved as frequently from symbol to symbol as from fact to fact." [12]

---

[11] *Summa Theologica*, Quaest. I, Art. x.
[12] *The Mediaeval Mind*, II, 43.

It is only in the recognition of these principles, it seems to me, that we can form an accurate opinion as to the conception of Piers in the mind of the author or his meaning for the medieval reader. If once more we may propose an answer to our original question, we may say that Piers is a symbol of the human race. That he is a symbol too, for a laborer, an overseer, a king, the pope, Adam, St. Peter, and Christ, sometimes individually, sometimes compositely. That in their humanness lies their unity and that in their symbolism for man lies their divergence.

The organization of this paper has necessitated a general statement of the principles involved before any examination of the text of the poem itself could be presented. In doing so it has been practical to assume an interpretation of Piers as a multifold character, before actually presenting the evidence. It is now necessary to examine the various aspects of Piers throughout the several episodes in which he appears or in which reference is made to him, to show how they relate to the principles suggested above, and to draw from them our conception of the Piers character and his general relation to the poem of *Piers the Plowman*.

II

For the sake of clarity we may divide our study of that part of the poem relating to Piers into (a) those passus or visions where Piers appears as an actual character, and (b) those passus or visions in which reference is made to Piers, but in which he does not actually appear as a character.

Piers assumes the rôle of a character in four of the visions.[13] We may group these passages as the episode of the pilgrimage to Truth, the episode of Hunger, the episode of the pardons, the brief episode in the C-text of Piers at the dinner of the Friar, the vision of the Tree of Charity, and the episode of Pentecost. In each case a character called Piers is present and assumes an active rôle in the vision.

(a) The pilgrimage episode, chronologically the first, is as strategic as any for our purpose. The incident itself relates simply. After the opening passus concerning the field-of-folk, the trial of Lady Mede, and the confession of the seven deadly sins,

> A thousand of men tho thrungen togyderes;
> Criede vpward to Cryst and to his clene moder
> To haue grace to go with hem Treuthe to seke.[14]

Because they had no guide, they blindly "blustreden forth as bestes ouer

---

[13] The second vision, B. v, vi, vii; the sixth vision, C. xvi; the seventh vision, B. xvi; and the tenth vision, B. xix.
[14] B. v, 517–20.

bankes and hilles" until they met a pilgrim who though he had many "signes of Synay and shelle of Galice" knew nothing at all of the great Saint Treuthe. Then one a plowman swore by St. Peter and "put forth his hed." He knew Treuthe for Treuthe was his master who paid him promptly for his faithful services. The pilgrims proffer him a reward if he will guide them to the dwelling place of Treuthe, but he rejects it angrily, for Treuthe would love him less if he took hire. Then he sets them the way. It runs through Meekness into Conscience, through the Ten Commandment country of "berghes and brakes" to the court of Truth, whose walls are of Wit and whose mote is of Mercy. The castle is buttressed by Bileve-so and roofed with Love. Grace is the gate-keeper and Amende-you lifts the Wicket, but Mercy is the maid, who has might over all.

A cutpurse objects that he has no kin there, and an apeward likewise; a pardoner sends for his brevets and his bull, and a common woman joins his company.

The significance of the story is less simple however than the mere tale, and the conventional interpretation of Piers as a simple plowman, pointing the way out to the author's fourteenth-century world, is almost at once inadequate. The thousand of men thronging together and crying to God may represent fourteenth-century England, but they also represent the human race. The plowman who "put forth his hed" is also a Nazarene carpenter, who also came from among men to show men the way to God. He too, was a plowman, though of the heart of man, and a perfect laborer whose will was submission to the will of the Father. He it was who gave himself willingly and without hope of gain to show men the way to God; he who came to fulfil the Old Law and lead men to God through the mercy of the New. If in simple aspect the story is that of a loyal plowman teaching his fellows the way to truth, the deeper significance of the incident lies in the moral teaching of the great plowman who gave himself unselfishly and without reward, and in the divine revelation of the mission of the Son of God among men. Which is to say as far as our interpretation of the symbol goes, that the rôle of Piers here in its very inception is more than that of a mere plowman. It is a symbol of multifold aspect revealing multifold truth.

There is at least one other aspect of Piers in this pilgrimage episode that merits attention in our consideration. His commission to both "sowe and to sette the while he might swynke" is reminiscent of God's words to Adam, and Piers in the immediate lines is less a plowman or Christ than he is the race. He "dykes" and "delves," he plants and harvests, he is a tailor, a tinker, and a weaver. All of these aspects we have noticed are important. We shall find them repeated throughout the poem.

The next passus, which has for its central interest the episode with Hunger, is somewhat more complicated in story. We have not yet finished with the idea of a pilgrimage, though it is a new kind of pilgrimage that now concerns us, for the word pilgrim as well as Piers is a symbol for many truths. Before it was a pilgrimage of man in search of God, now it is the pilgrimage of men in this life between the deep dale and high tower. Before Piers and his followers may see God, they have a half-acre to plow. To facilitate matters Piers sets them to work, each according to his station. With the knights he makes a covenant to supply them with sustenance in return for protection for himself and the church. When he becomes old and the pilgrimage of death (still another aspect of the pilgrimage symbol) awaits him, he writes his bequest. With the idea of death and the final pilgrimage, we have, however, gotten ahead of the story, so we return to the time when Piers and his followers are at work. At high prime Piers leaves the plow to supervise the work of others. Unfortunately he finds many wasters and gluttons who eat, but who do not produce. His rebuke to them ends in a quarrel, and when the Knight proves himself incapable of performing his part of the covenant he has with Piers, the latter perforce "houped after Hunger" and famine results. Only an old loaf of pea-bread saved Wastour from death and the insolent Britoner "loked like a lanterne al his life after." But Hunger drives men to work and then there is food enough. Piers learns two important principles from Hunger, and then he with the help of his neighbors feeds him and succeeds in putting him to sleep, only to find, of course, that once Hunger has been put to sleep, there are wasters and gluttons anew.

The rôle of Piers needs to be indicated in some detail. The predominating one is certainly the one already indicated in the earlier episode, that of man on his pilgrimage of life. It is Piers and his fellows who have the half-acre to plow ere they turn home in old age to the final pilgrimage to heaven. It is out of the experience of the race that the task of each has been assigned according to his station. It is man who is married to Worche-whan-tyme-is, whose daughter is Do-rizte-so-or-thy-dame-shall-the-beat, whose son is Suffre-thi-souerrynes-to-hauen-their-wille-deme-them-nouzte-for-if-thow-doste-thow-shalt-it-dere-abugge. It must have been man himself who when the gluttons and wasters lived upon the fat of the land "houped after Hunger," as it was man who after the famine with its lesson of moderation and its dictum of charity for the infirm, but only "horse-bread" and beans for the idle, had learned a little, and could say sometime later,[15]

---

[15] B. vii, 117–18.

> I shall cessen of my sowyng and swynk nouȝt so harde,
> Ne about my bely-ioye so bisi be namore!

And it is man who has perennially found that when food is plentiful and
Hunger put to sleep, the idlers and wasters return ever again.

If, however, the predominating aspect of Piers is the race, the rôle of
Piers narrows somewhat at times. It is more properly the function of the
state to set "each man in his manere" and to covenant with the Knights
to keep the church and commons from wastours and wicked men and the
fields from foxes and boars in exchange for their livelihood off the land.
Or did the fourteenth-century Englishman feel the social and political
status as ancient and ordered as society itself? It is in the function of an
overseer or Lord of a manor that Piers lets the plow stand to oversee the
work of others, to reprove the idle and those who feign infirmity, but to
feed the poor and needy.

> And yf thow be of power Peers, ich the rede,
> Alle that greden at they gate for godes loue, after fode,
> Parte with hem of thy payn of potage other of souel,
> Lene hem som of thy loof thauh thou the lasse chewe.
> And thauh lyers and lacchedrawers and lolleres knocke,
> Let hem abyde tyl the bord be drawe ac bere hem none cromes,
> Til alle thyn nedy neihebores haue none ymaked.[16]

It is too, in the function of a baron or king that Piers after the famine
is over realizes anew that it was the "defaute of her food" that put this
folk "at my will" and ponders how he might "amaistrien hem and make
hem to worche."

There are too, several places in the episode where the Piers rôle definitely suggests being that of Christ. The Piers of the passage beginning

> And I shal apparaille me, (quod Perkyn) in pilgrimes wise,
> And wende with ȝow I wil til we fynde Treuthe[17]

is more than the laborer, he is also the Son of God who became man to
lead man to God. It is he to whom Truth told once that "Iake the ioge-
loure, Ionet of the stues, Danyel the dysplayer, Denote the Bawde, Frere
the faytoure and folke of his ordre" were blotted out of the book of life,
a statement that becomes the precedent for refusing them material sustenance unless they reform their ways. Likewise the overseer who at high
prime leaves the plow

---

16 C. ix, 284–90.
17 B. vi, 59–60.

> To oversen hem hym-self and who-so bet wrouȝte,
> He shulde be huyred ther-after whan hervest-tyme come[18]

represents the Christ, who shall come at the last day to judge the quick and the dead. And the lines

> And I am his olde hyne and hiȝte hym to warne
> Which thei were in this worlde his werkemen appeyred[19]

are certainly suggestive of the pope or church.

We have then in this single episode at least six varying aspects of the Piers rôle, i.e., the race, individual man at death writing his bequest, an overseer on a manor ordering his laborers, the head of a state governing society, the church with her spiritual charge, and Christ the great pilgrim leading man to God. It would be perhaps impossible to indicate all of the truths the symbol of Piers yields in this episode in all its variants. One may note, however, to suggest only the most obvious of them, such material truths in Piers as the allegorical figure for the race, as the classes of society, the division of labor, the relation of industry to production, of moderation to health, such moral truths in Piers as representative of man in the functions of society as the care for the sick and the infirm, the support of the church, the maintenance of justice, the commendation of honest neighborliness, and such divine truths in Piers as Christ, as the incarnation, the stewardship of the church, the final judgment of man, and the equality in heaven.

The next episode is the one dealing with pardons. In simple outline Piers, still tilling his half-acre, is sent a pardon by Truth for "hym, and for his heires for euermore after." Included in it are all "kinges and knightes that kepen holycherche, and ryztfullych in reumes reulen the peple" and "bisshopes yblessed if thei ben as thei shulden," and

> Alle lybbing laboreres that lyuen with hondes,
> That trewlich taken and trewlich wynnen,
> And lyuen in loue and in lawe for her lowe hertis,
> Haueth the same absolucion that sent was to Peres.[20]

Merchants are not in the bull, but they have a gloss in the margin and some letters under seal. Men of law, especially those pleading for reward have no pardon, and beggars and "lolleres" unless honestly in need "beth nouzte in the bulle." There is great rejoicing among all included and the merchants praise Piers for purchasing this bull. Then a bit later a priest, in a dramatic moment, reduces the pardon to its first principle of

18 B. vi, 115–16.
19 B. vi, 133–34.
20 B. vii, 62–65.

Dowel, and haue wel and god shal haue thi sowle,
And do yuel, and haue yuel hope thow non other
But after thi ded-day the deuel shal haue thi sowle![21]

And Piers in the A and B version of the episode for "pure tene" pulls the pardon in two.

The significance of Piers is here less complicated than in the preceding episode. In simple aspect Piers is a laborer who is the recipient of a bull from the pope. He is more than that, however; Piers is also man, who while tilling his half-acre, was sent a pardon from God in the form of his son. And when the merchants praise him for purchasing the pardon, he is not only the laborer but also Christ, who gave his life for man. The incident of the tearing of the pardon is in simple aspect probably nothing more than the portrayal of a contemporary incident. Many a poor plowman in the indulgence traffic of the middle ages must have been imposed upon by unscrupulous pardoners, who preyed upon their gullible market with unwarranted eloquence as they went about vending their forged drafts on the heavenly exchequer. Many a poor plowman when informed of the imposition, must in chagrin have torn his pardon in two. On the other hand it is quite within the spirit of the poem and the general method of the author to suppose the inclusion of the incident because the author saw in it a deeper truth he meant to convey. Theologically men held a pardon from God in the atonement of Christ, but as the years went on men came more and more to rely on that pardon and less and less on the merits of their own deeds until they indeed believed themselves saved by it irrespective of their conduct. Though they were liars, bribetakers, wasters, and gluttons, they rejoiced with the faithful kings, knights, and bishops, until they in their own deception of themselves had destroyed any probability of receiving the grace which Christ's atonement had provided for them. And the plowman tearing his pardon was perhaps to be symbolic of how utterly futile the author felt men had made the atonement by their own lives, a view certainly not out of harmony with the note of despair on which the poem itself ends later on. Whether or not such an extreme interpretation is justified, it is apparent that the episode, as those preceding it, is one of multifold aspect. In addition to the moral lesson of the abuse of pardons, there is the revelation of the divine redemption of man in the pardon of Christ.

There are three distinct appearances of Piers as a character in the portion of the poem known as the *Vita*. The first, peculiar to the C-text, is on the occasion when Conscience and Clergy take the dreamer to dine with a friar. As they are sitting down to meat, a minstrel at the gate, one

21 B. vii, 113–15.

Patience, joins them, and is seated opposite the dreamer at a side table. When the conversation afer dinner has turned to the quest of Dowel, Dobet, and Dobest, Piers Plowman himself suddenly appears in the midst of the assembly. He urges the power of love and patience in words with a Sinaic ring, and then mysteriously disappears.

> And whanne he hadde worded thus wiste no man after,
> Where Peers Plouhman by-cam so priueliche he wente.[22]

The relation between Patience and Piers is not quite clear from the context. In the B-text it is Patience who plays the rôle allotted here to Piers, and there is, at least, a suggestion that the two rôles are identical.[23] At any rate in this incident so strongly remindful of the road to Emmaus both Patience and Piers obviously represent Christ. The incident as a whole is too brief and indefinite to add very much to our understanding of the Piers symbol. Perhaps the most interesting feature about it is this merging of the figures of Patience and Piers, which is only another illustration of the general method of the author.

The second appearance of Piers as a character in the *Vita* is in the vision of the Tree of Charity. Though there is a divergence in the C- and B-texts in the identity of the guide, the vision is otherwise essentially the same. The dreamer beholds the Tree of Charity or the Tree of True Love planted in the heart of man. The tree is sustained and upheld by the triple prop of the Trinity and produces the fruit of chastity. While the dreamer is still gazing, the image shifts into one of the Tree of Life, whose fruit is the patriarchs and prophets of the Old Testament. When the Tree is shaken, the patriarchs and prophets fall into the hands of the Devil, who carries them off to the "Lymbo inferni" from which they are rescued later by the *Filius*. In the B-text we are told that Piers Plowman is the guide showing the vision to the dreamer. It is he who rocks the Tree of Life when the patriarchs and the prophets fall into the hands of the Devil and he who cudgels the latter for his trouble.

The character of Piers as guide is an intricate one. It carries us back to the rôles he appeared in, in the *Visio;* Piers is our guide in multifold aspect. First of all it is the Piers-Christ who is our guide to the Father. It is, however, in men that the Tree of Charity or True Love grows,[24]

---

[22] C. xvi, 149–50.

[23] There is, for instance, the casual introduction of the speech of Piers as if it were the not unexpected speech of an ordinary member of the assembly, though his mysterious disappearance is carefully noted. The figure of Patience, as suggested, is quite like that of Christ on the road to Emmaus. It was not until after the blessing of the bread, one recalls, that the disciples recognized who spoke to them.

[24] B. xvi, 13–14.

as it is in Piers as man that Christ the great Tree of Charity became incarnate. Hence it is man that shows to us the divine, for it was in his own form that man once had the opportunity to see God. It is of Piers as the race that one may speak of the patriarchs and prophets of old as having been "Piers fruit the Plowman."

The incident in the B-text of Piers rocking the Tree of Life and then a minute later cudgeling the Devil for seizing the fruit thus shaken down, is an interesting version of the Eve and Mary relationship in medieval literature, and adds directly to our understanding of the Piers symbol. The meaning is obvious. As Adam the first man, brought death to mankind, so Jesus another man, brought deliverence from death. Both Adam and Christ are here represented by the symbol of Piers; that is to say, Piers is both Adam and Christ, for he is man. Since this point is quite pertinent to our entire discussion, it will not be out of the way to quote an exact parallel from the medieval *Stanzaic Life of Christ*.

> by mon came deth to al his kynde,
> and dede schul rise withouten wer
> thurgh him bodely, as I finde. . . .[25]

The final actual appearance of Piers in the poem which we shall need to consider is the pentecostal episode. After the resurrection, Conscience tells the dreamer how Christ taught Dobest and gave to Piers power

> To bynde and to unbynde bothe here and elles-where,
> And assoille men of alle synes saue of dettes one.[26]

A little later the dreamer sees the *spiritus paraclitus* [Holy Spirit (Paraclete)] descend on Piers and his fellows in the "lykeness of a liȝtning." Grace bestows upon them the gifts of the faithful life in all its callings. Piers is created the "procurator and reve" of the physical church; he is given a team of "foure gret oxen" to plow the hearts of men, "foure stottis" to harrow after, four virtues to plant there, a house against the harvest, the "holicherche on Englische," and a cart "hyzte Christendome to carye Pieres sheues." Piers goes to the plow, and "Pruyde it aspyde, and gadered hym a grete oest" to overthrow Piers. Conscience counsels all Christian people to come into Unity and hold themselves safe, and with it the final appearance of Piers as a character in the poem ends. The passage is quite obvious and the meaning throughout allows of less multifold interpretation than many. Piers is first of all St. Peter, and thereafter

25 Edited by F. A. Foster for the E.E.T.S., 1926. Ll. 7496–7500.
26 B. xix, 184–85.

he is the pope who inherited his power, "the procurator and reve of the physical church."

This completes a rather hurried survey of those parts of the poem in which Piers appears as an actual character. It has shown, it seems to me, that quite in accord with the principles suggested in the earlier part of the paper, the central and prevailing representation of Piers is man the race, and that within the generic symbol the representation sometimes narrows to a simple laborer, to an overseer or lord, to a king, to Adam, to St. Peter, to the pope, and to Christ.

(b) We may next confine our attention to passages in the poem in which Piers is referred to either by the dreamer or by characters appearing in the dream. In this case our interest will be to see whether or not the references to him corroborate in general such rôles as we have found him assume when he appeared in the poem. If this is true, it would seem to be an additional warrant for our interpretation.

There are no references to Piers in the *Visio* save those in the incidents where he himself appears, and the reference there is, of course, to the rôle he has assumed in its immediate context. In the *Vita* our first reference to him comes in the C-text in an incident already referred to. When the dreamer is dining with the friar in company with Conscience and Clergy, there is a stranger at the gate asking for charity.

> Pacience as a poure thyng cam and preide mete for charite,
> Ylike to Peers Plouhman as he a palmere were.[27]

Our question is, of course, who is the Piers Plowman to whom Patience is "ylike"? There are two rôles of Piers to which there is an obvious likeness. Patience was a palmer who wandered the continent of Europe; we have seen Piers as man, a pilgrim in this world between the deep dale and high tower. Patience came in poverty and humility, Piers as Christ had come likewise.

Our next reference to Piers comes again in the C-text, when Conscience having forsaken the company of the friar and his books for the companionship of Patience, they meet one Activa-vita who is, as he says, an apprentice to Piers Plowman. Again if we take only the more obvious suggestions of Activa-vita, we find the master of the apprentice one of multifold aspect. Activa-vita too, is a minstrel, type of the wanderer, and thus an apprentice to Piers as man on his pilgrimage. However he is also a wafer-seller, type of the food-provider, and thus an apprentice to Piers Plowman the laborer. Finally he comes "all peuple to comfortye" and is a provider of wafers for the sacrament, and so an apprentice to the Piers as Christ, who had given his body.

27 C. xvi, 33–34.

An interesting reference is the one in B Passus xv (C. xviii) where after a long discussion of abstractions, Anima finally tells the dreamer, who desires to know charity, that without the help of Piers Plowman his person can never be seen. Which is to say, had there been no incarnation all men would have been lost and should not see God. The B-text then goes on to quote *Petrus, id est, Christus.* This quotation was taken by Skeat as the key for the interpretation of the Piers symbol in the *Vita,* but, though it is obviously correct here, the applicability of the quotation to Piers at this point is no warrant for restricting the rôle elsewhere to this one aspect of the symbol.

There are a number of references to Piers by Conscience in the postpentecostal passage of B Passus xix (C. xxii) . Some of them refer to Piers the Christ and some of them to Piers the pope. Conscience counsels all Christians to pray for peace in the barn of Piers Plowman, which is, of course, the church of Christ. Then he bids men come and receive the sacrament.

> Here is bred yblessed and goddes body ther-vnder.
> Grace thorw goddes worde gaue Pieres power,
> And myztes to maken it and men to ete it after. . . .[28]

Here Piers is the pope and those to whom his power is delegated. However, only three lines later Conscience again refers to the Piers-Christ in his invitation to all those "that hadde ypayed to Pieres pardoun the Plowman, *redde quod debes*" [pay back what you owe].

One of the most interesting of all references to Piers comes in the abrupt tirade of the "lewd vicar" against the pope's cardinals, who make the country the worse for their sojourn in it. In an apocalyptical passage he asks that they hold themselves at Avignon or Rome, that Conscience stay at the king's court, that Grace be the guide for all clerks, and that the Piers-Christ with "his newe plow and eke with his olde" be emperor of all the world. Then he concludes with a direct admonition for the pope.

> Inparfyt is that pope that al peple shulde helpe,
> And sendeth hem that sleeth suche as he shulde saue;
> And wel worth Piers the Plowman that pursueth god in doynge,
> *Qui pluit super iustos et iniustos at ones,*
> [Who sends rain at the same time on the just and on the unjust,]
> And sent the sonne to saue a cursed mannes tilthe,
> As bryʒte as to the best man and to the beste woman.

---

28 B. xix, 383–86.

> Riȝte so Piers the Plowman peyneth hym to tulye
> As wel for a wastour and wenches of the stuwes,
> As for hym-self and his seruauntz saue he is firste yserued;
> And trauailleth and tulyeth for a tretour also sore
> As for a trewe tydy man al tymes ylyke.[29]

There is again in these references an interesting merging of the rôles within the Piers symbol. The first Piers the Plowman, cautioned in his conduct to follow God, whose rain falls on the just and unjust alike and whose son was sent to save the wicked as well as the good, is obviously the Piers-pope, as is clear from the preceding context. The second Piers who is set up as an example is a multifold figure. He is the Piers who is the perfect laborer and provides food for the wasters and traitors as well as for himself. He is the Piers who is the faithful priest administering the sacrament, after "he is firste yserued." And more than either he is also the Piers who is Christ, giving himself for all without respect to person.

There is one more reference to Piers that merits attention. In that strange last passus the author depicts once more the fourteenth-century field-of-folk. Only now he depicts it not in terms of bishops and kings, commoners and knights, feigning friars and unlearned priests, but as the forces of evil arrayed against the forces of good. Holy Church and Anti-Christ, Conscience and Covetousness, Contrition and Pride, Kynde Wit and Elde, Life and Death are in the struggle, and the picture the dreamer leaves with us is quite as despairing as the one at the end of the *Visio*. Here, deserted on all sides by his confederates, who have been put to sleep by the "phisick" of the friar, Conscience vows a new pilgrimage to seek Piers the Plowman. Not in fourteenth-century England had the quest for Christ-like men been completed. Morally, the world was still needing commoners and laborers, lords and kings, bishops and popes who could destroy pride and restore friars to sincerity. And the world was still awaiting the divine fulfilment of the promise of the great Piers Plowman, whom they contemplated coming in clouds of glory to receive his faithful.

There are several factors worthy of note concerning these references to Piers the Plowman. First, the references to him no more confine his figure to one rôle than do his appearances in the poem. Second, if we assume for the reference the interpretation obvious from the context, we find Piers referred to in practically every rôle in which we had previously seen him appear. And finally we may note that there is the same merging of rôles and the same shifting from one rôle to another as there is in the passages where he actually appears.

---

29 B. xix, 426–36.

III

After our analysis of the author's usage of the symbol throughout the poem we may revert to the question, who is Piers the Plowman? The examination has shown, it seems to me, that Piers is a multifold symbol. He is allegorically man the race. He is sometimes an individual man, who is in his integrity a picture of moral perfection in the functions of society which the race has developed. And he is also the great God-man, the highest achievement of the race in the figure of its own redeemer.

This interpretation has a significance for us in the title of the poem itself. It is apparent from the manuscripts that the poem early, if not from the very first, became known by the title, *Visio Willelmi de Petro le Plowman,* which was taken by Skeat to apply particularly to the *Visio,* and less particularly to the *Vita,* which was entitled *Vita de Dowel, Dobet, Dobest, Secundum Wit et Resoun.*[30] Skeat goes on to point out the slight ambiguity, as he calls it, since the author had in his earlier text already three separate visions, and suggests that the author later called his poem after his favorite character, *Liber de Petro Plowman.* In Skeat's own interpretation of the Piers symbol the appropriateness of such a title is less apparent. If Piers is no more in the *Visio* than a plowman and no less in the *Vita* than Christ, the rôle is after all limited to minor portions of the poem. If one considers the poem as a whole, in only four out of the twenty passus does Piers become an active figure, and in only nine out of the twenty does he receive any reference at all. It is as we see the organic unity of the Piers symbol uniting all of its variants, that we see the significance of the title *Visio Willelmi de Petro le Plowman,* for which the symbol standing for man, for humanity, the work becomes entitled for what it is—a vision concerning man in this life, in his attainment of economic and political well-being, and in his attainment of salvation and a free access to heaven, through the medium of the Son of God who became man to save men. In this sense the poem is truly a vision concerning Piers the Plowman.

[30] Vol. II, xxiv.

9. Lady Meed and the Art of
Piers Plowman
A. G. MITCHELL

ALLEGORY, in the most skilful practice of it, is an art of implications. Once name and establish certain characters and start them talking or acting, and everything that is said about them or by them and everything they do or allow to be done to themselves becomes significant. The challenge to the poet is to present character and action that are in themselves interesting and colourful and that enable the poet to convey his thought precisely and subtly. It is not, at its best, an easy art. If the action gets out of hand the thought may be obscured or left open to misinterpretation; if the poet works primarily at the communication of the thought the narrative may become insipid. If the poet's art is not equal to the fusion of action and thought, then we may expect to find the thought in speeches or other passages where it is explicitly and unmistakably stated and regard the situations, conflicts, and humour of the narrative, if they are present, as so many agreeable interludes. It follows that the more vigorous and varied the action the more exacting the art of allegory becomes, the greater the risks run by the unskilful allegorist and the greater the opportunities of the skilful writer. Through action and the intermingling and conflict of character in allegory it is possible to express finer shadings of thought than through any direct exposition.

An older way of approaching *Piers Plowman* was to enjoy the narrative, the dramatic situations and the human portraits and to leave the allegory aside as being, except in scattered passages where it was unmistakable, on the whole obscure and wandering. A newer method has been to expound the allegory by the aid of some key, whether of contemporary satirical reference or contemporary belief and doctrine, and to regard the action and the characterization as pleasant interludes to be enjoyed along the way.

But Langland was equal to the highest demands of the art of allegory. In *Piers Plowman* thought and action are fused. The pattern of one is

Reprinted by permission of the author and University College London. This paper was originally delivered at University College London on Feb. 27, 1956, as the Third Chambers Memorial Lecture, and was first published in 1956 by H. K. Lewis and Co., Ltd., London.
See also John A. Yunck, *The Lineage of Lady Meed: The Development of Medieval Venality Satire* (Notre Dame, 1963) .

the pattern of the other. If we are to share his insights and appreciate the nuances of the thought we must be responsive to the actions and reactions, even the gestures of the characters, attend to the overtones of what they say, never in interpreting what is said forget who the speaker is or the circumstances in which he speaks. We find out what Meed is, not by reasoning from the evidence of contemporary thought without reference to the poem; we get to know what force she represents just as we get to know a character in any good play or narrative, by observing what she says, about herself or about others, what she does, what others say about her, how she reacts to what is said about her and what is done to her.

It has always been clear that a side of Meed's activities was bribery and corruption, but it has been clear too that she represents something more general. Jusserand said that Meed means "à la fois récompense et corruption" [simultaneously reward and corruption].[1] Skeat[2] and Chambers[3] said she stands for reward in general and bribery in particular. Christopher Dawson has called her "the power of the purse." [4] Of Jusserand, Skeat, and Chambers, Father Dunning has said: "None of these scholars, however, has worked out this vague and mixed idea of Meed in the allegory; and I doubt if it could be so worked out." [5] Father Dunning's own interpretation is that in the early part of the allegory Meed represents gain, including the wages of honest labour, and she does this by a fallacy deliberately admitted into the poem by Langland. After the fallacy is revealed in the second speech by Conscience, says Father Dunning, Meed is shown to represent cupidity.

This interpretation does justice to neither the literary art nor the subtlety of thought in the poem. Langland tells us what he means by Meed not in one or two speeches or references, but through the action of the poem and the revelation of character and motive. We need only read the poem in the belief that every incident and every piece of dialogue, every clash of personality, is carefully planned and significant.

Some of the difficulties are caused by the apparent mixed nature of Meed, which is not merely Skeat's or Chambers's imagination, not something that confuses the portrayal, but something insisted upon by Langland himself. After all, if Meed were simply corruption or bribery or venality or cupidity the question would not be troublesome. But the question posed by Langland in the Vision of Meed is not a simple one

---

[1] J. J. Jusserand, *L'Epopée Mystique de William Langland* (1893) , p. 19.

[2] *The Vision of William concerning Piers Plowman*, ed. W. W. Skeat (Early English Text Society, Original Series, No. 67 [1885], p. 43) .

[3] R. W. Chambers and J. H. G. Grattan, "The Text of 'Piers Plowman' " in *Modern Language Review,* IV (1908–9) , 365.

[4] Christopher Dawson, *Mediaeval Essays* (1954) , p. 252.

[5] T. P. Dunning, *Piers Plowman: An Interpretation of the A-Text* (1937) , p. 69.

because Meed is not to the first plain view entirely evil or entirely good. In the trial of Meed before the King, Langland examines the moral issues involved in reward or payment with thoroughness and subtlety. He does not over-simplify the question, he relies on no ready-made answers, and the solution to it is not arrived at easily or superficially.

We need not be surprised that Holy Church at the outset condemns Meed. Meed has been so often found on the side of those who resist or find fault in the teaching of Holy Church that Holy Church without qualification disapproves of her. But it is Theology who insists upon the dual strain in Meed's ancestry. Her father was Wrong but her mother was Amends. Reward or payment may be offered falsely and with evil intention. But it may also be the means of making amends to one who has been wronged, a penance and a recompense. Meed—reward, *munus*—as Theology knows, is mentioned in the scriptures and with approval. He quotes the scriptures—*Dignus est operarius mercede sua* [The laborer is worthy of his hire]. It seems to Theology that Meed has qualities in her that would make her marriage to False an affront to Truth. God, he says, had granted her to Truth. He advises them to go to Westminster to test the validity of the proposed marriage.

As the dual strain in Meed's nature is insisted upon by Theology, so there is actually a slight palliation of her association with False. Even Holy Church lays the primary responsibility for it upon Guile and Flattery. Favel, she says, has brought them together. Guile has prevailed upon Meed, and it is all Liar's leading that they go together. When it is proposed to journey to Westminster to test the validity of the marriage Favel and Guile report to False that they have so prevailed upon Meed that "she granteth to go with a good will" (A. ii, 119). There is no sign of resistance from Meed, but the supporters of False apparently find it necessary to keep up these inducements.

When Meed is brought to trial before the King the first question to be settled is Whom is she to marry? While Meed is waiting for the King to enter the hall the justices assure her that they will do their best to see that she is allowed to marry whom she pleases. To them it is a simple matter of ensuring to Meed her freedom of choice. The King decides that she is to marry Conscience. Though she has often been found on the side of wrongdoing the King feels that married to Conscience she would become an influence for good. When the King asks Meed whether she will marry Conscience she immediately consents. God forbid, she says, that she should do other than the King's will. This reply is, of course, in keeping with Meed's character. She is always ready to do anyone's will.

But Conscience firmly declines the offer. If we read these lines on the human plane we may well sympathize with Conscience. He is invited to marry a faithless woman in order to make her honest. Conscience gives a catalogue of Meed's characteristic activities in which three types of misdeed are emphasized. Meed, says Conscience, is faithless, a bawd; she corrupts the law both civil and ecclesiastical; she protects the wrongdoer and causes the innocent to suffer. The indictment is so damaging that the King has little hope that Meed will be able to answer it.

> Excuse þe, ȝif þou const, I con no more seye;
> For Concience haþ a-cuiset þe to Congeye for euere.
>
> (A. iii, 166–67)

The meaning of an important part of the speech by Meed that follows has been obscured by some of the very theories which it has been hoped might illuminate it. Meed refers to the war in Normandy. Conscience, she says, like a coward, counselled the King to give up the fight and to sell his heritage of France for a little silver. But she stayed behind, kept up his spirits and comforted him. Conscience, like a robber, carried the brass of poor men on his back to Calais to sell.

> In Normandie nas he not a-nuyȝed for my sake;
> Ac þou þi-self soþliche schomedest him þere,
> Creptest in-to a Caban for Colde of þi nayles,
> Wendest þat wynter wolde haue last euere,
> And dreddest to haue ben ded for a dim Cloude,
> And hastedest hamward for hunger of þi wombe!
> Withouten pite, pilour! pore Men þou robbedest,
> And beere heor bras on þi Bac to Caleys to sulle.
> þer I lafte with my lord his lyf forto saue,
> Maade him murþe ful muche Mournynge to lete,
> Battede hem on þe Bakkes to bolden heore hertes,
> Dude hem hoppe for hope to haue me at wille.
> Hedde I be Marchal of his Men (bi Marie of heuene) !
> I durste haue I-leid my lyf and no lasse wed,
> He hedde beo lord of þat lond in lenkþe and in brede;
> And eke kyng of þat cuþþe his cun for to helpe;
> þe leeste barn of his blod a Barouns pere.
> Soþliche, þou Concience þou counseildest him þennes,
> To leue þat lordschupe for a luitel seluer,
> þat is þe Riccheste reame þat Reyn ouer houeþ!
> Hit bicomeþ For a kyng þat kepeþ a Reame
> To ȝiue meede to men þat mekeliche him seruen;
> To Aliens, to alle Men to honoure hem with ȝiftes.
>
> (A. iii, 182–204)

Much has been written on these lines in the belief that they might be made meaningful only by the identification of contemporary people at whom satire is being aimed. Professor Huppé identifies Meed with Alice Perrers, Conscience with John of Gaunt.[6] According to him the money borne off by Conscience to Calais is the exactions wrung from poor men in England to finance the wars. The comfort that Meed refers to is the comfort the King found in her company while Gaunt was abroad. When it is said that Conscience left the King this means that Gaunt had left for France to prosecute the war while the King remained in London. Dr. J. A. W. Bennett, accepting Professor Huppé's critical principles in the main, by a shift of emphasis identifies the King's mourning with Edward's grief at the death of Queen Philippa in 1369.[7]

All these interpretations are surely out of joint. Why should John of Gaunt, if he could be called a robber, be identified with Conscience? Robertson and Huppé offer the theological explanation of "the fallibility of Conscience, which, directed towards particulars, may err." [8] Dr. Bennett suggests that we must make allowance for the general tone of abuse and contempt in what Meed says and so discount her accusations against Conscience.[9] But this would be to assume that Meed is a fool, making wild charges in a speech in which she is trying hard to defend herself. It would be to place much too low an estimation upon Meed's intelligence to propose that she actually claims credit to herself, in a serious trial before the King, for having, as his mistress, comforted him after the death of his wife.

The matter goes further than our feeling for the odd implications that these theories carry. Such interpretations distort our understanding of the allegory as a whole and they imply a low estimate of both the poet's art and the precision and vigour of thought which he is expressing through that art. If Langland means to show Meed seriously justifying herself in a serious trial before the King, and if he causes her to make wild accusations and be simply abusive in her references to Conscience, then he is merely presenting Meed as black against Conscience's white in the manner of melodrama and not looking deeply or subtly at her character and motive. If he presents the allegorical characters thus crudely, then the thought running parallel to the action can be neither vigorous nor precise.

6 Bernard F. Huppé, "The A-text of *Piers Plowman* and the Norman Wars" in *Publications of the Modern Language Association of America*, LIV (1939), 37–64.

7 J. A. W. Bennett, "The Date of the A-text of *Piers Plowman*" in *Publications of the Modern Language Association of America*, LVIII (1943), 566–72.

8 D. W. Robertson, Jr., and Bernard F. Huppé, *Piers Plowman and Scriptural Tradition* (1951), p. 61.

9 J. A. W. Bennett, *op. cit.*, p. 569.

But if we simply read the lines, the difficulties of Professor Cargill,[10] Professor Huppé, and Dr. Bennett about Conscience the robber carrying the brass of poor men on his back to Calais and about Meed staying behind to comfort the King and prevent his mourning will be seen not to exist. The reference to the Norman wars here is not intruded abruptly so that it could be accounted for only as a contemporary satirical reference breaking the flow of the narrative. It comes in quite naturally. When the King had asked her whether she would marry Conscience, Meed had agreed. She always agrees. But now, when the King asks Conscience whether he will marry Meed, Conscience bluntly and insultingly refuses. If we read the beginnings of Meed's speech on the human plane we shall find undertones that Langland must have intended. Meed is not used to being scorned. She is always courted and sought after. Not only this—she is a woman who has expressed her willingness to marry a man who now scornfully rejects her. She is shocked and indignant. When she says that she cannot understand why Conscience should so abuse her, this is no pose and her speech is no mere abuse of Conscience. She believes what she says. She believes that she has helped Conscience in the past and expects that he, like all the others she has benefited, will be grateful. She has had no complaints from him before. Why is he so angry now?

> Whi þou wraþþest þe now wonder me þinkeþ.
> (A. iii, 176)

It was Conscience, she hints, who started it by unjustly defaming her. Then she sets out, not merely to defend herself but to turn the tables on Conscience:

> "Nay, lord," quaþ þat ladi, "leef him þe worse."
> (A. iii, 168)

She tries to show that it was Conscience who embarrassed and impeded and misadvised the King during the wars in France. "If it comes to advising the King," she seems to say, "you haven't much to boast about yourself. What about the war in Normandy? It wasn't *I* who caused the King trouble there. Because of the sufferings of the campaign and because of a bit of a storm, you made the King think the campaign was ill omened and persuaded him to sign away his heritage by the Treaty of Bretigny. Not only that—but you demoralized his men. Every man who through the sufferings of the winter lost heart and feared that the sufferings were perhaps a sign of God's disapproval, was influenced by you.

---

[10] Oscar Cargill, "The Date of the A-text of *Piers Plowman*" in *Publications of the Modern Language Association of America*, xlvii (1932), 354–62. If these difficulties turn out not to exist, the arguments for a later date of the A-text have no force.

You made cowards of them. They deserted and added to the shame of cowardice the crime of theft, robbing poor men as they made their way to Calais. Fine specimens! But I stayed with the King. Through reward and the hope of reward men's courage and spirits were kept high in spite of sufferings and disappointments and signs. Reward and the hope of reward would have ensured that the King's men saw it through. If I, Meed, had prevailed, if I had been in command, the outcome would have been very different."

Meed is advocating the principle that the King should ensure the loyalty and the morale of his followers by reward and the expectation of reward in rank, land, treasure, or money. Meed opposes herself to Conscience as adviser to the King and as influence upon his men. Conscience caused the King to give up. Meed would have ensured the success of the campaign. This is not Meed having put into her mouth a defence of Alice Perrers or criticism of Gaunt. It is the allegorical character making her own claims for her actions and influences.

That this is the whole purpose of the reference to the Norman wars is confirmed by the C-text. Professor Huppé remarks that "when the C-text came to be written, the significance of this (the campaign of 1373 as he believes) had passed, and consequently in that version all particular reference has been effaced." [11] It is true that in the C-text there is no reference to Conscience who leaves the King, or to Meed who remains with him to save him from despondency and there is no actual mention of Normandy. But this does not mean that contemporary satirical references were the primary purpose of the poet of A and B and that the C-text appears as it does without them because these references had ceased to be meaningful when it was written. The points that Meed tries to make in the A- and B-texts are still the points that she makes in the C-text. But in C she makes them more explicitly. In C she directly states the principle that the King should reward his followers. She says it is not merely good policy (to keep their loyalty) but it is the King's obligation. She goes further and says it is wrong for a king to give up or sell a territory that had been won by the help of his men. The soldiers by virtue of hardship and danger have their rights in it. This is saying what Meed had said in A and B but saying it more explicitly and even daringly. The accusation against Conscience is repeated—

Hast arwed meny hardy men that hadden wil to fyghte.

(C. iv, 237)

The reference is not exclusively and pointedly to the Treaty of Bretigny

[11] *Op. cit.*, p. 64.

"The story of Haukyn," says Stella Maguire, "is the story of the passage from self-satisfaction, through the growing awareness of the sinfulness of human nature, to final repentence." In the B-text, Haukyn is introduced at the second paragraph rubric on this folio from MS. Laud Misc. 581.

The "Book" passage is here reproduced from two folios of
MS. Laud Misc. 581. The crux with which E. Talbot
Donaldson deals, Passus xviii of the B-text,
lines 252-57 is in the last six full
lines shown.

and the campaign that preceded it. The principles are stated as applicable to all campaigns anywhere—"bothe her and elleswher"—and what Meed thinks happened at the Treaty of Bretigny is stated more generally—

> Vnconnyng ys þat conscience a Kyngdome to sulle,
> þat ys conqueryd þorw comune helpe.
>
> (C. iv, 244–45)

The C-text says exactly what the A-text says, only more expressively and by direct, general statement rather than through the images of Conscience deserting the King and Meed remaining with him.

> "For-þy ich counsayle no kyng eny counsayle aske
> At conscience, yf he coueyteþ to conquery a reome.
> For sholde neuere conscience be my constable,
> Were ich a kyng ycoroned by marye," quaþ mede,
> "Ne be mareschal of my men þer ich moste fyghte.
> Ac hadde ich, mede, be hus mareschal ouer hus men in fraunce,
> Ich dorst haue leid my lyue and no lasse wedde,
> He had be lord of þat londe in lengthe and in brede,
> And al-so kyng of þat cuth hus kyn to haue holpen,
> The leste brol of hus blod a barones pere.
> Vnkyndely þow, conscience consailedest hym þennes,
> To lete so hus lordshup for a lytel moneye.
> Hyt by-comeþ for a kyng þat shal kepe a reame,
> To ȝeue men mede þat meklyche hym serueþ,
> To alienes, to alle men to honoury hem with ȝyftes;
> Mede makeþ hym [be] by-loued and for a man yholde."
>
> (C. iv, 254–69)

A King, says Meed then, grapples his soldiers to him in loyalty by rewards given, and keeps their courage strong by the hope of rewards after victory is won. Then, by a natural transition, she goes on to say that everyone, from emperor to beggar, both gives reward and expects it for his services. She ends with the emphatic statement—

> þer may no wiht, as I wene with-outen Meede libbe.
>
> (A. iii, 220)

Meed claims for herself that she represents the universal principle by which kings, popes, and earls ensure the loyalty of servants, by which tradesman, labourer, and beggar live and for which they perform their services.

The relief and pleasure of the King at Meed's vindication of herself
are very clear as he says to Conscience:

> be *cri*st, as me þinkeþ,
> Meede is Worþi Muche Maystrie[12] to haue.
>   (A. iii, 221–22)

We must heed the exact words of the King. He does not say merely
that Meed has cleared herself against the charges laid by Conscience or
that she has some possibilities of good in her. He says she seems to him
worthy to have the mastery. This is a very different question from those
raised before. It is not now merely a question whom Meed shall marry
or whether she shall marry Conscience and be guided by him. It is a question whether she is to have the mastery.

Conscience is quick to feel the danger of this situation. It is not sufficient for him merely to list the misdoings of Meed. Meed can answer that
by pointing to the rewards she gives to necessary and honorable service in
every activity of life, so that she seems an indispensable power. Conscience is obliged to examine philosophically the meanings of this name
"Meed." He is like the man who gives a rough and ready explanation
expecting that this will satisfy his questioner, but who then finds his
questioner better informed or more persistent in his curiosity than he
thought and is consequently obliged to offer a more precisely reasoned
explanation. Meed and Conscience are not merely expressing opinions
at random. Each speaks according to his or her character and as circumstances seem to demand.

Conscience's answer is not merely that there are two kinds of reward,
one wrongful and the other lawful and good. True he begins by saying
that there are two kinds of reward and then mentions the heavenly reward given by God to the virtuous and the rewards given by masters who
maintain misdoers.

> "Nay," q*u*od Concience to þe kyng *and* knelede to grou*n*de;
> "þer beoþ twey man*er* of Meedes my lord, bi þi leue.
> þat on, good God of his grace ʒiueþ, in his blisse,
> To hem þat wel worchen whil þat þei ben here.
> þe Prophete hit p*r*echede and put hit in þe psauter,
> *Qui peccuniam suam non dedit ad vsuram, etc.* [Who has not
>   given his money to usury, etc.]
> Tak no Meede, mi lord of Men þat beoþ trewe;
> Loue hem, and leeue hem for vr lordes loue of heuene;
> Godes Meede and his M*er*ci þer-*with* þou maiht winne.

---

12 The Trinity manuscript reads "*þ*e maistrie."

Bote þer is a Meede Mesureles þat Maystrie desyret,
To Meyntene Misdoers Meede þei taken;
And þerof seiþ þe psauter in þe psalmes eende,
In quorum manibus iniquitates sunt; dextera eorum repleta est
muneribus [In whose hands are iniquities; their right hand
is filled with gifts];
[þat here riȝthond is hepid ful of ȝeftis],
And heo þat gripeþ heore ȝiftus (so me God helpe!)
þei schullen a-Bugge bitterly or þe Bok lyȝeþ!"

(A. iii, 223–36)

At first it might seem that these two kinds of reward are sharply contrasted. They are, it appears, the two extremes. But it becomes clear then
that the two are thought of together and both contrasted with other sorts
of payment commonly brought together under the same designation of
Meed. The distinction made by Conscience is between meed *mesurable*
and meed *mesurles*. Where there is an exact relationship between the
payment and the goods handed over or the work or service done, the
payment is said to be measurable, proportionate, in exact relationship.
When there is not this settled, exact relationship the reward is measure-
less, out of proportion. There is not this exact and settled relationship between the infinite reward of God to the virtuous and their deserts. There
cannot be. There is similarly not this exact and settled relationship between the reward and the services of the wrongdoer. The reward of God
is infinitely more than even the most virtuous can deserve. The reward
of the wrongdoer can have no relationship to desert when the position is
that he receives a reward for the wickedness for which he deserves punishment. The point that Conscience is trying to make is not that there
are good sorts of reward and bad sorts of reward, but rather that there are
only two things that deserve to be called by the name of Meed, reward,
at all, namely the heavenly reward of God and the rewards given to
wrongdoers.[13] All other sorts of payment are not properly called rewards.
The wages of labourers and "low folk" are a directly proportionate hire.
In trade there is no reward, but merely an exchange of one thing for another directly proportionate in value.

þat laborers and louh folk taken of heore Maystres,
Nis no Maner Meede bote Mesurable huyre.

[13] In the B-text there is a delicate emphasis added. The reward of heaven is for
those who do works of mercy and charity *without meed:*
And alle þat helpeth þe innocent and halt with þe ritztful,
With-oute mede doth hem gode and þe trewthe helpeth.
(B. iii, 241–42)

In Marchau*n*dise nis no Meede I may hit wel avoue;
Hit is a permutacion a peni for anoþer.

(A. iii, 240–43)

It is clear from the C-text that Langland thought long and anxiously about these divisions, kinds of reward or payment. Nothing can be plainer than that in the C-text we have the same mind brooding over the same problem in the same general context and starting from the same point as in the A- and B-texts. If we compare the B-text with the C-text we shall notice that the grouping of the heavenly reward with the reward given to evildoers is abandoned. The fine effect of the bold grouping of the two in B is given up, not, I think, because Langland felt it to be a little risky, but because he felt it would be unnecessary if another part of Conscience's argument could be developed further—that is the notion of the precise and settled relationship between reward and desert, service or goods and payment. This argument is pressed much further in the C-text than in the B-text. Langland even coins (it seems) and introduces another term, *mercede,* to designate the strictly proportionate reward or payment. He brings under this heading the rewards given to their followers by kings, emperors, earls, and popes, even the reward given by God to his faithful on earth. In any case, says Conscience, the motive for these rewards is love; they are not given to buy the loyalty or faithful service of their followers as Meed would have us believe. But he goes a step further and insists that these rewards are earned. They are given conditionally. If the servant fails in loyalty or service the reward is taken away.[14] The servant must continue to earn the reward by service, truth, and loyalty. The reward is earned afresh day by day in much the same way in which the workman earns his wages at the end of each day's work.

In order to press this argument further Langland uses a grammatical analogy in a passage that Moore said was "quite unintelligible and utterly barren of all interest" [15] and that Skeat described as "barely intelli-

---

14   And þauh þe kyng of hys cortesye kaiser, oþer pope,
           zeue loud oþer lordshup [or] oþer large ziftes,
           To here leelle [and] lyge loue ys þe cause.
           And yf þe leelle and þe lyge be luther men after,
           Boþe kyng and kayser and þe coroned pope
           May desauowe þat þey dude and douwe þer-with oþer,
           And a-non by-nymen hym hit and neuere [more] after
           Noþer þei ne here Ayres hardy to cleyme,
           That kyng oþer cayser hym gaf catel oþer rente.
                                    (C. iv, 317–25)

15 Samuel Moore, "Studies in *Piers the Plowman*" in *Modern Philology,* XI (1913–14), 192.

gible and very dull reading." [16] It is not, of course, extraordinary in an age that used all material to hand as analogies to point a moral lesson. There existed a moralized Donatus in French and we need not doubt that such existed in English as well. Langland takes the grammatical concepts of direct and indirect relation as means of making clear his distinction between *Meed* and *mercede*.[17]

Adjective and substantive, says the poet, agree with one another in gender, case, and number. They agree in every respect and agree truly. Each is firmly interlocked with the other so that each strengthens the other and strengthens, too, the basis of their relationship. This basis is truth, and truth is God. As the adjective agrees with the substantive in gender, case, and number, so, if the relationship between them is direct and based upon truth, the servant agrees with his lord. He knows that the lord will do right by him, pay him promptly and fully for his work, and have compassion if he (the servant) should fail. The loyal, truthful man is joined by direct relation fully, precisely, unwaveringly with his lord or his servant. But in indirect relationship the man wants the right to waver and shift in his loyalties and obligations. He wants to be able to choose any case, attach himself without being bound by number or gender. It is as if in a sentence an adjective sought to attach itself not merely to any noun in the sentence but partly to one noun and partly to another, to choose good or evil as it felt inclined.

As Langland's thought develops here one cannot help being reminded of the marriage contract—"for better for worse, for richer for poorer, in sickness and in health." "That," he says,

> Is [noʒt] reisonable ne rect to refusy my syres sorname,
> Sitth y, his sone and seruaunt suwe for his ryghte.
>
> (C. iv, 369–70)

It is not reasonable or right, that is, for the son to decline to bear his father's surname when he expects to enjoy his father's rights and privileges. Once the pact is made, the contract entered into, the disadvantages that it may entail must be accepted along with the advantages. If the direct relationship is accepted then it can be agreement in only one case, one number, and one gender. And this agreement may involve discomfort, labour, and hardship. But indirect relationship would seek to choose the gender, the number, and the case that involve advantage and no hardship—

---

[16] *Op. cit.,* p. 70.
[17] See C. iii, 335–409.

So indirect þyng ys Inliche to coueyte
To a-corde in alle kyndes and in alle kynne numbre,
With-oute cost and care in alle kynne trauaile.

(C. iv, 373–75)

Rights and duties as between classes, groups, and individuals are in direct relationship as Langland understands it. He gives the example of the King and the commune. The King may claim of the commune three things: that they should follow him, provide for him, and give him counsel. In return the commune may claim three things of the King: law, love, lealty. But, says Langland—

þe moste partie of þe puple pure indirect semeþ,
For þei wilnen and wolde as best were for hem-selue,
Thauh þe kyng and þe comune al þe cost hadde.

(C. iv, 386–88)

Once the relationship is entered into the parties must hold to it, accepting the labour and the disadvantage along with the benefits. Those who are indirect will seek the benefits, and allow others to bear the cost. They consult only their own self-interest. Provided they receive money they do not care whether their contract is imperfectly honoured or even broken. They are like the labourer who, although bound to a particular lord, will leave him if the lord is in difficulties or is short of workmen and go to another who can pay better. Such people are unsteadfast, says the poet. We recall that the dominant characteristic of Meed is her unsteadfastness, her lack of settled loyalty. And it is Meed, reward by money, that both tempts people to fail in their contracts and loyalties and makes it possible for them to deny their obligations. Meed tempts and enables men to live by self-interest.

This elaborate grammatical analogy, at once so puzzling and so dull to readers of the poem, so dull that it has seemed to many that a poet who had any thought for the art of his poem would never have introduced it, represents, as a matter of fact, the furthest precision that Langland had been able to reach in his brooding upon the manifestations of reward, payment, the character of Meed.

If all the forms of reward and payment mentioned here by Conscience come under the heading of *mercede*—the King's reward of faithful followers, the master's wages to his labourer, the buyer's payment to the merchant—then there is little left of which Meed is mistress. Indeed all that is left to her is the payment that supports and protects wrongdoers. She would find herself deprived of most of those activities in which she claimed that she worked so busily to the universal good.

With what reason does Conscience thus deprive Meed of so many of the activities that she claimed to her credit? One reason is that many of the things that Meed claimed would not go on but for her—deeds of mercy and truth, honest labour, loyal service—are, as a matter of fact, often enough done out of loyalty and love and not through hope of reward at all. Conscience might say that for Meed to claim that such things would not be done but for her is an impertinence and an affront to true men. Meed's reply to this, already given, is that in this society as it may be seen in operation, the labourer, the priest, the soldier, the lawyer *do* look for reward and would not perform their duties without it.

Conscience in the latter part of his speech answers this by saying that in the reign of Reason, which he predicts, Meed would cease to be the motive for which such things would be done. When people are ruled by love and lealty, law will be unnecessary. No man will be paid for pleading at the bar and money will have no power to influence the processes of the law. There will be universal peace and swords will be beaten into ploughshares.

Conscience is here raising another question about Meed. The first question about Meed was Whom shall she marry? The second was Can Meed be reformed by marrying Conscience? The third was Is Meed worthy to have the mastery? This fourth question, raised by Conscience, is Is Meed necessary? Conscience suggests that in the reign of Reason there would be no need, indeed no place, for Meed.

Though Langland clearly put a great deal of thought into these fine theoretical distinctions drawn by Conscience he does not present them as final or as settling the questions about Meed. To Meed, of course, all this pretentious hair-splitting is a meaningless irritation. She knows no Latin, she says in the B-text, but quotes a passage from scripture which says that he gains honour who gives rewards. Conscience with little trouble is able to point out that she has quoted only half the text. The other half is not so comfortable to those that receive meed.

Even more important is the reaction of the King. He has had enough of their wrangling, claim, counter-claim, hair-splitting and bandying about of texts. The matter is not settled for him. Though he cannot now have any faith in his plan for the marriage of Meed and Conscience, he holds to his conviction that they should be reconciled and that they should both serve him. He sees Meed as still necessary and desirable in the management of the kingdom. Conscience says that unless Reason advises him to do it he would rather die than kiss Meed and make up. The King orders Conscience to go and fetch Reason.

Langland times the entry of the *dramatis personae* into the narrative with forethought and precision. As Conscience and Reason ride together to the King's court they are followed "busily" by Warren Wisdom and Witty his companion. In the B-text Conscience remarks that the words of these two are full of guile and that they dwell with Meed. Where there is love and loyalty they have no interest. But where there is wrath and wrangling and where they may win silver by manipulating the processes of the law, there they will be found.

This affinity between Meed and Witty and Wisdom explicitly stated by Conscience is of great significance. Meed in all her activities works at the level of ordinary intellectual cunning and ingenuity, skill in the mere processes of thought, never restrained or guided by any moral consideration or settled principle of behaviour. Self-interest, the expediency of the moment, she cannot see beyond or above these. Warren Wisdom and Witty, scampering along behind Conscience and Reason in the hope of learning something to their advantage, have an important part to play in the dramatic climax of the episode which enables the King to reach his judgment about Meed.

Peace comes into parliament and puts forward an accusation against Wrong, who, in the person of the King's purveyor, has committed grievous crimes against Peace, adding physical injury, theft, and rape to his exactions in the name of the King. When he hears the indictment Wrong is afraid and straightway seeks help and advice from Wisdom. If he had the King on his side, he says, he would care nothing though Peace complained forever. Wisdom and Witty tell him that things look bad and that unless Meed can influence the judgment he is in for serious trouble. Wrong is persuaded to distribute his money about and Wisdom and Witty go with him to win mercy. But the King swears that Wrong will suffer for his crimes and commands a constable to cast him in irons.

But Wisdom and Witty, well deserving their names, have a plausible argument to put up. Why not, says Wisdom, let Wrong make amends and then let someone be surety for him? In this way amends would be made to the injured party and Wrong would be saved from his predicament. That way everyone would be better off. Wit chimes in with this opinion and Meed then busies herself to persuade Peace to accept payment as amends for his injury. The three act as a team in the emergency. Meed promises Peace that Wrong will not injure him again. The King is not inclined to have mercy on Wrong for the very good reason that if Wrong goes free this time he will be the bolder in future to flout the law. Unless Reason is prepared to have mercy on Wrong, says the King, he shall remain in the stocks.

Reason says he would have no man beseech mercy for Wrong until pride, covetousness, hypocrisy, and neglect of duty are banished from the kingdom. In particular, he says, he would have no mercy while

Meede haþ eny Maystrie to Mooten in þis halle.
(A. iv, 118)

If he were King, Wrong would never go unpunished. Reason weaves into an allegorical sentence some words from Innocent's *De Contemptu Mundi:*

For *nullum malum* þe mon mette [with] *inpunitum,*
And bad *nullum bonum* be *irremuneratum.*
(A. iv, 126–27)

He commends this to the King as a principle by which to rule his kingdom and suggests that the King's confessor construe the plain meaning of the words.

In the A-text things now happen very rapidly, but in the B-text and the C-text Langland exploits the dramatic pause while the clerks busy themselves to construe the words, and the King and Reason wait. Meed, impudent, self-secure, unaware of the possible significance of the words, winks upon men of law and many of them cluster round her and desert Reason. There is a retrospective irony in these winks and vows when it is agreed by all present that Reason had spoken truth and Meed suddenly finds herself rejected and despised, jeered at and called a quaint common whore.

What is there about these words that through them Meed should find herself so suddenly discredited and bereft of influence? It is that they express a principle that Meed by her action, not by her words or professions, is constantly ready to thwart. She is ready, indeed, to turn the principle upside down, make it work in a contrary direction.

Nullum malum inpunitum, nullum bonum irremuneratum [No evil unpunished, no good unrewarded]. As to the good man, not only does Meed deprive him of his reward; she causes him suffering without redress. As to the wicked man, not only does she save him from punishment; she enables him to enjoy the fruits of his ill deeds. It is not merely that through Meed the good man is deprived of his reward and the wicked man saved from punishment. Through her the good man is made to suffer and the wicked man is rewarded. If Reason's principle is a good one Meed offends against it in a double degree. To this the King has the evidence of his own eyes. Following the course of her own nature Meed has tried to thwart the King's will and impede the course of justice. As she has behaved in respect of the law so she would act in other things.

This construing of the words from the *De Contemptu Mundi* is the climax of the Meed episode. Meed is dramatically revealed for what she is. The three texts show an interesting contrast in their handling of the denouement. In the A-text Wisdom and Wit stare dumbfounded at the floor when Reason's quotation is expounded. The King agrees with Reason but says it would be very hard to bring about the state of affairs that Reason has described. Reason says it would not be difficult if only obedience was given him, and agrees to stay with the King provided Conscience is of the council. No more is said about Meed. In its concise way the A-text makes the point by saying nothing. There is no place for her in the reign of Reason. All turn their backs on her and her power has vanished. In the B-text some additions are made in which the reader's attention is kept a little longer on Meed. While she is being jeered at a Sisor and a Summoner go to Meed to comfort her and a sheriff's clerk abuses the crowd for their insults. The King looks sternly upon Meed and rebukes her for her perversion of the law. The poet is, clearly, a little more explicitly winding up the episode of Meed. The C-text is more explicit still and anticipates the reader's natural question: "What happened to Meed?" The Sisor and the Summoner are seen to be tiptoeing with Meed out of the hall. They decide it is no place for them and try to take Meed with them. A sheriff's clerk calls out to seize Meed and keep her in custody, and the King then rebukes Meed for her influence upon the course of law.

The character of Meed is consistent from beginning to end. One thing that we notice about her quite soon is her own unawareness of wrongdoing. She acts indiscriminately, without consideration of the moral law. She is ready to please and to help anyone. When False, Guile, and Liar flee on hearing the King's sentence, Meed is left alone. She does not scurry off into hiding because she has no conviction that she has done wrong, even though she has consorted with these rogues. In the last scene of all in parliament, even after the King's admonitions and after all that Conscience had said about her, in face of the King's obvious anger against Wrong, when it might seem that in her own interests she should be wary of such associates, she is just as ready to help Wrong as she had been to help any of the rogues who had solicited her help all through the story.

For this reason it seems to me quite wrong to interpret the speeches of Meed as if she were aware of wrongdoing in herself, and on the defensive in the same way as the wrongdoer aware of his guilt. Robertson and Huppé, for example, speaking of Meed's reply to Conscience, say: "Lady Meed's reply to these charges is a masterly evasion: her equivocations consist (1) in an attack on the fallibility of Conscience which, directed towards particulars, may err, (2) in an identification of herself with true hire." [18] This is to take the words out of context and to ignore the action

18 D. W. Robertson, Jr., and Bernard F. Huppé, *op. cit.*, p. 61.

and the characterization. Meed makes no subtle evasions or logical shifts in her own defence. She believes that she is useful, and helpful, even indispensable, to men, and sees no wrong in herself that needs to be defended.

This trait in Meed's character, so consistently brought out, is part of the thought that the allegory seeks to develop. Meed is almost morally neutral. She has no secure attachments and no antipathies that are dictated by moral principles. She is incapable of faithfulness. Langland represents Meed as a woman whose favours are readily and indiscriminately given, not merely because he wishes thus to emphasize her general wickedness, but because he wishes to express a meaning. Meed is

> As Comuyn as þe Cart-wei to knaues and to alle.
> (A. iii, 127)

Conscience will not entertain the thought of marrying her because she is a bawd and anyone who married her would soon be known for a cuckold. At the end of the episode the insult most insistently thrown at Meed, even by the most common, is that she is a quaint common whore. Her favours are freely available to all, no matter what the character of giver and receiver, no matter what the purpose of the payment.

Meed is always agreeable, compliant. She never says "no." Though she has been consorting with False she is quite ready to marry Conscience when the King asks her. She eagerly takes up and improves upon the Friar's hint to glaze a window in his house. She responds immediately to the appeal of Witty and Wisdom on behalf of Wrong.

Meed claims that in all this she is helping people. This is her constant cry. "Where mischief is great Meed may help," she says (A. iii, 170). She asks the Friar to be light upon those who commit lechery. She asks the mayor to let dishonest craftsmen and tradesmen take advantage of the law a little, "to sulle sumdel aȝeyn resoun" (A. iii, 83). In all this Meed is not seeing the punishment for sin lightened or the law strained and manipulated in the interests of the dishonest. She sees people who need her help, the lecher in danger of severe punishment who would like it lightened, the tradesman and shopkeeper who would like to make a bit more profit. When Wrong is accused before the King, Meed sees not a wrongdoer who deserves the severest punishment, but someone in difficulty who has appealed to her for help when her help alone can avail.

This help, indiscriminately given, makes Meed popular. She is courted everywhere, and this universal adulation confirms her belief in her own worth. In the C-text she says directly

Is no lede þat leueþ þat he ne loueþ mede,
And glad for to grype hure gret lord oþer poure.
(C. iv, 283–84)

Because she believes in the worth of her benevolence and helpfulness to
all, Meed is at a loss to understand criticisms levelled at her. When Conscience scorns her, Meed is at a loss to understand why he should thus de-
fame her. Langland gives us at the same time a reaction true to human
behaviour and a revelation of his underlying thought.

Meed is exposed before the King for her influence upon the law. In his
final stern rebuke to her the King tells her that she has almost destroyed
the law. This she has done not merely through bribery and corruption in
the ordinary sense, but in ways that today we should think no great cause
of complaint. By bail and surety she saves lawbreakers from the full
sharpness of the punishment due to them. The fact that legal processes
have to be paid for at all means that justice is denied the poor. Even if
the poor man does begin proceedings the law's delays are such that it is
the one with the greater wealth who will last longest and so prevail. But
all these manipulations of the law in the interests of the wealthy and to
the hurt of the innocent would be unnecessary if men governed their
lives by duty and love. Matters would then be settled according to the
manifest justice and merits of the case. Law would become lealty—that
principle that inspires men to act according to their known duties and
rights, claiming no more than their own. When Meed is discredited it is
Love and Lealty who laugh her to scorn. These two, who have feared
Meed and been thwarted and oppressed by her, are emboldened now to
express their feelings. In the reign of Reason there will be no place for
Law. He will become a labourer and lead afield dung. This large machin-
ery governing the relationships of men, which Meed claims as to her
credit that she keeps in operation, and on which she so clearly exercises a
bad influence, will disappear.

In the reign of Reason, too, no man shall take meed for pleading at the
bar. Langland regards it as a sort of simony, to carry into action only for
payment, that is to sell, things like justice, religious ministration, mercy,
loyalty. In the reign of Reason such things will be put into practice because they are enjoined by duty and charity. In the reign of Reason no
man in authority, mayor or magistrate, will accept gifts to wink at in-
fringements of the law and no man will think of offering such gifts. One
after the other the domains over which Meed says she rules beneficiently
and in which she claims to be indispensable are taken away from her,
even to this last domain in which Reason says Meed actively supports

wrongdoers and in which *she* says she helps people upon whom the law bears rather strictly or who stand in danger of sharp punishment for sin.

It is a satisfying conclusion both on the human plane of the story and the allegorical plane. Meed, the fine lady, once so confident and so sought after, is discredited, jeered and scoffed at by even the most common. Meed, reward, is shown to be unnecessary in the reign of Reason. Provided the people are obedient to Reason there is no use for Meed and no harm that she can do. In a dramatic and colourful story the great questions about Meed have been raised, thrashed out, and settled. Whom should Meed marry? Can Meed be reformed? Is Meed worthy to have the mastery? Is Meed necessary? The episode of Meed has the continuity, the sweep, the rising to a climax, and the denouement, the economy and proportion of any good story or drama. It is not that the allegory, the thought, is clear at this or that point where Meed acts or speaks or Conscience speaks in a way that suggests she may be venality or cupidity or something else and that the matter in between has only a loose connexion with these passages in which the allegory seems to be clear. The thought does not merely shine out in separate speeches and situations. It develops through the whole movement of the narrative.

Piers Plowman is not the work of a man only moderately educated who is likely to flounder about in his handling of philosophical or theological subjects that he is not properly equipped to manage, or of a man who is indifferent about or unskilled in securing the coherence of his thought and the relevance of his material, who leaves loose ends and wanders in his course. It is the work of a well-informed thinker, well acquainted with the subtleties of the schools, with a flair and a zest for the exercise of scholastic reasoning, who knows exactly what he wants to say, says it precisely and coherently, and because he is a poet movingly and strikingly as well. Our problem in reading him is not that of following one who rambles and wavers in his thinking but of catching the subtleties in the detail, the connexions and the general flow of his thought through the movement of the poem.

10. The Significance of Haukyn, *Activa Vita*, in *Piers Plowman*

STELLA MAGUIRE

IN SPITE OF ALL THE WORK which has been done on the interpretation of *Piers Plowman*, there still remains one figure who has never received the attention which he deserves, namely, Haukyn, *Activa Vita*.

Haukyn is only introduced once. After the *Visio* section of the poem has ended with the episode of Piers's pardon, the Dreamer sets out on his long search for Dowel. The search takes him into the company of Wit and Study, Clergy and Scripture, Reason and Ymagynatyf; and then, rather unexpectedly, he meets Active Life in the person of Haukyn, the "minstrel" and "wafrere." Haukyn makes his appearance half-way through Passus xiii, and the account of him occupies the rest of that passus and the whole of Passus xiv. Then he vanishes again and with his disappearance the *Vita de Dowel* comes to a close.[1]

What is the significance of Haukyn, and what are the poet's reasons for introducing him? These questions have never been really adequately answered. In the famous article "The Character of Piers Plowman considered from the B-Text," Haukyn is dismissed by Mr. Coghill as a "shadowy phantom": "Compare with the robustness of Piers those shadowy phantoms, Thought, Clergye, Imaginatyf, or even Haukyn." [2]

Mr. Carnegy[3] has a passing reference to Haukyn, but he is primarily interested in the part played by Patience in the Haukyn episode. Concerning Haukyn himself, he says only that he is "a worker who hates all idleness," adding that:

> In spite of this, his lot is one of cares and poverty, and in addition, his spiritual welfare leaves as much to be desired as does his earthly existence. . . . He believes in the teaching of the Church, but in spite of that, his soul is defiled with vices of all kinds.[4]

Reprinted by permission of the author and The Clarendon Press, Oxford, from *Review of English Studies*, XXV (1949) , 97–109.

For a recent partial analysis of the *Activa Vita* episode, see A. C. Spearing, "The Development of a Theme in *Piers Plowman*," RES, N. S., XI (1960) , 241–53.

1 All references are to the B-text.

2 *Medium Ævum*, ii (1933) , 118.

3 *The Relations between the Social and the Divine Order in William Langland's Vision of William concerning Piers the Plowman* (Breslau, 1934) .

4 P. 31.

The fullest consideration of Haukyn is that given by R. W. Chambers in the long study of *Piers Plowman* in *Man's Unconquerable Mind.*[5] There it is stated that:

Active Hawkyn is the servant of Piers: he bakes the food which the ploughman provides. He is the hard-working, Christian man, the Active Life. Why, it may be said, repeat the picture of the Active Life, which has already been depicted in Piers? I do not think that here we have mere repetition. As Walter Hilton explains, all men must *begin* with the Active Life. Piers had represented that almost perfect Active Life which is preparatory to the higher life. . . . Hawkyn is the inferior type of Active Man as Hilton defines him—ignorant, rough, untaught, with no savour of devotion, yet with a fear of God, and good will to his fellow-Christians.[6]

Chambers also emphasizes the fact that Haukyn is an allegorical and not merely a typical figure.

Literally, Hawkyn is a minstrel, a wafer-seller, a hard-working, industrious, cheerful soul, whose only fault is that his coat is untidy: . . . *Allegorically,* Hawkyn stands for the whole body of sinning, penitent laity.[7]

This view has been strongly criticized by Mr. Gerould,[8] who says that Chambers "strangely misrepresents what Langland wrote."

The long section devoted to [Haukyn] is in reality a powerful indictment of life devoted to material things, no matter how useful the objects in themselves. Hawkyn is self-important in boasting about what he has done for society. . . . Only when his obstinate folly has been overcome by Patience does he bitterly repent.[9]

This criticism seems to me, however, to arise from an incomplete realization of Haukyn's nature and function. I believe that Chambers's estimate is just, and that he rightly makes clear the three important facts, namely, that Haukyn is related in some way to Piers; that he represents an inferior form of Active Life; and that he has a hidden "significacio" as well as a place in the surface narrative of the poem. These facts provide the indispensable starting-points for the full consideration of Haukyn.

Little further interest has been aroused by Haukyn. Even Dr. Huppé,

5 London, 1939.
6 P. 151.
7 P. 152.
8 "The Structural Integrity of *Piers Plowman* B," *S.P.* xlv (Jan. 1948) , i.
9 P. 68 *n.*

in his admirable and exhaustive article, "The Authorship of the A- and B-Texts of *Piers Plowman*," [10] says only that:

> As Will's pilgrimage is actually to begin, he meets Active Life, who confesses his deadly sins. So in the *Visio* the confessions of the Sins were the prelude to the pilgrimage to Truth. The difference lies in the obvious sincerity of Active Life, who recognises his lack of worth and the tremendous obligations involved in leading a spiritual life. Thus, at the end of the *Vita de Dowel* (XIV) Active Life has reached the same conclusion as had Piers at the end of Will's dream in the *Visio:* that too close attention to the cares of making a living had blinded him to the only true purpose in life—Salvation. And just as this knowledge had prepared Piers, so it prepares Will—prefigured in Active Life—for Dobet.[11]

By this comparison of Haukyn's confession with the confessions of the Sins, and of the Dreamer's state of mind at the end of *Dowel* with Piers's state of mind at the end of the *Visio,* another important fact about the Haukyn episode is brought out, that is, its close connexion with the *Visio*. But this connexion is not limited to a likeness at certain points. It is not even limited to the general similarity of material—the problems of Active Life—which draws Haukyn and the *Visio* together, and sets them in contrast to the earlier part of the *Vita de Dowel,* which deals with the problems of the mind. It is, rather, a fundamental and indissoluble connexion. For Haukyn does not merely *belong* to the world of the *Visio* rather than to the more abstract world presented in the rest of *Dowel;* he is, in his own person, the *embodiment* of that world. So, it would seem, a close examination of Haukyn is indispensable for a proper understanding of the *Visio*.

The context of Haukyn's entry into the poem is important. He appears at the moment when the Dreamer has turned from the intellectual faculties, the states of mental achievement, and the fruits of learning—Wit and Clergy, Study and Scripture—to a guide of an entirely different nature: Patience. At the beginning of Passus xiii, the Dreamer still seems to hold to his faith in the possibility of an intellectual resolution of his problems. When

> there come Conscience . to comforte me that tyme,
> And bad me come to his courte . with Clergye sholde I dyne,

it is

10 *Speculum,* xxii (Oct. 1947) , 4.
11 P. 619.

And for Conscience of *Clergye* spake . I come wel the rather.
(xiii, 22–24)

Clergy is certainly present at the banquet, and so is a Doctor of Divinity;
but the third guest is Patience.

> Pacience and I . were put to be macches,
> And seten by owre selue . at a syde-borde.
(xiii, 35–36)

This introduction of Patience, and especially the placing of him in immediate contact with the Dreamer, is significant. It marks the beginning
of the change in the Dreamer's approach to his difficulties. For the difference between Patience, on the one hand, and Wit, Study, Scripture, Reason, and the rest, on the other, is a fundamental difference, a difference
of order and quality. Some or all of the figures who appear earlier in the
Vita de Dowel may have a moral bias, but none of them is a moral virtue
in the sense that Patience is a virtue. The appearance of Patience is the
first indication of a return from speculative to practical morality.

The banquet ends in disagreement among the guests, and Conscience
and the Dreamer set out on pilgrimage with Patience. It is then that they
meet with the "minstrel," Haukyn, *Activa Vita,* who says that:

> Alle ydel ich hatye . for of actyf is my name.
(xiii, 225)

The subsequent account of Haukyn is divided into four main sections:
the introduction, which is put into his own mouth; the description of his
"Coat of Christendom," soiled with the marks of the Seven Deadly Sins;
the advice given to him by Conscience; and finally, a long discourse between Haukyn and Patience.

In the first of these sections Haukyn is shown in his most favourable
light—not unnaturally, since this is Active Life's own estimate of itself.
He is seen here as a hard-working man, a "wafrere" and a minstrel, who
hates idleness, who feeds and entertains his fellow men, good and bad
alike, cheerfully and without questioning, even though he gets scanty reward. He has certain clear affinities with Piers, as Piers appeared in the
Visio, being occupied with the fundamental task of finding food for the
people. His industry, his scorn of wasters, are reminiscent of Piers. Nevertheless, he and Piers are carefully and explicitly differentiated.

> I haue none gode gyftes . . .
>
> saue a beneson on the Sonday,
> Whan the prest preyeth the peple . her pater-noster to bidde

> For Peres the Plowman . and that hym profite wayten.
> And that am I, Actyf . that ydelnesse hatye.
>
> (xiii, 234–38)

This distinction between the persons of Haukyn and Piers, and the accompanying suggestion of their servant-and-master relationship, is important when one remembers Mr. Coghill's argument that it is Piers, the original Piers of the *Visio,* who "fulfils emblematically the moral obligations of the Active Life." [12]

Haukyn, judged even by his own estimate of himself as given in the fifty lines of introduction, is not Active Life in its full connotation, but only its superficial aspect. He represents its most limited form, what one might call "Practical Life." He is included in Piers; the fulfilment of the "moral obligations of the Active Life" includes the honest, unimaginative decency of sound neighbourly conduct; but there can never be any question of identifying the two.

The real counterpart to Haukyn is to be found in the good element in the crowd who throng the Field of Folk in the Prologue, and in those of the pilgrims who loyally assist Piers in the ploughing of the half-acre in Passus vi. Moreover, through the relationship of these earlier characters to Haukyn, their relationship to Piers, who includes them in himself but transcends them, as he includes but transcends Haukyn, is made clearer. It is therefore especially interesting to note the obvious, and frequently remarked, reminiscence of the Prologue in Haukyn's description of his activities as a minstrel.

> Couthe I lye to do men laughe . thanne lacchen I shulde
> Other mantel or money . amonges lordes mynstralles.
>
> (xiii, 228–29)

As it is, he gets no rewards, because he has no aptitude for the more outrageous tricks associated with minstrelsy. The comparison with the description of the "true" minstrels in the Prologue clearly suggests itself.

> And somme murthes to make . as mynstralles conneth,
> And geten gold with her glee . synneles, I leue.
>
> (Prologue, 33–34)

Apart from his specific resemblance to these minstrels, Haukyn might well be considered to be the archetype of all those, in the Field of Folk who "pleyed ful selde" and "swonken ful harde," whatever their particular occupation. These phrases are admirably suited to describe his mode of living.

12 Op. cit., p. 131.

These links with the Prologue are important. When the Dreamer first beholds the scene of his initial vision, he does not understand the significance of its design. He observes the Tower and the Dungeon, but his attention is concentrated on the Field of Folk which lies between them. In other words, while realizing the existence of heaven and hell, his judgements of life on earth are based on temporal standards. He is able to differentiate between the good and the evil, but the reasons for his differentiation are inadequate, because they fail to take into account eternal values. The Dreamer, in the Prologue, sees the universe very much as it might be seen through the eyes of Haukyn. However, Holy Church intervenes to explain the real pattern of the scene, and in saying:

Of other heuene than here . holde thei no tale,

(i, 9)

she not only criticizes the behaviour of the majority of the Folk in the Field, but also subtly corrects the Dreamer's own attitude.

In consequence, there is a gap between the Prologue and the rest of the *Visio*. The Prologue presents the world as it appears to a spiritually unenlightened man; but, once Holy Church has admonished and instructed him, the Dreamer can never return to his original limited perception. All subsequent events must be judged by him in the light of her teaching. So, although the theme and subject-matter of the Prologue appear later in the *Visio*, its particular, partial comprehension of life does not, and an apparent loose end is left in the poet's reasoning. He fully develops the account of the life of the unjust, as they appeared among the Folk in the Field, but not the account of the life of the just. Against Mede and her followers, and later, against the Seven Deadly Sins, he does not put forward the conscientious honest toilers of the Prologue, who only reappear sporadically, but the great moral faculties, Conscience and Reason, and, finally, Piers himself. He begs the question of the adequacy of the good "practical life." Those who follow it are only reintroduced after the entrance of Piers, and even then, they are subordinate to Piers, and are shown simply as his servants or followers.

Can it, after all, be argued that this form of life, with its patient performance of hard work, and its faithful fulfilment of obligations, is sufficient for salvation? In the *Visio* the poet tacitly assumes that it cannot, but the doubt might still remain. In the Haukyn episode he triumphantly vindicates his own previous assumptions by first building up as favourable a picture as possible of this particular narrow form of Active Life, and then showing how inadequate it is to keep man from hell or to bring him to heaven.

Another obvious point of contact between the opening account of

Haukyn and the *Visio* is to be found in the mention of Haukyn's pardon. Haukyn complains that, although he finds bread for the Pope and "prouendre for his palfrey," he has never received any reward for his services

> Saue a pardoun with a peys of led . and two pollis amydde.
>   (xiii, 246)

The contents of this pardon are not stated, but Haukyn's rather sceptical attitude towards it suggests to the reader its possible affinity with the "bulle with bishopes seles" flourished by the Pardoner in the Prologue (Prologue, 69).

Haukyn then describes the pardon that he would himself like to dictate.

> Hadde iche a clerke that couthe write . I wolde caste hym a bille,
> That he sent me vnder his seel . a salue for the pestilence,
> And that his blessyng and his bulles . bocches miȝte destroye:
> *In nomine meo demonia eicient, et super egros manus imponent, et bene habebunt.*
> [In my name they shall cast out devils, and they shall lay their hands upon the sick, and they shall recover.]
>   (xiii, 247 ff.)

This clearly shows the nature and the limits of Haukyn's good intentions. His pardon would be a "practical" one, a simple cure for men's physical infirmities. It is inevitable that the reader should call to mind here that other pardon, which Piers received from Truth:

> Al in two lynes it lay . and nouȝt a leef more,
> And was written riȝt thus . in witnesse of treuthe:
> *Et qui bona egerunt, ibunt in vitam eternam;*
> *Qui vero mala, in ignem eternum.*
> [And those who have done good will go into eternal life; Those who have done evil, into eternal fire.]
>   (vii, 110 ff.)

The difference between the two pardons is symptomatic of the whole difference between Haukyn and Piers. It is symptomatic of the difference between a decent, well-intentioned life based on, and judged by, purely temporal conceptions of goodness, and a life lived in the light of eternity directed by the bidding of God. Man, unassisted by the grace of enlightenment, desires to cure men's bodies, the mortal and temporal element of human nature. God, revealing His will to men, teaches that men must consider eternity, and that temporal affairs are important only because they determine the eternal end.

Haukyn is given the chance to state his opinion of what constitutes the highest good (and I think he may be regarded, in this, as the representative and spokesman of all the honest toilers in the *Visio*). That opinion, voiced in the form of this imaginary pardon, is in itself proof of his inadequacy. It justifies the poet in his earlier assumption that this form of life, admirable though it may be in many ways, is not sufficient to ensure salvation for those who follow it.

When Haukyn's initial account of himself is ended, attention is turned to the "Coat of Christendom" which he wears, a coat:

> moled in many places . with many sondri plottes,
> (xiii, 275)

—the stains of the Seven Deadly Sins. In the description of these stains the poet completes the task of proving the inadequacy of the good practical life as a means of reaching heaven. He reveals here its utter inability to refrain from sin of all kinds.

The episode of the Coat of Christendom is apt to cause Langland's apologists some difficulty. It is highly reminiscent of the Sins' own confessions in Passus v, and at first glance seems to be an instance of unwarrantable repetition for moral instruction's sake. Nevertheless, it is misleading to dwell too much on the repetitions and near-repetitions of material previously used. Some of the most striking similarities between the account of the stains on Haukyn's coat and earlier passages relating to the Sins are similarities of detail. The same particular manifestations of the Sins are recounted; the same subdivision of them into specific "branches" is made. For example, the Dreamer, noticing the stains of Envy on the Coat of Christendom, says that Haukyn has:

> made of frendes foes . thorugh a false tonge.
> (xiii, 328)

This is a clear reminiscence of Envy's own confession:

> I haue a neighbore neyȝe me . I haue ennuyed hym ofte,
> And lowen on hym to lordes . to don hym lese his siluer,
> And made his frendes ben his foon . thorw my false tonge.
> (v, 94–96)

Or, to take another example, the same "branch" of Sloth is instanced twice. We are told in Passus xiii that this particular branch

> Is, whanne a man morneth nouȝte for his mysdedes . ne maketh no sorwe,
> Ac penaunce that the prest enioigneth . perfourneth yuel.
> (xiii, 411–12)

This repeats, almost word for word, Sloth's own confession that

> I parfourned neure penaunce . as the prest me hiȝte,
> Ne ryȝte sori for my synnes . ȝet was I neuere.
>
> (v, 405–6)

These are typical examples of the sort of reminiscence of the Sins' confessions to be found in the account of Haukyn's Coat. (It need hardly be mentioned that the device of the stained coat is not consistently preserved. The whole passage is, of course, really Haukyn's own confession of his sins.)

Now, whatever view one may take of the poet's originality of phrase in describing the Sins, I think it must be admitted that his subject-matter here is traditional. In appending certain definite "branches" when mentioning the main sin, he simply follows contemporary custom. Didactic works of the type of the *Ayenbite of Inwyt* abound in instances of the habit. If, then, one wishes to object to the repetitions in the account of Haukyn's coat, it must be because the Sins are reintroduced at all, rather than because they are represented under the same aspects as in earlier parts of the poem.

The real reason for the reappearance of the Sins at this point is given in Chambers's remark, already quoted: "*Allegorically,* Haukyn stands for the whole body of sinning, penitent laity." This states the important truth. Haukyn is *not* a typical, representative human being; he is the personification of a whole manner of life. He is one of the most subtle of the allegorical figures created by the poet, and it is not always easy to keep his full significance clearly in mind.

As was seen in the examination of Haukyn's own account of himself, he has affinities with the simple, good-living labourers in the Prologue, and with the well-intentioned pilgrims who gather round Piers. Nevertheless, although he represents them, and speaks for them, he is not of their physical company. He is not merely "An Active Man."

Activa Vita is the assumed but unstated background to which all the events of the *Visio*—the whole abstract interplay, the three passus of drama and argument that centre around Mede, the episode of the Sins, the instruction given by Holy Church, the guidance offered by Piers—are to be referred. It is the composite whole from which many of the figures who appear in the *Visio* are abstracted. Not only the majority of the flesh-and-blood Folk, but certain of the allegorical figures also—Cyuile, for example—represent one aspect or another of Active Life. In addition, it may be regarded as the setting of the *Visio,* the world in which the events described take place. Then, too, it is also the material which many of the allegorical figures work upon and influence; we are certainly shown the effects of Mede and the Sins, of Conscience, Reason, and Kynde Witte, upon Active Life. So, since Haukyn is Active Life personified, he stands in an important but complex relationship to the *Visio*.

No single term will serve exactly to define this relationship. Haukyn is neither a simplification nor a recapitulation of the *Visio*. The connexion resembles rather that between commentary and original theme, but the apportioning of the parts is constantly shifting. At one minute Haukyn "explains" certain points in the *Visio;* at the next, recourse to the *Visio* is necessary in order to "explain" Haukyn. The background of the *Visio*—the continuity of argument linking the various episodes and figures—is assumed rather than stated; one is shown conclusions rather than the processes of arriving at them. The accounts of Mede, Conscience, Reason, the Sins, Piers, the pilgrims, have an essential fundamental connexion which the reader is expected to supply mentally, but they are treated episodically and separately. In the account of Haukyn, on the other hand, it is the fundamental connexion which is stressed, while the incidents and characters which were developed in the *Visio* are only touched upon comparatively briefly.

The introduction of the Seven Deadly Sins into the account of Haukyn is an instance of the way in which this episode serves to draw together the separate strands of the *Visio*. The association of Haukyn, who recalls the good elements among the Folk, with the Sins, helps to level the just and the unjust. It reminds the reader that no man is capable of claiming heaven by reason of his own righteousness, and that Reason's call to repentance in Passus v is necessarily addressed to *all* men, not merely to the more open sinners among them. Not only the "wasters," but those who "swonken ful harde" wear a "Coat of Christendom" stained with the marks of sin.

With the close of Passus xiii, the description of Haukyn ends. The next passus deals with the advice he receives from Conscience, and with the discourse between himself and Patience. Once again, one finds that the study of Haukyn involves a study of his relationship to the *Visio,* and once again it is necessary to remember the complexity of this relationship.

The material of the *Visio* is re-viewed in Haukyn. Its elements are regrouped by a process of allusion now to one passus, now to another. What was implicit is made explicit. But, it must also be remembered, there are abruptnesses and apparent *non sequiturs* in Haukyn which are only explicable if the poet's intentions are faithfully observed—that is, if the reader obeys his implied reminders to refer back constantly to the *Visio*.

Passus xiv opens with Haukyn's reply to the gentle rebuke given by Conscience in the last lines of the preceding passus:

> Thus Haukyn the actyf man . hadde ysoiled his cote,
> Til Conscience acouped hym there-of . in a curteise manere,
> Whi he ne hadde wasshen it . or wyped it with a brusshe.
>
> (xiii, 458–60)

The reply is an attempt to justify himself, and to make excuses for the state of his coat. It is his only garment, he wears it by night and by day; besides, his wife and children

> "wolen bymolen it many tyme . maugre my chekes!"
> [will spot it many times in spite of my efforts!]
>
> (xiv, 4)

His repentance of his sins is not yet absolute and without reservation; the urging of Conscience is still needed to bring him to true penitence. He regrets his inability to keep his coat free from stains:

> And couthe I neuere, by Cryste . kepen it clene an houre,
> That I ne soiled it with syʒte . or sum ydel speche,
> Or thorugh werke or thorugh worde . or wille of myn herte,
>
> (xiv, 12–14)

whereupon Conscience comes to his assistance with the promise to teach him Contrition,

> That shal clawe thi cote . of alkynnes filthe.
>
> (xiv, 17)

Then, through Confession (Dowel) , Purpose of Amendment (Dobet) , and Satisfaction (Dobest) , the cleansing shall be completed, and

> Shall none heraude ne harpoure . haue a fairere garnement
> Than Haukyn the actyf man . and thou do by my techyng.
>
> (xiv, 24–25)

Conscience teaches Haukyn to repent, and Patience teaches him to suffer God's will gladly and with trust.

> "And I shal purueye the paste," quod Pacyence . "though no plow
>   erie [is stirring],
> And floure to fede folke with . as best be for the soule,
> Though neuere greyne growed . ne grape vppon vyne.
> Alle that lyueth and loketh . lyflode [livelihood] wolde I fynde,

And that ynough shal none faille . of thinge that hem nedeth.
We shulde nouȝt be to busy . a-bouten owre lyflode."

(xiv, 28–33)

Then, drawing something from his bag, he offers it to Haukyn, saying:

"lo! here lyflode ynough . if owre byleue be trewe."

(xiv, 38)

The Dreamer studies this thing so praised by Patience, and finds that it is:

a pece of the pater-noster . *fiat voluntas tua* [thy will be done].

(xiv, 48)

Patience bids Haukyn take it, and eat it when he is hungry or cold or thirsty, and no earthly pain will be able to grieve him, for "pacientes vincunt" [the patient conquer]. But he must be sober of sight and speech, and in the use of all his five wits, and must "take no thought for the morrow." Then, after the exposition and illustration of the theme that "God will provide," Patience says:

And if men lyued as mesure wolde . shulde neuere more be defaute
Amonges Cristene creatures . if Crystes wordes ben trewe.
Ac vnkyndnesse *caristia* [dearth] maketh . amonges Crystene peple,
And ouer-plente maketh pruyde . amonges pore and riche;
Ac mesure is so moche worth . it may nouȝte be to dere.

(xiv, 71–74)

Here we have clearly both a reminiscence and an expansion of the words spoken by Holy Church to the Dreamer in the *Visio:*

Mesure is medcyne . thouȝ thow moche ȝerne.

(i, 35)

Patience then continues:

For-thi mesure we vs wel . and make owre faithe owre scheltroun,

(xiv, 81)

and concludes with a virtual repetition of the counsel given by Conscience, the need for contrition, the value of confession, and the supreme power of satisfaction:

satisfaccioun seketh oute the rote . and bothe sleeth and voideth,
And, as it neuere had ybe . to nouȝt bryngeth dedly synne.

(xiv, 94–95)

As soon as Patience's speech is ended, Haukyn asks abruptly:

> Where woneth charite?
>
> (xiv, 97)

The point of this sudden question can only be seen if one refers once again to the *Visio*.

In Passus v the whole pattern of repentance, as Langland sees it, is made abundantly clear. First come the confessions of the Sins, then the intervention of Repentance, who pities the sinners; then Hope's horn is blown with: *"beati quorum remisse sunt iniquitates"* [Blessed are they whose iniquities are forgiven] (v, 515) ; and finally, the throng of people:

> Criede vpward to Cryst . and to his clene moder
> To haue grace to go with hem . Treuthe to seke.
>
> (v, 518–19)

In other words, for Langland repentance is not an end in itself but a beginning. It is a preliminary, a condition which must be fulfilled in order to set the soul free for its real task: the search for God.

The same conception of the function of penitence must be presupposed in the account of Haukyn. Otherwise, the immediate transition from the theme of repentance to the apparently irrelevant question: "Where is charity to be found?" would be inexplicable.

Haukyn, like the Folk in Passus v, has been taught the need to repent and confess his sins. Like the Folk, he immediately passes on from the thought of penitence to the desire to seek for God. Although the pilgrims in Passus v ask the way to "truth," while Haukyn asks the way to "charity," it is the same question in another form. For here again there is to be seen an instance of the drawing together of the different strands of the *Visio*. The themes of repentance and the turning towards God (Truth) belong to Passus v; but much earlier in the poem Holy Church has shown that Truth and Love are bound together. It is Truth (which, in Passus i, stands both for God Himself and for the gift of God to men) that

> telleth that loue . is triacle of heuene,
>
> (i, 146)
>
> And alle his werkes he wrouȝte . with loue as him liste,
> And lered it Moises for the leuest thing.
>
> (i, 148–49)

So Haukyn, in wishing to seek for God after he has repented of his sins, recalls the theme of Passus v, but in asking the way to "charity" rather than to "truth" he recalls the tremendous teachings of Passus i.

The link between Truth and Love is finally closed by Patience, who answers Haukyn by saying:

> There *parfit treuthe* and pouere herte is . and pacience of tonge,
> There is Charitee, the chief chaumbrere . for god hymselue.
>
> (xiv, 99–100)

Haukyn then inquires:

> Whether paciente pouerte . . . be more plesaunte to owre driȝte
> Than ricchesse riȝtfulliche ywonne . and resonablelich yspended?
>
> (xiv, 101–2)

and the rest of the passus is taken up with Patience's discussion of the proposition. This discussion introduces yet another of the themes of the *Visio:* the theme of Mede, of worldly goods and their right use.

The main points in Patience's reply to Haukyn's question are these. His immediate answer is "Yes"; and he goes on to give his reasons for it. The rich

> han her hyre here . an heuene as it were;
>
> (xiv, 128)

and although Christ will

> rewarde alle dowble ricchesse . that reuful hertes habbeth,
>
> (xiv, 148)
>
> it nys but selde yseyn . . .
> That god rewarded double reste . to any riche wye.
>
> (xiv, 155–56)

Finally he says:

> For seuene synnes that there ben . assaillen vs euere,
> The fende folweth hem alle . and fondeth hem to helpe,
> Ac with ricchesse that ribaude . rathest men bigyleth.
>
> (xiv, 201–3)

This, I think, makes the poet's attitude towards temporal goods abundantly clear, and explains the reason for the judgement finally given against Mede in Passus iv. He does not condemn riches as being intrinsically evil, but while admitting the possibility of their meritorious use, he distrusts them; he is afraid of them because they are dangerous to the soul of their possessor. They are not sinful in themselves, but they incite men to sin.

After this discourse on riches, the passus closes with the spectacle of

Haukyn weeping and lamenting and wishing that he had died as soon as he was christened, since it is so grievous to have to live and to sin.

The story of Haukyn, then, is the story of the passage from self-satisfaction, through the growing awareness of the sinfulness of human nature, to final repentance; and repentance, when it is complete, involves the desire to seek for God and the things which are His. The placing of such a story, with its strong reminiscences of the events and lessons of the *Visio,* at the end of five passus of discussion of the speculative and intellectual problems of salvation, is a sharp reminder that knowledge and intellectual power do not absolve one from the necessity of meeting certain plain moral requirements which must be satisfied by all men, "lered" and "lewed" alike. Study, Clergy, and the rest of the learned company have their place in the search for salvation, but the fundamental obligations remain; Conscience must still be obeyed, and Patience must still be acquired.

This episode has therefore a double significance. In the first place, it is integral to the main structure of the poem. Coming where it does, it shows that the arguments established in the *Visio* are not to be discarded; they are not nullified or superseded by the speculations of the earlier part of the *Vita de Dowel.* Secondly, in its methods, in its linking together of the various themes and episodes of the *Visio* by referring them in turn to the unifying central figure of Haukyn, it makes clear the fundamental wholeness and singleness of the first part of the poem. The problems and teaching of the *Visio* are, obviously, concerned with various aspects of Active Life: the right use of temporal goods, the fact of sin and the need for repentance, the urge of the penitent soul to seek for God, the difficulties to be overcome in that search; but each aspect is considered separately. They are only synthesized when the poet, in the richness and completeness of his allegorical perception, personifies, in the figure of Haukyn, the very life, the whole of which they are the parts.

11. The Action of Langland's
Second Vision
JOHN BURROW

I

THE SECOND of the ten visions in the B version of *Piers Plowman* contains some of the poem's most famous episodes. It has the confession of the Seven Deadly Sins in Passus v, the ploughing of the half-acre in Passus vi, and the tearing of the pardon in Passus vii. Critics have devoted a good deal of attention to these episodes; but they have generally failed to see them as parts of that whole to which they most immediately belong—the action, that is, of the second vision. I hope to show that, so far as its action is concerned, this vision *is* a whole, and that its more difficult episodes make better sense if we see them as parts of it. This is in the general belief that readers and critics of Langland have made too little of his vision-structure. I suppose that many people do not even know that the B version has ten visions.

One cannot appreciate the wholeness of the second vision if one starts from the three famous episodes just mentioned. It may be worth recalling what Aristotle says about wholeness: "A whole is that which has beginning, middle, and end. A beginning is that which is not itself necessarily after anything else, and which has naturally something else after it; an end is that which is naturally after something itself, either as its necessary or usual consequent, and with nothing else after it; and a middle, that which is by nature after one thing and has also another after it. A well-constructed plot, therefore, cannot either begin or end at any point one likes" *(Poetics,* translated Bywater, Chap. 7) . But an action which begins with a confession, proceeds with a ploughing and ends with a pardon can hardly be called usual or natural, let alone necessary. On the contrary, it seems quite arbitrary. One feels one could extend it indefi-

Reprinted by permission of the author and F. W. Bateson from *Essays in Criticism,* XV (1965) , 247–68.

For some interesting approaches to medieval allegory, see Morton W. Bloomfield, "A Grammatical Approach to Personification Allegory," *MP,* LX (1963) , 161–71; Edward Bloom, "The Allegorical Principle," *ELH,* XVIII (1951) , 163–90; Angus Fletcher, *Allegory, the Theory of the Symbolic Mode* (Ithaca, N. Y., 1964) ; and Robert W. Frank, Jr., "The Art of Reading Medieval Personification Allegory," *ELH,* XX (1953) , 237–50.

nitely, with masses, sea-voyages, community singing and the like, "beginning and ending at any point one likes."

The feeling that the whole thing could be otherwise is not unfamiliar
to readers of *Piers Plowman*, perhaps; but in the second vision at least
there is a well-constructed plot, however incoherent our usual memories
of it may be. The parts of this plot are not confession, ploughing and pardon, but sermon, confession, pilgrimage and pardon.

This series may itself seem somewhat arbitrary; but Langland wrote
for readers who would appreciate its coherence. A sinful man hears a
SERMON. This is the beginning of the action: it is "not itself necessarily
after anything else"; but it "has naturally something else after it" insofar as it moves its hearer to contrition and so sends him on to CONFES-
SION. This is a middle, not an end, because the priest's absolution,
though it wipes away the guilt ("culpa") and the eternal punishment,
leaves a debt of temporal punishment to be paid. Hence penance necessarily follows confession; and a usual form of penance, in hard cases, is
PILGRIMAGE. But a pilgrimage is not an end either, for it is not normally thought sufficient in itself to pay off the whole debt of temporal
punishment. This is done by the plenary PARDON (or indulgence), the
usual object of major fourteenth-century pilgrimages. The pardon is a
true end, both because it follows the pilgrimage as its "usual consequent," and because it requires nothing else after it. By its power the
penitent is freed from the last consequences of his sin; and the arc of
penitential action is therefore complete.

Before going on to examine what Langland does with this plot, let me
briefly suggest a reason why he chose it for this particular vision. The
story of Lady Meed, in the first vision, concludes with the triumph of
Conscience and Reason in the King's court at Westminster. This represents a major reformation of society—the reformation of law; but Conscience's response to the King's enthusiasm suggests that it is not enough.
The King says:

> "I wil have leute in lawe and lete be al yowre ianglyng,
> And as moste folke witnesseth wel wronge shal be demed;"

to which Conscience replies:

> "but the comune wil assent
> It is ful hard, bi myn hed, here-to to brynge it,
> Alle yowre lige leodes to lede thus evene."
>   (Passus iv, 180–84) [1]

---

[1] All quotations are from W. W. Skeat's two-volume edition (Oxford, 1886).

This is the cue for the second vision: the "comune"—that is, the whole of the community, not just the King and his judges—must assent to the rule of Reason. What Langland has in mind here is not a total, apocalyptic transformation of society: that event, prophesied by Conscience in Passus iii (282 ff.) , is placed in the future, out of the range of the *Visio*. He means rather to show the kind of change, or conversion, that can be expected of people here, now, and in England. His problem was to find some form of action which would represent such a change. This cannot have been easy; and the course of the second vision, as we shall see, suggests that the solution he adopted caused him some misgivings. But the sermon-confession-pilgrimage-pardon sequence had definite advantages. It was a familiar and at the same time a dramatic way of turning from sin to righteousness; and it was a way which a whole society—or at least a representative "thousand of men"—could plausibly be shown as taking.

One should realise that it was quite common in the Middle Ages for great public sermons to be followed by mass confession and a mass pilgrimage in search of pardon. An early example is the First Crusade (1095) . After the Pope's sermon at Clermont, the audience knelt, recited the Confiteor, and undertook an armed pilgrimage to Jerusalem, the Pope promising plenary pardon to all who took part. Norman Cohn, in his book *The Pursuit of the Millennium,* discusses this and many other examples of what he calls the "collective quest for salvation." The quest was often associated, as in the case of the First Crusade, with a period of natural calamity. People were specially ready at such times to "cluster in devotional and penitential groups"—just like Langland's thousand men—and set out on crusades, or on other more pacific kinds of pilgrimage. It is perhaps worth noticing here that the very calamities referred to by Langland's Reason in his sermon—the winds and pestilences of 1361-2—provoked just such a reaction. John of Bridlington, a contemporary of Langland's, reports that "on account of the pestilence certain English lords received the sign of the Cross to go to the Holy Land." [2] Such movements were less frequent in England than on the Continent, where "hordes" of penitential pilgrims seem to have been almost commonplace; but Langland must have known about them. For his presentation of the conversion of the "comune" as a collective or horde response to natural calamity implies knowledge, if not approval.

II

The plot described in the last section provides the essential ground-

2 See *Political Poems and Songs,* ed. Thomas Wright, Vol. I (London, 1859) , p. 183.

plan of the second vision: unless one perceives it the whole structure will remain unintelligible. But it is no more than the ground-plan. The vision does not give a straight, literal account of a collective quest for salvation. Langland, rather, uses the customary sequence of events as a base from which to derive his allegorical action. The reader must know the original sequence, obviously; but most of the interest lies in the process of cut, addition and substitution by which it is transformed. In the case of the second vision, as I hope to show, it is specially important to attend to the substitutions. Since these do not become really interesting until we reach the third and fourth stages of the story, I shall deal with the sermon and the confession rather briefly.

The vision begins with Reason's sermon to the "comune" (identified with the "felde ful of folke" of the Prologue). Reason preaches to "alle the reume," with a cross, and in the King's presence. These details suggest a great episcopal occasion, rather than an ordinary parochial one; and the character of the sermon itself rather supports this impression. It is a "sermo ad diversos status hominum," such as fourteenth-century bishops are known to have preached on special occasions—an address to the various "states" of men, calling upon husbands, fathers, priests etc. to amend their ways. Yet the preacher is Reason, not a fourteenth-century bishop; and his homely tone suggests the personification rather than the parson:

> "My syre seyde so to me and so did my dame,
> That the levere childe the more lore bihoveth,
> And Salamon seide the same that Sapience made,
> *Qui parcit virge, odit filium.*
> [He who spares the rod hates his son.]
> The Englich of this Latyn is, who-so wil it knowe,
> Who-so spareth the sprynge spilleth his children."
>
> (v, 37–41)

This represents what any man's reason will tell him about his duties; and it is this reasoning with oneself, rather than any grand public preaching, which Langland sees as the beginning of the conversion of the folk of the field. People have only to take thought to see that all is not as it should be. Yet we should note, in view of developments later in the vision, that the substitution of Reason for the usual priest or bishop is not polemical. Langland, that is, does not seem concerned to score points off the priests and bishops by suggesting that self-examination is *better* than sermon-going.

There is a like absence of polemic in the second stage of the action—the confession. Here Langland substitutes the personifications of the Seven

Deadly Sins (representing the sins of the folk) for the penitents, and the personification of Repentance for the confessor. The latter substitution is not an altogether happy one: "confessing to Repentance," unlike "listening to Reason," makes little sense when one tries to convert it into literal terms. But the general point of the episode is quite clear. Once a man has taken thought and recognised his imperfections, he must then repent and confess. It must be admitted that Langland is vague about the externals of the confession. For example, Repentance speaks, in the manner of a confessor, of absolving the Sins individually (v, 186 & 276) ; but his actual absolution, which must be looked for in v, 486–513, is of a purely general and supplicatory character. He simply prays that God may have mercy on them all. The fact that this prayer ends with Hope blowing his horn of "Deus tu conversus vivificabis nos" [You will turn, O God, and bring us to life] (514) suggests that Langland is here thinking of public liturgical, rather than private sacramental, penance; for this verse from the Psalms occurs after the Confiteor and the absolution-prayer Misereatur in the Mass.[3] But such inconsistencies are typically Langlandian. We do not conclude that he thought sacramental absolution unnecessary or *merely* external.

It is, I want now to argue, exactly because he did think this way about pilgrimages that the third stage of his action presented him with a special challenge. The fact is beyond dispute. Langland, to put it bluntly, though he believed in sermons and confessions, did not believe in pilgrimages. His opinion of pilgrims is clearly stated in the Prologue:

> Pilgrymes and palmers plighted hem togidere
> To seke Seynt Iames and seyntes in Rome.
> Thei went forth in here wey with many wise tales,
> And hadden leve to lye al here lyf after.
>
> (Prol. 46–49)

Later in the first vision Reason says that, in his ideal society, St. James would be sought "there I shal assigne" (iv, 126) . The point of this enigmatic remark is made clear in the C-text, where Reason requires that

> "Seynt Iame be souht ther poure syke lyggen,
> In prisons and in poore cotes for pilgrymages to Rome."
>
> (C. v, 122–23)

Reason, in other words, tells us that it is better to do good works at home than to travel abroad on pilgrimages. The B-text has a very similar passage later on, when Anima, speaking of Charity, says that it is his custom

---

[3] I owe this information to Mr. S. Tugwell, who also points out that the source of the verse (wrongly given by Skeat) is Psalm 84.7 (Vulgate) .

> "to wende in pilgrymage
> There pore men and prisones liggeth her pardoun to have."
>
>   (xv, 177–78)

Good works *instead of* pilgrimage: this is surely also the point of the pilgrimage to Truth proclaimed by Reason at the end of his sermon in the second vision:

> "And ye that seke Seynte Iames and seintes of Rome,
> Seketh Seynt Treuthe for he may save yow alle."
>
>   (v, 57–58)

Seeking St. James and the saints of Rome is not an acceptable form of penance—the echo of the Prologue is sufficient proof of that. So the substitution of St. Truth (i.e., God) for these saints, unlike the substitutions of Reason and Repentance for preacher and confessor, *is* polemical. There is a new tension here between the allegorical action and that which it signifies. The pilgrimage proposed by Reason signifies, one might almost say, *anything but* actual pilgrimage.

Langland makes this point dramatically in the last part of his long fifth passus. After the confession of the Sins and Repentance's great prayer, a thousand men from the field full of folk cluster (Langland uses the word "thrungen") into a devotional and penitential group, and set out on the expiatory pilgrimage proclaimed by Reason. But they are not yet real pilgrims by any standards—Langland's or the world's—for they have no sense of where they are going. So they just roam about like a herd of animals, until they meet the Palmer:

> blustreden forth as bestes over bankes and hilles,
> Til late was and longe that thei a lede mette,
> Apparailled as paynym in pylgrymes wyse.
>
>   (v, 521–23)

The Palmer is a pure grotesque, embodying everything Langland most hated in the pilgrims of his day—the worldliness, the meaningless rigmarole of place-names and keepsakes, and above all the bland complacency:

> "Ye may se bi my signes that sitten on myn hatte,
> That I have walked ful wyde in wete and in drye,
> And soughte gode seyntes for my soules helth."
>
>   (v, 536–38)

The Palmer knows all the "good saints," it appears, except Truth. He represents the business of worldly pilgrimage, and so stands to be contrasted with Piers, the representative of the true or spiritual pilgrimage, who "puts forth his head" for the first time at this point in the poem. The contrast is boldly stated, and there is no need to enlarge upon it. Piers knows Truth well, and he knows the way to his place. It leads through Meekness, Conscience, Love of God, Love of Neighbour, and the Ten Commandments.

By the end of the fifth passus, then, Langland has established his third substitution—that of St. Truth for St. James and the saints of Rome—and has made sure, one would have thought, that the reader sees its polemical point. So we have every reason to expect, as we begin the sixth passus, that he will proceed with his account of the conversion of the commune by showing them following the road described by Piers, reaching Truth's shrine, and receiving his pardon. The actual course of events in the sixth passus is therefore disturbing—and, I think, deliberately so.

The opening of the passus gives no particular cause for alarm. Piers offers to guide the people on the way to Truth; but first he has a "half-acre bi the heighe way" to plough and sow. One may not quite see the point of this interruption; but it does not seem to matter very much. Ploughing and sowing a single half-acre cannot take very long—it seems in fact to have been no more than a customary "long morning's work" [4] —and the land is right "bi the heighe way," the road which the pilgrims are to travel (described in the C-text as the "alta via ad fidelitatem"). So one expects the company to resume its journey very shortly. True, when Piers enlists the help of the pilgrims and instructs them in their various duties—the ladies to sew church vestments, the common women to spin and weave, the knight to hunt and fight, etc.—he seems to be treating the long morning's interruption in the half-acre as if it were a lifetime in the world; but we are comforted by his repeated assurances that he will lead the pilgrims on shortly, as soon as he is ready:

> "Hadde I eried this half-acre and sowen it after,
> I wolde wende with yow and the way teche"
>
> (vi, 5–6)
>
> "And I shal apparaille me," quod Perkyn, "in pilgrimes wise
> And wende with you I wil til we fynde Treuthe"
>
> (59–60)
>
> "I wil sowe it myself and sitthenes wil I wende
> To pylgrymage as palmers don pardoun forto have"
>
> (65–66)

---

[4] See G. C. Homans, *English Villagers of the Thirteenth Century* (Cambridge, Mass., 1941), p. 49.

> "To penaunce and to pilgrimage I wil passe with thise other.
> For-thi I wil, or I wende, do wryte my biqueste"
>
> (86–87)

The "bequest," or will, which these last lines introduce seems at first to provide further reassurance; for the making of a will was a customary part of the preparations for a pilgrimage, it being necessary to set one's house in order in case one did not get back safely. Surely, we feel, Piers *is* going to set out on the journey. Yet it is the will which, in its closing passage, first positively suggests that this is not so. After bequeathing his soul to God, his body to the Church and his lawful winnings to his wife and children, Piers speaks of what is left:

> "And with the residue and the remenaunte, bi the rode of Lukes,
> I wil worschip ther-with Treuthe bi my lyve,
> And ben his pilgryme atte plow for pore mennes sake.
> My plow-fote shal be my pyk-staf and picche atwo the rotes,
> And helpe my culter to kerve and clense the forwes."
>
> (vi, 102–6)

This noble passage strongly suggests that Langland has in mind, however bewilderingly, a second polemical substitution. The opening lines recall a bit of anti-pilgrimage polemic in the confession of Sloth in the previous passus (a parallel which is even closer in the A-text where Piers refers, like Sloth, to the rood of Chester) :

> "And with the residue and the remenaunt, bi the rode of Chestre,
> I shal seke Treuthe arst ar I se Rome."
>
> (v, 467–68)

But the present passage goes further than that. Having substituted the pilgrimage to Truth, proclaimed by Reason and described by Piers, for the false and meaningless Rome-running represented by the Palmer, Langland now has Piers talk of a "pilgrimage at the plough," as if the ploughing of the half-acre was to be substituted for the pilgrimage to Truth.

The rest of the sixth passus, together with the beginning of the seventh, seems to me to provide decisive evidence that this was indeed Langland's intention, despite the opinion of several good recent critics (T. P. Dunning and R. W. Frank among them) to the contrary. The main point to note in Passus vi is the disintegration of the time-scheme proposed in its opening passage. The long morning's work stretches out to a whole year. The action of the passus begins round about Michaelmas, at the beginning of the husbandman's year, with the ploughing and sowing of the winter corn field—Piers' half-acre. Then, after the intervention of Hunger, there follows a threshing:

> Faitoures for fere her-of flowen into bernes,
> And flapten on with flayles fram morwe til even.
> [The false men fled in terror to the barns
> And flapped with flails from morning to evening.]
>
> (vi, 186–87)

This comes in its right place, for, as Homans observes in his excellent account of the medieval farming year, "after the sowing of the winter corn field, the husbandman would be likely to turn from the land to the barn, where he would busy himself with the sheaves of the last harvest" (op. cit., p. 356). There follows the discussion between Piers and Hunger about poor-relief, after which we learn from Piers that the people are to live sparsely until Lammas (August 1st).

> "And bi that, I hope to have hervest in my croft."
>
> (292)

Then, with dream-like suddenness, "hervest" or autumn (the period between Lammas and Michaelmas) approaches once more, bringing the wheel round in a full circle:

> By that it neighed nere hervest newe corne cam to chepynge;
> Thanne was folke fayne and fedde Hunger with the best.
>
> (301–2)

So the people, it would seem, are no longer merely pausing by the highway on their pilgrimage to Truth. They are living, under Piers' guidance, through the whole yearly cycle of dearth and abundance which determined the everyday life of the medieval "commune."

But the decisive indication that the pilgrimage is not to be resumed comes at the beginning of the following passus:

> Treuthe herde telle her-of and to Peres he sent
> To taken his teme and tulyen the erthe,
> And purchaced hym a pardoun *a pena et a culpa* [from
>   punishment and from guilt]
> For hym, and for his heires for evermore after;
> And bad hym holde hym at home and eryen his leyes,
> And alle that halpe hym to erie to sette or to sowe,
> Or any other myster that myghte Pieres availle,
> Pardoun with Pieres Plowman Treuthe hath ygraunted.
>
> (vii, 1–8)

Two things, for the moment, are particularly to be noticed in this passage. First, Truth sends a message to Piers telling him to "holde hym at home" and plough his lands once more—in preparation for another year of sowing and reaping. This surely means that on one level—the literal level—the pilgrimage is abandoned. For St. Truth himself, the very object of the proposed pilgrimage, commands his servant to stay at home. At the same time, the fact that Truth obtains a plenary pardon for Piers, his heirs and his helpers, suggests equally clearly that the pilgrimage is, in another sense, completed. Critics have not generally drawn this inference; but it seems quite unavoidable. Piers himself said, towards the beginning of the sixth passus, that he would go.

> "To pylgrymage as palmers don *pardoun forto have*."
>   (vi, 66)

Truth's pardon is the object of the pilgrimage to Truth; so the granting of it can only mean that the object of the pilgrimage has been attained. There seems no alternative to this simple explanation of why the pardon comes at this point in the action. We are forced to recognise a second substitution. Piers will not lead the folk on a pilgrimage "as palmers don." *His* pike-staff is a plough-foot, *his* scrip a seed-hopper, and *his* pilgrimage a pilgrimage at the plough.

In the third stage of his action, then, Langland first substitutes an allegorical pilgrimage for a real one, and then substitutes for that allegorical pilgrimage something which is not a pilgrimage at all, even in the allegorical action. "Pilgrimage" first becomes an allegorical form or "vehicle," then dwindles into a mere metaphor. The point of both transformations is essentially the same; but the second involves a more explicit emphasis on the idea of "holding oneself at home."

In the forty-fifth chapter of Rabelais' *Gargantua*, Grangousier addresses the following "good words" to a company of pilgrims recently swallowed by Gargantua in a salad: "Go your ways, poor men, in the name of God the Creator, to whom I pray to guide you perpetually; and henceforward be not so ready to undertake these idle and unprofitable journeys. Look to your families, labour every man in his vocation, instruct your children, and live as the good Apostle St. Paul directeth you: in doing whereof God, his angels and sancts, will guard and protect you, and no evil or plague at any time shall befall you." This view of pilgrimage—which is exactly Langland's—can be traced right back to the Fathers. Typical statements are to be found in Jerome—"the palace of heaven can be reached as well from Britain as from Jerusalem; for the Kingdom of God is within you"—and in Augustine—"one must travel to Him who is everywhere present and everywhere all, not with one's feet but with one's conduct *(non pedibus, sed moribus)*." In another passage, Augustine finds scriptural authority for the idea in the words of Christ to the woman of Samaria: "Woman, believe me, the hour cometh when ye shall neither in this mountain, nor yet at Jerusalem, worship the Father. . . . God is a Spirit: and they that worship him must worship him in spirit and in truth" (John IV. 21 & 24) .

This biblical antithesis between worshipping God "at Jerusalem" (interpreted by Augustine, evidently, as a reference to pilgrimages) and worshipping him "in spirit and in truth" is particularly close, I believe, to Langland's thought in the fifth and sixth passus. We must recall that in Passus i Holy Church uses the word "truth" not only of God ("Truth" with a capital T) , but also of a way of life. The word has a subjective reference to conduct, as well as an objective one to supernatural reality. She also says that the life of truth is the best way of reaching Truth. I think that Langland intended the experiences of Piers and his pilgrims to illustrate this very biblical paradox ("I am the way, the truth, and the life") .

This implies that the life of the half-acre is to be identified with the life of truth, as defined by Holy Church. There are two main arguments in support of this identification. Both Passus i and Passus vi stress the importance of labouring honestly ("truly") in one's vocation: compare, for example, the discussions of a knight's vocation in i, 94–97 and vi, 28 ff. Again, both passus are much concerned with charity. Piers' concern for his "blody bretheren,"

> "Treuthe taughte me ones to lovye hem uchone,
> And to helpen hem of alle thinge ay as hem nedeth"
>
> (vi, 211–12)

recalls the teaching of Holy Church in such passages as i, 177–82. It is true that charity takes a somewhat mundane form in the half-acre, where it is a question of those who can labour in their vocations helping those of their neighbours who cannot (or will not) ; but this is quite proper, for the half-acre represents the life of truth as it is lived "day by day" (see vii, 190) .

I hold, then, that Piers and his faithful followers—"alkyn crafty men that konne lyven in treuthe"—are on the highway to Truth, "non pedibus, sed moribus," when they stay at home labouring in their vocations and helping their neighbours, since this is the way of truth which Truth himself taught. They are worshipping him not in Jerusalem but in spirit —"by their lives" as Piers says (vi, 103) . It is therefore not surprising that they win his pardon. Holy Church promised that they would:

"Tho that worche wel as holiwritt telleth,
And enden as I ere seide in treuthe, that is the best,
Mowe be siker that her soule shal wende to hevene,
Ther treuthe is in Trinitee and troneth hem alle."
                                        (i, 128–31)

III

I believe that many of the difficulties in the controversial fourth stage
of the vision, to which I now turn, will disappear once we realise that
Langland handles the pardon in very much the same way as he handled
the pilgrimage. In each case there is a tension between the literal action
and that which it signifies; and in each case Langland eases this tension
by a twice-repeated gesture of substitution.

It cannot be said of pardons, as of pilgrimages, that Langland simply
did not believe in them. In the epilogue to the second vision he goes out
of his way to assert that the Pope *has* power to grant pardon:

And so I leve lelly (lordes forbode ellis!)
That pardoun and penaunce and preyeres don save
Soules that have synned sevene sithes dedly.
                                        (vii, 176–78)

The protestation is doubtless sincere; yet it seems clear that Langland's
deepest feelings on the matter are represented in the following lines
(where "triennales," despite Skeat's note, refers to pardons) :

Ac to trust to thise triennales, trewly me thinketh,
Is nought so syker for the soule, certis, as is Dowel.
                                        (179–80)

Langland's fear, as so often, is that the external form or institution—even
though it is acceptable in itself—may come to usurp the place of the inner
spiritual reality. It is this fear which determines his treatment of the pardon in Passus vii. His chosen action required that the final reward for the
converted members of the commune should take the form of a pardon.
But this was no more than a "form," embodying the spiritual truth,
stated by Holy Church in the first vision and spelt out in the epilogue to
the second, that those who turn from their wickedness and do well will
receive their reward in heaven. And Langland explicitly says that this
Dowel—represented, again, in the life of the half-acre[5]—is more "syker for

5 See Nevill Coghill, "The Character of Piers Plowman," *Medium Aevum* II
(1933) , 108–35, passim. Several recent critics have disputed Coghill's contention that
Dowel is represented in the half-acre. But the second vision is (among other things)

the soule" than any pardon. So Truth's pardon, like his pilgrimage, is not—emphatically not—to be taken literally. It is in his anxiety to make this point that Langland resorts once more to a somewhat bewildering double transformation of his primary action.

The first of these transformations is basically quite straight forward, in that it follows directly from the substitution of St. Truth for St. James and the saints of Rome as the object of the pilgrimage. But it led Langland into certain complications, to understand which the reader must know that a pardon involves three parties—a producer, a distributor, and a consumer. The producers are Christ and the saints, who by their lives and deaths have accumulated a "treasury of merit" which is available to the faithful. The distributor is the Pope, who as God's vicar alone has the power—though he can delegate it—of distributing the treasure by the grant of pardons. The consumers are those who obtain such grants. Now Langland's original intention, if that is what the A-text represents, was simply to introduce Truth as the saint who by his life and death "purchased" the pardon which the penitent commune obtain. This works out well, since Truth is God, and God did purchase a pardon for the faithful in the redemption. Christ founded the treasury of merit. So the A-text has Truth "purchase" the pardon (A. viii, 3) and the Pope "grant" it (A. viii, 8 & 21). This is entirely consistent; but the B author was apparently not satisfied with it, for he substituted (if Skeat's text is to be trusted) Truth for the Pope in line 8. This also works out, since Truth/ God not only purchased man's pardon in the person of Christ; he also grants it through his vicar the Pope (compare xix, 177 ff.). It was left for C to regularise the alliteration of line 8 (where B has "*P*ardoun with Pieres *P*lowman *T*reuthe hath ygraunted") and make the corresponding change, neglected by B, in A. viii, 21—thus eliminating the Pope altogether and creating a new unmetrical line.

This comparison between the three texts is of interest because it allows one a glimpse, seemingly, of Langland—or his atelier—actually at work on the kind of substitution with which this essay is largely concerned. But the changes in question are of relatively minor importance. The main points are the same in all three versions: that the pardon is purchased by St. Truth, and that it is available (whoever actually "grants" it) to all who help Piers:

---

a story of how some people, instead of going on a pilgrimage to win an indulgence, stay at home and win salvation there; and I cannot see why Langland should draw from this the conclusion that Dowel surpasses indulgences unless he meant "Dowel" to refer to the people's life at home. Subsequent definitions of Dowel, especially viii, 80–83, ix, 107–8 and xii, 33 f., support this view. Passus vi does not say the last word on Dowel; but that is another matter.

> Alle that halpe hym to erie to sette or to sowe,
> Or any other myster that myghte Pieres availle,
> Pardoun with Pieres Plowman Treuthe hath ygraunted.

The essence of the first substitution is here. This is not an ordinary saint's pardon, such as could be obtained at any registered shrine; it is *Truth's* pardon.

After a longish passage (vii, 9–105) specifying the various benefits the pardon brings for various classes of men—kings, knights, bishops, merchants, etc.—Langland proceeds to dramatise his point by confronting Piers with a representative of "ordinary pardons": the Priest. There have been considerable differences of opinion about this character, whom Langland seems rather to have taken for granted; but I would agree with Mr. Coghill that he is "a sophist who understands the letter but not the spirit." [6] Those who share this view will see here a notable parallel between the third and fourth stages of the action. The Priest stands to Piers with respect to the pardon exactly as the Palmer stands to Piers with respect to the pilgrimage. In each case a representative of the unsubstituted, literal institution challenges the spiritual version for which Piers stands. The Palmer does not recognize the pilgrimage to Truth:

> "I seygh nevere palmere with pike ne with scrippe
> Axen after hym er til now in this place";
>
> $\qquad\qquad\qquad\qquad$ (v, 542–43)

and the Priest does not recognise Truth's pardon:

> "Peter!" quod the prest tho "I can no pardoun fynde,
> But 'Dowel, and have wel and God shal have thi sowle,
> And do yvel, and have yvel, hope thow non other
> But after thi ded-day the devel shal have thi sowle!' "
>
> $\qquad\qquad\qquad\qquad$ (vii, 112–15)

It is natural that a priest should want to see the pardon, since priests were responsible for seeing that false pardons were not distributed in their parishes. But this priest, it would seem, is so much concerned with proper drafting and proper sealing that he does not recognise the word of God.

Some critics have held that the Priest's attack on the pardon is supported by the author; but I cannot believe that this is right. The pardon is "purchased" by Truth/God, and, in the B- and C-texts, "granted" by him too; and it carries a message from the Athanasian Creed:

---

6 See "The Pardon of Piers Plowman," *Proceedings of the British Academy*, XXX (1944), p. 319 [see above, p. 53].

"Et qui bona egerunt, ibunt in vitam eternam;
    Qui vero mala, in ignem eternum."
[And those who have done good (well) will go into eternal life;
Those who have done evil, into eternal fire.]

This recalls the words of Holy Church in Passus i (126–31, quoted in part
above), and harmonises with the whole argument of the second vision,
especially Passus vi. Those who "worche wel" (live the life of truth, do
well, "bona egerunt") will, by the grace of God, be saved; those who
don't, won't. It is true that the message is very simple, and can be reduced, as the Priest reduces it, to a common proverb: "Do well and have
well . . ." ("est notandum quod proverbialiter solet dici, 'bene fac et bene
habe' " [It has been observed that one is accustomed to say proverbially,
"Do well and have well."], Brunton, 1376). But Langland respected proverbs and admired simplicity.

In the C-text the second vision ends with the Priest's attack on the pardon. This is a possible, if not a very satisfactory, ending. What Imaginative later calls God's "gret mede to treuthe" has, notwithstanding the
Priest's misguided objections, been demonstrated by the pardon. The arc
of penitential action is complete. But in the A- and B-texts the vision continues for another twenty-odd lines (B. vii, 116–37) before the dreamer
wakes. This closing passage, cut by the C poet, requires some discussion
here.

First, Piers responds to the Priest's attack on the pardon by tearing it
up:

And Pieres for pure tene pulled it atweyne.

This is, of course, the most notorious crux in the whole vision. If I treat
it rather briefly here, it is because I believe that R. W. Frank, in his
article on the pardon scene in *Speculum* volume XXVI (1951), to which
I refer the reader, has already made the essential points better than I can.
I can claim only that the argument of this essay provides new support for
his case. Frank believes, as I do, that the pardon is valid and that Piers
does not reject it. He explains the tearing in terms of a "clash between
form and content" (on pages 322–3 of his essay). The pardon, he argues,
"contains a message which is by implication an attack on pardons and
which does in fact lead to such an attack by the Dreamer" (in the epilogue). It is definitely not an ordinary pardon. Indeed, "in trusting its
message, Piers is *rejecting* bulls with seals. In tearing the parchment,
Piers is symbolically tearing paper pardons from Rome." So the tearing,
"because of the special character of the pardon, was intended by Lang-

land as a sign that Piers had rejected indulgences and accepted the command to do well. Unfortunately, it was a very confusing sign."

This reading enables us to see a clear parallel between the tearing of the pardon and the shelving of the pilgrimage. The "clash between form and content" is the same in each case; for the pilgrimage, like the pardon, contains a message which is by implication an attack on itself. And in each case Langland responds in the same fashion. First he allegorises the "form" polemically (pilgrimage to *Truth, Truth's* pardon) ; then, as if not content with this, he has Piers turn against even the allegorised version. And the significance of this "second substitution" is the same in each case. Piers does not reject the "content" of Truth's pardon (Dowel etc.) when he tears it up, any more than he rejects the content of Truth's pilgrimage (Meekness, Conscience, etc.) when he distracts the folk from that. He is demonstrating angrily ("for pure tene") , and on Langland's behalf, against the "form."

What makes the pardon-tearing a somewhat obscure demonstration, however, is that in this case Langland could find nothing concrete or dramatic—no vehicle, form, objective correlative, or what you will—to convey positively what was to be substituted *for* pardon-mongering, as the ploughing of the half-acre conveys what is to be substituted for pilgrimage. It is one thing to show Piers living "truly" at home, quite another to show—really *show*—him trusting in Dowel. Trust in Dowel is an idea not easy to present dramatically. In the event, Langland was content to follow the tearing with a single quotation from the Psalms:

> And Pieres for pure tene pulled it atweyne,
> And seyde, *"si ambulavero in medio umbre mortis, non*
> *timebo mala; quonian tu mecum es."*
>
> (vii, 116)

Langland, I think, cuts a corner here. I would suggest that he is trying to convey in a single verse Piers' trust in the saving power of Dowel or Truth. The evidence for this is that Imaginative expresses the same trust with the very same verse at the end of Passus xii:

> "Ne wolde nevere trewe God but treuth were allowed;
> And where it worth or worth nought the bileve is grete of
>   treuth,
> And an hope hangyng ther-inne to have a mede for his
>   treuthe.
> For, *Deus dicitur quasi dans vitam eternam suis, hoc est,*
>   *fidelibus; et alibi:*
> *Si ambulavero in medio umbre mortis, etc.*

[It is said that God will give eternal life to His own, that is, to the
   faithful; and elsewhere:
Though I walk through the valley of the shadow of death, etc.]
   The glose graunteth upon that vers a gret mede to treuthe."

                                                        (xii, 287–90)

The relevant passage from Psalm 23 runs as follows: "He leadeth me
in the paths of righteousness for his name's sake. Yea, though I walk
through the valley of the shadow of death, I will fear no evil: for thou art
with me." Peter Lombard, author of the most widely used commentary
("glose") on the Psalms, takes "thou art with me," following Augustine,
to refer to the reward enjoyed after death by the man who walks "in the
paths of righteousness." [7] The "gret mede to treuthe" is God's company
in heaven. This, surely, is the point of Piers' enigmatic quotation: that
righteousness ("truth") can be trusted, as pardons cannot, to win the reward of eternal life.

The remainder of Piers' speech (vii, 117–29) raises questions which
reach beyond the scope of this essay, for it points forward from the *Visio*
to the *Vita de Dowel, Dobet & Dobest*. Langland seems to be trying to
link *Visio* and *Vita* by starting issues for the one at the end of the other:

"I shal cessen of my sowyng," quod Pieres, "and swynk nought
   so harde,
Ne about my bely-ioye so bisi be namore.
Of preyers and of penaunce my plow shal ben herafter,
And wepen whan I shulde slepe, though whete-bred me
   faille."

These lines open up new perspectives; but the reader of the second vision should be familiar at least with the *movement* of the thought. "Of
preyers and of penaunce my plow shal ben herafter": this is the movement of substitution which Langland uses so often when he is in the process of advancing, serpent-like, from something which is, or may be, no
more than an externality towards a more inward statement of his theme.
So in Passus vi he advanced from the pilgrimage to Truth—itself representing an advance on real-life pilgrimage, but seen in retrospect as itself
"formal"—to the pilgrimage at the plough: "My plow-fote shal be my
pykstaf." That is, essentially, as far as the second vision takes us; but in
the lines quoted above Langland is preparing for a further advance. As a
substitute for the pilgrimage, the ploughing of the half-acre is sufficient
to embody Dowel; but it too can be seen critically, in retrospect, as just
"a way of putting it—not very satisfactory." Langland certainly did be-

---

[7] See Frank's article cited in the text, p. 323, for quotation and references.

lieve that the life of labour and love could be trusted to save a man's soul—that is the main message of the second vision. Yet the action of the half-acre cannot adequately represent that life without an indeterminate degree of metaphor and metonymy. A "bisi" ploughman may, after all, be little better than a busy palmer. So the plough comes to figure, in the context of Piers' new resolution, as another externality, like the pike-staff; and it suffers the same fate: "Of preyers and of penaunce my plow shal ben herafter." It is as if the images which carry Langland along are consumed in the process.

IV

Perhaps the most peculiar and perplexing feature of the second vision, as I have described it, is the degree of "interference" on the literal level of the allegory. This is sufficiently common in Langland's work to be con-sidered characteristic. It contributes to the general "lack of a sustained literal level" noted by Miss Woolf among the chief "non-medieval quali-ties" of *Piers Plowman*.[8] A good example, to add to the shelving of the pilgrimage and the tearing of the pardon, is provided by Passus xviii. By the beginning of this passus Langland has already made quite elaborate preparations for presenting the passion as a joust between Jesus and the powers of evil. Jesus is a young knight, instructed by Piers and wearing his mentor's armour, who rides into Jerusalem, announced by the herald Faith, to do battle with his enemies in a joust presided over by Pilate. Langland could easily have sustained this allegory, as other medieval writers, such as Bozon, had done before him. Instead, he allows such in-terference from the Bible story that the joust is almost forgotten. There are references to the apocryphal story of Longinus, the blind knight who "jousted" with the dead body of Jesus (see xviii, 78–91) ; but the joust between Jesus and Satan, the expected climax of the action, simply never takes place. The few remaining references to the matter (e.g., in line 365) therefore strike the reader as sustaining a metaphor rather than carrying on an allegory.

Serious objections can undoubtedly be raised against this mode of pro-ceeding. It is foreign, one might say, not only to the "typical medieval allegories" of which Miss Woolf speaks, but also to the very nature of allegory itself. An allegorical story is, in one very simple way, unlike a metaphor. A metaphor, however long it may be sustained, has no exclu-sive rights: the author is always free to dispense with it whenever he feels that his "real" subject would be better served that way. An allegorical

8 "Some Non-Medieval Qualities of *Piers Plowman*," *Essays in Criticism*, XII (1962) , p. 112.

story, on the other hand, has itself a kind of "reality"—the reality of the literal level—and for that reason the author, however much he may digress and delay, cannot simply dispense with it. If he chooses to represent the good life allegorically as a pilgrimage or the passion as a joust, one might say, he must stand by his choice. A full-scale allegorical action can perhaps never be in all its parts equally congruous with, or adequate to, its creator's intended meanings; so an author who wants to write allegory at all must be prepared just to tolerate some incongruity and inadequacy. Otherwise, if he allows his intended meanings to interfere with the course of his chosen action whenever it suits him, he may well fail to communicate altogether. When the discarded parts of his allegory return to haunt him in the shape of metaphors, for example, his literal level will become hopelessly confused. For as Eliot says in his essay on Dante, "allegory and metaphor do not get on well together."

It cannot be denied that Langland's two interferences with the chosen action of his second vision have both given rise to confusions of this sort among his modern readers; and the C poet's omission of the tearing of the pardon suggests that one of them at least puzzled his contemporaries too. Clearly there has been some failure of communication here. Yet it seems to me equally clear that the vision would be a poorer thing if Lang-Land had *not* interfered as he did. I fear that this paradoxical opinion needs more justification than I have been able to find for it. Perhaps it is partly that the gradual supersession of the pilgrimage and the sudden tearing of the pardon are both, in their different ways, such authentically dream-like inventions. Langland's visions do, as Miss Woolf contends, have a greater sense of true dream about them than most medieval visions; and that is a good reason for valuing them. But more important, perhaps, is that the two inventions in question represent so powerfully, in their dream-like way, that peculiar movement of Langland's thought which I have already tried to describe as a "serpent-like" movement towards more inward statements. This mode of movement, as the case of the second vision shows, runs counter to the demands of the "sustained literal level"; but it seems essential to the progress of Langland's poem. Without the tearing of the pardon, the second vision would in itself be a more perfect whole; but it would, after all, stop the poem dead.

12. *"Ex vi transicionis"* and Its Passage in *Piers Plowman**

R. E. KASKE

IN THE B-TEXT OF *Piers Plowman,* near the end of the episode featuring the gluttonous friar, the character Patience is invited by Conscience to define Dowel, Dobet, and Dobest (xiii, 133–34), and replies in a passage of notorious difficulty:

"At ȝowre preyere," quod Pacyence tho . "so no man displese hym;
   Disce [*Learn* (imperative)]," quod he, *"doce . dilige inimicos*
      [*Teach* (imperative) . *love your enemies*].
Disce, and Dowel . *doce,* and Dobet;
Dilige, and Dobest . thus tauȝte me ones
A lemman that I loued . Loue was hir name.
'With wordes and with werkes,' quod she . 'and wille of thyne herte,
Thow loue lelly thi soule . al thi lyf-tyme;
And so thow lere the to louye . for the lordes loue of heuene,
Thine enemye in al wyse . euene-forth with thi-selue.
Cast coles on his hed . and al kynde speche,
Bothe with werkes and with wordes . fonde his loue to wynne;
And lay on hym thus with loue . til he laughe on the;
And but he bowe for this betyng . blynde mote he worthe!
Ac for to fare thus with thi frende . foly it were,
For he that loueth the lelly . lyte of thyne coueiteth;
Kynde loue coueiteth nouȝte . no catel but speche.'
With half a laumpe lyne in latyne . *ex vi transicionis* [from the
      power of transitivity],
I bere there in a bouste . fast ybounde Dowel,

Reprinted, with some revisions by the author, by permission of the author and the University of Illinois Press from *Journal of English and Germanic Philology,* LXII (1963) , 32–60.

See also Ben H. Smith, Jr., *Traditional Imagery of Charity in Piers Plowman* (The Hague: Mouton and Company, 1966) .

* This study is greatly indebted to the Research Council of the Graduate School at the University of North Carolina and to the Research Board of the Graduate College at the University of Illinois, for grants allowing the extensive use of microfilm in my research. Parts of the following interpretation have appeared in a paper entitled "Allusion in Middle English Poetry," presented as part of the Medieval Colloquium at the University of Michigan, 15 February 1962, and as part of the Pennsylvania State University Conference on Bibliography, 30 November 1962.

In a signe of the Saterday . that sette firste the kalendare,
And al the witte of the Wednesday . of the nexte wyke after;
The myddel of the mone . is the miȝte of bothe.
And here-with am I welcome . there I haue it with me."

(ll. 135–56) [1]

Though it seems generally agreed that the cryptic lines 151–56 are a deliberate riddle presented dramatically under the figurative guise of a charm (xiii, 167–68), this realization in itself does not greatly advance our understanding of them. In line 151 particularly, the phrase *ex vi transicionis* and the accompanying reference to "half a laumpe lyne in latyne" constitute what may well be the most baffling individual crux in the poem. Skeat speculates that the "laumpe lyne" may refer to "a Latin inscription on such a lamp as was often kept burning in old churches," but has no explanation to offer for *ex vi transicionis*.[2] Henry Bradley calls attention to the Classical use of *transitio* as a term designating grammatical inflection, and suggests that *ex vi transicionis* may have been "a current phrase, parallel with *ex vi termini* [from the power of the ending], and employed to indicate that a particular interpretation of a proposition is necessitated by the grammatical form (the case, number, tense, or the like) of one of the words contained in it"; for "half a laumpe lyne in latyne," he offers as an admittedly desperate solution the ablative *corde*—that is, "half" of the Latin word *cordella,* which he further conjectures may have been used to designate a "laumpe lyne," or cord from which a lamp is hung.[3] J. F. Goodridge, in an extended analysis of xiii, 135–71, interprets *ex vi transicionis* as an allusion to the "passing-over" of the Israelites through the Red Sea, "a symbol of Baptism—the passing over from the bondage of the Old Law, to the freedom of that love which is the 'fulfilling of the law' "; the "laumpe lyne" he takes as a figurative reference to the words *ex vi transicionis* themselves, relating them to "the lamp which burns in a church before the Sacrament," which "may be re-

1 Ed. W. W. Skeat (Oxford, 1886) , 1, 394–96; further references are to the B-text unless otherwise noted. In the first half of line 152, I have replaced Skeat's reading, "I bere there-inne aboute," with the probable reading of the forthcoming critical edition, for which I am indebted to Professor E. Talbot Donaldson of Yale University. In lines 149–51, I have revised the punctuation so as to make line 151 the opening line of Patience's resumed speech, rather than (as in Skeat's text) the closing line of Love's speech reported by Patience. My initial basis for this change is that the enigmatic line 151 seems much more plausible as the beginning of an acknowledged riddle (l. 152 ff.) than as a single riddling line at the end of Love's speech—the rest of which (ll. 140–50) presents a noticeable contrast in this respect to the speech of Patience which follows (ll. 152–56) . Further support for this proposal will appear in my interpretation of the passage itself.

2 Skeat, 11, 196.

3 Henry Bradley, "Some Cruces in *Piers Plowman,*" *MLR,* v (1910) , 340–41.

garded as a token of man's love for Christ, or of His love for him." [4]
Finally, Ben H. Smith, Jr.—in an article to which this one is in part complementary—proposes for lines 150–51 a number of mutually related
meanings depending on the medieval grammatical concept of *transicio*
(transitivity) as employed in commentary on Psalm 4:7, and paraphrases
the most basic meaning of the two lines, "Unobstructed charity, stamped
not only with reason but also with grace, desires nothing but self-expres-
sion." [5]

Let us begin with what I take to be the closing line in the speech that
Patience attributes to his *lemman,* Love (l. 150). I do not think it has
ever been pointed out that the first half of this line, "Kynde loue coueiteth nouȝte," is a virtual translation of the words "Charitas non æmulatur" [Charity covets not] in I Corinthians 13:4, from a famous characterization of charity:

> Charitas patiens est, benigna est. Charitas non æmulatur, non agit
> perperam, non inflatur; non est ambitiosa, non quærit quæ sua sunt,
> non irritatur, non cogitat malum; non gaudet super iniquitate, con-
> gaudet autem veritati; omnia suffert, omnia credit, omnia sperat,
> omnia sustinet. [Charity is patient, is kind. Charity covets not, deals
> not perversely, is not puffed up; is not ambitious, seeks not her own,
> is not provoked to anger, thinks no evil; rejoices not in iniquity, but
> rejoices in the truth; bears all things, believes all things, hopes all
> things, endures all things.] (13:4–7)

In the second half of line 150, the "coveting" of speech is strongly suggested by the theme of the following chapter, I Corinthians 14:

> Sectamini charitatem, æmulamini spiritalia, magis autem ut pro-
> phetetis. Qui enim loquitur lingua, non hominibus loquitur, sed
> Deo, nemo enim audit. Spiritus autem loquitur mysteria. Nam qui
> prophetat, hominibus loquitur ad ædificationem, et exhortationem,
> et consolationem. Qui loquitur lingua, semetipsum ædificat; qui au-
> tem prophetat, ecclesiam ædificat. . . . Sic et vos, quoniam æmula-

---

4 J. F. Goodridge, trans., *Piers the Ploughman* (Penguin Books, 1959), pp. 299–308,
especially pp. 304–306. Though Goodridge's explanation of the phrase *ex vi transi-*
cionis can hardly be maintained in view of the evidence presented below, his interpretation of the passage as a whole should not be discounted in future study.

5 Ben H. Smith, Jr., "Patience's Riddle, *Piers Plowman* B, XIII," *MLN,* LXXVI
(1961), 675–82; the quotation is from p. 679. Our two studies were originally planned
as a complementary pair; but since the bulk of my own research was done after Professor Smith's article had already been completed, some points of difference have inevitably emerged. As the two interpretations now stand, they complement one another
in some respects, and in others offer what we hope will be illuminating alternatives.

tores estis spirituum, ad ædificationem ecclesiæ quærite ut abunde-
tis. Et ideo qui loquitur lingua, oret ut interpretetur. . . . [Follow
after charity, covet spiritual gifts, but rather that you may prophesy.
For he that speaks in a tongue, speaks not to men, but to God: for
no man hears. Yet, by the Spirit he speaks mysteries. But he that
prophesies, speaks to men for their edification, and their exhortation, and their comfort. He that speaks in a tongue, edifies himself;
but he that prophesies, edifies the church. . . . So you also, forasmuch
as you are zealous of spirits, seek to abound for the edification of the
church. And therefore, he that speaks by a tongue, let him pray that
he may interpret. . . .] (14:1–4, 12–13) [6]

The subject of this whole chapter is the "gifts of the Spirit" referred to
in the command "æmulamini spiritalia" [covet spiritual gifts] (14:1), all
of which are directly connected with speech—are, in fact, the *prophetia,
genera linguarum,* and *interpretatio sermonum* [prophecy, kinds of
tongues, and interpretation of speeches] first introduced in I Corinthians
12:10 among the *dona* [gifts] or *charismata* [the "gifts" enumerated in I
Corinthians 12] of the Holy Ghost (12:4–11), Whose first and greatest
"gift" is *charitas* [charity (love)] itself.[7] Commentators like Hugh of St.
Cher distinguish the contrasting senses of the verb *æmulor* [to covet] in

[6] See also the rest of I Corinthians 14, along with the related 12:31, "Æmulamini
autem charismata meliora" [But covet better gifts]. For the connection between *charitas* and speech elsewhere, see I Thessalonians 5:13, 20; II Peter 1:7, 9; and especially
the quotations below.
[7] A universal interpretation; see for example Hugh of St. Cher on I Corinthians
12:4, *Opera omnia in universum Vetus et Novum Testamentum* (Venice, 1732), vii,
fols. 106ᵛ–107ʳ. Note Langland's own expansion of the *charismata*, B. xix, 224–45; they
are not, of course, to be identified with the seven Gifts of the Holy Ghost, whose origin
is Isaias 11:2–3. Though space forbids a detailed listing at every point, my references
to commentary on the Pauline Epistles throughout are supported by all or most of the
following: "Ambrosiaster," *PL*, 17, cols. 45–508; John the Deacon (ps.-Jerome), *PL*, 30,
cols. 645–902; ps.-Primasius, *PL*, 68, cols. 415–794; Florus of Lyon, ed. with Bede, *Opera
omnia* (Basle, 1563), vi, 2–1133; Sedulius Scottus, *PL*, 103, cols. 9–270; Rabanus Mau-
rus, *PL*, iii, cols. 1273–1616, and *PL*, 112, cols. 9–834; Haimo of Auxerre (ps.-Haimo of
Halberstadt), *PL*, 117, cols. 361–938; Hatto of Vercelli, *PL*, 134, cols. 125–834; Lanfranc
of Canterbury *et al.*, *PL*, 150, cols. 101–406; ps-Bruno the Carthusian, *PL*, 153, cols. 11–
566; ps-Hugh of St. Victor, *PL*, 175, cols. 431–634; Hervé of Bourgdieu, *PL*, 181, cols.
391–1692; Peter Lombard, *PL*, 191, cols. 1297–1696, and *PL*, 192, cols. 9–520; *Biblia
latina cum glossa ordinaria Walafridi Strabonis et glossa interlineari Anselmi Lauden-
sis* (Strassburg, 1481); a *Commentarius Cantabrigiensis in Epistolas Pauli e schola
Petri Abaelardi*, ed. Artur Landgraf (Publications in Mediaeval Studies, ii; Notre
Dame, 1937–45); Hugh of St. Cher, *ed. cit.*, vii, fols. 2ʳ–277ᵛ; Thomas Aquinas, *Exp. in
omnes S. Pauli Epp.*, in *Opera omnia* (Parma, 1852–73), xiii; Peter Aureoli, *Compendium sensus litteralis totius Divinæ Scripturæ* (Quaracchi, 1896), pp. 244–380; Nicolas
of Lyra, *Postilla litteralis in universa Biblia*, ed. John de La Haye, *Biblia maxima*
(Paris, 1660), xv–xvi; and Denis the Carthusian, *Opera omnia* (Montreuil, 1901), xiii,
3–531.

13:4 and 14:1, in a way that bears directly on the concept of love "covet-ing" nothing but speech:

> *Non æmulatur:* id est, non invidet, contra invidos. Gilbertus: "Invi-dam animam non potest intrare æstimatio bona. Quare? Quia livor dum privatam excellentiam cogitat, alienam obscurat." *Non æmula-tur:* Contra *infra* 14, "Æmulamini spiritualia." Solutio: Æquivoca est æmulatio: hic pro invidentia. . . . Et *infra* 14 pro desiderio chari-tatis. . . . ["Expositio Glossæ" on 14:1:] *Æmulamini,* id est, desider-ate alia dona; sed post charitatem. . . . Charitas est melior quam alia dona, de quibus hic specialiter est sermo, ut donum linguarum et do-num prophetiæ. . . . [*Non aemulatur:* that is, it does not envy, in op-position to the envious. Gilbert: "Good esteem is not able to enter an envious soul. Why? Because envy, as long as it considers its own excellence, obscures the excellence of another." *Non aemulatur:* As opposed to chapter 14, *Aemulamini spiritualia.* Solution: *Aemula-tio* is ambiguous: here it means envy. . . . And in chapter 14, it means the desire for charity. . . . (Exposition on the *Glossa ordinaria,* on 14: 1:) *Aemulamini,* that is, desire other gifts; but after charity. . . . Charity is better than the other gifts, which are, in particular, dis-cussed here, such as the gift of tongues and the gift of prophecy. . . .][8]

The meaning crowded into Langland's one-line adaptation, then, is that the Christian ruled by *charitas* will not covet earthly goods ("Chari-tas non æmulatur," 13:4), but will "covet" only the further gifts of *charitas* itself ("æmulamini spiritalia," 14:1) —here represented, in ac-cordance with the whole of I Corinthians 14, as the gifts of speech. This intimate dependence of line 150 upon I Corinthians 13:4 is confirmed by two further important connections with the opening words of the verse: "Charitas patiens est, benigna est." The declaration "Charitas patiens est" provides the obvious Scriptural basis for the close connection be-tween *charitas* and the personification Patience in this part of Passus xiii.

8 Hugh of St. Cher, *ed. cit.,* VII, fols. 110[r], 111[v]; "Gilbertus" is evidently either Guibert de la Porrée or Gilbertus Universalis. Nicolas of Lyra, *ed. cit.,* xv, 559, 570: "Ideo dicit: *Non æmulatur,* id est, inuidet. Habet enim *æmulari* plures significationes quæ continentur in hoc versu: 'Æmulor, inflatur, amat, inuidet, ac imitatur'. . . . *Sectamini charitatem:* . . . dicit quod præ cæteris [donis] debent charitatem sequi. . . . *Æmulamini spiritalia:* Id est, desiderate seu amate talia dona, vt est prophetiæ donum, & linguarum." [Thus the author says: *Non æmulatur,* that is, envies not. For *æmulari* has more meanings which are contained in this verse: "*Æmulor* is puffed up, loves, envies, and imitates". . . . *Sectamini charitatem:* . . . he says that they should seek charity before the other gifts. . . . *Æmulamini spiritalia:* That is, desire or love such gifts, such as the gift of prophecy and of tongues.] Besides the commentaries on these verses, see *Le laie Bible,* 2048–57, 2230–34, ed. John Alfred Clarke (New York, 1923), pp. 77–78, 83. This same Scriptural theme seems relevant to Wit's remarks about the use of speech, ix, 96–103.

The following statement, "Charitas . . . benigna est," clarifies the meaning of Langland's troublesome *Kynde loue* (usually rendered as "natural love" or "natural affection") into *"kind* love"—the *charitas* which, according to I Corinthians 13:4–5, "non æmulatur, non agit perperam, non inflatur; non est ambitiosa, non quærit quæ sua sunt, non irritatur, non cogitat malum . . ." [covets not, deals not perversely, is not puffed up; is not ambitious, seeks not her own, is not provoked to anger, thinks no evil . . .].[9] And this recognition of the first half of line 150 as a paraphrase of the words "Charitas . . . benigna est. . . . non æmulatur" throws light, in turn, on a detail at the close of the episode, where Patience takes with him food

> To conforte hym and Conscience . if they come in place
> There Vnkyndenesse and Coueytise is . hungrye contrees bothe.
>
> (ll. 218–19)

Coueytise, though equated with *avaricia* in the Confession of the Deadly Sins (v, 188 ff.) , appears in Passus xiv as *invidia* [envy] or *æmulatio* [covetousness] (ll. 238–43) —a fact that speaks strongly for the rendering of *Vnkyndenesse* here as "unkindness" rather than "unnaturalness," completing the parallel with the first half of line 150.

If my argument so far has been convincing, it seems clear that line 150 is to be read not as a simple restatement of the two lines preceding it (148–49) , but as an expression of the universal principle upon which their particular observation is based: "whoever truly loves you, covets little of what is yours; [for it is a Scriptural truth that] kindly charity itself covets nothing, etc." A similar relationship can be found between the "coveting" of speech in line 150, and Love's several earlier remarks about the use of the gifts of speech (ll. 140, 144, 145) . These compressed Scriptural allusions in line 150 seem, in fact, to be related in much the same way to the whole of Love's reported discourse (ll. 140–49) —which has emphasized particularly the love of one's enemies in accord with Luke 6:27–35 and Romans 12:20 (ll. 142–47) , and the absence of covetousness between friends bound by love (ll. 148–49) . The twelfth-century exegete Hervé of Bourgdieu, for example, comments on our basic text, I Corinthians 13:4,

> Quæ charitas habet in se virtutes, quæ nunc enumerantur. Est enim

---

[9] For *kynde* corresponding generally to *benigna,* see Love's "al kynde speche" a few lines earlier (xiii, 144) ; and *OED,* "Kind," *a.,* ii.5.a. Presumably the same meaning is to be attached to *kynde loue* in *Piers,* iii, 297. Note, however, C. xviii, 151–53; my suggestion (p. 247 and n. 39, below) of a reference to the *lex naturalis* in line 153 of our present passage; and the resulting possibility of a meaningful play on the word *Kynde* in line 150: *"Kindly* charity (which, as it happens, is also *natural*) . . . ."

patiens, id est patientiam servans. Patientiam vero servare, est aliena mala æquanimiter perpeti; contra eum quoque qui mala irrogat, nullo dolore morderi. . . . Sed *charitas est patiens,* quoniam aliena mala æquo animo tolerat, et *est benigna,* quia ipsos etiam a quibus mala patiuntur, amat. *Patiens,* quia illata a proximis mala æquanimiter portat; *benigna* vero, quia pro malis bona largiter administrat. . . . *Charitas non æmulatur,* id est non invidet, quia ubi est invidia, ibi fraternus amor esse non potest. *Non æmulatur,* quia per hoc quod in præsenti modo nil appetit, invidere terrenis successibus nescit. *Non æmulatur,* quoniam alterius bonum diligit ut suum. . . . [This charity has within itself certain virtues, which are now enumerated. For it is patient, that is, it preserves patience. To preserve patience is to suffer evils from another with equanimity, and to be stung by no resentment against him who inflicts the evils. . . . But *charitas est patiens,* because it suffers evils from another with equanimity, and *est benigna,* because it loves even the very ones from whom evils are suffered. *Patiens,* because it bears with equanimity the evils inflicted by one's neighbors, but *benigna,* because it returns abundantly good things for evil. . . . *Charitas non aemulatur,* that is, it does not envy, because where envy is, there brotherly love cannot be. *Non aemulatur,* because since it desires nothing in the present world, it does not know how to envy earthly successes. *Non aemulatur,* because it loves the good of another as it own. . . .][10]

If line 150 can also be allowed such connotations, it seems to function within Love's speech as a kind of allusive epitome of her teachings on *amor proximorum* [love of neighbors], set forth more circumstantially in her preceding exhortation (142–49).[11]

[10] Hervé of Bourgdieu, *PL,* 181, col. 954; much of this passage is heavily dependent on Gregory's *Hom. in Evang.,* xxxv, quoted below at n. 45. See also Bonaventura's comment relating Luke 6:33—one of the verses obviously underlying Love's lines 142–49—to the theme of I Corinthians 13:4 (*Opera omnia* [Quaracchi, 1895], vii, 157) : "Et eo ipso, si vult Domino reconciliari, oportet, quod ipse benefaciat non tantum benefacienti, sed etiam adversanti, et tale est beneficium caritatis secundum illud primae ad Corinthios decimo tertio: 'Caritas patiens est, benigna est' " [And on that very point, if one wishes to be reconciled with the Lord, it is necessary that he do good not only to his benefactor, but also to his enemy; and such is the beneficence of charity according to that verse of chapter thirteen of I Corinthians: "Caritas patiens est, benigna est"]. Gregory's *Hom. in Ezech.,* II, ix, on Ezechiel 40:38–43 (*PL,* 76, cols. 1041–58) , offers promising connections between I Corinthians 13:4 together with its subjects *charitas* and *patientia* (cols. 1042–43, 1052) , the two tables at the banquet in Passus xiii (ll. 36 ff.) , and the theme of the doctor "qui bona loquitur, sed non operatur" [who speaks of good works, but does not do them] (col. 1051) . Note, incidentally, Langland's more obvious expansion of I Corinthians 13:4–7 in xv, 152–70; and the brief quotation from 13:7 at C. xviii, 5.

[11] The love of self mentioned in Love's first two lines (140–41) may, in this context,

We are now confronted by the mysterious line 151—which I take to be uttered directly by Patience as a part of the following riddle, rather than reported as part of Love's speech. For the decisive evidence concerning the phrase *ex vi transicionis,* we must begin with the concept of grammatical *regimen,* developed particularly during the thirteenth century.[12] Already in the twelfth century, the commentary of Peter Elias on Priscian's *Institutiones* contains a significant explanation of the verb *regere,* as employed by contemporary grammarians to express the "rule" imposed by one word upon the grammatical form of another:

> Ubi gramatici huius temporis dicunt quod dictio regit dictionem, ibi dicit Priscianus quod dictio exigit dictionem, et quod alii dicunt regimen, ipse dicit exigentiam, magis aperta utens locutione. Non tamen culpo nostrorum gramaticorum locutionem, quia metaphorice dictum est quod regat dictio dictionem; et est metaphora satis congrua. Sicut enim dux regit exercitum, sic verbum regit nominativum in constructione positum. [Where grammarians of this time say that one form rules another form, there Priscianus would say that one form demands another form, and what others call *regimen,* he calls *exigentia,* using a clearer expression. Nevertheless, I do not find fault with the expression of our own grammarians, because it is a metaphorical expression that one form rules another form; and the metaphor is sufficiently appropriate. For just as a leader rules an army, so the verb placed in a grammatical construction rules the nominative case.][13]

In an anonymous thirteenth-century epitome of *regimen,* this metaphoric *regere* has become a more or less straightforward grammatical term: "Sicut in natura illud dicitur regere aliud, quod non sinit illud deviare, similiter in arte illa dictio dicitur regere aliam, que non sinit illam poni in alio casu vel genere vel numero. Unde regere est conferre dictioni poni in tali casu in quo stare debet. . . ." [Just as in nature that thing is said to

---

be a synecdoche for *amor Dei,* the other "precept" of *charitas;* see William Peraldus, *Summæ virtutum ac vitiorum,* tom. I, pars II, tract. 4, cap. 8 (Antwerp, 1588), I, fol. 89[v]: "Notandum quod licet debeamus amare Deum, & nos, & proximum, tamen non habemus speciale præceptum de amore nostri . . . eo quod amare Deum sic amare seipsum" [It should be noted that although we ought to love God, and ourselves, and our neighbor, nevertheless we do not have any special command about the love of ourselves . . . because to love God is to love oneself]. But see also n. 35 below.

12 See the definitive study by Charles Thurot, *Notices et extraits de divers manuscrits latins, pour servir á l'histoire des doctrines grammaticales au Moyen Âge* (Notices et extraits des manuscrits de la Bibliothèque Impériale [Nationale] et autres bibliothèques, XXII; Paris, 1868), particularly pp. 239–46.

13 Peter Elias, MS Paris, Bibl. Arsenal 711, fol. 177[v]. Thurot's quotation of the passage (pp. 239–40) is based on MS B.N. lat. 15121 (old Saint-Victor 798), fol. 149[r].

rule another thing which does not allow it to deviate, so likewise in art, that form is said to rule another form which does not allow it to be put into another case or gender or number. Hence *regere* is to cause a form to be put into the case in which it ought to stand. . . .][14] The "ruling" or "governing" power implicit in such grammatical relationships is commonly designated by the word *vis.* As Thurot explains,

> La métaphore que présentait le terme *regere* avait conduit à considérer le terme gouvernant comme régissant le terme gouverné en vertu d'une certaine puissance, d'une certaine force qui contraint le terme gouverné à être à tel cas plutôt qu'à tel autre. Ainsi on disait qu'un verbe régit l'accusatif *ex vi transitionis.* [The metaphor which introduced the term *regere* had led to considering the governing term as ruling the governed term by virtue of a certain power, of a certain force which compels the governed term to be in such a case rather than in another. So they said that a verb rules the accusative *ex vi transitionis.*][15]

This phrase *ex vi transitionis,* referring to the "power" of transitivity by which a verb "rules" its direct object in the accusative case, can be found with no great difficulty in unpublished thirteenth- and fourteenth-century works on syntax. An anonymous *Summe gramaticales* from the thirteenth century offers the example, "Cum enim dicitur 'ego video omne quod currit,' hic accusativus *omne* regitur ab hoc verbo *video* ex vi transitionis" [For when one says, "ego video omne quod currit," this accusative *omne* is ruled by this verb *video* ex vi transitionis].[16] A fragmentary treatise on *regimen,* preserved in a fourteenth-century manuscript, employs the expression several times in a brief passage beginning, "Plures regule ponuntur de regimine accusativi cum verbo. . . . Secunda est in his exemplis, *video te, percuro socrum.* Que pars regit *socrum? Percuro.* Quare? Quia omne verbum ex vi trancicionis potest regere accusativum." [Many rules are proposed about the rule of the accusative with the verb. . . . The second rule is in these examples, *video te, percuro socrum.* Which word rules *socrum? Percuro.* Why? Because every verb can rule the accusative "ex vi trancicionis."] A few lines later, the example under discussion is *Doceo te gramaticam:*

> omne [verbum] passivum cuius activum construitur cum gemino accusativo ex vi trancitionis, construitur cum ablativo; unde congrue

14 Quoted by Thurot, *Notices,* pp. 243–44.

15 Thurot, p. 244. See also pp. 298–301; and Thurot, *De Alexandri de Villa-Dei Doctrinale ejusque fortuna . . .* (Thesis, University of Paris, 1850), pp. 35–36.

16 *Summe gramaticales,* MS Paris, B.N. lat. 2572, fol. 287ᵛ (in the older foliation unnumbered, between fols. 934 and 935). For a brief description of the work itself, see Thurot, *Notices,* p. 43.

dicitur, "Iste docetur gramatica." Que pars regit *gramaticam? Doce-tur.* Quare? Quia omne verbum passivum cuius activum construitur cum gemino accusativo ex vi trancitionis, construitur cum ablativo. Item sic obicitur in his exemplis, *efficio te militem, voco te Socra-tem,* "Construitur cum gemino accusativo, ergo eius passivum con-struitur cum ablativo." Non sequitur, quia hec verba non constru-untur cum sequenti accusativo ex vi trancitionis. . . . [every passive verb, whose active form is constructed with a double accusative "ex vi trancitionis," is constructed with the ablative; hence it is proper-ly said, "Iste docetur gramatica." What word rules *gramaticam? Docetur.* Why? Because every passive verb, whose active form is con-structed with a double accusative "ex vi trancitionis," is constructed with the ablative. In similar fashion an objection is raised thus in these examples, *efficio te militem, voco te Socratem,* "It is con-structed with the double accusative, therefore its passive should be constructed with the ablative." It does not follow because these verbs are not constructed with a following accusative "ex vi tranci-tionis". . . .]17

The phrase is closely approximated twice in the influential *Doctrinale,* written in the thirteenth century by Alexander of Villedieu:

> Hinc datur exemplum tibi triplex: "Dico magistrum
> discipulos mores placidos de iure docere."
> Infinitivi natura regit praeeuntem,
> doctrinam capiens regitur vi transitionis;
> hocque gerundivum *tradendo* dic ibi clausum,
> cuius vi regitur casus, qui non variatur,
> dum per passivi vocem volo dicta resolvi;
> aut illic positi regit hunc vis propria verbi.
> Accusativis data per vim transitionis,
> si vox concordet, activa frequenter habebis.

[Hence is given you a triple example: "Dico magistrum discipulos mores placidos de iure docere." The nature of the infinitive rules that which precedes it, the receiver of learning (i.e., "discipulos") is ruled "vi transitionis"; take also to be included there this gerun-dive *tradendo,* by whose power *(vi)* the (accusative) case is ruled— which is not varied, so long as I wish the utterance to be set forth through the voice of a passive verb; or there the proper power *(vis)*

---

17 Fragmentary treatise on *regimen,* MS Paris, B.N. lat. 8314, fol. 88r; the work is described by Thurot, *Notices,* p. 50. The phrase *ex vi transicionis* is found also, for example, in a brief treatise on *regimen (inc.,* "Regimina") included in MS Worcester Cathedral F. 123, fols. 40r–52r.

of a verb placed in a grammatical construction rules this case (the accusative.) To nouns in the accusative case through the power of transitivity *(per vim transitionis),* you will have, if the voice agrees, many active verbs assigned.][18]

And an important thirteenth-century gloss on the *Doctrinale,* known from its *incipit* as the "Admirantes" gloss, employs the words "ex vi transitionis" at least twice: in a summary of the types of *regimen* treated in Alexander's section on the accusative case (ll. 1234–87) ,[19] and as an interlinear gloss on the word *transitione* in line 1259.[20]

It seems hardly open to question, then, that Langland's *ex vi transicionis* is a direct incorporation of this term from late medieval grammar. As such, it falls within a recognized medieval tradition of grammatical metaphor[21]—exemplified also in an extended passage of the Lady Meed episode in the C-text (iv, 335–409) , where rightful and unrightful material profit are compared respectively to "direct" and "indirect" grammatical relationship. It would be pleasant at this point to offer an equally compelling solution to the first half of line 151, "With half a laumpe lyne in latyne"; unfortunately, I must here follow previous interpreters at least partly into the realm of conjecture. One obvious possibility would be to take the expression as a wry fling at the learned origin of *ex vi transicionis* itself, meaning, in effect, "If I may resort to a Latin tag smelling of the lamp . . . !" A more promising suggestion is that of Professor Smith, who finds in the "half a laumpe lyne" an allusion to the first half of Psalm 4:7, "Signatum est super nos lumen vultus tui, Domine" [The light of thy countenance, O Lord, is signed upon us]; and in *ex vi transicionis,* a reference to what some medieval commentators explain as the "transitive" interpretation of this half-verse: "Vultus Dei dicitur ratio; lumen hujus vultus, est gratia . . . ratio nostra deformis est, donec per gratiam Dei illustretur." [The countenance of God means reason; the light of this countenance is grace. . . . Our reason is deformed until it is

---

[18] Lines 1245–54, ed. Dietrich Reichling, *Das Doctrinale des Alexander de Villa-Dei* (Monumenta Germaniae Paedagogica, xii; Berlin, 1893) , p. 81; note lines 1248 and 1253. The fifteenth-century commentary of Ludovicus de Guaschis on the *Doctrinale* (Milan and Vicenza, 1481) , uses "ex vi transitionis" several times in explaining this passage.

[19] Quoted by Thurot, *Notices,* pp. 294–95. On the "Admirantes" gloss, see Thurot's brief description, *ibid.,* pp. 32–34; and Reichling, p. lxii.

[20] Alexander of Villedieu, *Doctrinale,* with the "Admirantes" gloss, MS Paris, B.N. lat. 8422, fol. 37ᵛ.

[21] E. R. Curtius, *Europäische Literatur und lateinisches Mittelalter* (Bern, 1948) , p. 417; and note the example from Trevisa cited by David C. Fowler, *Piers the Plowman: Literary Relations of the A and B Texts* (Seattle, 1961) , p. 253. The theological significance of medieval grammar is surveyed by M.-D. Chenu, O.P., *La théologie au douzième siècle* (Études de philosophie médiévale, xlv; Paris, 1957) , pp. 90–107.

illuminated through the grace of God.]²² This explanation seems plausible enough in itself, and may very well turn out to be correct; since the allusion remains a difficult one, however, I add the following further possibility.

In view of the emphasis concentrated on *charitas* in the immediately preceding line (150), as well as in Love's speech as a whole and in the enveloping speeches of Patience and Conscience (ll. 136–39; and 158–63, Romans 8:35–39, and I John 4:18), it seems reasonable to expect that *charitas* will play some part also in the meaning of line 151. Let us therefore begin by observing the close connection of lamps with both *charitas* and *æmulatio*—two of the governing concepts of line 150—in Canticles 8:6–7:

> fortis est ut mors dilectio,
> dura sicut infernus æmulatio:
> lampades ejus lampades ignis atque flammarum.
> Aquæ multæ non potuerunt extinguere charitatem,
> nec flumina obruent illam.
>
> [love is strong as death,
> covetousness hard as hell:
> its lamps are lamps of fire and flames.
> Many waters could not quench charity,
> nor will rivers overwhelm it.]

These *lampades* [lamps], which in early medieval exegesis generally signify the hearts of the elect filled with the fire of *charitas*,²³ are in the later Middle Ages explained also as the motions of *charitas* in the heart, or sometimes as *charitas* itself; the last interpretation appears, for example, in the thirteenth-century *Distinctiones* by Maurice of Ireland (or England): "Item [est lampas] caritatis ignee, Canticorum ultimo: 'Lampades eius lampades ignis atque flammarum' " [Again, there is the lamp of fiery charity in the last chapter of Canticles: "Its lamps are lamps of fire and flames"].²⁴ Now in Priscian's *Institutiones*—a grammatical

---

²² Smith, pp. 675–78; the quotation (p. 677) is from Hugh of St. Cher, *ed. cit.*, ii, fol. 9ᵛ.

²³ See for example Thomas of Citeaux, *PL*, 206, cols. 815–16 (with several references to I Corinthians 13:4) ; and Peter Riga's *Aurora*, quoted by J. B. Pitra, *Spicilegium Solesmense* (Paris, 1852–55), ii, 182–83. Similar meanings are often attached to the *lampades* of Ezechiel 1:15, and to those of the wise and foolish virgins in Matthew 25:1–12; some such interpretation seems to underlie Holy Church's remark in *Piers*, i, 86.

²⁴ Maurice of Ireland, MS Paris, B.N. lat. 15945, fol. 155ʳ. For the lamps as *motus* [motions] or *inflammationes* [kindlings] of *charitas*, see Hugh of St. Cher, *ed. cit.*, iii, fol. 137ʳ, "Lampades dilectionis, motus sunt charitatis," followed by a long explanation; and Denis the Carthusian, *ed. cit.*, vii, 434—along with his explanation of *æmulatio*, pp. 433–34.

work whose importance had by no means disappeared in the fourteenth century[25]—a section "De accusativo singulari tertiae declinationis" includes the following discussion of Greek accusatives:

> In Graecis autem frequenter invenimus auctores tam in hac quam in aliis declinationibus Graecos plerumque serventes accusativos, ut *Titana, Sirena, thoraca, lampada* pro *Titanem, Sirenem* et *thoracem, lampadem,* quamvis Plautus "hanc lampadem" dixit in *Casina* [IV, iv, 24]:
>
> > Tene hanc lampadem!—Immo ego hanc tenebo.

[Among the Greeks, however, we often discover authors who, in this as well as in the other declensions, often preserve Greek accusatives, such as *Titana, Sirena, thoraca, lampada* in place of *Titanem, Sirenem* and *thoracem, lampadem,* although Plautus said in the *Casina: hanc lampadem:*

Hold this lamp! *(Tene hanc lampadem!)*—Nay I will hold her.][26]

In this final quotation from Plautus, the words "Tene hanc lampadem!" [Hold this lamp!] could be described accurately enough as "half a laumpe lyne in latyne"; while the grammatical origin of *ex vi transicionis,* demonstrated above, would of course speak for the plausibility of this further grammatical allusion in the same line. It may also be worth

---

25 The replacement of *Priscianus maior* (*Inst.,* I–XVI) and *Priscianus minor* (*Inst.,* XVII–XVIII) by the *Doctrinale* of Alexander and the *Grecismus* of Évrard of Béthune, though a prominent development in French universities of the later Middle Ages, seems never to have really occurred in England. A *forma incoepturis in artibus Oxoniae* in an early fourteenth-century hand (ed. Hastings Rashdall, *The Universities of Europe in the Middle Ages,* re-ed. by F. M. Powicke and A. B. Emden [Oxford, 1936], III, 480–81), includes "Priscianus magni voluminis. . . ." and "Priscianus de constructionibus partium." A summary of the chief requirements for the B.A. and the M.A. at Oxford in the fifteenth century (*ibid.,* pp. 153–55) includes "Grammar, i.e. Priscian, *De constructionibus,* twice" (with the further provision, "Determiners *pro aliis* who had not previously determined *pro se* were required further to have heard the *Magnum* of Priscian . . ."), and again, "Grammar: Priscian 'in majore vel minore.'" (One term.) "; see also p. 352. Louis John Paetow (*The Arts Course at Medieval Universities* [University Studies of the University of Illinois, III, 7; Champaign, 1910]), who lays great emphasis on the radical changes in the teaching of grammar in French universities during the thirteenth and fourteenth centuries, adds (p. 61) that at the end of this period at Oxford, "the course in arts . . . still bore the general features of the conventional thirteenth-century course." A document edited by M. Fournier (*Les statuts et privilèges des universités françaises depuis leur fondation jusqu'en 1789* [Paris, 1890], I, 770–71), indicates that even at Toulouse, *Priscianus maior* and *minor* still enjoyed some currency in 1426.

26 VII, 53 (*i.e.,* a part of *Priscianus maior*), ed. Martin Hertz (Grammatici latini, ed. Heinrich Keil, Vol. II; Leipzig, 1855), I, 330. In the second half of the line from Plautus, *hanc* refers not to *lampadem* but to the supposed bride; the situation bears small relation to *charitas.*

noticing that the very construction of this half-line from Plautus by way of Priscian—in which the accusative *lampadem* is governed directly by the transitive verb *Tene*—illustrates grammatical "rulership" by the verb *ex vi transitionis*. We have found, then, on the one hand a strong *a priori* likelihood that the "half a laumpe lyne" will be somehow related to *charitas,* together with a promising traditional connection between lamps and *charitas;* and on the other, a quotation that would not only fit Langland's allusion in line 151, but would also bear a general topical relation to *ex vi transicionis* through its own context outside the poem—whether in the *Institutiones* itself, in medieval commentary on it, or possibly in some independent grammatical work.[27] What meaningful connection, if any, might have existed for Langland between these seemingly unrelated correspondences?

It happens that the command "Tene hanc lampadem!" is itself paralleled more or less closely by various traditional injunctions to *charitas.* The precise parallel "tene charitatem" [hold charity] occurs in a well-known passage of one of Augustine's sermons, quoted for example in the thirteenth-century *Summæ virtutum ac vitiorum* of William Peraldus (italics mine, here and in the five quotations following) : "Si non voles omnes paginas perscrutari, omnia inuolucra sermonum euoluere, omnia secreta Scripturarum penetrare, *tene charitatem* vbi pendent omnia" [If you do not wish to examine all the pages, to unroll all the windings of words, to penetrate all the secrets of the Scriptures, *hold charity* upon which all things depend].[28] Similar expressions are found in certain pseudo-Augustinian sermons on *charitas:*

> In his enim omnibus quæ ad corporis fatigationem pertinent, nullus Christianorum invitus cogitur . . . qui vero non potest implere, *charitatem* veram *teneat,* et in ipsa habebit omnia. . . . Et ideo qui veram *charitatem* noluerit *tenere,* non invenit quod in veritate aliis, sed quod sibi debeat imputare. *Tenete* ergo, fratres charissimi, dulce ac salubre *vinculum charitatis.* . . . Amate ergo et *tenete charitatem,* fratres charissimi, sine qua nullus unquam Deum videbit. [For in all

27 For example, an anonymous twelfth-century commentary on Priscian, preserved in the fourteenth-century MS Paris, B.N. lat. 15130 (old Saint-Victor 930; described by Thurot, *Notices,* pp. 52–53) , fol. 54ᵛ, contains the rather confused echo, "Quamvis dico *lampadem* tercie declinationis, tamen [quamvis, *MS*] Plautus dixit 'lampadam [*sic*] tene'. . . ." [Although I place *lampadem* in the third declension, still Plautus says, "lampadam tene". . . .] I have not pursued the quotation further; but such grammatical warhorses, once accepted as dependable, were not soon retired (in the passages quoted above, cf. the venerable *Doceo te gramaticam* and *Voco te Socratem*) .

28 William Peraldus, tom. I, pars II, tract. 4, cap. I (see n. II; I, fol. 78ʳ) . The quotation of Augustine—found also in the *Glossa ordinaria* on I Timothy 1:5—is from the popular Sermo 350 on *charitas* (*PL*, 39, col. 1534) , which, among other themes pertinent to our passage, contains an extended analysis of I Corinthians 13:1–8.

these things, which lead to the fatigue of the body, no Christian is thought unwilling . . . but he who is unable to fulfill them, let him *hold* true *charity,* and in that he shall have all. . . . And therefore he who does not wish to *hold* true *charity,* does not discover what in truth he ought to credit to others, but what he ought to credit to himself. *Hold,* therefore, dear brethren, the sweet and saving *bond of charity.* . . . Love, therefore, and *hold charity,* dear brethren, without which no one shall ever see God.][29]

The *Summa Abel,* a *distinctiones* compiled in the late twelfth century by Peter Cantor, includes in its exposition of *charitas* four quotations of the maxim, *"habe charitatem* et fac quicquid vis" [*have charity* and do what you wish].[30] The command is approximated also in several Scriptural exhortations—most of them followed at no great distance by references to speech: "Super omnia autem hæc, *charitatem habete.* . . . Verbum Christi habitet in vobis abundanter . . ." [But above all things, *have charity.* . . . May the word of Christ dwell in you abundantly . . .] (Colossians 3:14, 16); *"Sectamini charitatem,* æmulamini spiritalia, magis autem ut prophetetis . . ." [*Follow after charity,* covet spiritual gifts, but rather that you may prophesy . . .] (I Corinthians 14:1) ; and "Ante omnia autem, mutuam in vobismetipsis *charitatem* continuam *habentes.* . . . Si quis loquitur, quasi sermones Dei [loquatur] . . ." [But above all things, *having* unfailing *charity* for one another. . . . If anyone speak, let him speak, as it were, the words of God . . .] (I Peter 4:8, 11) .[31] My suggestion, then, is that Langland's "half a laumpe lyne in latyne" may allude immediately to the command "Tene hanc lampadem!" as quoted in the *Institutiones* or elsewhere; and that through Langland's own whimsical but purposeful association of this command with formulas of the kind quoted above—supported by connotations of *lampades* like those attached to Canticles 8:6—"Tene hanc lampadem!" may in turn be a deliberately enigmatic vehicle for the fundamental Christian injunction to *charitas.*

Bypassing line 152 temporarily, I proceed to Patience's declaration that he bears Dowel bound fast

---

[29] Sermo 269 *(PL,* 39, cols. 2246–47) ; see also Sermo 112 *(PL,* 39, col. 1968) : *"Tenete* ergo et custodite . . . dulce ac salubre *vinculum charitatis.* Sed ante omnia veram *charitatem tenete.* . . ." [Therefore *hold* and guard . . . the sweet and saving *bond* of charity. But above all things *hold* true *charity.* . . .]

[30] Peter Cantor, MS Paris, B.N. lat. 3388, fols. 25ᵛ–26ᵛ. This whole section (fols. 24ᵛ–30ᵛ) is a useful brief assembly of medieval commonplaces on *charitas.*

[31] See also I Corinthians 16:14, II Timothy 2:22, and II Peter 1:5–7, 19; and the Sarum Missal (ed. J. W. Legg [Oxford, 1916], p. 226) : *"Habete vinculum charitatis* et pacis. . . ." [*Have the bond of charity* and peace. . . .]

In a signe of the Saterday . that sette firste the kalendare,
And al the witte of the Wednesday . of the nexte wyke after;
The myddel of the mone . is the miȝte of bothe.

(ll. 153–55)

The essential difficulty in the first lines is explained, I think, by Professor
Smith's brilliant suggestion that they allude respectively to the "weeks"
of Creation and Redemption, elaborated in certain medieval works on
charitas;[32] the following interpretation of the lines, though differing
slightly from Professor Smith's in some of its emphases, is directly indebted to this important discovery. Among the various spiritual exegeses
of God's six days of creation and final day of rest (Genesis 1–2:3) is a
scheme associating them with seven "days" in the work of redemption,
exemplified in the *De charitate Dei et proximi* by Peter of Blois:

> Verum omne Sabbatum habet sex præambulos dies. . . . Isti sex dies
> sunt, Christi conceptio, nativitas, prædicatio, passio, resurrectio, as-
> censio. Istis sex diebus operatus est Dominus salutem in medio terræ,
> et requiescens ab omni opere quod patrarat [cf. Genesis 2:2], sedens-
> que in gloria Dei Patris ad illud Sabbatum, quod est in illius dilec-
> tione celeberrimum, misericorditer nos invitat. [Every true Sabbath
> has six preceding days. . . . Those six days are the conception, birth,
> preaching, passion, resurrection, and ascension of Christ. In those
> six days the Lord worked salvation in the midst of the earth; and
> resting from all the work he had done and sitting in the glory of God
> the Father, he mercifully invites us to that Sabbath, which is cele-
> brated in love of him.][33]

In terms of such a scheme, Langland's "Saterday that sette firste the kalendare" would allude to the first Sabbath, on which God rested from His
six days of creation (Genesis 2:2–3) ; while "the Wednesday of the nexte
wyke after" would allude to the fourth "day" of man's redemption by
Christ—here signifying the Passion, which constitutes the specific work
of atonement. If so, one pattern that emerges from lines 153–54 is a refer-

32 Smith, pp. 680–82.

33 Peter of Blois, *De charitate Dei et proximi*, cap. 17 (*PL*, 207, col. 915) . See also
an anonymously compiled *Tractatus de charitate*, cap. 18 (*PL*, 184, cols. 612–13) ; and
for further references, Smith, pp. 680–82. The idea that God's original Sabbath "sette
firste the kalendare" (below) seems borne out, for example, in a *Summa sententiarum*
traditionally attached to the name of Hugh of St. Victor and now doubtfully attributed
to Otho of Lucca (III, I; *PL*, 176, col. 91) : ". . . fuit [in septima die] aliquis status
rerum . . . et ideo usque ad eam procedimus, et post eam statim reincipimus" [. . .
there was on the seventh day a certain established state of things . . . and therefore we
continually proceed toward this state, and after it immediately begin again]. See also
Bede's *Hexaemeron,* I (*PL*, 91, col. 33) .

ence to the beginnings of the two greatest divisions of history: the time of
the Old Testament, which may be thought of as dating from the completion of the Creation; and that of the New Testament, which may be
thought of as dating from the completion of the Atonement. The "myddel of the mone" in line 155 has been generally recognized as an allusion
to the Paschal moon, and so to Easter and the Resurrection;[34] its obvious
relevance to the pattern just proposed would be as the central event in
human history, by which the two great periods are decisively separated
and from which both draw their ultimate significance in the plan of salvation.

More immediately important for our passage, however, is a detailed
correspondence between the original seven days and the familiar group
of seven virtues, comprising the three Theological Virtues (*fides, spes,*
and *charitas*) and the four Cardinal Virtues (*prudentia, justitia, temperantia,* and *fortitudo*). Peter of Blois, for example, associates the first day
of creation with *fides,* the second with *spes,* the third with *temperantia,*
the fourth with *prudentia,* the fifth with *fortitudo,* the sixth with *justitia,*
and the final day of rest with *charitas;* our particular concern is with his
discussions of the seventh day (the Sabbath, or Saturday) and of the
fourth day (Wednesday):

> Vere verum est in charitate Sabbatum, cum enim cæteræ virtutes
> vicem vehiculi vel viatici gerant ad requiem obtinendam, omnes in
> charitate requiescunt. . . . Sicut autem charitas est vera mentis hu-
> manæ requies, perfectumque Sabbatum, sic et sex prædictæ virtutes,
> fides, spes, temperantia, prudentia, fortitudo, justitia sunt quasi qui-
> dam dies operationis. Charitas vero quædam luminosissima dies est
> quietis, tranquillitatis et pacis. . . . Prudentia quasi dies quartus fac-
> iat scientiæ lumen erumpere, ut inter facienda et non facienda dis-
> cernens dividat inter diem et noctem, quatenus sapientiæ lumen
> velut solis splendor, effulgeat. Lux vero scientiæ spiritualis in qui-
> busdam crescit, et in quibusdam deficit, quasi lunæ lux minor ap-
> pareat. . . . Dies enim septimus est charitas, dies Sabbati, dies requie-
> tionis, jocunditatis et pacis. . . . [Truly, in charity we have the true
> Sabbath; for while the other virtues perform the function of vehicle
> or provisions for finding rest, all come to rest in charity. . . . More-
> over, just as charity is the true rest and the perfect Sabbath of the
> human soul, so also the six aforesaid virtues—faith, hope, temper-
> ance, prudence, fortitude, justice—are, as it were, the individual days
> of labor. Charity indeed is the shining day of quiet, tranquillity, and
> peace. . . . Let prudence, as it were the fourth day, make the light of

34 Skeat, ii, 196–97; Goodridge, p. 307; Smith, p. 682.

knowledge break forth, so that, distinguishing between what should
be done and what should not be done, it may make division between
day and night, in order that the light of wisdom, like the splendor
of the sun, may shine forth. Indeed the light of spiritual knowledge
grows in some and fails in others, as if the lesser light of the moon appeared. . . . For charity is the seventh day, the day of Sabbath, the
day of rest, joy, and peace. . . .][35]

In the light of this traditional theme, together with the context of our
passage in *Piers Plowman,* it seems quite probable that Langland's "signe
of the Saterday" is a riddling circumlocution for *charitas;* that his "witte
of the Wednesday" is a slightly less oblique reference to *prudentia, sapientia, scientia,* or some combination of them; and that these meanings
are somehow more immediate and important than the historical pattern
discussed above. What, then, is their relation to the "myddel of the
mone" in the following line (155), and to the statement on which lines
153–55 grammatically depend—"I bere there in a bouste . fast ybounde
Dowel . . ." (l. 252) ?

The likeliest point of synthesis—not only for the allusions in these
lines, but for all the themes I have proposed in the passage so far—is
found in Colossians 3, already quoted briefly in connection with the
"half a laumpe lyne":

Igitur, si consurrexistis cum Christo, quæ sursum sunt quærite, ubi
Christus est in dextera Dei sedens. . . . Nolite mentiri invicem, ex-
spoliantes vos veterem hominem cum actibus suis, et induentes novum eum, qui renovatur in agnitionem, secundum imaginem ejus
qui creavit illum. . . . Induite vos . . . viscera misericordiæ, benignitatem, humilitatem, modestiam, patientiam. . . . Super omnia autem
hæc, charitatem habete, quod est vinculum perfectionis. . . . Verbum
Christi habitet in vobis abundanter, in omni sapientia, docentes et
commonentes vosmetipsos. . . . [Therefore, if you have risen with
Christ, seek the things that are above, where Christ is sitting at the
right hand of God. . . . Do not lie to one another, having put off the
old man with his practices and having put on the new one, who is
renewed in knowledge after his image who created him. . . . Put you
on . . . the bowels of mercy, kindness, humility, modesty, patience.
. . . But above all these, have charity, which is the bond of perfec-

[35] Peter of Blois, cap. 11–13 *(PL,* 207, cols. 906, 908–909). See also Aelred of Rievaulx,
Speculum charitatis, I, 32 *(PL,* 195, cols. 526–27); and the *Tractatus de charitate,* cap.
14 *(PL,* 184, cols. 608–09). Peter adds in cap. 14 *(PL,* 207, col. 909), "Et notandum
quod in charitate hoc triplex Sabbatum . . . invenitur." The three "Sabbaths" are
love of self, love of one's neighbor, and love of God—the first two of which correspond
to Love's instructions in lines 140–41 and 142 ff., respectively.

tion. . . . Let the word of Christ dwell in you abundantly, in all wisdom, teaching and admonishing one another. . . .]

(1, 9–10, 12, 14, 16)

Besides the obvious importance of *patientia* and *charitas* in our passage
as a whole, and the potential relevance of "docentes . . . vosmetipsos"
[teaching . . . one another] to Patience's definition of Dobet as *doce* (136–
37) , the references here to *charitas, benignitas,* and the *Verbum Christi*
approximate the subjects of line 150 discussed earlier; those to *charitas,*
to *sapientia* and *agnitio* [knowledge], and to the Resurrection as inspira-
tion and source of the prescribed regeneration, parallel generally the significances just proposed for lines 153–55;[36] and the image of *charitas* as
the *vinculum perfectionis* (3:14) is reflected in lines 152–53 by the description of Dowel as "fast ybounde . . . In a signe of the Saterday," or
charitas—particularly in the light of comments like that by Hervé of
Bourgdieu, who explains that *charitas* is the *vinculum perfectionis*
[*bond of perfection*] "quia per hanc ligatur omnis virtutum perfectio,
ne dissoluta defluat et dilabatur ac dispereat. Perfectionis vinculum est
charitas, quia omne bonum quod agimus [cf. Dowel] per hanc, ne pereat,
ligatur." [because through it every perfection of the virtues is bound, lest
dissolved, it should flow away and collapse and perish. The bond of perfection is charity, because every good we do is bound through it lest it
should perish.][37] The point of lines 152–55, then, seems to be that Dowel—here conceived of as the harmonious perfection of the virtues envi-
sioned by Paul, along with the Christian well-doing that it implies—is
created and maintained through the vital power of *charitas* ("a signe of
the Saterday") , supported by *prudentia/sapientia/scientia* ("the witte
of the Wednesday") ;[38] and that these master-virtues, in turn, draw their

[36] For a pertinent epitome of the significance of Colossians 3:1-17—with particular
emphasis on the imagery of clothing in verses 9–12, suggesting the allegorical clothing
of Haukyn *Activa-vita* which follows shortly (xiii, 272–460; xiv, 1-27) —see Peter
Aureoli, *Compendium sensus litteralis*, pp. 311–12.

[37] *PL*, 181, col. 1347. See also Denis the Carthusian, *ed. cit.*, xiii, 367; and Hugh of
St. Cher, *ed. cit.*, vii, fol. 193ᵛ: "Cætera [dona] enim perfectum faciunt, *charitas autem
omnia ligat ne abeant.* Dicitur ergo secundum hoc vinculum perfectionis, quia perfectionem ligat & conservat in Sanctis." [For other gifts make one perfect, *but charity
binds them all lest they depart.* Therefore, in accord with this, it is called the bond of
perfection because it binds and preserves perfection among the Saints.] The clause
that I have italicized appears in the *Glossa ordinaria* as an interlinear gloss on Colossians 3:14–from which it is quoted by Peraldus, tom. I, pars II, tract. 4, cap. 2 (*ed. cit.*,
I, fol. 82ʳ) . Note Langland's own explicit reference to the "cheyne of charyte," v, 616;
Osee 11:4; and footnotes 29 and 31 above.

[38] For the considerable flexibility in the use of these terms, see Peraldus, tom. I, pars
II, tract. 2, cap. i, "De diuersis modis quibus sumitur nomen Prudentia" (*ed. cit.*, i, fol.
100ᵛ) ; a likely association here, of course, would be with the *sapientia et scientia* of
Colossians 2:3. For the probable relation of this *witte* to the Redemption itself, see

power from the central Christian fact of the Resurrection (155) , without which "vana est fides vestra" [vain is your faith] (I Corinthians 15:13, 17) . The relation of this set of meanings to the historical one proposed earlier depends, I would suggest, on a kind of loose analogy between them: historically, Dowel can be analyzed as "bound up in" the teachings of the Old and New Laws; morally, Dowel can be analyzed as virtue it- self "bound up in" *charitas,* aided by *prudentia/sapientia/scientia;* but to be meaningful at all, either pattern must be validated by the Redemp- tion, conclusively manifested in the Resurrection. The implicit union of the Old Law and *charitas* in "a signe of the Saterday" finds a parallel in Langland's later conflation of the tables of the Law and the *præcepta charitatis* [*precepts of charity*] (xvii, 10–18) —also described, significantly enough, as a "charme" (17) . Our specific allusion to the Creation in this "signe of the Saterday," however, suggests that what I have been calling broadly "the Old Law" may here embrace not only the Mosaic Law but also the *lex naturalis,* established at the Creation and generally thought of (in accord with Romans 2:14–15 and 5:13–14) as ruling mankind from Adam to Moses.[39]

Smith, p. 681. Writers on the "weeks" of Creation and Redemption—among others— stress the close harmony between *prudentia/sapientia/scientia* and *charitas;* Peter of Blois, cap. II (*PL,* 207, col. 906) : "In charitate est perfecta scientia, ideoque nullus error quem prudentia eliminet. . . . Quid est prudentia, nisi amor, quem error non seducit?" [In charity is perfect knowledge and therefore no error which prudence might eliminate. . . . What is prudence, unless love, which error does not seduce?] And see Peraldus, tom. I, pars II, tract. 4, cap. 2 (*ed. cit.,* I, fol. 82ʳ) , with potential rele- vance also to Patience's *Disce* and *Doce* in lines 136–37.

39 See for example Hugh of St. Cher, *ed. cit.,* VII, fols. 19ᵛ, 34ʳ. A relation of this *lex naturalis* to the Mosaic Law and the New Law, as well as to *charitas* itself, is illus- trated by Hugh's critical analysis of the *Glossa ordinaria* on the *epistola . . . Christi . . . scripta . . . Spiritu Dei vivi, non in tabulis lapideis sed in tabulis cordis carnalibus* [*letter . . . of Christ . . . written . . . with the spirit of the living God, not on tablets of stone but on fleshly tablets of the heart*] of II Corinthians 3:3 (*ibid.,* fol. 125ᵛ) : "Item super illud Rom. 2:[14], *Ipsi sibi sunt lex,* dicit *Glossa:* 'Lex naturalis scripta est in cordibus hominum, sed lex naturalis nihil aliud est quam illa decem mandata, quæ scripta sunt in tabulis lapideis.' . . . & quia lex Euangelii omnia illa [cæremonialia et judicia] removet, docens legem naturalem, de qua constat quod digito Dei scripta est, ideo dicitur [Lex] Nova & digito Dei scripta. . . . [*Glossa:*] 'Hæc lex naturalis est chari- tas Dei.' Imo ratio potius." [Similarly, on Romans 2: 14, *They are a law unto them- selves,* says the *Glossa:* "The natural law is written in the hearts of men, but the natural law is nothing other than those ten commandments, which are written on tablets of stone" . . . and because the law of the Gospel takes away all those ceremonies and judgments, teaching the natural law which it is certain was written by the finger of God, therefore it is called a New Law and written by the finger of God. . . . "This natural law is the charity of God." Or even reason.] In the printed edition of the *Glossa,* this last quotation appears as "hec lex [noua] est charitas dei" [this new law is the charity of God]. Within *Piers Plowman,* note Holy Church's earlier definition of *treuthe* as "a kynde knowynge . . . that kenneth in thine herte / For to loue thi lorde . leuer than thi-selue . . ." (i, 140–41) .

A final detail in line 152 is the *bouste* (*boiste,* or box) in which Patience carries Dowel "fast ybounde." If we allow Patience himself the importance that his role here seems to justify, one promising lead toward the meaning of this *bouste* is offered by Luke 21:19, as allegorized for example in the *Dictionarius pauperum,* a popular thirteenth-century compendium by Nicolas de Byard:

Primo in patientia vt in arca anima custoditur, Lucas xxi: "In patientia vestra possidebitis animas vestras." Multum deberet diligere homo illum qui faceret ei talem arcam gratis; sic debet diligere tribulationem que fabricat arcam istam. . . . Quot contumelie tibi dicuntur, quot iniurie fiunt, tot bende et claui ad fortificandum arcam tuam apponuntur [oppununtur, *ed.*]: vnde magnas gratias deberes illi agere qui tibi talem arcam fabricaret, non contumelias reddere. Si ergo venit operarius quem tibi Deus mittit, qui tibi arcam fabricet in qua thesaurus anime conseruetur, non est repellendus sed amplectendus. Dominus vult multum fortificare arcam amicorum suorum, et ideo multos operatores mittit qui multas bendas et clauos apponant; sic patientiam tribulatio fabricat, sed infirmitas perficit. . . . Unde sicut sollicite custodit homo arcam in qua habet magnam pecuniam, sic debet custodire patientiam in qua tam preciosus thesaurus anime custoditur. . . . Et sicut latrones facile habent thesaurum postquam fregerint arcam, ita diabolus animam postquam turbauerit hominem et abstulerit patientiam, quia "cor fatui quasi vas confractum, omnem sapientiam non retinebit" [First, in patience the soul is guarded as in a chest, Luke xxi: "You shall possess your souls in your patience." One ought to love very much that man who makes for him such a chest free of charge; so he should love the tribulation which constructs this chest. . . . As many insults as are spoken against you, as many injuries as are done to you, just so many bonds and locks are added to strengthen your chest: hence you should give great thanks to him who makes such a chest for you and not return him insults. If then a workman whom God sends to you, comes to construct a chest for you in which the treasure of your soul is preserved, he should not be driven off, but embraced. The Lord wishes greatly to strengthen the chest of his friends, and so he sends many workmen to add many bonds and locks; thus tribulation builds patience, but weakness perfects it. . . . And so just as a man carefully guards the chest in which he has great wealth, so he should guard the patience in which the very precious treasure of the soul is guarded. . . . And just as robbers easily have the treasure after they have broken the chest, so the devil has the soul after he has confused a man and stolen his patience, because "the heart of a fool is like a broken vessel, no wisdom at all shall it hold"] (Ecclesiasticus 21:-17).[40]

Again, in the popular Old Testament account of the return of the Ark to Bethsames by the Philistines, there is the *capsella* [*little box*] into which the Philistines are ordered to place certain rather unlikely golden images (I Kings [Samuel] 6:8, 11, 15); Denis the Carthusian, for example, interprets this detail in a way that immediately suggests the concept of Dowel: "Hi itaque in capsella, hoc est in conscientia humili vel poenitentia salutari, custodiunt et reponunt bona quæ operantur" [Therefore they guard and place the good they do in a little box; that is, in a humble conscience or saving penitence].[41] In the *Promptorium Parvulorum* and the *Catholicon Anglicum*, "boyste" or "buyste" is defined by the word *alabastrum* [*alabaster box*][42]—whose most prominent medieval context, so far as I know, is the Gospel episode in which an *alabastrum unguenti* [*alabaster box of ointment*] is broken open by a woman universally identified as Mary Magdalene, in order to anoint the feet of Christ (Matthew

[40] Nicolas de Byard, cap. 85, "De patientia (Strassburg, 1518), fols. 128ᵛ-129ʳ. Though *boiste/bouste* originally meant a small jar or box for holding ointment and the like, by the later fourteenth century it could certainly have approximated the meaning of *arca* [*chest*]. See *Piers*, A. xii, 69; *MED*, B.4, p. 1015, "boist(e)," I(b); *OED*, "Boist," *sb.*, and "Buste"; and as a possible earlier example, *Ancrene Wisse* (sel.), ed. Fernand Mossé, *A Handbook of Middle English* (Baltimore, 1952), p. 148, line 140.

[41] Denis the Carthusian, *ed. cit.*, III, 293. See also Peter Riga's *Aurora*, rev. Gilles of Paris, MS Oxford, Bodl. 822, fols. 94ᵛ-95ʳ:

Ex auro quinos faciunt anos, totidemque
Mures, hos et eos portet ut archa Dei,
Ut tam deformis illorum plaga quiescat,
Et sanent turpes splendida dona notas.
Sic qui sunt maculis per sensus quinque notati
Ad veniam veniunt si sua facta gemunt,
Si quinos sensus convertant ad cor, et intra
Capsellam mentis dona precesque locent;
Et licet inviti se convertant, tamen illos
Reddit devotos gratia sepe Dei.

[They make five hemorrhoids from gold, and just as many mice, so that the ark of God might carry the one and the other, and their very ugly plague might subside and the splendid gifts might heal the foul marks. Thus those marked by strains because of their five senses come to forgiveness if they bemoan their deeds, if they convert their five senses to the heart and place gifts and prayers within the little box of the mind. And though they turn themselves unwillingly, nevertheless the grace of God often renders them faithful.] For the frequent appearance of this *capsella* in medieval illustration of I Kings 6, see the Princeton Index of Christian Art.

[42] *Promptorium*, ed. A. Way (Camden Society, No. 89; London, 1865), p. 42; *Catholicon*, ed. S. J. H. Herrtage (EETS 75; London, 1881), p. 49. In the fourteenth-century Scottish *Magdalena*, line III (ed. W. M. Metcalfe, *Legends of the Saints* [STS 13, 18; Edinburgh, 1896], I, 259), the *alabastrum* broken by Mary Magdalene (see below) is called "a bouste of precius vngument."

26:7, Mark 14:3, Luke 7:37). The incident is expressly mentioned some forty lines later in this passus of the B-text (xiii, 194); the breaking of the box itself could, I suppose, be reflected in the line (apparently spoken by Conscience) which immediately follows our passage: " 'Vndo it, late this doctour deme . if Dowel be therinne . . .' " (l. 157); and an earlier quotation by Conscience, *Cor contritum et humiliatum, deus, non despicies* [*A contrite and humbled heart, God, you will not despise*] (l. 58; Psalm 50:19) bears latent relevance to a typical interpretation of the *alabastrum* by Hugh of St. Cher: "Alabastrum in quo unguentum est, [est] ipsum cor penitentis, quo fracto, unguentum effunditur. . . . Frangitur autem alabastrum, quia cor in oratione comminuendum est, si larga sit effusio unguenti. . . ." [The alabaster box in which is ointment is the very heart of the penitent; when it is broken, the ointment is poured out. . . . The alabaster box is broken, because the heart in prayer must be shattered, if the flow of ointment is to be generous. . . .][43]

With some guidance from these not altogether consistent hints, as well as from my interpretation of the passage thus far, I would suggest that the imagery of line 152 presents Dowel not only "bound" by *charitas* as explained above, but also enclosed within a *bouste;* and that this *bouste* is to be understood either as *patientia* itself, or as the heart of the Christian fortified by *patientia*—traditionally the "guard" or "protector" of all the other virtues. The *Summæ* of Peraldus supports this function of *patientia* from one of our basic Scriptural texts, Colossians 3:12: "*Induite vos sicut electi Dei viscera misericordiæ, benignitatem, humilitatem, modestiam, patientiam. Patientia ultima ponitur quasi ordinans & protegens ceteras virtutes.*" [*Put on as God's chosen the bowels of mercy, kindness, humility, modesty, patience. Patience is placed last as if ordering and protecting the other virtues.*][44] A famous analysis by Gregory, quoted profusely throughout the Middle Ages, emphasizes the same function of *patientia* along with its relationship to *charitas,* employing

---

[43] Hugh of St. Cher, *ed. cit.,* VI, fol. 80[r], on Matthew 26:7; *ibid.,* fol. 115[v], on Mark 14:3. Bede supplies a possible connection with the concept of Dowel by remarking (*PL,* 92, col. 426, on Luke 7:37) that we pour ointment on the Lord's body "si igitur recta opera agimus" [if we do good works]. See also the detailed analysis by Albertus Magnus (on Luke 7:37), ed. A. Borgnet, *Opera omnia* (Paris, 1894), XXII, 500–501; the *De vita B. Mariæ Magdalenæ* ascribed to Rabanus (*PL,* 112, col. 1438); Odo of Cluny's hymn on Magdalene (*PL,* 133, col. 514); and the *Allegoriæ in universam Sacram Scripturam* (*PL,* 112, col. 1085).

[44] Peraldus, tom. I, pars III, tract. 4, pars 6, cap. 2 (*ed. cit.,* I, fol. 138[r]). Peter Cantor, *Summa Abel,* MS Paris, B.N. lat. 3388, fol. 130[v]: "Patientia non tantum bona custodit, sed repellit adversa. . . . Cum patientia relinquitur, etiam bona reliqua que gesta sunt destruuntur." [Patience not only guards good things, but drives off hostile things. . . . When patience is abandoned, even the other good works which have been done are destroyed.] The first sentence is found in Cyprian's *De bono patientae,* cap. 14 (ed. W. Hartel, *CSEL,* III, I, 407).

two more of our basic texts (Luke 21:19 and I Corinthians 13:4) as well as the Scriptural prototype of Patience's *Dilige inimicos* [*Love your enemies*] (l. 136) :

In patientia vestra possidebitis animas vestras [Luke 21:19]. Idcirco possessio animæ in virtute patientiæ ponitur, quia radix omnium custosque virtutum patientia est. Per patientiam vero possidemus animas nostras, quia dum nobis ipsis dominari discimus, hoc ipsum incipimus possidere quod sumus. Patientia vero est aliena mala æquanimiter perpeti, contra eum quoque qui mala irrogat nullo dolore moderi. . . . Scriptum quippe est: *Charitas patiens est, benigna est* [I Corinthians 13:4]. Patiens namque est ut aliena mala toleret, benigna vero est ut ipsos etiam quos portat, amet. Hinc namque per semetipsum Veritas dicit: *Diligite inimicos vestros, benefacite his qui oderunt vos, orate pro persequentibus et calumniantibus vos* [Matthew 5:44; cf. Luke 6:27–28, 35]. Virtus itaque est coram hominibus adversarios tolerare, sed virtus coram Deo diligere, quia hoc solum Deus sacrificium accipit, quod ante oculos in altari boni operis flamma charitatis incendit. [*In your patience you shall possess your souls.* Therefore possession of the soul is placed in the virtue of patience, because patience is the root and guardian of all the virtues. Through patience we indeed possess our souls, because when we learn to be ruled by our very selves, we begin to possess the very thing which we are. Patience is to suffer evils from another with equanimity, to be stung by no resentment against him who inflicts the evils. . . . For it is written: *Charity is patient, is kind.* It is patient so that it may suffer evils from others, it is kind so that it may love even those from whom it suffers. For hence Truth speaks through Himself: *Love your enemies, do good to those who hate you, for those who persecute and calumniate you.* Thus it is a virtue before men to endure one's enemies, but a virtue before God to love them, because God accepts this sacrifice alone which the flame of charity burns before his eyes on the altar of good works.][45]

---

[45] Gregory, *Hom. in Evang.*, xxxv, 4 (*PL*, 76, cols. 1261–62) ; see also his *Hom. in Ezech.*, ii, v, 14 (*PL*, 76, cols. 993–94) . Albertus Magnus on Luke 21:19 (*ed. cit.*, xxiii, 639) , confronted by Gregory's characterizations of *patientia* and *humilitas* each as the "radix et custos virtutum" [root and guardian of the virtues], and of *charitas* as the "radix virtutum," explains: "Est autem patientia radix, quantum ad illam radicis proprietatem, quod est arborem firmare contra impulsus exteriores. Humilitas autem custos est, quantum ad occultationem ab insidiantibus. Sed charitas, quantum ad succi et nutrimenti ministrationem, est radix." [Patience is the root insofar as pertains to that property of a root, which is to strengthen the tree against exterior attacks. Humility, however, is the guardian insofar as pertains to concealment from attackers. But charity is the root insofar as pertains to the office of supplying strength and nourish-

A dependence of *charitas* itself upon *patientia* is clearly implied in Langland's later figure of the Tree:

Pacience hatte the pure tre . and pore symple of herte,
And so, thorw god and thorw good men . groweth the frute Charite.

(xvi, 8–9) [46]

So far, we may seem to be little the wiser with regard to the noncommittal syntax of "With half a laumpe lyne in latyne . *ex vi transicionis . . ."* (1. 151) , or its relation to the lines which follow. I would propose, first of all, that this part of Patience's speech (ll. 151–56) is essentially a definition of his own role in the preservation of Dowel through *charitas*. His reported speech of Love (140–50) has descriptively defined *amor proximorum,* the second "precept" of *charitas,* ending with a summary of the great pronouncement on *charitas* in I Corinthians 13–14—"Kynde

---

ment.] In the *Glossa ordinaria,* the interlinear gloss on "Charitas patiens est" [*Charity is patient*] in I Corinthians 13:4 adds, "scilicet habitu patientie in anima" [namely by the habit of patience in the soul]. The relationship between *patientia* and *charitas* is, of course, developed particularly in commentary on this verse; that between *patientia* and *prudentia/sapientia* is prominent in commentary on Luke 21:19. See for example— with additional reference to *Piers,* xiii, 205–10—Hugh of St. Cher, *ed. cit.,* vi, 254ᵛ: "*Possidebitis animas vestras:* . . . Nota duæ virtutes maxime sunt necessariæ predicatoribus, scilicet, sapientia & patientia. Nam per sapientiam respondetur verbis, per patientiam verberibus. . . . Veruntamen [in patientia vestra possidebitis animas vestras], quia patientia radix est, & omnium virtutum custos, etiam sapientie. Unde Prov. cap. 19:[11], 'Doctrina viri per patientiam noscitur.' " [*You shall possess your souls . . . .* Note that two virtues are most necessary for preachers, namely wisdom and patience. For through wisdom one answers to words, through patience to blows. . . . But in your patience you shall possess your souls because patience is the root and the guardian of all the virtues, even of wisdom. Whence Proverbs, 19:11: "The learning of a man is known through patience."] Maurice of Ireland, *Distinctiones,* MS Paris, B.N. lat. 15945, fol. 208ᵛ: "[Patientia] generat sapientiam, Prov. [14:29]: 'Qui patiens est [multa gubernatur prudentia].' " [Patience generates wisdom, Proverbs 14:29: "He who is patient is governed by much prudence."]

[46] See also xiv, 99–100, 191–92; xviii, 414–15; and E. Talbot Donaldson, *Piers Plowman: The C-Text and Its Poet* (New Haven, 1949) , pp. 178–79. Compare the early expression of the same idea by Cyprian, cap. 15 (*CSEL,* iii, i, 407–408) : "Caritas fraternitatis uinculum est, fundamentum pacis, tenacitas ac firmitas unitatis. . . . Tolle illi patientiam, et desolata non durat, tolle sustinendi tolerandique substantiam, et nullis radicibus ac uiribus perseuerat. Apostolus denique cum de caritate loqueretur, tolerantiam illi et patientiam iuncxit . . . [I Corinthians 13:4–7; Ephesians 4:2]. Probauit nec unitatem seruari posse nec pacem, nisi se inuicem fratres mutua tolerantia foueant et concordiae [i.e., caritatis] uinculum patientia intercedente custodiant." [Charity is the bond of fraternity, the foundation of peace, the tenacity and strength of unity. . . . Take from it patience and, forsaken, it does not endure; take away the substance of bearing and enduring, and it continues without roots and strength. Finally, the Apostle, when he spoke of charity, joined endurance and patience to it. . . . He proved that neither unity nor peace can be preserved, unless brothers cherish each other with mutual long-suffering and guard the bond of concord (i.e., of charity) with mediating patience.]

loue coueiteth nouȝte . no catel but speche" (l. 150). Patience now adds
that his own closely related function is to protect, as in a *bouste,* the
whole complex of virtues (Dowel) bound together by *charitas,* the *vinculum perfectionis* of Colossians 3:14. If, as I have suggested, the phrase
"With half a laumpe lyne in latyne" can be understood as alluding to the
command "Tene hanc lampadem!" and so indirectly to *charitas* itself,
the point of lines 151–52 seems to be that by means of this command (i.e.,
by keeping the Christian aware of and receptive to it), the virtue *patientia* maintains the heart in *charitas* and so makes possible the "binding"
(the attainment and preservation) of Dowel. *Ex vi transicionis,* I suspect,
carries some force as a modifier of both the verb *bere* and the participle
ybounde in line 152: through a process as inevitable as the "ruling" of a
direct object by a transitive verb *ex vi transicionis* (or as the "ruling" of
the accusative *lampadem* by the verb *Tene*), the possession of Dowel is
governed ultimately by *patientia;* but through a similarly inevitable process, the possession of Dowel is governed more directly by *charitas,* which

> primo habet bonitatem inter virtutes, & per eam habent bonitatem
> cæteræ. Et secundum hoc intelligendum est quod dicit *Glossa* super
> I Tim. 1, quod charitas est radix omnium bonorum inquantum scili-
> cet sunt bona. Et illud similiter super Galat. 5. Ex charitate nascun-
> tur omnia bona, inquantum scilicet sunt bona. Et sicut radix hu-
> morem mittit ad ramos, sic charitas bonitatem ad opera cæterarum
> virtutum. [first has goodness among the virtues, and through it the
> others have goodness. And in the light of this must be understood
> what the *Glossa ordinaria* says on I Timothy 1, that charity is the
> root of all good things insofar as they are good. And that similarly
> on Galatians 5. From charity are born all good things insofar as they
> are good. And just as the root sends moisture to the branches, so
> charity sends goodness to the works of other virtues.][47]

The grammatical imagery of line 151, however, seems to function also

---

[47] Peraldus, tom. I, pars II, tract. 4, cap. 1 (*ed. cit.,* I, fol. 78ᵛ). The first citation
from the *Glossa* refers to part of the gloss on I Timothy 1:5, ultimately from Augustine's Sermo 350 (*PL,* 39, col. 1534); the second apparently refers to that on Galatians
5:22. See also, for example, the elaborations of the parallel between the week of creation and the seven virtues (notes 33 and 35 above), where the theme is especially
prominent; *Le laie Bible* (ll. 2072–2104; pp. 78–79), where it is expounded in a passage
beginning, "Carités est le droite fourme / Qui toutes les viertus enfourme . . ." [Charity
is the true form / Which informs every virtue]; and the related exegesis of Colossians
3:14 (note 37 above). Besides constituting a commonplace whose popularity defies
meaningful documentation, this concept of *charitas* as *causa, radix, mater,* or *forma
virtutum* [*cause, root, mother,* or *form of virtues*] was a subject of detailed theological
analysis; for a general account, see Dom Odon Lottin, *Psychologie et morale aux XIIᵉ
et XIIIᵉ siècles* (Louvain, 1942–60), III, 199–215.

as a topical development of Love's final reference to *speche* in line 150, while a possible pun on the word *lyne* in line 151 (either "line of a text" or "cord") might contribute an additional figurative suggestion to the "binding" of Dowel in line 152.

In the light of this whole relentless exegesis, lines 151–56 may at last be paraphrased somewhat as follows: "By means of the fundamental Christian injunction to charity (epitomized rather whimsically in the Latin grammatical tag *Tene hanc lampadem!*), and through a relationship comparable to that by which a transitive verb 'rules,' *ex vi transicionis,* its direct object in the accusative case, I, Patience, contain and guard as if in a protective box the other virtues (identified, along with their results, as 'Dowel'), which are themselves interrelated and maintained, as if tightly bound, by charity, with the support of prudence/wisdom/knowledge (alluded to respectively as 'a sign of the Saturday' and 'the wit of the Wednesday,' which constitute also an analysis of Dowel in terms of the 'Old Law' [the *lex naturalis* and/or the Mosaic Law] and the New Law) —both of which virtues (like also the Laws) receive their power ultimately through the Redemption, conclusively manifested by Christ's resurrection on Easter morning; and I, Patience, am esteemed along with this complex of virtues, in the hearts where I enter bringing it with me." If it should be thought that line 151 is, after all, more plausible as Love's final line than as the beginning of Patience's resumed speech (see footnote 1 above), lines 150–51 could be paraphrased satisfactorily, though I think somewhat less naturally, "Just as a noun ruled by a transitive verb *ex vi transicionis* 'covets' its proper grammatical case (*or* just as a transitive verb 'covets,' *ex vi transicionis,* the completion of its own meaning through a direct object), so the Christian ruled by the kindly power of charity covets no wordly goods, but instead 'covets' only the further gifts of charity, like those of speech—along with, of course, the abiding injunction to charity itself, which I epitomize in the Latin tag *Tene hanc lampadem!*" There are, in fact, two arguments that might favor such a construction: first, the fact that its resulting interpretation is almost completely independent of my conjecture about the "half a laumpe lyne"; second and more substantial, the parallel presented by the elaborate grammatical metaphor of the C-text, in which proper and improper relationship between a substantive and its adjective are made to illustrate rightful and unrightful forms of figurative "coveting" (iv, 365–68, 373–76, 397–406). As to why so enigmatic a speech should come from the mouth of Patience, I can offer only the hesitant conjecture that a passage like the following might have been enough to identify *patientia* figuratively with marvels, and so perhaps with marvelous utterance: "[Patientia] mira facit. Gregorius: 'Ego virtutem patientiæ signis & miraculis maiorem puto.' Si patientiam habens aliquid mortiferum biberit, non ei nocebit [cf. Mark 16:18]. Sermo venenatus quem audit, in medicinam ei vertitur. . . ." [Patience works marvels. Gregory: "I consider the virtue of patience greater because of signs and miracles." If one having patience drink something fatal, it shall not harm him. The enchanted word which he hears turns for him into medicine. . . .][48]

In any case, this reading of our crucial passage implies strongly that its use of the term "Dowel" (l. 152; again 157) embraces Patience's earlier "Dowel" or *Disce* [*Learn* (imperative)], "Dobet" or *Doce* [*Teach* (imperative)], and "Dobest" or *Dilige inimicos* [*Love your enemies*] (ll. 136–38) —a conclusion almost inevitable on other grounds as well, since this emphatic introduction of the trio at the beginning of Patience's speech would make it difficult to account for his climactic fastening upon the lowest of them here, in a passage emphasized still further by its enigmatic cast. The speech immediately following our passage (ll. 157–71) — punctuated with some appearance of symmetry by the significant *Caritas nichil timet* [*Charity fears nothing*] (l. 163) and *Pacientes vincunt, &c.* [*The patient conquer, etc.*] (l. 171), and paralleled abundantly in conventional eulogies of *charitas* and *patientia*—I take to be Conscience's praise of the "charm" resulting from the combined might of these two virtues, assisted by the virtues of the intellect. In line 168, the statement that this *redeles* will work "Nouȝt thoruȝ wicche-craft, but thoruȝ wit" may be a synecdoche employing as its vehicle the *veneficia* [*witchcrafts*] of Galatians 5:20, which are introduced as one of a series of *opera carnis* [*works of the flesh*] (5:19–21) opposing the *fructus Spiritus* (5:22–23). Among these "fruits of the Spirit" are the familiar *charitas, patientia,* and *benignitas;* and at least one commentator, Nicolas of Lyra, explains the *veneficia* themselves with the help of the "vocem . . . venefici incantantis sapienter" [the voice . . . of a wizard charming wisely] of Psalm 57:6 [49]—a juxtaposition carrying some suggestion of Langland's antithe-

---

[48] Peraldus, tom. I, pars III, tract. 4, pars 6, cap. 2 (*ed. cit.*, I, fol. 137ᵛ). I have not found the quotation in Gregory; note *Speculum Christiani*, ed. G. Holmstedt (EETS, 182; London, 1933), pp. 196–97, 200–201.

[49] *Ed. cit.*, XVI, 80: "*Veneficia.* Id est, sortilegia quæ ex ardore libidinis solent fieri. In hac significatione dicitur, Psalm. 57: *Venefici incantantis sapienter.*" [*Veneficia.* That is, magic which is wont to come from the ardor of libido. It is used with this meaning in Psalm 57: *Venefici incantantis sapienter.*] The meaning of this *veneficus,* however, is clearly favorable; Hugh of St. Cher, *ed. cit.*, II, fol. 146ᵛ, explains him as Christ charming wisely "ut [peccatores] de occultis extrahat ad lucem gratiæ [in order to draw sinners from the darkness into the light of grace]. If the proposed synecdoche is plausible, the second half of line 168, " (and thow wilt thi-selue) ," may conceivably reflect in some way Galatians 5:17, "ut non quæcunque vultis, illa faciatis" [so that you do not the things that you would]. Note also *æmulationes* among the *opera carnis* of 5:20.

sis between *wicche-craft* and *wit.* In Patience's speech the dependence of Dowel upon *charitas,* supported by *prudentia/sapientia/scientia,* anticipates the discussion in which *patientia*—clearly still bearing its intimate association with *charitas*[50]—is praised by Conscience, while the intellec-

[50] The importance of *charitas* in this passage, along with its general density of allusion, may be illustrated by lines 192–93, "The good wille of a wiȝte . was neuere bouȝte to the fulle; / For there nys no tresore therto . to a trewe wille." Augustine's *Enarratio in Psalmum 36:21 (CCL,* xxxviii, 355–56; *PL,* 36, col. 371) associates *voluntas bona* [*good will*] figuratively with *thesaurus* [*treasure*] (cf. line 193), comments on its inexhaustibility (cf. line 192), and identifies it literally with *charitas:* "Videte egestatem, uidete diuitias. Ille accipit, et non soluet; iste miseretur, et commodat; abundat illi. Quid si pauper est? Etiam sic diues est. Tu tantum ad diuitias eius pios oculos intende. Respicis enim arcam inanem, conscientiam Deo plenam non respicis. Non habet extrinsecus facultatem, sed habet intrinsecus caritatem. De caritate quanta erogat, et non finitur! Etenim si habet foris facultatem, dat ipsa aritas, sed ex quo quod habet; si autem non inuenit foris quod det, dat beneuolentiam, praestat consilium, si potest; praestat auxilium, si potest; ad extremum si nec consilio nec auxilio adiuuare potest, uel uoto adiuuat, uel orat pro contribulato, et forte magis ipse exauditur quam qui porrigit panem. Habet semper unde det, cui plenum pectus est caritatis, Ipsa est caritas, quae dicitur et uoluntas bona. Plus a te Deus non exigit, quam quod tibi intus dedit. Vacare enim non potest uoluntas bona. Non enim habens uoluntatem bonam, etsi nummus tibi supersit, non porrigis pauperi; ipsi inter se pauperes praestant sibi de uoluntate bona, non sunt inter se infructuosi. Vides caecum duci a uidente; quia nummos non habuit quos daret egenti commodauit oculos non habenti. Vnde hoc factum est, ut membra sua commodaret ei qui non habet, nisi quia intus inerat uoluntas bona, thesaurus pauperum? In quo thesauro dulcissima requies et uera securitas." [Behold poverty, behold riches. One man receives, and does not give; another has pity and lends; that man abounds. What if he is poor? Still he is rich. Only turn your pious eyes to his riches. For you see an empty money box, you do not see a conscience full of God. Externally he does not have abundance, but internally he has charity. How much he expends of charity, and it is not exhausted! Even if he has abundance from without, it is charity that gives, but from what he has; but if he does not find externally what he might give, he gives benevolence, he grants counsel, if he is able; he grants aid if he is able; finally, if he is able to help neither by counsel nor by aid, he either helps by his good wish or prays for the one in tribulation, and perhaps he is heard more in his prayer than he who offers bread. Whose heart is full of charity always has whence he might give. It is charity itself which is also called good will. God does not demand from you more than he has given you internally. A good will is unable to be idle. For when you do not have a good will, although you have an extra coin, you do not offer it to the poor; the poor care for themselves among one another from a good will, they are not fruitless among themselves. You see a blind man led by a seeing man; because he does not have money to give to a needy man, he lends his eyes to the man who has none. Whence has it happened that he has lent his bodily parts to another who does not have them, unless it is because there was within him a good will, the treasure of the poor? In that treasure is most sweet rest and true security.] A close relation between this "treasure" of *voluntas* [*good will*] or *intentio bona* [*good intention*] and the action of *charitas* appears also in later commentary on Matthew 12:35 (Luke 6:45), "Bonus homo de bono thesauro profert bona. . . ." [The good man from a good treasure brings forth good things. . . .] Nicolas of Lyra, for example, in his *Postilla litteralis (ed. cit.,* xiii, 140) explains, "Id est, de bona voluntate, quæ sicut thesaurus absconditus latet interius in mente, profert bona verba scilicet & facta" [That is, from a good will, which lies hidden like buried treasure within the mind, he brings forth good works as well as deeds]; in his *Moralia super totam*

tual virtues are defended by Clergy (ll. 179–214; and cf. I Corinthians 13:2). The friar's arrogance and explicit repudiation of *patientia* (ll. 177–78) gain somewhat in point from my analysis of Patience's speech, which reveals them as an even more precise index to the absence of *charitas* and a corresponding inability to attain Dowel. In larger terms, I suspect that the very situation of Patience's speech within Passus xiii may establish it as a major turning point in the poem, at which Will's quest for truth becomes, merges into, or is significantly combined with a quest for *charitas*. If this should be true, the pronouncements of Patience and Love—particularly the compact figurative analysis of *charitas* and its relation to *patientia,* the intellectual virtues, and Dowel itself (ll. 150–56) —would seem to function as a kind of preliminary abstract definition, introducing the more detailed presentations of *charitas* in the passus which follow.

If this interpretation has been at all convincing, our recognition of so intricate and precise a pattern of learned allusion in lines 150–56 speaks strongly for the likelihood of similar patterns in the other "riddling" or "prophetic" passages of *Piers Plowman,* and suggests that the intellectual texture of the poem itself may be much more complex, and much more dependent on learned allusion, than some of us are yet ready to admit. To this disquieting prospect, of course, there are by good fortune a number of less demanding alternatives. The lines in question may be a meaningless babble; they may have a patent and therefore congenial surface meaning; their "meaning" may reside primarily in some elusive sensuous pattern, to be experienced rather than understood; or, best of all, their peculiarities may have been dictated simply by the poet's need for alliterating syllables. One awaits with special enthusiasm the application of these hypotheses to the crucial line, "With half a laumpe lyne in latyne . *ex vi transicionis.*"

As a sort of concluding footnote, let us now glance briefly at the drastic revision of this passage in the C-text (xvi, 138 ff.). The substance of Patience's opening lines and most of Love's speech in the B-text are here assigned to Piers himself (C. xvi, 141–48);[51] lines 151–56 of B do not

---

Bibliam (Cologne, 1478), he adds, "Iste tesaurus est fides caritate formata, de qua procedit operatio bona" [This treasure is faith formed by charity, from which proceeds good work]. See also Albertus on Luke 6:45 (*ed. cit.*, xxɪɪ, 453).

[51] If, as seems to me rather likely, Piers at this point in C is to be recognized as somehow analogous to Christ, the expression "tho Peers was thus passed" (xvi, 153) may echo the concept of the *transitus Christi* [*passings of Christ*] as developed, for example, in Augustine's Sermo 349, cap. 6 (*PL,* 39, col. 1532). And if such an analogy should extend also to Patience in the B-text—in accord with the traditional idea of Christ as the supreme exemplar of *patientia* (Peraldus, tom. I, pars III, tract. 4, pars 6, cap. 3 [*ed. cit.*, ɪ, fol. 138ᵛ]) —the allegorizing of Love as Patience's *lemman* (xɪɪɪ,

appear, but are more or less replaced by another crux worthy of their company: Patience's guarantee of immunity to misfortune

> and thow take Pacience,
> And bere hit in thy bosom . abowte wher thou wendest,
> In the corner of a cart-whel . with a crowe croune.
>
> (ll. 160–62)

Since the avowed subject here is the bearing of Patience in one's bosom, it does not seem unreasonable to expect that the riddle of line 162 may bear some relation to that subject. In the first half-line, the concept suggested most immediately by "the corner of a cart-whel" would surely be the wedge-shaped interstice between two of its spokes. A painting of around 1400 once visible in the Church of Mary and Edmund, Ingatestone (Essex), represented a seven-spoked "wheel of vices," with each interstice occupied by one of the Deadly Sins.[52] The illustrations of the twelfth-century treatise *De rota vere et false religionis* by Hugh of Folieto include both a "wheel of vices" and a "wheel of virtues"; in the latter, the virtues *puritas, voluntas, charitas, humilitas, sobrietas,* and *paupertas* [*purity, good will, charity, humility, sobriety,* and *poverty*] occupy sections of the rim *(canti),* while the twelve spokes *(radii)* are *bona intentio, discretio, nolle malum, velle bonum, amor Dei, amor proximorum, contemptus sui, contemptus mundi, mensura cibi, modus edendi, nil proprium habere,* and *nil alienum appetere* [*good intention, discretion, to will no evil, to will good, love of God, love of neighbors, contempt of self, contempt of the world, moderation in regard to food, self-control in the manner of eating, to possess nothing as one's own,* and *to desire nothing of someone else's*]. The accompanying text explains in part: "Rotunditas rote circumspectio vite, volubilitas est vite varietas. Hec rota aliquando silet, aliquando stridet. Silet quando adversa paciente sustinet;

---

139) might gain in significance from comments on I Corinthians 13:4 like that of Bonaventura, *De Purificatione B. V. Mariæ,* serm. I (*ed. cit.,* IX, 638) : "Caritas, in quantum *patiens,* origo est virtutum activarum; in quantum amatrix est Christi, origo est virtutum contemplativorum" [Charity, inasmuch as it is *patient,* is the origin of the active virtues; inasmuch as it is the mistress of Christ, it is the origin of the contemplative virtues].

52 J. Charles Wall, *Mediæval Wall Paintings* (London, [1920?]) , pp. 198–99 and fig. 85; I am indebted for this reference to Miss R. B. Green, Director of the Princeton Index of Christian Art. The church at Arundel apparently contains a similar figure (Wall, p. 195) , as well as a "wheel" portraying the Seven Corporal Works of Mercy (p. 200) . For other "wheels" illustrating the Deadly Sins, see Morton W. Bloomfield, *The Seven Deadly Sins* (East Lansing, Mich., 1952) , p. 379, n. 310; and for an apparently unique "wheel" of the five senses governed by Reason, E. W. Tristram, *English Wall Painting of the Fourteenth Century* (London, 1955) , pl. 64 (b) and pp. 107–108.

stridet dum conqueritur et dolet. Silet dum ungitur; stridet dum artius coartatur." [The roundness of the wheel is the circumspection of life, the turning (rolling) is the variety of life. This wheel sometimes is silent, sometimes squeaks. It is silent when it patiently endures adversities; it squeaks when it complains and grieves. It is silent when it is oiled; it squeaks when it is too tightly joined.] [53] Though the virtues here do not occupy the interstices and do not include *patientia* explicitly, I would venture the suggestion that to bear Patience in one's bosom "In the corner of a cart-whel" is to possess *patientia* as part of some such visualized scheme of interrelated virtues—an idea approximated fairly closely in my interpretation of lines 151–56 in the B-text. Such a figure might also be indebted less directly to late medieval commentary on the famous *rotæ* [wheels] of Ezechiel 1, which are explained as consisting of two circles or discs set at right angles to one another and intersecting each other along their vertical diameters, so as to form four *angulos* (angles, "corners") or *semicirculos*.[54] These *anguli* or *semicirculi* are identified with the *quatuor facies* [four faces] of Ezechiel 1:15, and elaborately allegorized; Hugh of St. Cher, for example, attaches to the above explanation the medieval commonplace of the three *currus Dei* [cars of God]—the first of which is the *currus patientiæ* [car of patience], having as its wheels "benigna temporalium administratio, operosa infirmantium compassio, tentatorum blanda consolatio, injuriarum læta toleratio" [the kind administration of temporal matters, the painstaking compassion for the weak, the pleasant consolation of temptors, the joyful toleration of injuries]; and the third, the *currus charitatis,* having as its wheels "zelus Dei, amor proximi, maceratio carnis, devotio vel liquefactio cordis" [zeal for God, love of neighbor, the punishment of the flesh, the devotion or melting of the heart].[55]

In the second half of line 162, we are told either that Patience is to be carried in one's bosom along with or by means of "a crowe croune," or

[53] Hugh of Folieto, MS Heiligenkreuz, Stiftsbibl. 226, fol. 146ᵛ. On fol. 147ʳ, this allegory is further developed by a list of twelve means through which "ungitur axis ne strideat" [the axle is oiled lest it squeak], followed by the summarizing comment, "Hac unctione axis perunctus silet, quia huiusmodi monitis instructus, quilibet conversus pacienter omnia sustinet" [The axle oiled with this oil is silent, because whoever is instructed by such advice, when he is turned, patiently endures everything], and a list of nine such actions, all generally related to *patientia*. The illustrations themselves (fols. 146ʳ, 149ᵛ) are reproduced by Adolf Katzenellenbogen, *Allegories of the Virtues and Vices in Mediaeval Art* (Studies of the Warburg Institute, X; London, 1939), pl. XLIV–XLV, figs. 70–71; and see pp. 71–72. Note also the wheel-like representations of sets of vices and virtues in his pl. XXXVI, fig. 60, and pl. XXXVII, fig. 62.

[54] Hugh of St. Cher, *ed. cit.,* v, fol. 7ᵛ; Nicolas of Lyra, *ed. cit.,* xi, 10–11; Denis the Carthusian, *ed. cit.,* ix, 417.

[55] Hugh of St. Cher, *ed. cit.,* v, fol. 7ᵛ; the second chariot is the *currus pudicitiæ* [car of modesty].

that "the corner of a cart-whel" or the "cart-whel" itself is to have "a crowe croune"; in any case, it is again difficult to see how the expression could be unrelated to the maintenance either of *patientia,* of some accompanying virtue, or of virtue generally. An embarrassing assortment of potentially appropriate meanings can of course be found in medieval exegeses of *corona [crown];*[56] but what, precisely, is a *crow*-crown? The probable explanation, I believe, depends on a detail in Canticles 5:11, describing the *sponsus [spouse]:*

> Comæ ejus sicut elatæ palmarum, nigræ quasi corvus.
> [His hair is as the upright branches of palm trees, black as a raven.]

The first image here carries a natural suggestion of a crown; and the conventional association between the fronds of the palm and the crown of victory is not overlooked by commentators on the verse: "Ea [*i.e.,* palma] etiam coronantur triumphantes. . . . in corona triumphatorum [palma nos invitat] ad victoriam. . . . [De hoc:] 'Qui vicerit, dabo illi coronam vitæ' [Apocalypse 2:10]" [Also the triumphant are crowned with (the palm). . . . in the crown of the triumphant (the palm invites us) to victory. . . . (Concerning this:) "To him who conquers I shall give the crown of life"].[57] We may notice in passing that the *Liber floridus,* composed in the twelfth century by Lambert of St. Omer, contains what might even be

---

56 The galaxy of such meanings attached to *corona* includes, for example, *virtutes, sapientia, timor Domini, bona opera, religiositas, gratia,* and *spes . . . æternitatis in mente* [*virtues, wisdom, fear of the Lord, good works, religiousness, grace,* and *hope . . . of eternity in the mind*] (Hugh of St. Cher on Psalm 102:4, Lamentations 5:16–17, and Ezechiel 16:12; *ed. cit.,* ii, fol. 263ʳ, iv, fol. 309ᵛ, v, fol. 58ᵛ) ; *misericordia [mercy]* (William Durandus, *Rationale divinorum officiorum,* I, 3 [Lyon, 1540], fol. 7ᵛ) ; *iusticia* (Maurice of Ireland, *Distinctiones,* MS Paris, B.N. lat. 15945, fol. 57ᵛ); *fides* and *perfectio et ornatus omnium virtutum [faith* and *the perfection and embellishment of all the virtues*] (Ludolph of Saxony on Psalm 20:3, *In Psalterium expositio* [Paris, 1520], fol. 29ʳ) ; *infusa caritas mentis, spirituale sertum ex virtutum floribus contextum,* and *dominatio rationalis* [*the infused charity of the mind, a spiritual garland woven from the flowers of the virtues, and rational domination*] (Denis the Carthusian on Lamentations 5:16 and Ezechiel 16:12; *ed. cit.,* ix, 377, 477) . Particularly interesting in view of my intended interpretation is Hugh of St. Cher on Lamentations 5:16 (iv, fol. 309ᵛ) , who explains the crown itself as the *corona gratiæ [crown of grace]* in which are set four *lapides pretiosi [precious stones]:* "In fronte est charitas, quæ nos inflammat ad coelestia appetenda. . . . Item in occipite est humilitas, quæ bona sua nec videt, nec numerat. . . . Item in parte dextera est obedientia, quia quicquid nobis praecipit, debet esse prosperum nobis. . . . Item in sinistra parte est patientia in adversis." [On the front is charity, which inflames us to desire the things of heaven. . . . also on the back is humility, which neither sees nor enumerates its own goods. . . . Also on the right side is obedience, because whatever it orders, ought to be prosperous for us. . . . Also on the left side is patience in adversity.]

57 Thomas of Citeaux, *PL,* 206, col. 571; see also Hugh of St. Cher, *ed. cit.,* iii, fol. 130ᵛ. Nicolas of Lyra, *ed. cit.,* vii, 454, glosses the immediately preceding words of Canticles 5:11, "Caput ejus aurum optimum" [His head is the best gold], by "ornatum corona aurea" [established by a golden crown].

thought of as a visual combination of the palm, the crown, and the wheel of virtues: a full-page illustration of a palm tree (though not that of Canticles 5:11), topped with a crownlike semicircle of fronds resembling also the spokes of a wheel—the interstices of which contain individual virtues, including *patientia* as well as *karitas, prudentia,* and *humilitas.*[58] In any case, the appropriateness of Canticles 5:11 is completed by the word *corvus,* rendered by modern translators with its Classical meaning "raven," but also the normal fourteenth-century term for a crow—as illustrated by the Wycliffite translation, "hise heeris *ben* as the bowis of palm trees, *and ben* blake as a crowe." [59] Medieval commentators consistently associate this crow with the humble, and so with *humilitas* itself:

Qui *nigræ* etiam dicuntur sicut *corvus,* nigredo bonorum est, quod peccatores se reputant, et peccatorum suorum verecundiam in vultu portant. Despectionem quippe eligunt, contemptum æquanimiter ferunt, vilia opera et sordidum habitum non solum non refugiunt, sed etiam appetunt, scientes in hac humilitate pretiosum thesaurum latere. Hæc est nigredo bonorum in qua se corvis similant, ut Christo quoque assimilentur. Est enim humilitas virtus Christi, quam qui habuerit, Christi quoque similitudinem habebit, et quantum per hanc fuerit nigrior, tantum erit Christo similior, et apud seipsum humilior. Boni namque nigri sunt, et despecti apud se, sed pulchri et pretiosi ante Deum. [Who are also called *black* as a *raven,* their blackness is the blackness of the good, because they consider themselves sinners, and carry on their face the shame of their sins. Indeed they choose disdain, they suffer contempt with equanimity; they not only do not flee from vile jobs and a dirty garment but desire them, knowing that in this humility lies hidden a precious treasure. This is the blackness of the good by which they liken themselves to ravens, that they may be also like Christ. For humility is the virtue of Christ, which the one who has will have also the likeness of Christ; and the more black one is because of this, the more like to Christ he will be, and the more humble in his own sight. For the good are black, and despised in their own sight, but beautiful and precious in the sight of God.][60]

58 Lottlisa Behling, "Ecclesia als Arbor Bona," *Zeitschrift für Kunstwissenschaft,* xiii (1959), 143, fig. 3; note also fig. 7 on p. 153. This reference is also due to the kindness of Miss R. B. Green.

59 *The Holy Bible . . . by John Wycliffe and His Followers,* ed. Josiah Forshall and Frederic Madden (Oxford, 1850), iii, 79; see also *MED,* D.i, p. 770, "croue," i (b). The explanation of "croue coroune" as "the skull or head of a crow [as a charm]," *ibid.,* 2 (a), seems based on this single occurrence in *Piers.*

60 Richard of St. Victor, *Explicatio in Cant. Cantic.,* cap. 37 (*PL,* 196, cols. 509–10). See also, among others, Gilbert Foliot, *PL,* 202, col. 1279; Philip of Harvengt, *PL,* 203,

The inevitable contrast between *humilitas* and the connotations of a crown seems pointed not only by the familiar Christian paradox of present lowliness as the means to an eternal crown, but also by the common exegetical significance of the crown as *superbia,* the vice directly opposed to *humilitas.*[61] At one level of spirituality, the relationship between *humilitas* and *patientia* is of course an intimate and necessary one.[62] Bernard of Clairvaux is more demanding:

> Est autem humilis, qui humiliationem convertit in humilitatem.... Nemini prorsus, quod patienter fert, bonum est, sed plane molestum. Scimus autem quod *hilarem datorem diligit Deus* [II Corinthians 9:7].... Etenim sola gratiam, quam præfert, meretur læta et absoluta humilitas. Quæ enim coacta fuerit vel extorta, qualis utique est in viro patiente illo qui possidet animam suam; hæc, inquam, humilitas, etsi vitam obtinet propter patientiam, propter tristitiam tamen gratiam non habebit.... Vis autem videre humilem recte gloriantem, et vere dignum gloria? *Libenter,* inquit, *gloriabor in infirmitatibus meis, ut inhabitet in me virtus Christi* [II Corinthians 12:9]. Non dicit patienter se ferre infirmitates suas; sed et sibi

col. 434; Thomas of Citeaux, *PL,* 206, col. 569; Peter Riga, *Aurora,* rev. Gilles of Paris, MS Oxford, Bodl. 822, fol. 127ᵛ; Hugh of St. Cher, *ed. cit.,* III, fol. 130ᵛ; and *Allegoriæ, PL,* 112, cols. 902–903.

61 The latter is exemplified by Alanus of Lille, *Distinctiones (PL,* 210, col. 752) ; the former, by Peraldus, tom. I, pars V, tract, "De beatitudine," pars 4, cap. 3 (*ed. cit.,* I, fol. 234ʳ) : "Humilibus qui se cinerem reputant, specialiter debetur corona, Esaiæ 61:[1, 3]: *Ad annuntiandum mansuetis misit me, vt darem eis coronam pro cinere"* [The crown is especially owed to the humble who consider themselves as ash: *He sent me to preach to the meek, that I might give them a crown for ashes*].

62 See for example medieval commentary on Ecclesiasticus 2:4, "et in humilitate tua patientiam habe" [and in your humility have patience]; and Ephesians 4:1, "Obsecro itaque vos . . . ut digne ambuletis vocatione qua vocati estis, cum omni humilitate et mansuetudine, cum patientia, supportantes invicem in charitate, solliciti servare unitatem spiritus in vinculo pacis" [And so I beg you . . . to walk worthy of the vocation in which you are called, with all humility and meekness, with patience, supporting each other in charity, careful to preserve the unity of the Spirit in the bond of peace]. Maurice of Ireland, *Distinctiones,* MS Paris, B.N. lat. 15945, fol. 209ʳ: "Primam pacienciam tria operantur: gracia divina . . . magnanimitas discreta . . . humilitas devota, Ecclesiastici ii: *in humilitate tua pacienciam habe"* [Three things bring about initial patience: divine grace . . . discreet magnanimity . . . devoted humility, Ecclesiasticus ii: *in your humility have patience*]. Peraldus as in the preceding footnote, cap. 5, fol. 236ʳ: "Quartus [gradus humilitatis secundum sanctum Benedictum] est, si in ipsa obedientia contra aspera patientiam amplectatur" [The fourth grade of humility, according to St. Benedict, is if one embraces patience out of sheer obedience in the face of adversity]. Concerning the virtue of *humilitas* generally, see Bernard, *De gradibus humilitatis et superbiæ (PL,* 182, cols. 941–72) ; Peraldus as above, cap. 1–5, fols. 227ᵛ–236ʳ; and *Le laie Bible,* 1781–1991, pp. 70–76. Its common role as the antithesis of *superbia* and the root of all virtues (cf. n. 45 above) is graphically illustrated in Katzenellenbogen, pl. XLI, fig. 67.

bonum esse, quod humiliatur; nec sufficere omnino, ut possideat animam suam tanquam patienter humiliatus, nisi et gratiam accipiat
tanquam sponte humiliatus. [But he is humble who turns humilia-
tion into humility. . . . What one suffers patiently is completely good
to no one, but simply annoying. We know, however, that *God loves
a cheerful giver.* . . . For truly only cheerful and absolute humility
earns grace, which it anticipates. For the humility which is forced or
extorted, such as is certainly in that patient man who possesses his
own soul, this humility, I say, although it gain life because of patience, nevertheless will not win grace because of sadness. . . . But do
you wish to see the humble man rightly glorying, and truly worthy
of glory? He says, *Gladly, therefore, will I glory in my infirmities,
that the power of Christ may dwell within me.* He does not say that
he patiently suffers his infirmities; but that it is even good for him
that he is humiliated; that it is not enough at all that he possess his
soul as one patiently humiliated, unless he also receive grace as one
willingly humiliated.][63]

These facts, taken together, suggest that Langland's "crowe croune" is
an oxymoron designed to express *humilitas,* the lowly virtue which exalts—perhaps with the further implication that *patientia* itself remains
imperfect unless "crowned" by *humilitas.* Visually, *humilitas* might be
thought of as "crowning" the wheel of virtues either by sitting above it,
or by appearing as its center or hub.[64] If this explanation can be accepted, the terms of Patience's assurance in lines 160–62 may finally be
paraphrased, "if you will adopt the virtue of patience and carry it in your
heart wherever you go, as part of a unity of virtues like that sometimes
represented in a 'cartwheel' (and alluded to in B. xiii, 152, as 'Dowel') —
along with its natural concomitant (*or* its necessary completion) humility, which, though 'black as a crow,' bears promise of a crown and is itself
paradoxically a 'crown.' "

[63] Bernard of Clairvaux, *Serm. in Cant.,* XXXIV (*PL,* 183, col. 961) . For *humilitas*
as the virtue that exalts (mentioned below) , see Bernard, *ibid.;* and Peraldus as in
n. 61, cap. 2, fol. 232^r. Note the special pertinence of the quoted passage for *Piers,* B.
xiii, 59–60; C. xvi, 63–64.

[64] In the *rota vere religionis* (Katzenellenbogen, pl. XLV, fig. 72) , these positions
are occupied respectively by the good abbot (top) and by the words "hic axis est cura
fratris" [this axle is the care of a brother] (center) ; the central importance of *humilitas,* however, seems implied by Katzenellenbogen's description (p. 72) : "The abbot
sits at the top and gives the benediction, a model abbot. With becoming modesty he
has inclined his crozier. At the bottom of the wheel, the monk who has voluntarily
humbled himself is reading." The text, MS Heiligenkreuz, Stiftsbibl. 226, fol. 148^v,
comments: "In altum vero humilitas se elevat, dum se humiliat" [Humility raises itself
on high, while it humbles itself]. A fourteenth-century painting on the north wall of
the nave in the church at Padbury (Bucks.) depicts a "wheel of vices" with pride, the
antithesis of humility, at its center.

13. The Grammar of Book's Speech
in *Piers Plowman*
E. TALBOT DONALDSON

And I boke wil be brent but ih*e*sus rise to lyue
In alle my3tes of man & his moder gladye
And conforte al his kynne & out of care brynge
And al *þ*e iuwen ioye vnioignen & vnlouken
And but *þ*ei reuerencen his Rode & his resurexiou*n*
And beleue on a newe lawe be lost lyf & soule
(Piers Plowman, B. xviii 252–57) [1]

THUS BOOK concludes his prophecy. But as is perhaps inevitable with prophecies, his meaning is not the same for all readers — a fact demonstrated in recent articles on the passage by R. E. Kaske and R. L. Hoffman.[2] Apart from the broader issues of theology in which these scholars are interested, Book's speech presents to the modern reader a number of syntactical problems. There are at least four of these in the first four lines quoted above. I shall list them separately, though they are in fact interdependent:

(1) Is *but* in 252 a subordinating conjunction governing a verb in the subjunctive ("unless Jesus rise"), or is the coordinating adversative followed by a future indicative in which the future auxiliary must be understood from the preceding clause ("but Jesus [will] rise")?

(2) Is *to lyue* in 252 an infinitive, or is it a prepositional phrase with "petrified" inflection of the noun ("to life")?

(3) Are the verbs *gladye, conforte,* and *brynge* in 253–54 subjunctives parallel with the possible subjunctive *rise,* or are they infinitives parallel with the unmistakably infinitival verbs *unioignen* and *vnlouken* in 255?

(4) On what do the infinitives in 255, as well as the verbs in 253–54 (if they are infinitives) , depend?

Reprinted, with some revisions by the author, by permission of the author and the publishers from *Studies in Language and Literature in Honour of Margaret Schlauch,* ed. Mieczyslaw Brahmer, Stanislaw Helsztyński, and Julian Krzyżanowski (Warszawa: Państwowe Wydawnictwo Naukowe, 1966) , pp. 103–109.

1 Skeat's B-text, *EETS* OS 38; I have removed the punctuation from all citations.
2 Kaske, "The Speech of 'Book' in *Piers Plowman,*" *Anglia,* LXXVII (1959) , 117–44; Hoffman, "The Burning of 'Boke' in *Piers Plowman,*" *MLQ,* XXV (1964) , 57–65.

In the case of (1), Kaske follows Wells[3] in reading the future indicative, while Hoffman follows Skeat and Goodridge[4] in preferring the subjunctive: that is, the first two believe that Book is prophesying that he will be burnt in any case, the last three that he will be burnt only if Christ fails to rise. To try to settle the matter, let us ask what a contemporary of Langland's would have understood when he heard the words, "And I, Book, will be burnt but Jesus rise." Middle English lacked the conjunctions *unless* and *except:* to express a negative condition one had to choose among *but, but if,* and *if . . . not.* The last of these is, I believe, limited to contexts where the speaker wishes to emphasize the negative probability of the condition, and would be stylistically unattractive here as a means of expressing the idea "unless." [5] If Langland had wanted to make it absolutely clear — to the modern reader — that he meant "unless" he should have written the second alternative, *but if.* Since, however, he was writing for a Middle English audience, all he had to do was write, *but* with the subjunctive in order to express "unless." For *but* is by all odds the commonest way of saying "unless" in Middle English, and its meaning is unmistakable when it is followed by a recognizable subjunctive. The evidence furnished by the B-MSS of *Piers Plowman* suggests that the author almost employed *but,* although cautious scribes have often inserted *if* in positions where ambiguity is conceivable, especially when the *but*-clause precedes the main clause and where the following verb may be read as an indicative.[6] In the present example no ambiguity would arise — a fact that is reinforced by the failure of any B-scribe to insert an *if.*[7] All readers would have understood "unless" because *but* plus the subjunctive was the usual way of saying "unless." On the other hand, *but Jesus rise* seems an entirely impossible way of expressing the idea "but Jesus will rise." Professor Kaske admits that he has found no other example in Middle English where the auxiliary *will* has to be understood as being carried over from the first clause to a coordinate adversative clause with a different subject.[8] This means that if Langland meant to say, "I, Book, will be burnt, but Jesus will rise," he chose not only a

[3] Kaske, pp. 133–38; H. W. Wells's translation (New York, 1935), p. 247. Kaske, p. 136, n. 1, says that Nevill Coghill in his translation (London, 1949), p. 101, also uses the future indicative, but what Coghill actually writes is "but Jesus rise."

[4] Hoffman, pp. 57–60; Skeat, *EETS* OS 91, 556 (gloss to equivalent line in the C-text); J. F. Goodridge's translation (Penguin, 1959), p. 262.

[5] As a glance at Goodridge's translation will suggest.

[6] In Chaucer, the alternation *but / but if* seems largely a matter of metrics.

[7] As Kaske notes, p. 136, n. 3, at least one C-MS reads *but if* in the equivalent line.

[8] See Kaske, p. 136. His examples of the construction with *and*-clauses are not really relevant, for the adversative idea in *but* puts an added strain on the possibility of carrying the auxiliary over from the first clause.

unique way to express it, but also a way uniquely designed to give readers exactly the opposite sense to what he intended. Of such is not, one hopes, the kingdom of poets.

It is true that the reading "unless Jesus rise" causes difficulties later in the passage, but since these are also involved with the meaning of *to lyue,* let us look at that first. Langland and his hearers knew whether he meant the verb "live" or the noun "life," since one had a short vowel and the other a long; but there is no way for us to decide which he meant from the written shape of the phrase. Nor is there much grammatical evidence for either alternative. It is true that *rise* is a verb which does not take the infinitive without a fairly strong sense of purpose, so that one must be prepared to accept the heavy-handed translation, "unless Jesus rise in order to live," if one prefers the infinitive. There can be no grammatical objection to the prepositional phrase *to lyue,* since Middle English *lif* very commonly retained its old inflections in certain usages: compare *on lyue,* giving Modern English *alive,* and Chaucer's *al my lyue* rhyming with a long vowel. But as positive evidence for the meaning "to life" in the present context Professor Kaske has collected from Middle English poetry celebrating the Resurrection a number of examples of the phrase *rise to lȳue* (pp. 134–35, especially 135, n. 3) and this seems to have been the common idiom for translating the Latin *resurgere* [to rise up again]. In my own recent reading of Middle English lyrics I have failed to find a single example of a surely identifiable *rise to lȳue (n).* Furthermore, as Kaske has already pointed out (p. 139), in the line under discussion no B-scribe reads the unequivocal infinitive *lyuen;* and while, as he says, such evidence is negative, it is nevertheless weighty, for there are extremely few infinitive forms in the B-text of *Piers Plowman* which are not spelled by at least one scribe with a final -*n*.[9] Apparently the scribes here recognized a familiar formula "rise to life," and I agree with Kaske that modern readers should do the same.

If we take 252 to read, "And I, Book, will be burnt unless Jesus rise to life," then the verbs in 253–54 are easily interpreted as subjunctives parallel with *rise.* But this leaves the infinitives of 255 in an anomalous position, and it was indeed their anomaly that encouraged Professor Kaske (pp. 59–60) to defend the alternative I have rejected: "but Jesus [will] rise." For if the auxiliary is to be understood before *rise,* then it may also be understood before all the other verbs and, in his opinion, it has to be understood before the last two in order to explain why they are infinitives. In opposition, Mr. Hoffman argues that while *rise* is a sub-

---

[9] Nor does any B-MS read *libbe (n),* which is a common alternate form for the verb *lyue(n).*

junctive, *to lyue* is an infinitive[10] and that the subsequent verbs are infinitives parallel to it. The position I have taken, rejecting in part both Kaske's and Hoffman's explanation for 252, leaves the infinitives of 255 unexplained.

The explanation lies, I believe, in a usage of the infinitive in Middle English for which there is no really descriptive name. Both Mustanoja and Einenkel discuss it under the heading of the "Absolute Infinitive," and Mustanoja describes it as "a construction with a nominative subject, occasionally used to express futurity, expectation, purpose, or even command.[11] He lists two examples from Chaucer,[12] two from *Cursor Mundi*,[13] and one from the charter of False in *Piers Plowman:*

> Glotonye he gaf hem eke and grete othes togydere
> And alday to drynke at dyuerse tauernes
> (And . . . to iangle and to iape and iugge . . . And . . . to frete . . .
> And . . . to sitten and soupen . . . And breden . . . and bedden . . .)
> And þanne wanhope to awake hym so with no wille to amende
> For he leueth be lost þis is here last ende
> And þei to haue and to holde and here eyres after
> A dwellyng with þe deuel and dampned be for eure
>   (B. ii, 92–102)

The infinitives from *drynke* in the second line above through *bedden* in the fourth may be construed as objective, dependent on *gaf*, "granted," but it is difficult to construe *wanhope to awake* in the same way, and impossible so to construe *þei to haue and to holde*. The charter ceases to be an enabling instrument and becomes rather a prediction of the future behavior of the grantees. Einenkel notes that this type of infinitive is

---

10 The only evidence he provides in favor of the infinitive is the necessity to explain the infinitives in 255.

11 Tauno F. Mustanoja, *A Middle English Syntax. Part I: Parts of Speech* (Helsinki, 1960), p. 542; Eugen Einenkel, *Geschichte der Englischen Sprache. II: Historische Syntax,* 3d ed. (Strassburg, 1916), pp. 18–22. Einenkel's categories μ, ν, and π all contain examples of the construction under discussion, and I do not think his attempted distinctions are valid; furthermore, under π he places what Mustanoja (p. 538) clearly distinguishes as the historical infinitive, a quite different usage represented by Chaucer's *And she to laughe it thoughte hire brest* (*TC*, II, 1108).

12 *CT* E 354: *that I frely may . . . do yow laughe or smerte, And nevere ye to grucche it;* and E 105: *I dar the bettre aske of yow a space Of audience to shewen oure requeste And ye my lord to doon right as yow leste.* Further examples from Chaucer may be consulted in Einenkel, *Streifzüge durch die Mittelenglische Syntax* (Münster, 1887), pp. 80–82; see also J. S. Kenyon, *The Syntax of the Infinitive in Chaucer,* Chaucer Society, 2d Series (London, 1909), pp. 137–40.

13 *Cursor* 7121: *he het men to gyve mede If þei coude hit riȝtly rede and þei to gyve þe same aȝeyn;* and 10795; *Oure lord wolde for resoun þilke Be fed of a maydenes mylke So hir maydenhede to be hid And hir husbonde wide kid.*

characteristic of decrees and wills (p. 20) . On the strength of the above passage we ought to add charters; and on the strength of the following, from Conscience's speech to Meed and the Court, we ought to add prophecies:

> (Alle þat bereth baslarde . . . Shal be demed to þe deth . . .)
> Eche man to pleye with a plow pykoys or spade
> Spynne or sprede donge or spille hym-self with sleuthe
> Prestes and parsones with *placebo*[14] to hunte
> And dyngen vpon dauid eche a day til eue.
>
> (B. iii, 303–10)

Although both of these passages have fairly strong elements of futurity, as Mustanoja notes (p. 542) , futurity is not absolutely essential to the usage. In the following passages, from the description of Hawkin's sins, the infinitives seem to be describing a typical present action:

> . . . a lyer in soule
> With Inwit and with outwitt ymagenen and studye
> As best for his body be to haue a badde name
> And entermeten hym ouer-al þer he hath nouȝt to done
>
> And if he gyueth ouȝte pore gomes telle what he deleth
>
> Baldest of beggeres a bostour þat nouȝt hath
> In towne and in tauernes tales to telle
>
> And segge þinge þat he neuere seigh and for soth sweren it
> Of dedes þat he neuere dyd demen and bosten
> And of werkes þat he wel dyd witnesse and seggen
>
> . . . leue tonge to chyde
> Al þat he wist wykked by any wiȝte tellen it
> And blame men bihynde her bakke and bydden hem meschaunce
> And þat he wist bi wille tellen it watte
>
> (B. xiii, 288–91, 300, 303–7, 323–26)

Some of the infinitives in these passages may be rationalized under the heading of better known usages, though not without considerable wrenching from the norm; but the majority seem to represent a conscious stylistic device that violates usual speech practices with regard to the infinitive. What all the passages quoted seem to express is either a future action strongly hypothesized by the speaker or a present action strongly visualized by him; in both cases the effect is one of inevitability, whether

---

[14] [Literally, "I will please": in this instance, *placebo* refers ot the Office for the Dead.]

that of an action legally, prophetically, or otherwise bound to take place in the future or that of an action generically bound—that is, by the nature of things and people—either to take place in the future or to be taking place now. With regard to Book's prophecy, I suggest that once the negative condition "unless Jesus rise" has been stated, the rest of Jesus's actions become, in Book's mind, inevitable, and that he expresses this inevitability by a recourse to the infinitive. At precisely what point the mood of doubt implied in *rise* gives way to the assurance implied in *vnioignen* and *vnlouken* perhaps neither Langland nor Book could tell us.[15] It might be wise to describe *gladye, conforte,* and *brynge* as "subjunctives, becoming infinitives."

There is one further point about the passage. Mr. Hoffman, having chided Professor Kaske for twisting syntax to achieve a preconceived meaning, does precisely the same thing himself with 256–57! These he reads as meaning, "And unless they [the Jews] reverence His Rood and His Resurrection, And believe on a New Law [I, Book, will] be lost life and soul (p. 60) ." Now it is true that the subject of the verb *be lost* is not expressed, and true that in Middle English pronoun subjects are often omitted. This is especially true of subjects in the third person, far rarer with the second and first persons.[16] But the overriding consideration is clarity: pronoun subjects are omitted when the meaning is perfectly clear without them. In the present case, the subject of the main verb *be lost* is unmistakably the same as the subject of the preceding subordinate clause—a common enough construction in Middle English. No reader of Langland would have carried over to *be lost* a first person subject that has appeared only once, five lines previously, and is separated from its putative verb by two other subjects: Middle English syntax frequently differs from Modern English, and its logic is more elliptical, but it is no less logical. If Langland had meant that Book would be lost, he would have written, "I wil be lost lyf & soule." Actually, if we could get Langland's ghost to fill out the line so that it would be entirely unambiguous for modern readers, I suspect that he would use the infinitive:

> And but þei reuerencen his Rode & his resurexiou*n*
> And beleue on a newe lawe þei to be lost lyf & soule.

---

[15] MS C² reads *gladen,* MSS MHmCr read *conforten;* in the C-text, which omits B253, MS P reads *conforten.* It is possible, of course, that the transition of the verbs into the infinitive was aided by the visual identity of the prepositional phrase *to ꝉyue* with the infinitive *to ꝉyue,* but in view of the other infinitive usages noted, this is not a necessary assumption.

[16] See Mustanoja, pp. 138–44; Einenkel, *Historische Syntax,* pp. 130–31.

It was Dame Study who first caused grammar to be written; and since it is the ground of all, she will beat us with a birch unless we learn it.[17]

---

[17] Mr. Hoffman's attempt to equate *lyf* in 257 with the word *lef* ("leaf") is based on a misunderstanding of Skeat's gloss to A. vii, 241; according to George Kane's edition of A (London, 1960), vii, 238 [241] reads: *Eny l[ef] of lechecraft lere it me my dere* [lef] WUJLKN; lif TRChVAMH3; lyst D; lessoun H. Skeat followed MS V and read *lyf*; but when he came to make his gloss he apparently realized his error and listed, as a separate word, "Lyf (*put for* leef)" in order to explain the spelling, in A. vii. It is simply not true that the "word 'lyf' was sometimes a variant of 'leef' " or that the two words were "sometimes . . . pronounced alike" (Hoffman, p. 61). One might easily be written for the other through scribal error, and, as Kane notes (p. 449), *lyf* is conceivably a bad spelling for *leef*—though hardly, I think, a common one; but the words in Middle English were just as far apart phonetically as they are in Modern English.

Index

Style and Symbolism in *Piers Plowman*

has been set on the Linotype in 10-point Baskerville with two points spacing between the lines. The paper on which this book is printed is designed for an effective life of at least three hundred years.